Scale 1: 500,000
or 8 miles to 1 inch
(5km to 1cm)

15th edition August 2015

© AA Media Limited 2015

Cartography:
All cartography in this atlas edited, designed and produced by the Mapping Services Department of AA Publishing (A05331).

This atlas contains Ordnance Survey data © Crown copyright and database right 2015.

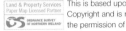 This is based upon Crown Copyright and is reproduced with the permission of Land & Property Services under delegated authority from the Controller of Her Majesty's Stationery Office, © Crown copyright and database right 2015. PMLPA No. 100497.

 © Ordnance Survey Ireland/ Government of Ireland. Copyright Permit No. MP000115.

Publisher's notes:
Published by AA Publishing (a trading name of AA Media Limited, whose registered office is Fanum House, Basing View, Basingstoke, Hampshire RG21 4EA, UK. Registered number 06112600).

ISBN: 978 0 7495 7735 3

A CIP Catalogue record for this book is available from the British Library.

Disclaimer:
The contents of this atlas are believed to be correct at the time of the latest revision, it will not include any subsequent amended, new or temporary information including diversions and traffic control or enforcement systems. The publishers cannot be held responsible or liable for any loss or damage occasioned to any person acting or refraining from action as a result of any use or reliance on material in this atlas, nor for any errors, omissions or changes in such material. This does not affect your statutory rights.

The publishers would welcome information to correct any errors or omissions and to keep this atlas up to date. Please write to the Atlas Editor, AA Publishing, The Automobile Association, Fanum House, Basing View, Basingstoke, Hampshire RG21 4EA, UK.
Email: *roadatlasfeedback@theaa.com*

Printer:
Printed by 1010 Printing International Ltd.

AA
GLC
B
WITI

GW00672233

Atlas contents

Map pages	II
Road map symbols	1
Road atlas Britain 1:500,000 scale	2–65
Index to places in Britain	66–80
County, administrative area map	66–67
Distance charts	81 & 90
Britain	81
Ireland	90
Road atlas Ireland 1:1 million scale	82–89
Index to places in Ireland	91–94
County, administrative area map	91
Town plan section	95–191
Index to town plans	95
Key to town plans	96
Central London	97–107
Town plans	108–191
Major airports	192–197
Channel tunnel	198

Map pages

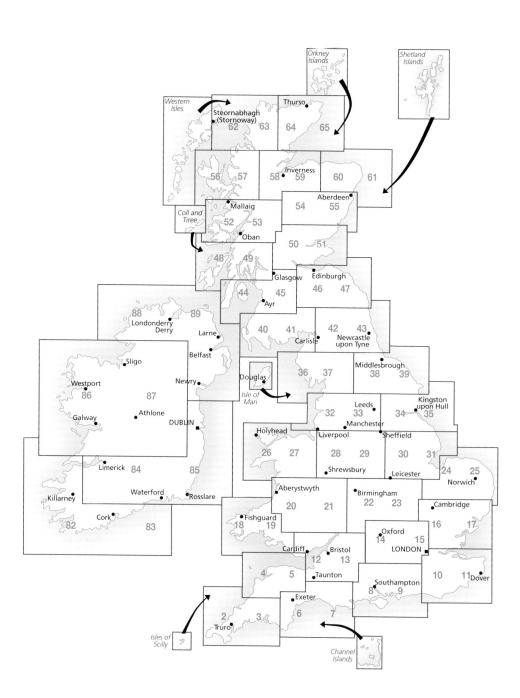

Britain

M4	Motorway with number
Toll 74	Toll motorway with junction
10	Motorway junction with and without number
40	Restricted motorway junction
S Fleet	Motorway service area
	Motorway under construction
A40	Primary route single/dual carriageway
16	Primary junction with and without number
25	Restricted Primary junction
S	Primary route service area
A33	Other A road single/dual carriageway
B4224	B road
	Unclassified road
	Road under construction / approved
	Narrow Primary, other A or B road with passing places (Scotland)

5	Distance in miles between symbols
Toll	Road toll
or V	Vehicle ferry
	Fast vehicle ferry or catamaran
	National boundary
	County, administrative boundary
H	Heliport
BRISTOL	Airport
	Viewpoint
SNAEFELL 620	Spot height in metres
	River, lake and coastline
	National Park or National Scenic Area
27	Page overlap with number

1: 500 000

0	5	10 miles
0	5	10 15 kilometres

8 miles to 1 inch

Ireland

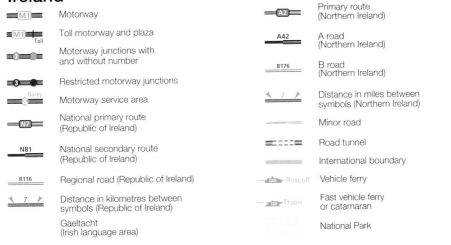

M1	Motorway
M1 Toll	Toll motorway and plaza
3	Motorway junctions with and without number
3	Restricted motorway junctions
S Gorey	Motorway service area
N7	National primary route (Republic of Ireland)
N81	National secondary route (Republic of Ireland)
R116	Regional road (Republic of Ireland)
7	Distance in kilometres between symbols (Republic of Ireland)
	Gaeltacht (Irish language area)

A2	Primary route (Northern Ireland)
A42	A road (Northern Ireland)
B176	B road (Northern Ireland)
7	Distance in miles between symbols (Northern Ireland)
	Minor road
	Road tunnel
	International boundary
Roscoff	Vehicle ferry
Troon	Fast vehicle ferry or catamaran
	National Park

1: 1 000 000

0	10	20 miles
0	10 20	30 kilometres

16 miles to 1 inch

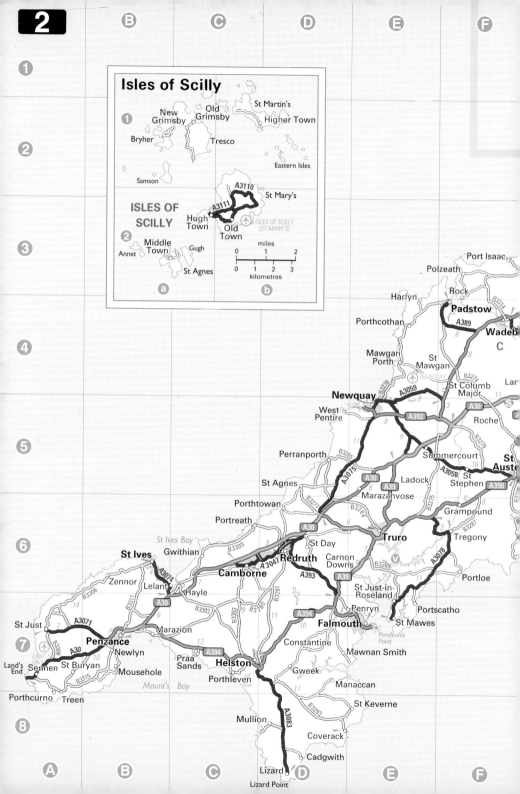

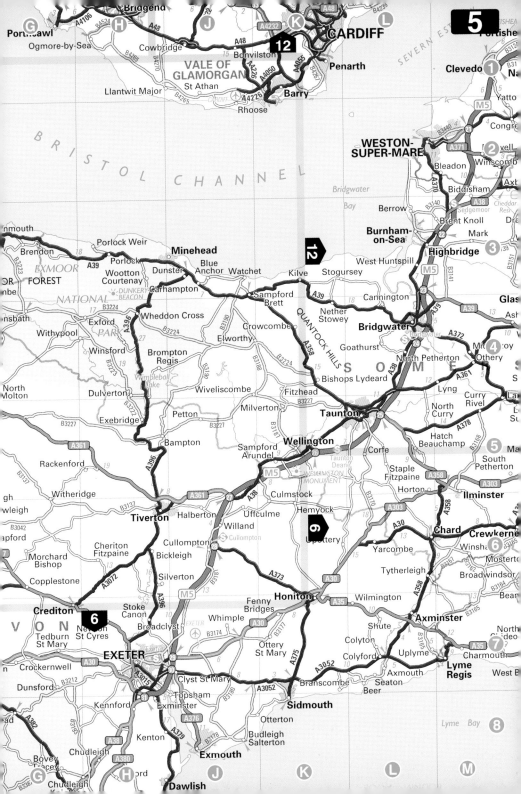

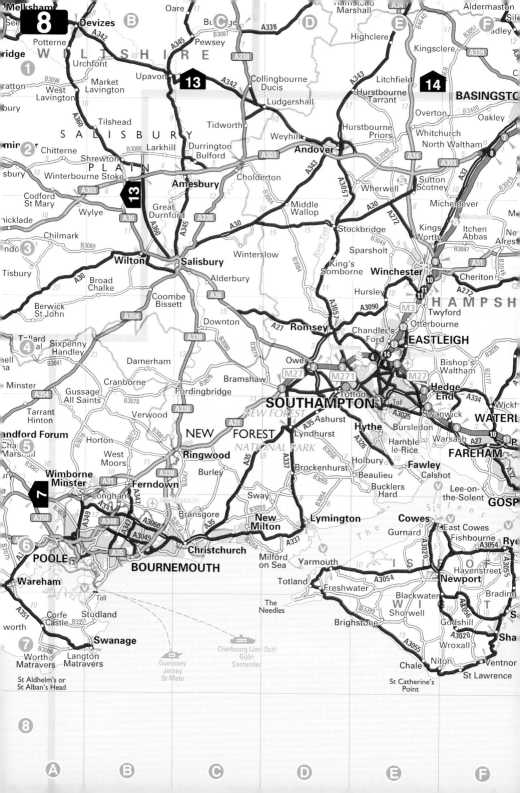

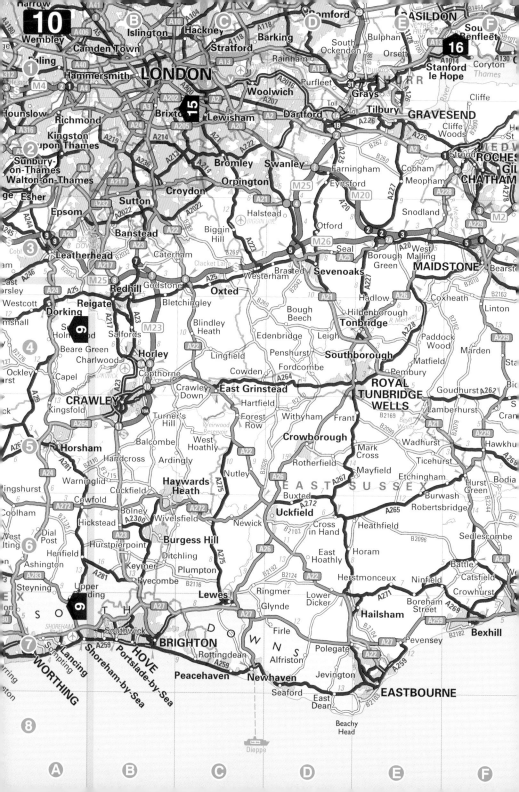

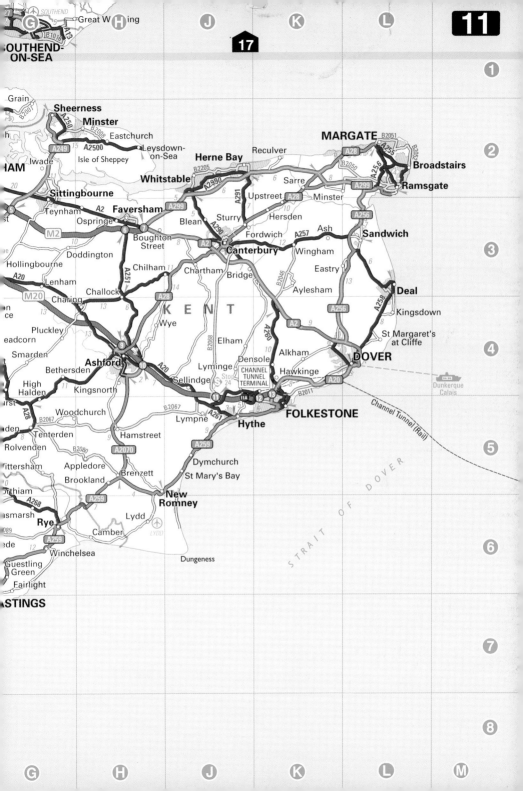

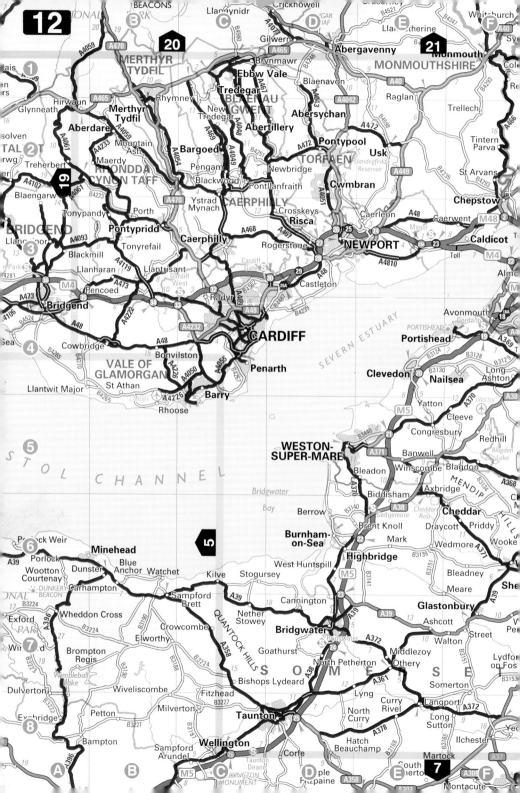

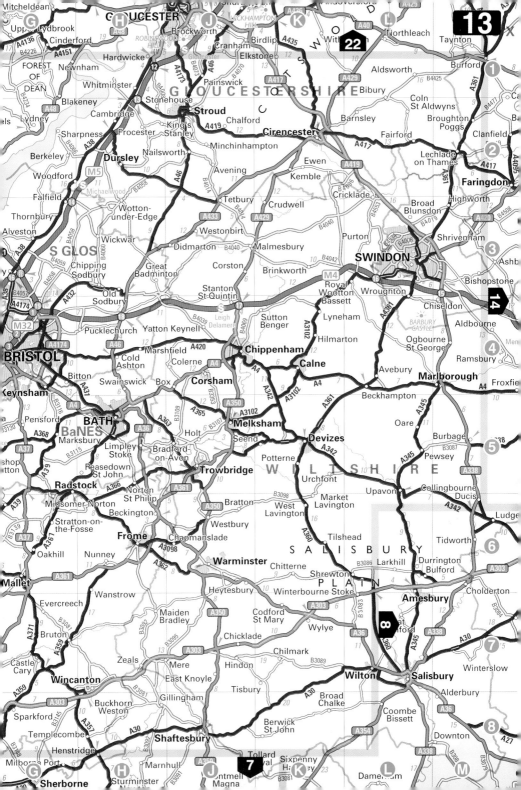

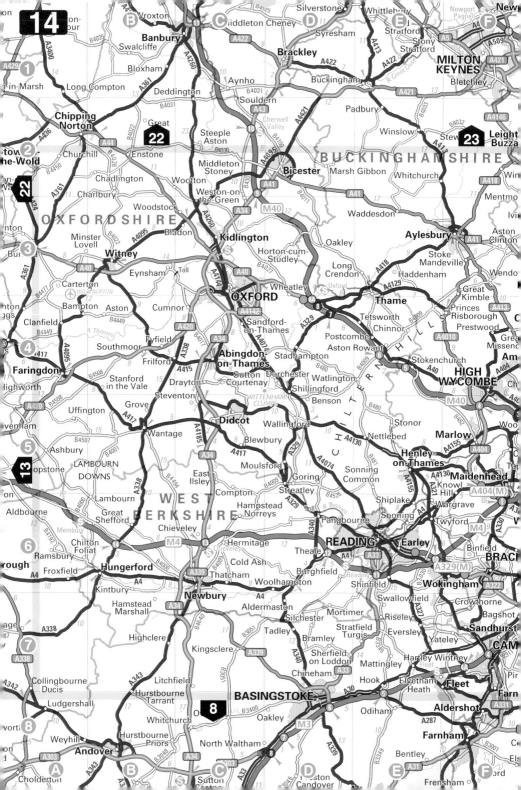

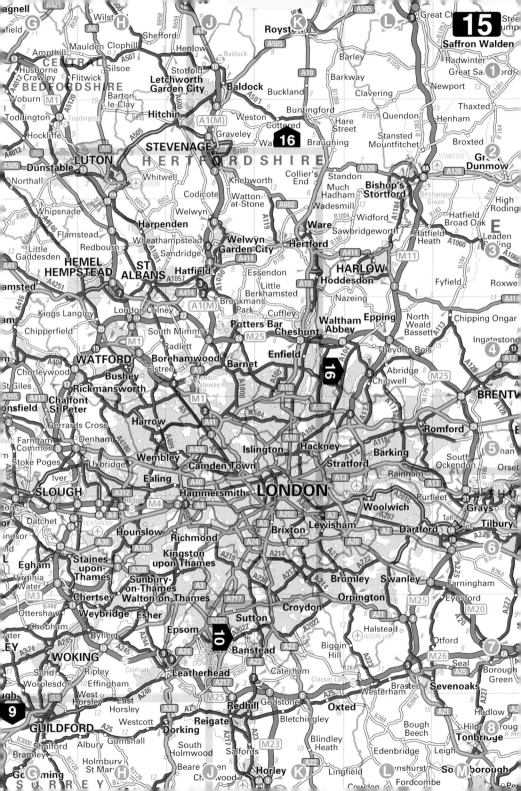

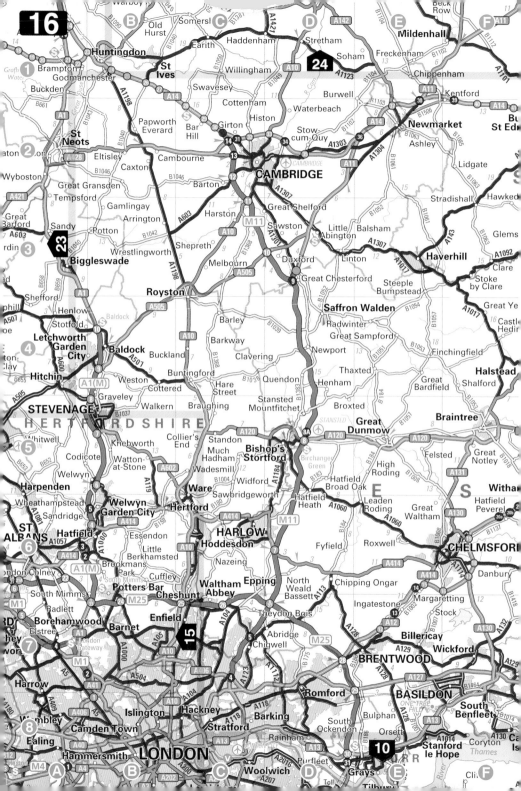

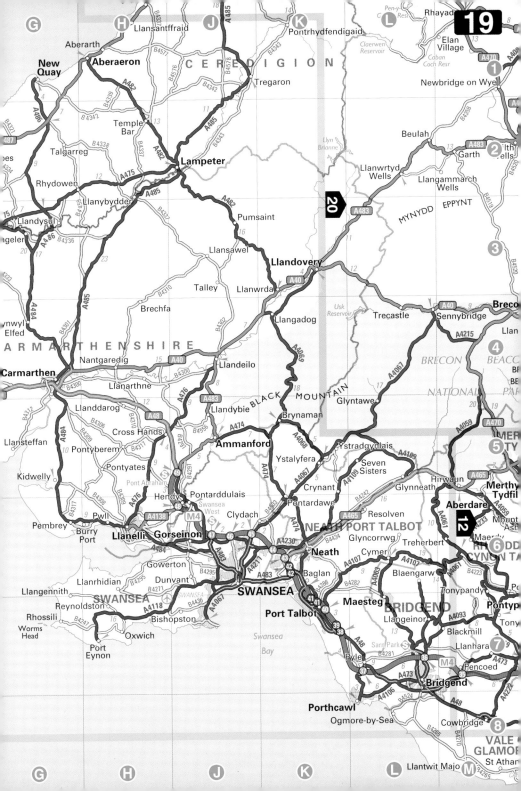

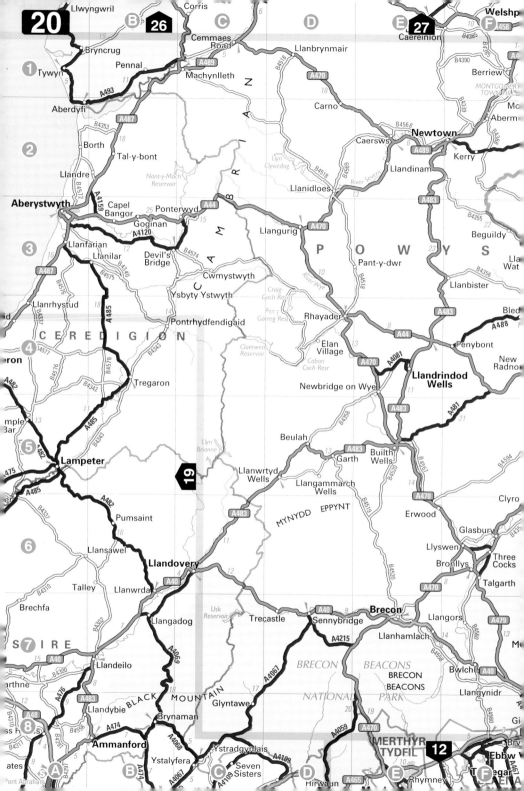

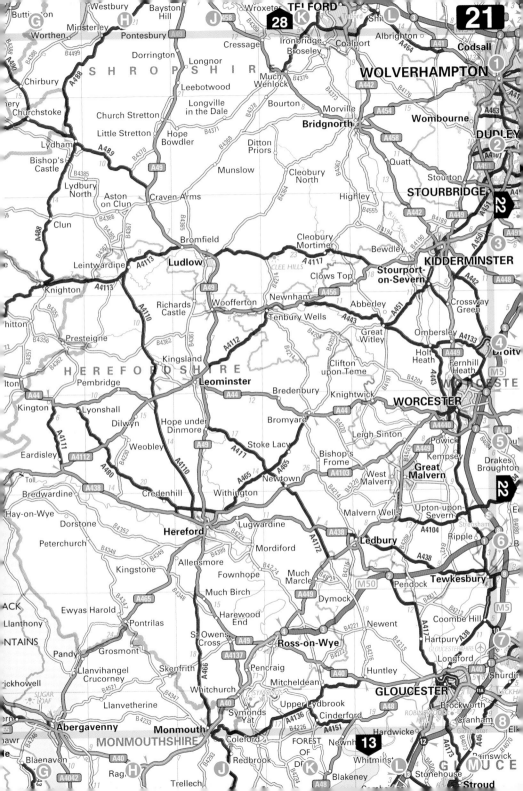

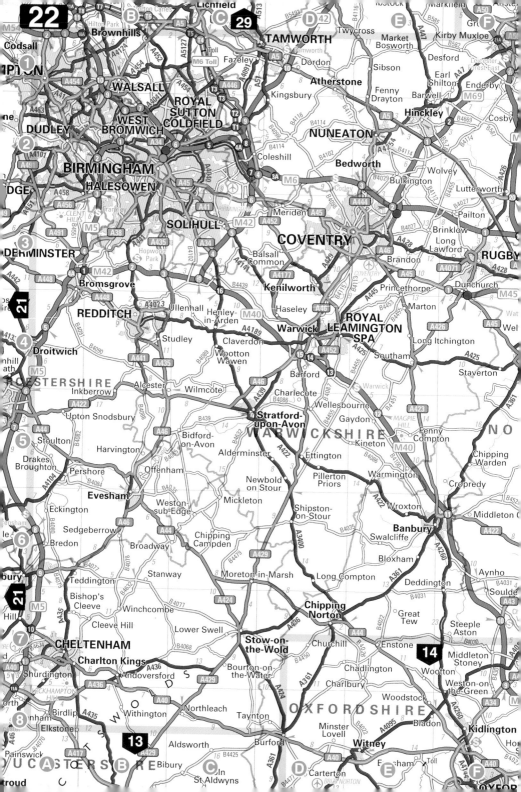

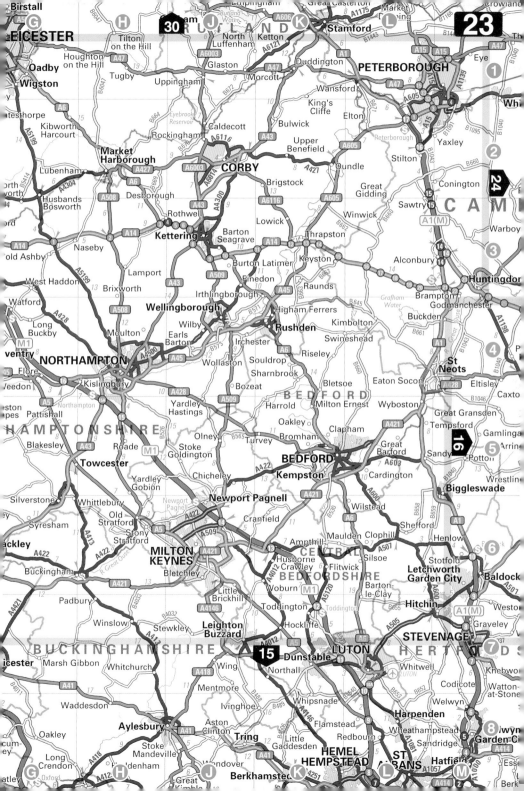

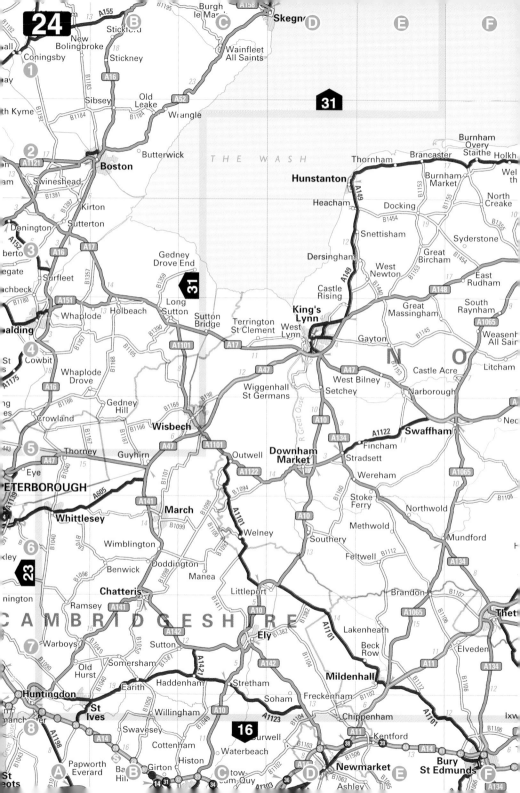

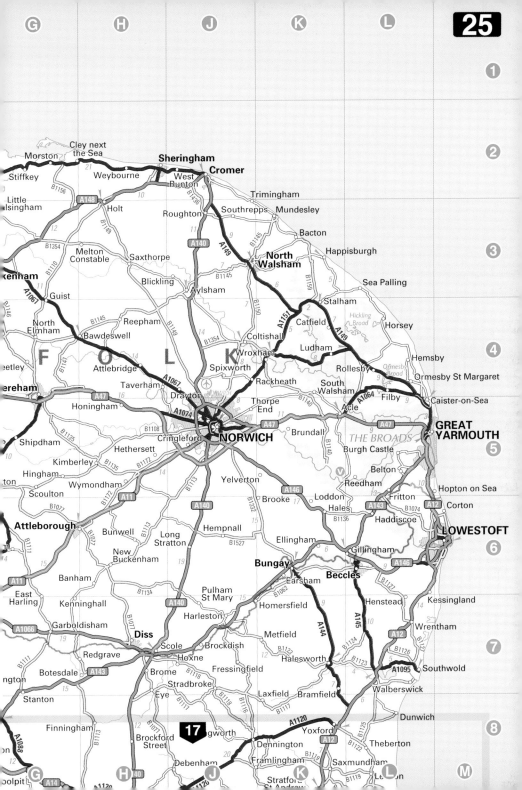

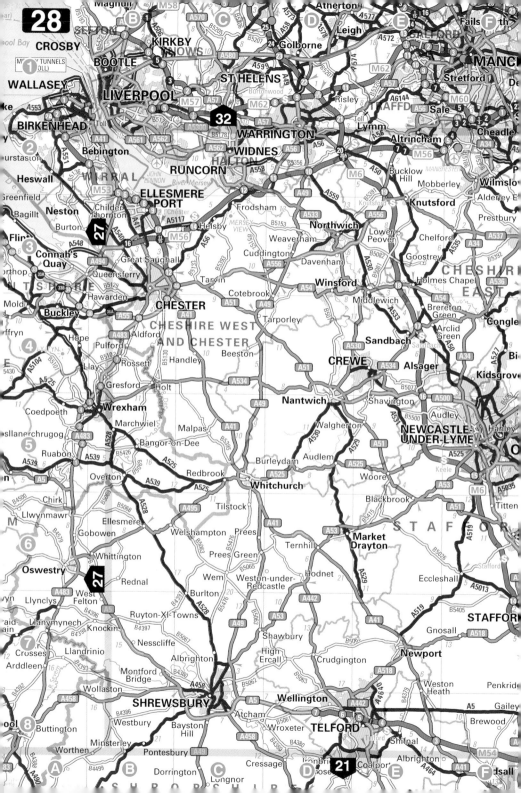

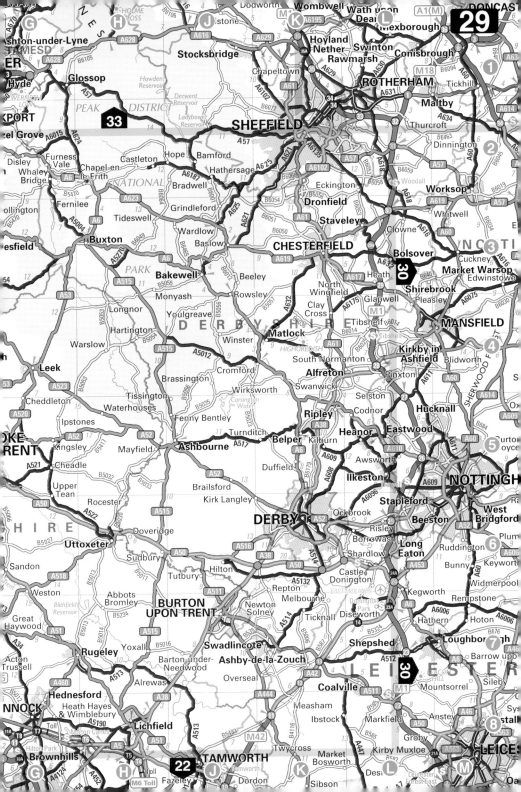

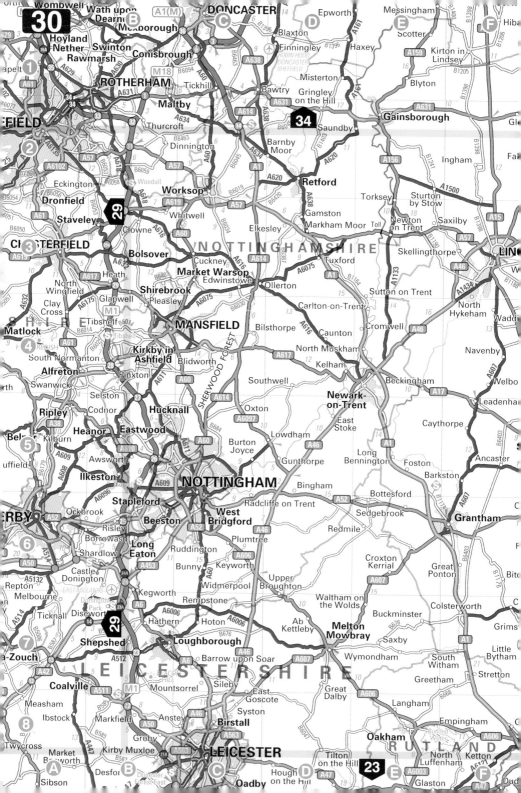

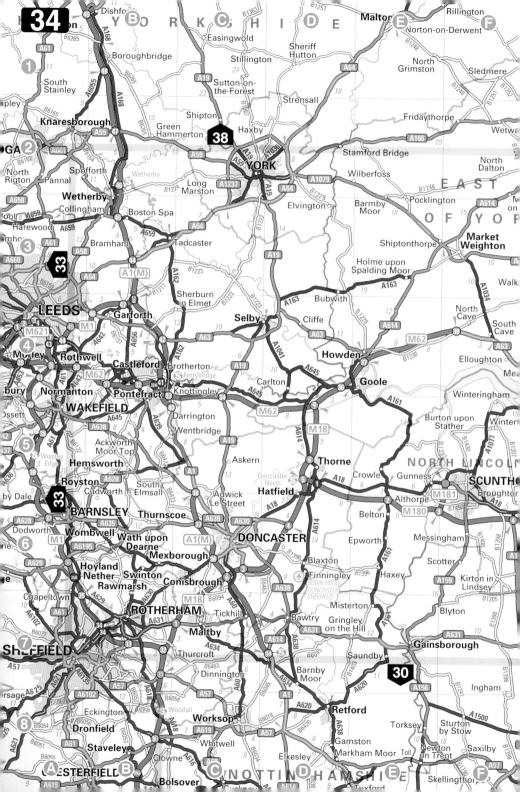

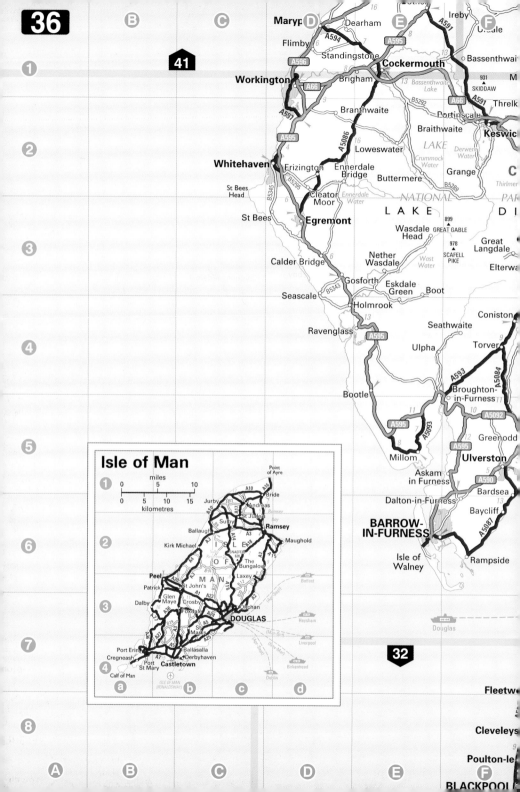

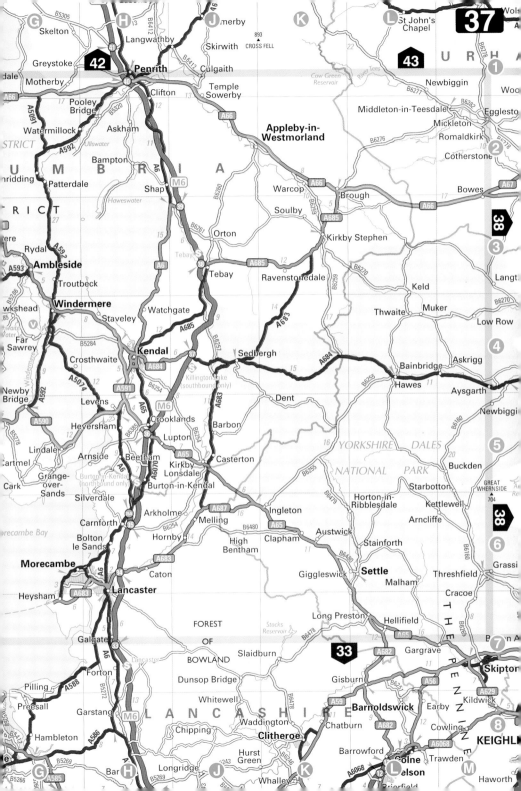

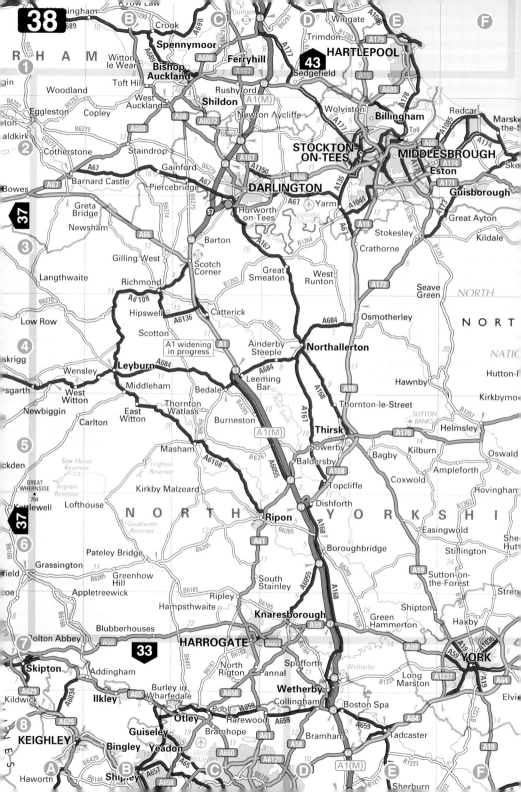

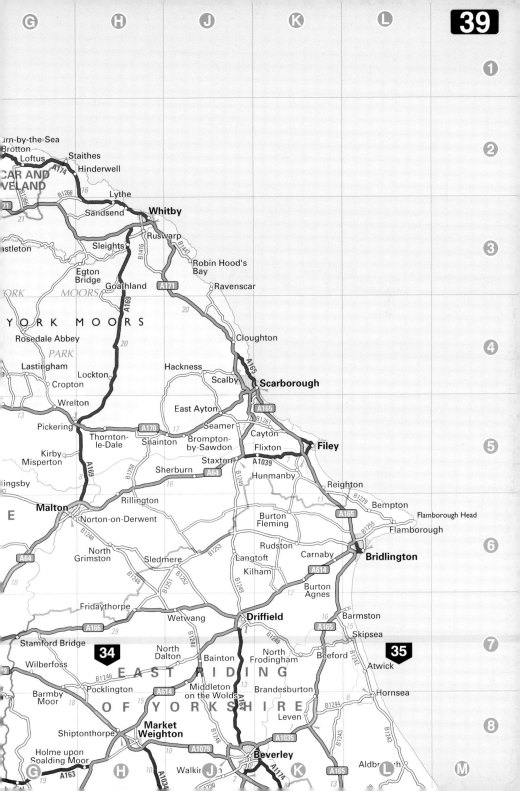

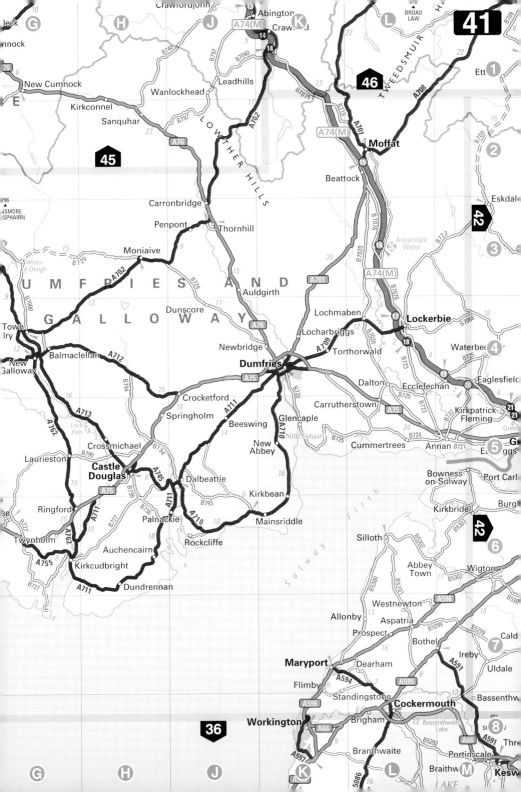

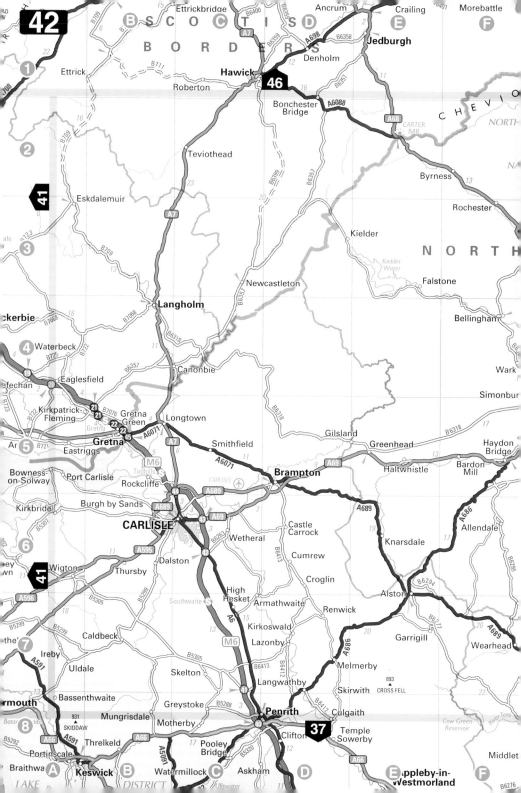

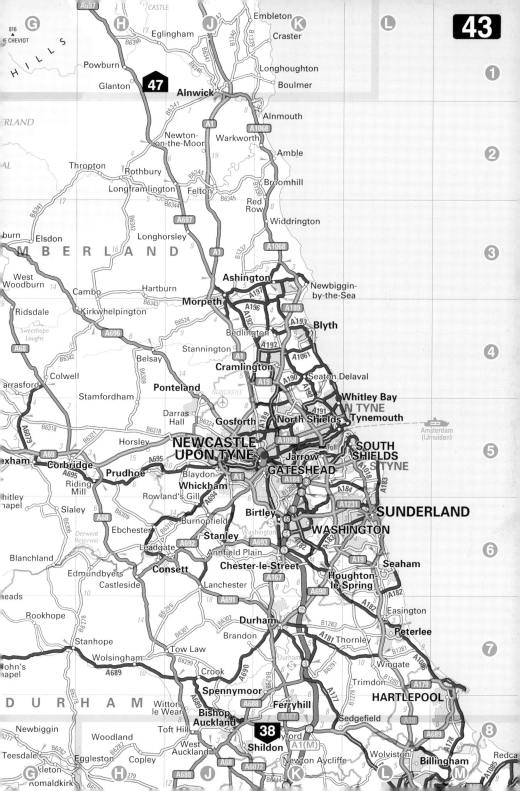

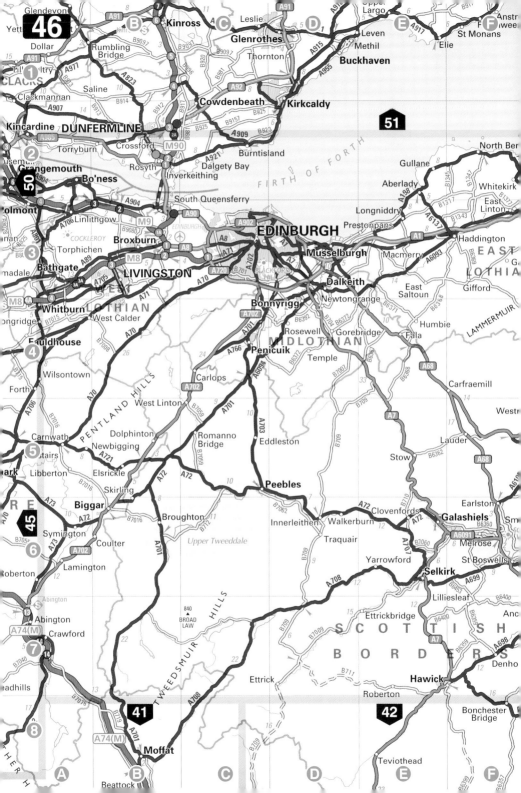

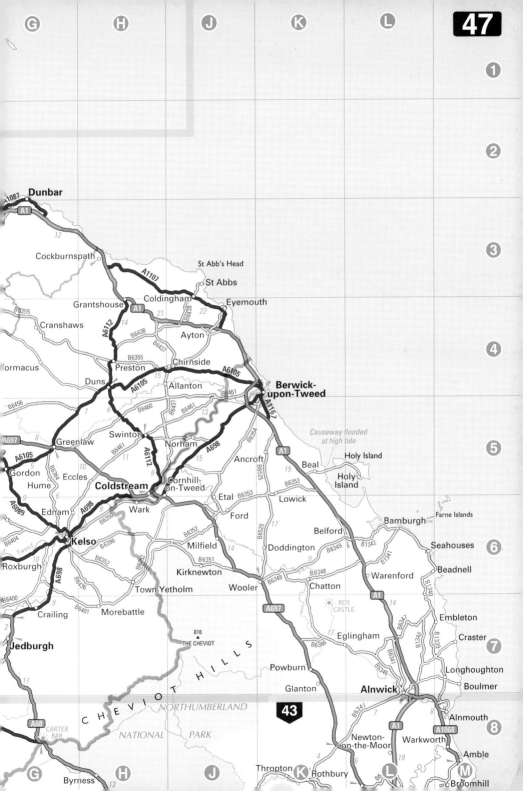

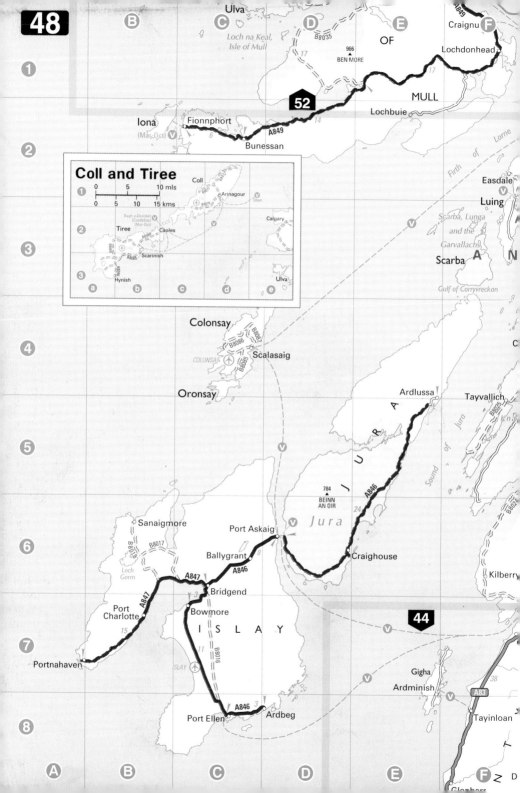

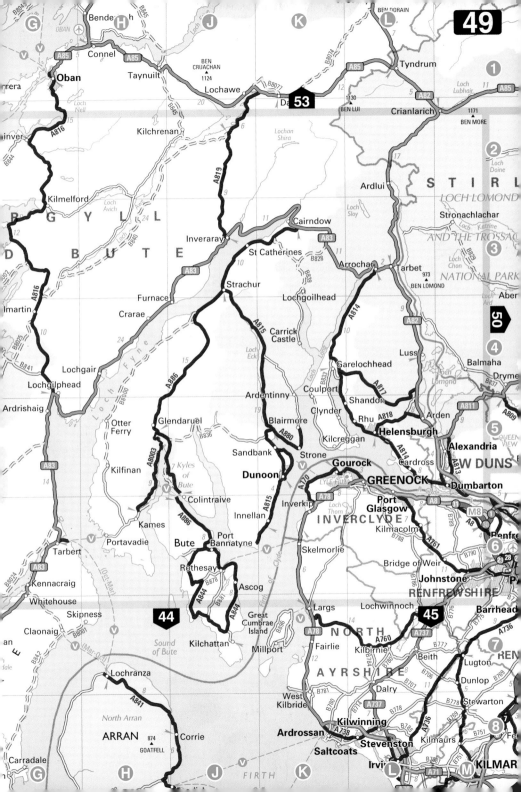

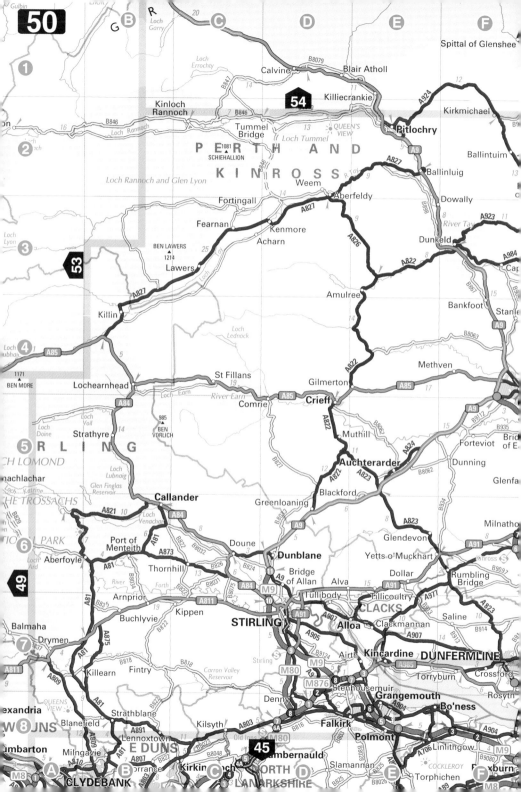

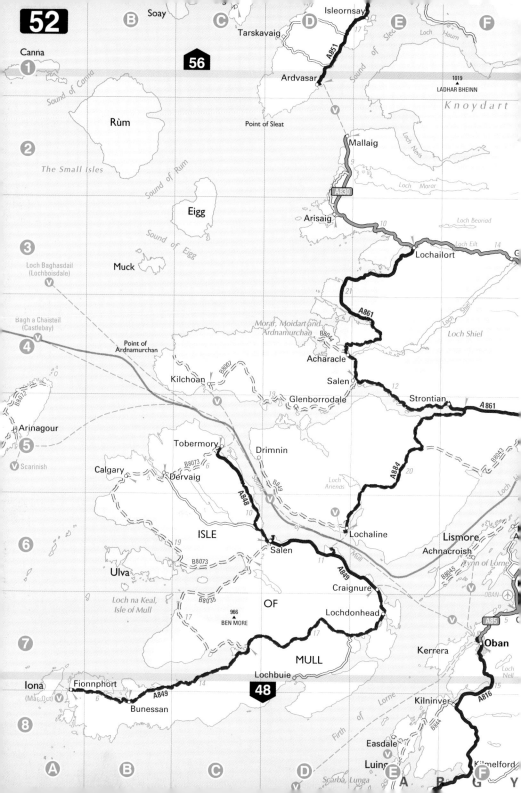

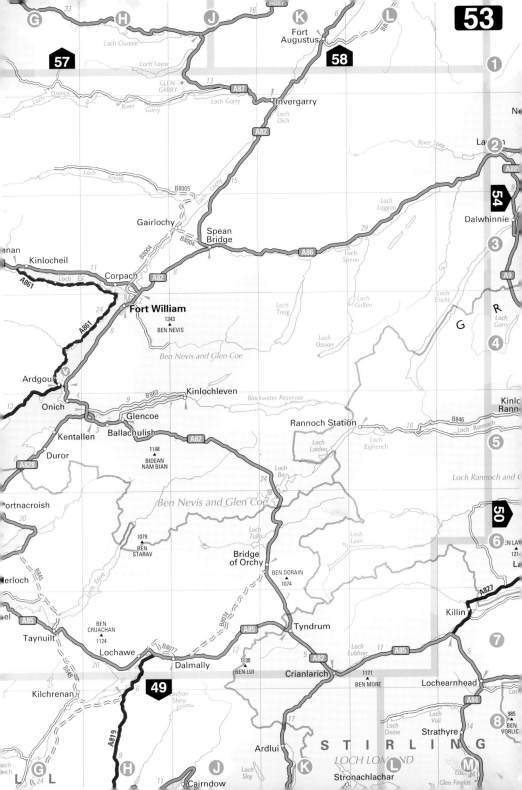

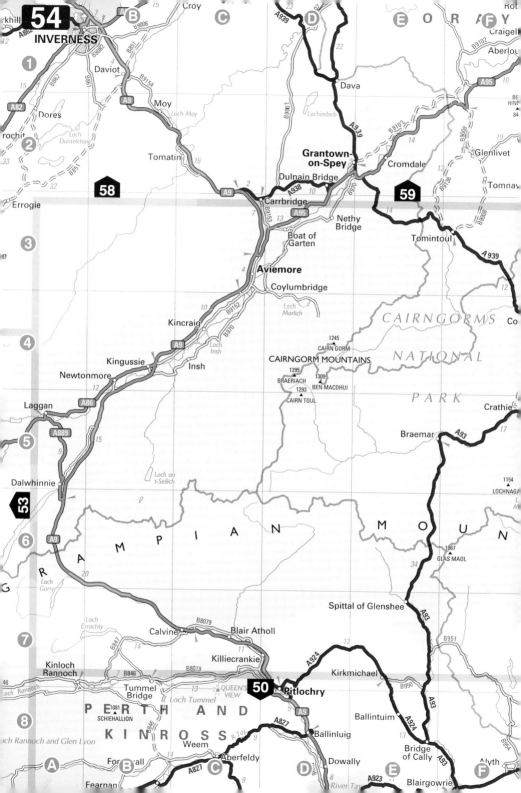

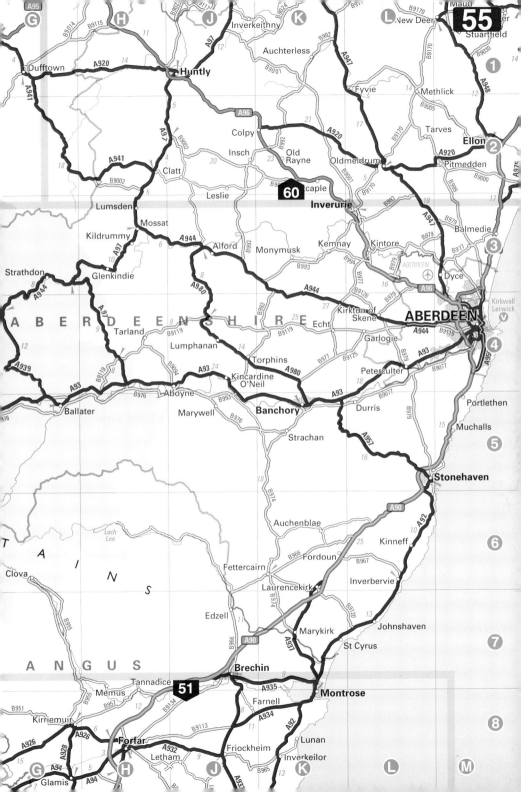

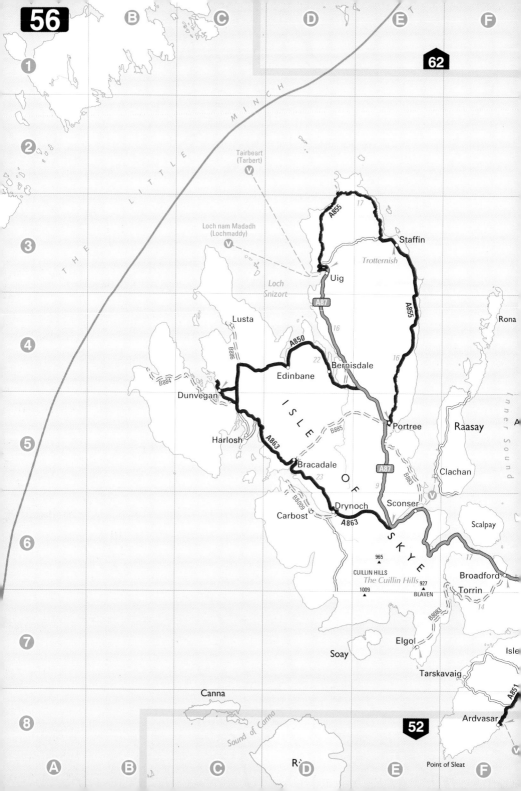

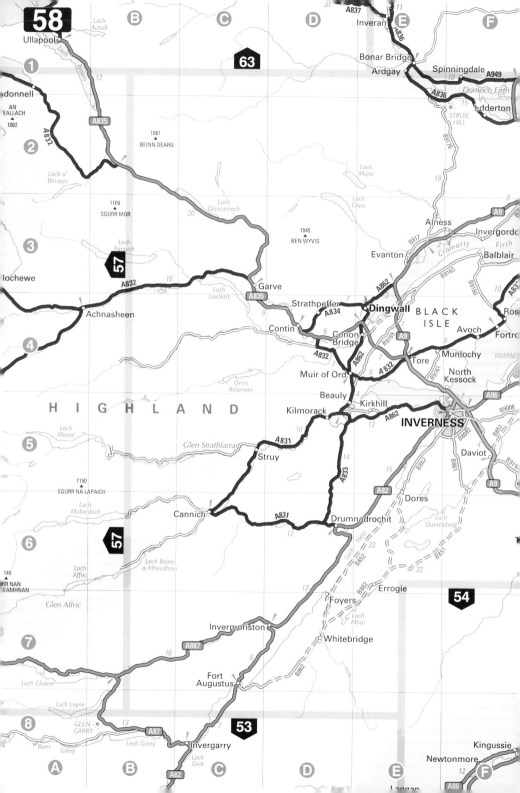

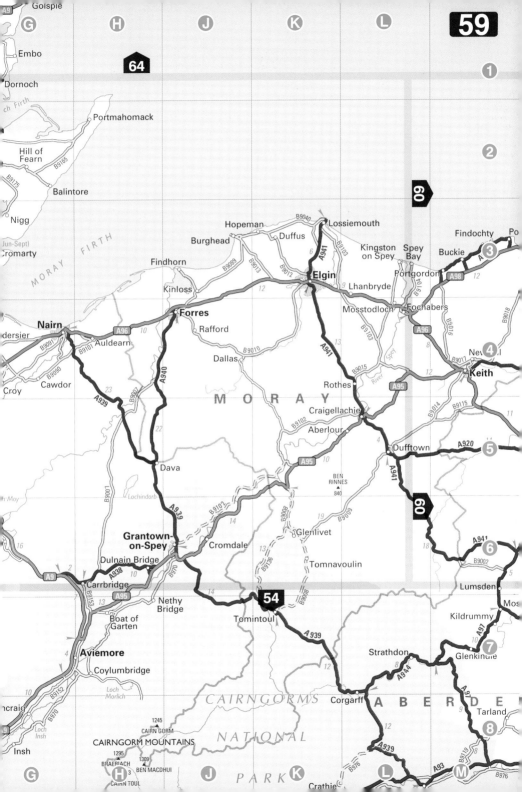

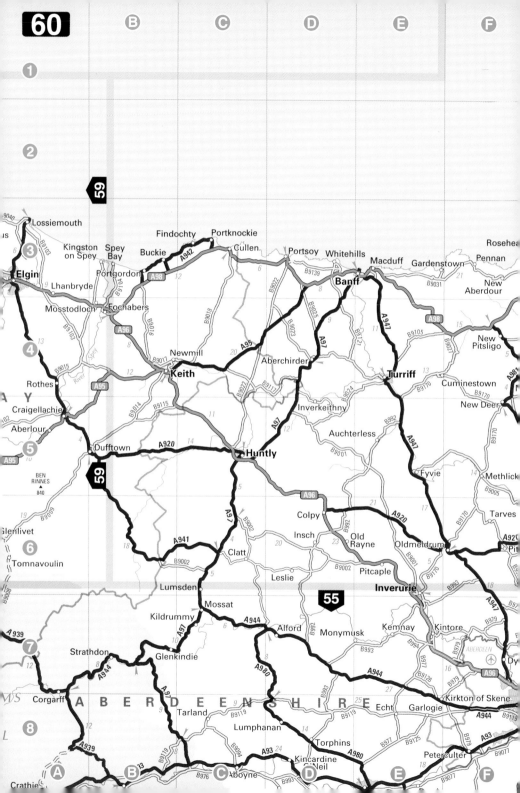

G   H   J   K   L

1
2
3

Sandhaven
Fraserburgh
B9032   Inverallochy
B9033   St Combs
A90
lemsie   Rathen
B9033
12   Strichen   Crimond
B9093   18
A952   12
St Fergus
50   6   Mintlaw
Id Deer   A950   PETERHEAD   H   **Peterhead**
artfield   Longside   9
A952
Clola   Boddam
14
A952   Hatton   A90
A948   Cruden Bay
A975
n.   17   Collieston
000   A975   32
Newburgh
17
Balmedie
A90
V
Kirkwall
Lerwick
ABERDEEN
A956
lethen

Shetland Islands

0   5   10   15 mls   *Herma Ness*
1   0   5   10   15   20 kms

Haroldswick
Unst   A968   Baltasound
2   Gutcher   Uyeasound
Yell   V
West   Mid
Sandwick   Yell   Fetlar
A970   A968   V
B9081
3   Ollaberry   Ulsta
B9078   V   Burravoe
Hillswick   Toft   Out
SHETLAND   Skerries
Brae
4   Muckle   Vidlin
Roe   Whalsay
Voe   V   Symbister
Sandness   ISLANDS
A971   V
5   Walls   A970
LERWICK
Scalloway   **Lerwick**
6   Kirkabister
MAINLAND   Bressay
V   Fladdabister
A970
7   Sandwick
V
Kirkwall
Aberdeen
8   Sumburgh
Head   SUMBURGH

a   b   c   d   e

1
2
3
4
5
6
7
8

G   H   J   K   L   M

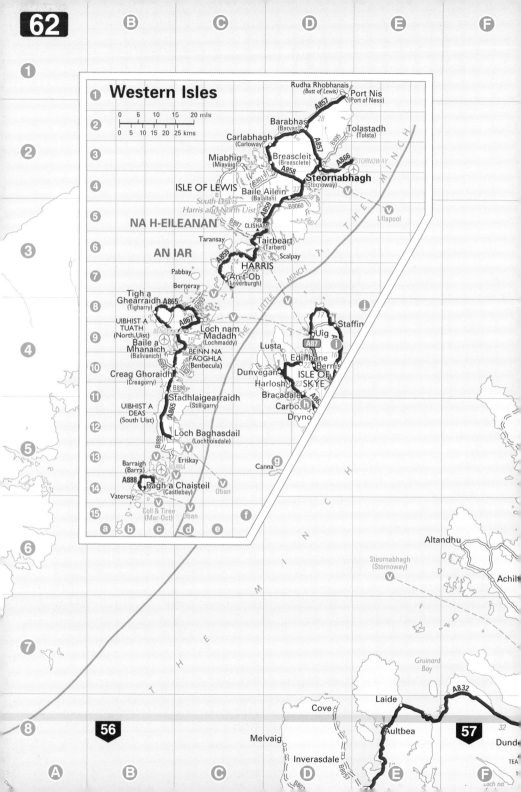

Western Isles

NA H-EILEANAN

AN IAR

ISLE OF LEWIS

South Lewis
Harris and North Uist

HARRIS

UIBHIST A TUATH
(North Uist)

BEINN NA FAOGHLA
(Benbecula)

UIBHIST A DEAS
(South Uist)

Rudha Rhobhanais
(Butt of Lewis)
Port Nis
(Port of Ness)

Barabhas
(Barvas)

Carlabhagh
(Carloway)

Tolastadh
(Tolsta)

Breascleit
(Breasclete)

Miabhig
(Miavaig)

Steornabhagh
(Stornoway)

Baile Ailein
(Balallan)

CLISHAM

Tairbeart
(Tarbert)

Taransay

Scalpay

Pabbay

An t-Ob
(Leverburgh)

Berneray

Tigh a Ghearraidh
(Tigharry)

Loch nam Madadh
(Lochmaddy)

Baile a Mhanaich
(Balivanich)

Lusta

Uig

Staffin

Dunvegan

Edinbane

Bernis

Creag Ghoraidh
(Creagorry)

ISLE OF SKYE

Harlosh

Bracadale

Stadhlaigearraidh
(Stilligarry)

Carbo

Dryno

Loch Baghasdail
(Lochboisdale)

Barraigh
(Barra)

Eriskay

Canna

Oban

Bagh a Chaisteil
(Castlebay)

Vatersay

Coll & Tiree
(Mar-Oct)

Oban

Altandhu

Steornabhagh
(Stornoway)

Achil

Gruinard
Bay

Laide

A832

Cove

Aultbea

Melvaig

Dund

Inverasdale

THE MINCH

THE LITTLE MINCH

Ullapool

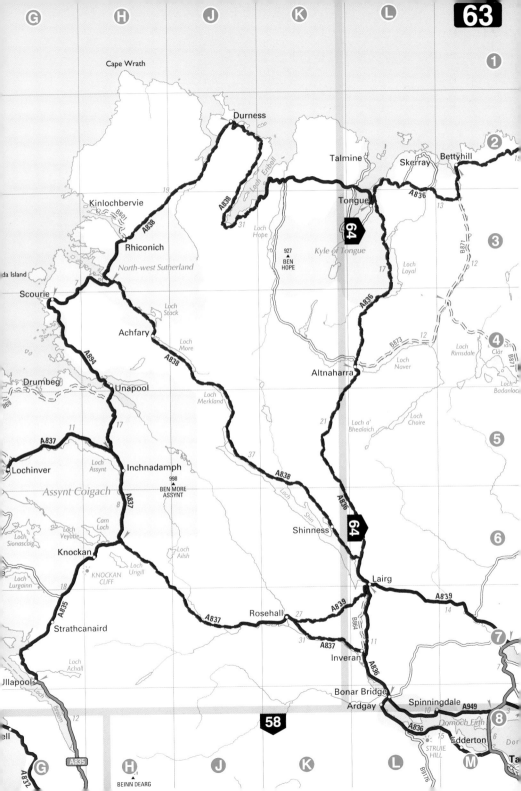

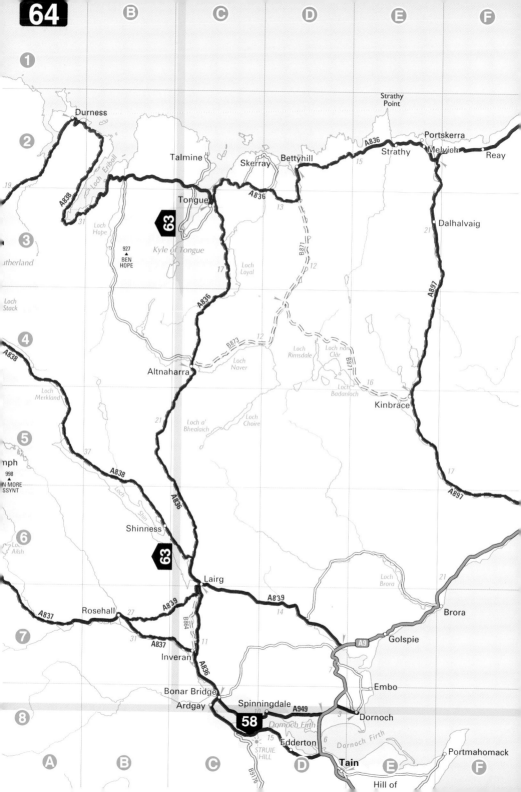

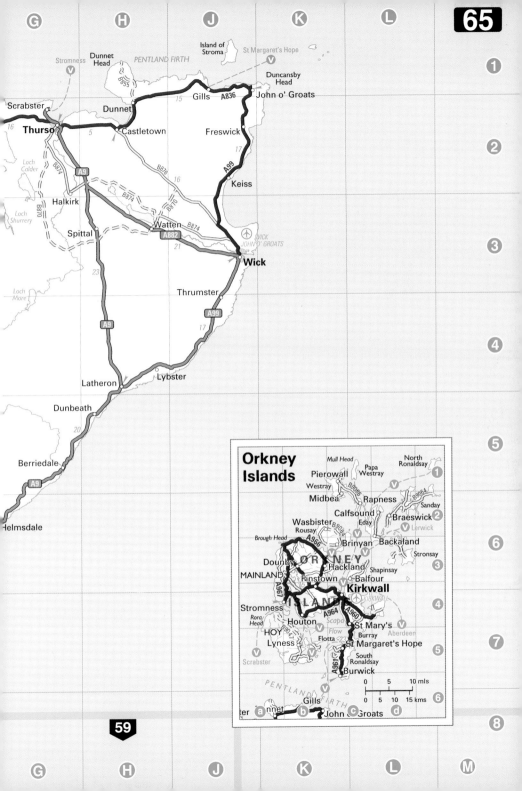

G   H   J   K   L

1
2
3
4
5
6
7
8

Stromness
Dunnet Head
Island of Stroma
St Margaret's Hope
PENTLAND FIRTH
Duncansby Head
B855
Scrabster
Gills
A836
John o' Groats
Dunnet
15
Thurso
Castletown
5
Freswick
16
B876
A99
17
Loch Calder
A9
B874
Keiss
Halkirk
B874
B870
B874
Loch Shurrery
Spittal
Watten
A882
B874
WICK JOHN O' GROATS
21
A9
Thrumster
23
Wick
Loch More
A99
A9
17
Latheron
Lybster
Dunbeath
20
Berriedale
A9
Helmsdale

Orkney Islands

Mull Head
Papa Westray
North Ronaldsay
Pierowall
1
Westray
B9066
Midbea
Rapness
B9064
Sanday
Calfsound
Braeswick
2
Wasbister
Eday
Lerwick
Rousay
A966
Brough Head
Brinyan
Backaland
Stronsay
Dounby
ORKNEY
Hackland
Shapinsay
3
MAINLAND
Finstown
Balfour
A967
Kirkwall
Stromness
KIRKWALL
4
Rora Head
Houton
A964
A960
St Mary's
HOY
Scapa Flow
Burray
Lyness
Flotta
St Margaret's Hope
5
Scrabster
A961
South Ronaldsay
Aberdeen
Burwick
A961
PENTLAND FIRTH
6
Gills
0   5   10 mls
a   nnet   b   c   Groats   d
John o' Groats
0   5   10   15 kms

G   H   J   K   L   M

Index to places in Britain

This index lists places appearing in the main-map section of the atlas in alphabetical order. The reference following each name gives the atlas page number and grid reference of the square in which the place appears. The map shows counties, unitary authorities and administrative areas, together with a list of the abbreviated name forms used in the index.

England

BaNES	**Bath & N E Somerset (18)**
Barns	**Barnsley (19)**
Bed	**Bedford**
Birm	**Birmingham**
Bl w D	**Blackburn with Darwen (20)**
Bmouth	**Bournemouth**
Bolton	**Bolton (21)**
Bpool	**Blackpool**
Br & H	**Brighton & Hove (22)**
Br For	**Bracknell Forest (23)**
Bristl	**City of Bristol**
Bucks	**Buckinghamshire**
Bury	**Bury (24)**
C Beds	**Central Bedfordshire**
C Brad	**City of Bradford**
C Derb	**City of Derby**
C KuH	**City of Kingston upon Hull**
C Leic	**City of Leicester**
C Nott	**City of Nottingham**
C Pete	**City of Peterborough**
C Plym	**City of Plymouth**
C Port	**City of Portsmouth**
C Sotn	**City of Southampton**
C Stke	**City of Stoke-on-Trent**
C York	**City of York**
Calder	**Calderdale (25)**
Cambs	**Cambridgeshire**
Ches E	**Cheshire East**
Ches W	**Cheshire West and Chester**
Cnwll	**Cornwall**
Covtry	**Coventry**
Cumb	**Cumbria**
Darltn	**Darlington (26)**
Derbys	**Derbyshire**
Devon	**Devon**
Donc	**Doncaster (27)**
Dorset	**Dorset**
Dudley	**Dudley (28)**
Dur	**Durham**
E R Yk	**East Riding of Yorkshire**
E Susx	**East Sussex**
Essex	**Essex**
Gatesd	**Gateshead (29)**
Gloucs	**Gloucestershire**
Gt Lon	**Greater London**
Halton	**Halton (30)**
Hants	**Hampshire**
Hartpl	**Hartlepool (31)**
Herefs	**Herefordshire**
Herts	**Hertfordshire**
IoS	**Isles of Scilly**
IoW	**Isle of Wight**
Kent	**Kent**
Kirk	**Kirklees (32)**
Knows	**Knowsley (33)**
Lancs	**Lancashire**
Leeds	**Leeds**
Leics	**Leicestershire**
Lincs	**Lincolnshire**
Lpool	**Liverpool**
Luton	**Luton**
M Keyn	**Milton Keynes**
Manch	**Manchester**

Medway	**Medway**
Middsb	**Middlesbrough**
NE Lin	**North East Lincolnshire**
N Linc	**North Lincolnshire**
N Som	**North Somerset (34)**
N Tyne	**North Tyneside (35)**
N u Ty	**Newcastle upon Tyne**
N York	**North Yorkshire**
Nhants	**Northamptonshire**
Norfk	**Norfolk**
Notts	**Nottinghamshire**
Nthumb	**Northumberland**
Oldham	**Oldham (36)**
Oxon	**Oxfordshire**
Poole	**Poole**
R & Cl	**Redcar & Cleveland**
Readg	**Reading**
Rochdl	**Rochdale (37)**
Rothm	**Rotherham (38)**
Rutlnd	**Rutland**
S Glos	**South Gloucestershire (39)**
S on T	**Stockton-on-Tees (40)**
S Tyne	**South Tyneside (41)**
Salfd	**Salford (42)**
Sandw	**Sandwell (43)**
Sefton	**Sefton (44)**
Sheff	**Sheffield**
Shrops	**Shropshire**
Slough	**Slough (45)**
Solhll	**Solihull (46)**
Somset	**Somerset**
St Hel	**St Helens (47)**
Staffs	**Staffordshire**
Sthend	**Southend-on-Sea**
Stockp	**Stockport (48)**
Suffk	**Suffolk**
Sundld	**Sunderland**
Surrey	**Surrey**
Swindn	**Swindon**
Tamesd	**Tameside (49)**
Thurr	**Thurrock (50)**
Torbay	**Torbay**
Traffd	**Trafford (51)**
W & M	**Windsor and Maidenhead (52)**
W Berk	**West Berkshire**
W Susx	**West Sussex**
Wakefd	**Wakefield (53)**
Warrtn	**Warrington (54)**
Warwks	**Warwickshire**
Wigan	**Wigan (55)**
Wilts	**Wiltshire**
Wirral	**Wirral (56)**
Wokham	**Wokingham (57)**
Wolves	**Wolverhampton (58)**
Worcs	**Worcestershire**
Wrekin	**Telford & Wrekin (59)**
Wsall	**Walsall (60)**

Channel Islands & Isle of Man

Guern	**Guernsey**
Jersey	**Jersey**
IoM	**Isle of Man**

Scotland

Abers	**Aberdeenshire**
Ag & B	**Argyll and Bute**
Angus	**Angus**
Border	**Scottish Borders**
C Aber	**City of Aberdeen**
C Dund	**City of Dundee**
C Edin	**City of Edinburgh**
C Glas	**City of Glasgow**
Clacks	**Clackmannanshire (1)**
D & G	**Dumfries & Galloway**
E Ayrs	**East Ayrshire**
E Duns	**East Dunbartonshire (2)**
E Loth	**East Lothian**
E Rens	**East Renfrewshire (3)**
Falk	**Falkirk**
Fife	**Fife**
Highld	**Highland**
Inver	**Inverclyde (4)**
Mdloth	**Midlothian (5)**
Moray	**Moray**
N Ayrs	**North Ayrshire**
N Lans	**North Lanarkshire (6)**
Ork	**Orkney Islands**
P & K	**Perth & Kinross**
Rens	**Renfrewshire (7)**
S Ayrs	**South Ayrshire**
Shet	**Shetland Islands**
S Lans	**South Lanarkshire**
Stirlg	**Stirling**
W Duns	**West Dunbartonshire (8)**
W Isls	**Western Isles (Na h-Eileanan an Iar)**
W Loth	**West Lothian**

Wales

Blae G	**Blaenau Gwent (9)**
Brdgnd	**Bridgend (10)**
Caerph	**Caerphilly (11)**
Cardif	**Cardiff**
Carmth	**Carmarthenshire**
Cerdgn	**Ceredigion**
Conwy	**Conwy**
Denbgs	**Denbighshire**
Flints	**Flintshire**
Gwynd	**Gwynedd**
IoA	**Isle of Anglesey**
Mons	**Monmouthshire**
Myr Td	**Merthyr Tydfil (12)**
Neath	**Neath Port Talbot (13)**
Newpt	**Newport (14)**
Pembks	**Pembrokeshire**
Powys	**Powys**
Rhondd	**Rhondda Cynon Taff (15)**
Swans	**Swansea**
Torfn	**Torfaen (16)**
V Glam	**Vale of Glamorgan (17)**
Wrexhm	**Wrexham**

ORKNEY ISLANDS

SHETLAND ISLANDS

WESTERN ISLES (Na h-Eileanan an Iar)

SCOTLAND

HIGHLAND

MORAY

ABERDEENSHIRE

Aberdeen

ANGUS

PERTH & KINROSS

Dundee

ARGYLL & BUTE

STIRLING

FIFE

1

FALK

Edinburgh

8 2 W
4   LOTH   E LOTH
7   3
6   5

Glasgow

NORTH AYRSHIRE

S LANS

E AYRS

SCOTTISH BORDERS

S AYRS

DUMFRIES & GALLOWAY

NORTHUMBERLAND

Newcastle upon Tyne 35
29   11
                      Sunderland

CUMBRIA

DURHAM

31
26 40 R & CL
     Middlesbrough

IoM

NORTH YORKSHIRE

Blackpool

LANCASHIRE

Bradford

York

EAST RIDING OF YORKSHIRE

Kingston upon Hull

Leeds

25

53

N LINC

N E LIN

20
21 24 37
36
55 47
44
33 42 49
54 51
56 30 48

32   19   27

Liverpool

Manchester

38
Sheffield

IoA

CONWY

FLINTS

CHES W

CHES E

DERBYS

NOTTS

LINCOLNSHIRE

DENBGS

WREXHAM

Stoke-on-Trent

Derby

Nottingham

GWYNEDD

STAFFS

59

SHROPSHIRE

58 60
28 43
46

LEICS

RUTLAND

Leicester

Peterborough

NORFOLK

POWYS

WORCS

WARWKS

Birmingham

Coventry

NHANTS

CAMBS

SUFFOLK

CERDGN

HEREFS

Milton Keynes

BED

PEMBKS

CARMTH

WALES

ENGLAND

BEDS Luton

HERTS

ESSEX

12 9
13   16
15 11
10   14
Cardiff
17

MONS

GLOUCS

OXON

BUCKS

Reading 52 45
57 23

GREATER LONDON

50

Southend-on-Sea

MEDWAY

Swansea

Bristol

39

Swindon

W BERK

SURREY

KENT

34 18

WILTSHIRE

HAMPSHIRE

W SUSX

E SUSX

SOMERSET

DORSET

Southampton

22

DEVON

Bournemouth
Poole

Portsmouth

IoW

CORNWALL

Torbay

CHANNEL ISLANDS

Guernsey

Jersey

Plymouth

IoS

A

Abberley Worcs 21 L4
Abbey Town Cumb 41 L6
Abbots Bromley
  Staffs............................29 H7
Aberaeron Cerdgn 19 H1
Aberarth Cerdgn 19 H1
Aberchirder Abers 60 D4
Aberdare Rhondd 12 B2
Aberdaron Gwynd 26 B6
Aberdeen C Aber 55 M4
Aberdyfi Gwynd 20 A2
Aberfeldy P & K 50 D2
Aberffraw IoA...............26 C3
Aberfoyle Stirlg 50 B6
Abergavenny Mons 21 G8
Abergele Conwy...........27 H3
Aberlady E Loth............46 E2
Aberlour Moray 59 L5
Abermule Powys 20 F2
Abernethy P & K............51 G5
Aberporth Cerdgn 18 F2
Abersoch Gwynd 26 C6
Abersychan Torfn 12 D2
Abertillery Blae G 12 D2
Aberystwyth Cerdgn....20 A3
Abingdon-on-
  Thames Oxon 14 C4
Abington S Lans............45 M5
Ab Kettleby Leics 30 D7
Aboyne Abers 55 J4
Abridge Essex 16 D7
Accrington Lancs 33 G4
Acharacle Highld 52 D4
Acharn P & K 50 C3
Achfary Highld..............63 H4
Achiltibuie Highld 62 F6
Achnacroish Ag & B 52 F6
Achnasheen Highld.......57 L4
Ackworth Moor Top
  Wakefd 34 B5
Acle Norfk.....................25 K5
Acton Trussell Staffs ...29 G7
Addingham C Brad.........33 J2
Adwick Le Street
  Donc 34 C6
Ainderby Steeple
  N York 38 D4
Airdrie N Lans................45 L2
Airth Falk 50 E7
Albrighton Shrops........21 L1
Albrighton Shrops.........28 C7
Albury Surrey 9 K2
Alcester Warwks 22 B4
Alconbury Cambs.........23 M3
Aldbourne Wilts 14 A6
Aldbrough E R Yk 35 J3
Aldeburgh Suffk 17 M2
Alderbury Wilts 8 C3
Alderley Edge Ches E ...28 F3
Aldermaston W Berk 14 D7
Alderminster Warwks ...22 D5
Aldershot Hants 9 H2
Aldford Ches W.............28 B4
Aldham Essex 17 G5
Aldsworth Gloucs 13 L1
Alexandria W Duns 49 M5
Alfold Surrey 9 K3
Alford Abers 55 J3
Alford Lincs 31 K3
Alfreton Derbys 29 L4
Alfriston E Susx 10 D7
Alkham Kent 11 K4
Allanton Border 47 H4
Allendale Nthumb.........42 F6
Allenheads Nthumb......42 F7
Allensmore Herefs 21 J6
Alloa Clacks..................50 E7
Allonby Cumb 41 L7
Alloway S Ayrs 45 G6
Almondsbury S Glos 13 G3
Alness Highld 58 F3
Alnmouth Nthumb 43 K2
Alnwick Nthumb 47 L7
Alrewas Staffs..............29 J7
Alsager Ches E..............28 E4
Alston Cumb 42 E6
Altandhu Highld 62 F6
Althorpe N Linc.............34 E5
Altnaharra Highld 64 C4
Alton Hants 9 G2
Alton Pancras Dorset ...7 K2
Altrincham Traffd.........28 E2
Alva Clacks...................50 E6
Alveston S Glos 13 G3
Alyth P & K 51 G3
Amberley W Susx 9 K4
Amble Nthumb..............43 K2
Ambleside Cumb...........37 G3

Amersham Bucks 15 G4
Amesbury Wilts 8 C2
Amlwch IoA...................26 D1
Ammanford Carmth 19 J5
Ampleforth N York........38 F3
Ampthill C Beds 23 K6
Amroth Pembks 18 E5
Amulree P & K...............50 E3
Ancaster Lincs..............30 F5
Ancroft Nthumb............47 K5
Ancrum Border..............47 G7
Andover Hants................8 D2
Andoversford Gloucs ...22 B7
Andreas IoM 36 c1
Angle Pembks 18 C6
Angmering W Susx.........9 K5
Annan D & G 41 M5
Annfield Plain Dur.........43 J6
Anstey Leics 30 C8
Anstruther Fife 51 K6
An t-Ob W Isls 62 e7
Anwick Lincs 31 G5
Appleby-in-
  Westmorland
  Cumb 37 J2
Applecross Highld 57 G5
Appledore Devon 4 D4
Appledore Kent.............11 H5
Appletreewick
  N York 38 A7
Arbroath Angus............51 L3
Arclid Green Ches E 28 E4
Ardbeg Ag & B 48 D8
Arddleen Powys 27 L7
Arden Ag & B.................49 L5
Ardentinny Ag & B 49 K4
Ardersier Highld 59 G4
Ardgay Highld 64 C8
Ardgour Highld 53 G4
Ardingly W Susx 10 C5
Ardleigh Essex 17 H4
Ardlui Ag & B.................49 L2
Ardlussa Ag & B 48 E4
Ardminish Ag & B 44 A3
Ardrishaig Ag & B 49 G5
Ardrossan N Ayrs..........44 F4
Ardvasar Highld............52 D1
Ardwell D & G................40 C7
Arinagour Ag & B 48 d1
Arisaig Highld...............52 D3
Arkholme Lancs 37 J6
Armadale W Loth 45 M2
Armathwaite Cumb 42 C7
Arncliffe N York............37 M6
Arnprior Stirlg 50 B7
Arnside Cumb 37 H5
Arrington Cambs...........16 B3
Arrochar Ag & B 49 L3
Arundel W Susx 9 K5
Ascog Ag & B.................49 J6
Ascot W & M..................15 G6
Ash Kent.......................11 K3
Ashbourne Derbys 29 J5
Ashburton Devon............6 B5
Ashbury Oxon 14 A5
Ashby-de-la-Zouch
  Leics 29 K7
Ashcott Somset 12 E7
Ashford Kent.................11 H4
Ashington Nthumb........43 K3
Ashington W Susx 9 L4
Ashley Cambs 16 E2
Ashton-under-Lyne
  Tamesd........................33 H6
Ashurst Hants 8 D5
Ashwater Devon 4 D7
Askam in Furness
  Cumb 36 F5
Askern Donc 34 C5
Askham Cumb 37 H2
Askrigg N York 37 M4
Aspatria Cumb..............41 L7
Aston Oxon 14 B4
Aston Clinton Bucks.....14 F3
Aston on Clun Shrops...21 J4
Aston Rowant Oxon......14 E4
Atcham Shrops..............28 C8
Atherstone Warwks 22 D1
Atherton Wigan............32 F6
Attleborough Norfk 25 H6
Attlebridge Norfk 25 H5
Atwick E R Yk................35 H2
Auchenblae Abers........55 K6
Auchencairn D & G 41 H6
Auchinleck E Ayrs 45 J5
Auchterarder P & K.......50 E5
Auchterless Abers........60 E5
Auchtermuchty Fife......51 G5
Audlem Ches E 28 E5
Audley Staffs 28 E5
Auldearn Highld 59 H4

Auldgirth D & G............41 J3
Aultbea Highld..............57 H1
Austwick N York 37 K6
Avebury Wilts 13 L4
Avening Gloucs 13 J2
Aveton Gifford
  Devon 6 A6
Aviemore Highld...........54 C3
Avoch Highld.................58 F4
Avonmouth Bristl.........12 F4
Awsworth Notts............30 B5
Axbridge Somset..........12 E5
Axminster Devon 6 F3
Axmouth Devon 6 F3
Aylesbury Bucks...........14 F3
Aylesham Kent..............11 K3
Aylsham Norfk 25 J3
Aynho Nhants...............22 F6
Ayr S Ayrs 45 G5
Aysgarth N York 38 A4
Ayton Border 47 J4

B

Backaland Ork 65 d2
Bacton Norfk 25 K3
Bacup Lancs 33 H4
Bagby N York 38 E5
Bagh a Chaisteil W Isls..62 b14
Bagillt Flints 27 K3
Baglan Neath 19 K6
Bagshot Surrey.............14 F7
Baile Ailein W Isls.........62 g4
Baile a Mhanaich
  W Isls 62 c10
Bainbridge N York 37 M4
Bainton E R Yk..............34 F2
Bakewell Derbys 29 J3
Bala Gwynd...................27 H6
Balallan W Isls..............62 g4
Balbeggie P & K............51 G4
Balblair Highld 58 F3
Balcombe W Susx.........10 B5
Baldersby N York..........38 D5
Baldock Herts 16 B4
Balfour Ork 65 c3
Balintore Highld 59 G2
Balivanich W Isls.........62 c10
Ballachulish Highld 53 H5
Ballantrae S Ayrs..........40 B4
Ballasalla IoM...............36 b4
Ballater Abers 55 G5
Ballaugh IoM 36 c2
Ballinluig P & K 50 E2
Ballintuim P & K 50 F2
Ballygrant Ag & B..........48 C6
Balmaclellan D & G 41 G4
Balmaha Stirlg 49 M4
Balmedie Abers 55 M3
Balsall Common
  Solhll..........................22 D3
Balsham Cambs............16 E3
Baltasound Shet 61 d1
Bamber Bridge Lancs ...32 E4
Bamburgh Nthumb 47 L6
Bamford Derbys 29 J2
Bampton Cumb.............37 H2
Bampton Devon 5 H5
Bampton Oxon 14 A4
Banbury Oxon 22 E6
Banchory Abers............55 K5
Banff Abers 60 E3
Bangor Gwynd 26 E3
Bangor-on-Dee
  Wrexhm 28 B5
Banham Norfk 25 H6
Bankfoot P & K..............50 F4
Banstead Surrey...........10 B3
Banwell N Som 12 E5
Barabhas W Isls...........62 h2
Barbon Cumb 37 J5
Bardney Lincs 31 G3
Bardon Mill Nthumb 42 F5
Bardsea Cumb 36 F5
Barford Warwks 22 D4
Bargoed Caerph 12 C2
Bar Hill Cambs 16 C2
Barking Gt Lon 16 C8
Barkston Lincs 30 F5
Barkway Herts 16 C4
Barley Herts 16 C4
Barmby Moor E R Yk......34 D3
Barmouth Gwynd 26 F7
Barmston E R Yk 39 L7
Barnard Castle Dur.......38 A2
Barnby Moor Notts........30 D2
Barnet Gt Lon................15 J4
Barnetby le Wold
  N Linc 35 G6

Barnoldswick Lancs......33 H3
Barnsley Barns.............33 M6
Barnsley Gloucs 13 L2
Barnstaple Devon 4 E4
Barr S Ayrs....................40 D3
Barrasford Nthumb.......43 G4
Barrhead E Rens...........45 H3
Barrhill S Ayrs 40 D4
Barrowford Lancs 33 H3
Barrow-in-Furness
  Cumb 36 E6
Barrow upon Soar
  Leics 30 C7
Barry V Glam..................5 K1
Barton Cambs 16 C2
Barton Lancs.................32 E3
Barton N York 38 C3
Barton-le-Clay
  C Beds.........................23 L7
Barton Seagrave
  Nhants 23 J3
Barton-under-
  Needwood Staffs........29 J7
Barton-upon-
  Humber N Linc 35 G5
Barvas W Isls 62 h2
Barwell Leics 22 E2
Basildon Essex 16 F7
Basingstoke Hants 9 G1
Baslow Derbys 29 J3
Bassenthwaite
  Cumb 42 A8
Bassingham Lincs 31 G7
Bath BaNES...................13 H5
Bathgate W Loth...........46 A3
Batley Kirk 33 L4
Battle E Susx 10 F6
Baumber Lincs 31 H3
Bawdeswell Norfk 25 H4
Bawdsey Suffk..............17 L4
Bawtry Donc 34 D7
Baycliff Cumb................36 F6
Bayston Hill Shrops......28 C8
Beaconsfield Bucks......15 G5
Beadnell Nthumb..........47 L6
Beaford Devon 4 E5
Beal Nthumb 47 K5
Beaminster Dorset.........7 H2
Beare Green Surrey........9 L2
Bearsted Kent...............10 F3
Beattock D & G 41 L2
Beaulieu Hants 8 E5
Beauly Highld 58 D5
Beaumaris IoA 26 E3
Beaumont Jersey 7 b2
Beaworthy Devon 4 D7
Bebington Wirral 27 L2
Beccles Suffk................25 L6
Beckhampton Wilts 13 L4
Beckingham Lincs.........30 E4
Beckington Somset 13 H6
Beck Row Suffk 24 E7
Bedale N York 38 C4
Beddgelert Gwynd 26 E5
Bedford Bed 23 K5
Bedlington Nthumb 43 K4
Bedworth Warwks.........22 E2
Beeford E R Yk 35 H2
Beeley Derbys 29 J3
Beer Devon 6 F3
Beesands Devon 6 B7
Beeston Ches W 28 C4
Beeston Notts 30 B6
Beeswing D & G 41 J5
Beetham Cumb 37 H5
Beetley Norfk 25 G4
Beguildy Powys 20 F3
Beith N Ayrs..................45 G3
Belford Nthumb 47 L6
Bellingham Nthumb......42 F4
Bellochantuy Ag & B.....44 A5
Bellshill N Lans 45 K2
Belper Derbys...............29 K5
Belsay Nthumb..............43 H4
Belton N Linc.................34 E6
Belton Norfk 25 L5
Bembridge IoW 9 G6
Bempton E R Yk.............39 L6
Benderloch Ag & B........52 F6
Benenden Kent..............10 F5
Benllech IoA 26 D2
Benson Oxon 14 D5
Bentley Hants 9 H2
Benwick Cambs 24 B6
Bere Alston Devon..........3 K4
Bere Ferrers Devon 3 K4
Bere Regis Dorset 7 L3
Berkeley Gloucs 13 G2
Berkhamsted Herts 15 G3
Bernisdale Highld..........56 D4
Berriedale Highld 65 G3

Berriew Powys..............20 F1
Berrow Somset...........12 D6
Berwick St John Wilts...13 K8
Berwick-upon-
Tweed Nthumb.......47 K1
Bethersden Kent........11 G4
Bethesda Gwynd........26 E3
Bettyhill Highld...........64 D2
Betws-y-Coed Conwy...27 G4
Betws-yn-Rhos
Conwy.....................27 H3
Beulah Powys..............20 D5
Beverley E R Yk..........35 G3
Bewdley Worcs............21 L3
Bexhill E Susx.............10 F7
Bibury Gloucs.............13 L1
Bicester Oxon.............14 D2
Bickleigh Devon............5 H6
Biddenden Kent..........11 G4
Biddisham Somset.......12 E6
Biddulph Staffs...........28 F4
Bideford Devon............4 D5
Bidford-on-Avon
Warwks....................22 C5
Bigbury-on-Sea
Devon.......................3 M6
Biggar S Lans.............46 B6
Biggin Hill Gt Lon.......10 C3
Biggleswade C Beds....23 M5
Bildeston Suffk...........17 H3
Billericay Essex...........16 E7
Billingborough Lincs...31 G6
Billingham S on T........38 E2
Billinghay Lincs...........31 H4
Billingshurst W Susx.....9 K3
Bilsby Lincs.................31 K3
Bilsthorpe Notts.........30 C4
Binbrook Lincs............35 H7
Binfield Br For............16 F6
Bingham Notts............30 D5
Bingley C Brad...........33 K3
Birdlip Gloucs.............22 A8
Birkenhead Wirral.......32 C7
Birmingham Birm........26 B2
Birstall Leics..............30 C8
Birtley Gatesd............43 K6
Bishop Auckland Dur...38 C1
Bishop's Castle
Shrops.....................21 G2
Bishop's Cleeve
Gloucs......................22 A7
Bishop's Frome
Herefs......................21 K5
Bishops Lydeard
Somset.....................12 C7
Bishop's Stortford
Herts........................16 D5
Bishopsteignton
Devon.......................6 C4
Bishopston Swans......19 J7
Bishopstone Swindn....13 M3
Bishop Sutton BaNES...13 G5
Bishop's Waltham
Hants.........................8 F4
Bitchfield Lincs...........30 F6
Bitton S Glos..............13 G4
Blaby Leics.................22 F1
Blackbrook Staffs........28 E6
Blackburn Bl w D........32 F4
Blackford P & K...........50 E6
Blackmill Brdgnd.........19 M7
Blackpool Bpool..........32 C3
Black Torrington
Devon........................4 D6
Blackwater IoW.............8 F6
Blackwaterfoot
N Ayrs.....................44 C5
Blackwood Caerph......12 C2
Blackwood S Lans......45 L4
Bladon Oxon..............14 C3
Blaenau Ffestiniog
Gwynd.....................26 F5
Blaenavon Torfn.........12 D1
Blaengarw Brdgnd......19 L6
Blaenporth Cerdgn.....18 F2
Blagdon N Som..........12 F5
Blair Atholl P & K........54 C7
Blairgowrie P & K........51 G3
Blairmore Ag & B........49 K5
Blakeney Gloucs.........13 G1
Blakesley Nhants........23 G5
Blanchland Nthumb.....43 G6
Blandford Forum
Dorset........................7 L2
Blanefield Stirlg..........50 B8
Blaxton Donc..............34 D6
Blaydon Gatesd..........43 J5
Bleadney Somset........12 F6
Bleadon N Som...........12 E5
Blean Kent.................11 J3
Bleddfa Powys............20 F4

Bletchingley Surrey.....10 B3
Bletchley M Keyn........23 J6
Bletsoe Bed................23 K4
Blewbury Oxon...........14 C5
Blickling Norfk............25 J3
Blidworth Notts..........30 C4
Blindley Heath
Surrey.....................10 C4
Blisland Cnwll...............3 G4
Bloxham Oxon............22 E6
Blubberhouses
N York.....................38 B7
Blue Anchor Somset.....5 J3
Blyth Nthumb..............43 K4
Blyton Lincs................34 E7
Boat of Garten
Highld.....................54 D3
Boddam Abers............61 H5
Bodfari Denbgs...........27 J3
Bodfuan Gwynd..........26 C6
Bodiam E Susx...........10 F5
Bodmin Cnwll...............3 G4
Bognor Regis W Susx....9 J6
Bollington Ches E.......29 G3
Bolney W Susx...........10 B6
Bolsover Derbys.........29 L3
Bolton Bolton..............32 F6
Bolton Abbey N York...33 J2
Bolton le Sands
Lancs......................37 H6
Bolventor Cnwll............3 H3
Bonar Bridge Highld...64 C8
Bonchester Bridge
Border......................42 D1
Bo'ness Falk..............46 A2
Bonnyrigg Mdloth.......46 D4
Bontnewydd Gwynd....26 D4
Bonvilston V Glam......12 B4
Boot Cumb.................36 E3
Bootle Cumb...............36 E4
Bootle Sefton.............32 C7
Bordeaux Guern...........6 b1
Boreham Street
E Susx....................10 E6
Borehamwood Herts...15 J4
Boroughbridge
N York.....................38 D6
Borough Green Kent...10 E3
Borrowash Derbys......29 L6
Borth Cerdgn..............20 A2
Borth-y-Gest Gwynd...26 E6
Boscastle Cnwll............3 G2
Bosham W Susx...........9 H5
Bosherston Pembks....18 D6
Boston Lincs...............31 J5
Boston Spa Leeds......34 B3
Botesdale Suffk..........25 H7
Bothel Cumb...............41 M7
Bottesford Leics.........30 E6
Bough Beech Kent......10 D4
Boughton Street
Kent........................11 H3
Boulmer Nthumb........47 M7
Bourne Lincs..............31 G7
Bournemouth
Bmouth......................8 B6
Bourton Shrops..........21 K2
Bourton-on-the-
Water Gloucs...........22 C7
Bovey Tracey Devon.....6 B4
Bowes Dur.................37 M3
Bowmore Ag & B........48 C7
Bowness-on-Solway
Cumb......................41 M5
Box Wilts...................13 J4
Boxford Suffk.............17 H4
Bozeat Nhants...........23 J4
Bracadale Highld........56 D5
Brackley Nhants.........23 G6
Bracknell Br For.........14 F6
Bradford C Brad.........33 K4
Bradford-on-Avon
Wilts........................13 J5
Brading IoW.................8 F6
Bradwell Derbys.........29 J2
Bradwell-on-Sea
Essex......................17 H6
Bradworthy Devon........4 C6
Brae Shet..................61 b4
Braemar Abers...........54 E5
Braeswick Ork............65 d2
Braidwood S Lans......45 L3
Brailsford Derbys.......29 J5
Braintree Essex..........16 F5
Braithwaite Cumb.......36 F2
Bramdean Hants..........8 F4
Bramfield Suffk...........25 K7
Bramham Leeds.........34 B3
Bramhope Leeds........33 L3
Bramley Hants...........13 D7
Bramley Surrey............9 K2

Brampton Cambs........23 M3
Brampton Cumb..........42 D5
Bramshaw Hants..........8 D4
Brancaster Norfk........24 E2
Brandesburton
E R Yk....................35 H3
Brandon Dur..............43 J7
Brandon Suffk............24 E6
Brandon Warwks........22 E3
Branscombe Devon......6 E3
Bransgore Hants..........8 C6
Branston Lincs...........30 F3
Branthwaite Cumb......36 D2
Brassington Derbys....29 J4
Brasted Kent..............10 D3
Bratton Wilts..............13 J6
Bratton Clovelly
Devon........................3 K2
Bratton Fleming
Devon........................4 F4
Braughing Herts.........16 C5
Braunton Devon............4 E4
Brayford Devon............4 F4
Breascleit W Isls........62 g3
Breasclete W Isls.......62 g3
Brechfa Carmth..........19 H4
Brechin Angus............55 J7
Brecon Powys............20 E7
Brede E Susx..............11 G6
Bredenbury Herefs.....21 K5
Bredhurst Kent...........10 F3
Bredon Worcs.............22 A6
Bredwardine Herefs....21 G6
Brendon Devon............5 G3
Brent Knoll Somset.....12 E6
Brentwood Essex........16 E7
Brenzett Kent.............11 H5
Brereton Green
Ches E....................28 E4
Brewood Staffs...........28 F8
Bride IoM...................36 c1
Bridestowe Devon........3 L2
Bridge Kent................11 J3
Bridgend Ag & B.........44 C4
Bridgend Ag & B.........48 C6
Bridgend Brdgnd........19 L7
Bridge of Allan Stirlg...50 D6
Bridge of Cally P & K...51 G2
Bridge of Earn P & K...51 G5
Bridge of Orchy
Ag & B....................53 K6
Bridge of Weir Rens...49 M6
Bridgnorth Shrops......21 L3
Bridgwater Somset.....12 D7
Bridlington E R Yk......39 L6
Bridport Dorset............7 H3
Brierfield Lancs...........33 H3
Brigg N Linc...............35 G6
Brigham Cumb............41 L8
Brighouse Calder........33 K4
Brighstone IoW.............8 E7
Brightlingsea Essex....17 J5
Brighton Br & H..........10 B7
Brigstock Nhants........23 K2
Brinklow Warwks........22 E3
Brinkworth Wilts.........13 K3
Brinyan Ork................65 c3
Bristol Bristl...............13 G4
Brixham Torbay............6 C6
Brixton Devon..............3 L5
Brixton Gt Lon............15 K6
Brixworth Nhants........23 H3
Broad Blunsdon
Swindn....................13 L3
Broad Chalke Wilts.....13 K8
Broadclyst Devon.........6 D3
Broadford Highld........56 F6
Broad Haven Pembks...18 C5
Broadstairs Kent........11 L2
Broadway Worcs.........22 C6
Broadwindsor
Dorset........................7 G2
Brockdish Norfk..........25 J7
Brockenhurst Hants......8 D5
Brockford Street
Suffk.......................17 J1
Brockworth Gloucs.....21 M8
Brodick N Ayrs...........44 D4
Brome Suffk...............25 H7
Bromfield Shrops........21 J3
Bromham Bed............23 K5
Bromley Gt Lon..........10 C2
Brompton-by-
Sawdon N York........39 J5
Brompton Regis
Somset......................5 H4
Bromsgrove Worcs.....22 A3
Bromyard Herefs........21 K5
Bronllys Powys...........20 F6
Brooke Norfk..............25 K6
Brookland Kent...........11 H5

Brookmans Park
Herts.......................15 J4
Broomfield Nthumb.....43 K2
Brora Highld...............64 F7
Broseley Shrops.........21 K1
Brotherton N York......34 B4
Brotton R & Cl...........39 G2
Brough Cumb.............37 K2
Broughton Border.......46 B6
Broughton N Linc.......34 F6
Broughton-in-
Furness Cumb........36 F5
Broughton Poggs
Oxon.......................13 M2
Brownhills Wsall.........29 H8
Broxburn W Loth........46 B3
Broxted Essex............16 D5
Brundall Norfk............25 K5
Bruton Somset...........13 G7
Brynamman Carmth....19 K5
Bryncrug Gwynd.........20 A1
Brynmawr Blae G.......12 C1
Bubwith E R Yk..........34 D3
Buchlyvie Stirlg..........50 B7
Buckden Cambs.........23 M4
Buckden N York.........37 M5
Buckfastleigh Devon.....6 B5
Buckhaven Fife...........51 H6
Buckhorn Weston
Dorset.....................13 H8
Buckie Moray.............60 B3
Buckingham Bucks.....23 G6
Buckland Herts...........16 C4
Bucklers Hard Hants.....8 E5
Buckley Flints.............27 L4
Bucklow Hill Ches E....28 E2
Buckminster Leics......30 E7
Bude Cnwll...................4 B6
Budleigh Salterton
Devon........................6 D4
Bugle Cnwll..................2 F5
Builth Wells Powys.....20 E5
Bulford Wilts................8 C2
Bulkington Warwks.....22 E2
Bulphan Thurr............16 E6
Bulwick Nhants..........23 K2
Bunessan Ag & B.......48 C2
Bungay Suffk.............25 K6
Bunny Notts...............30 C6
Buntingford Herts.......16 C4
Bunwell Norfk.............25 H6
Burbage Wilts............13 M5
Bures Essex...............17 H4
Burford Oxon..............13 M1
Burgess Hill W Susx...10 B6
Burgh by Sands
Cumb......................42 B6
Burgh Castle Norfk.....25 L5
Burghead Moray.........59 J3
Burghfield W Berk......14 D6
Burgh le Marsh Lincs...31 K4
Burley Hants................8 C5
Burleydam Ches E......28 D5
Burley in
Wharfedale
C Brad.....................33 K3
Burlton Shrops...........28 C7
Burneston N York.......38 C5
Burnham Market
Norfk.......................24 F2
Burnham-on-Crouch
Essex......................17 H7
Burnham-on-Sea
Somset....................12 D6
Burnham Overy
Staithe Norfk...........24 F2
Burnley Lancs.............33 G4
Burnopfield Dur..........43 J6
Burntisland Fife..........46 C2
Burravoe Shet............61 d3
Burrelton P & K..........51 G3
Burrington Devon.........4 F5
Burry Port Carmth......19 H6
Burscough Bridge
Lancs......................32 D5
Bursledon Hants..........8 E5
Burton Ches W...........27 L3
Burton Agnes E R Yk...39 K6
Burton Bradstock
Dorset........................7 H3
Burton Fleming
E R Yk....................39 K6
Burton-in-Kendal
Cumb......................37 H6
Burton Joyce Notts....30 C5
Burton Latimer
Nhants....................23 J3
Burton upon
Stather N Linc........34 F5
Burton upon Trent
Staffs......................29 J7

Burwash E Susx 10 E5
Burwell Cambs 16 E1
Burwick Ork 65 c6
Bury Bury 33 G5
Bury St Edmunds
  Suffk 17 G2
Bushey Herts 15 H4
Butley Suffk 17 L3
Buttermere Cumb 36 E2
Butterwick Lincs 31 J5
Buttington Powys 27 K8
Buxted E Susx 10 D6
Buxton Derbys 29 H3
Bwlch Powys 20 F7
Byfleet Surrey 15 H7
Bylchau Conwy 27 H4
Byrness Nthumb 42 F2

C

Cadgwith Cnwll 2 D8
Caerleon Newpt 12 E3
Caernarfon Gwynd 26 D4
Caerphilly Caerph 12 C3
Caersws Powys 20 E2
Caerwent Mons 12 F3
Caerwys Flints 27 J3
Cairndow Ag & B 49 K3
Cairnryan D & G 40 B5
Caister-on-Sea Norfk 25 L5
Caistor Lincs 35 H6
Caldbeck Cumb 42 B7
Caldecott Rutlnd 23 J2
Calder Bridge Cumb 36 D3
Caldercruix N Lans 45 L2
Caldicot Mons 12 F3
Calfsound Ork 65 d2
Calgary Ag & B 52 B5
Callander Stirlg 50 B6
Callington Cnwll 3 J4
Calne Wilts 13 K4
Calshot Hants 8 E5
Calvine P & K 54 C7
Camber E Susx 11 H6
Camberley Surrey 14 F7
Cambo Nthumb 43 H4
Camborne Cnwll 2 C6
Cambourne Cambs 16 B2
Cambridge Cambs 16 C2
Cambridge Gloucs 13 H2
Cambuslang S Lans 45 K2
Camden Town Gt Lon 15 K5
Camelford Cnwll 3 G3
Campbeltown Ag & B 44 B5
Candlesby Lincs 31 K3
Cannich Highld 58 C6
Cannington Somset 12 D7
Cannock Staffs 29 G8
Canonbie D & G 42 C4
Canterbury Kent 11 J3
Canvey Island Essex 16 F8
Caoles Ag & B 48 b2
Capel Surrey 9 L2
Capel Bangor Cerdgn 20 B3
Capel Curig Conwy 26 F4
Capel St Mary Suffk 17 J4
Caputh P & K 50 F3
Carbost Highld 56 D6
Cardiff Cardif 12 C4
Cardigan Cerdgn 18 E2
Cardington Bed 23 L5
Cardross Ag & B 49 L5
Carew Pembks 18 D6
Carfraemill Border 46 F4
Carhampton Somset 5 J3
Cark Cumb 37 G5
Carlabhagh W Isls 62 g3
Carlisle Cumb 42 C6
Carlops Border 46 C4
Carloway W Isls 62 g3
Carlton N York 34 D4
Carlton N York 38 A5
Carlton-on-Trent
  Notts 30 E4
Carluke S Lans 45 L3
Carmarthen Carmth 19 G4
Carnaby E R Yk 39 K6
Carnforth Lancs 37 H6
Carno Powys 20 D2
Carnon Downs Cnwll 2 E6
Carnoustie Angus 51 K4
Carnwath S Lans 46 A5
Carradale Ag & B 44 C4
Carrbridge Highld 59 H6
Carrefour Jersey 7 b1
Carrick Castle Ag & B 49 K4
Carronbridge D & G 41 J3
Carrutherstown
  D & G 41 L5

Carsphairn D & G 40 F3
Carstairs S Lans 45 M3
Carterton Oxon 14 A3
Cartmel Cumb 37 G5
Castel Guern 6 a2
Casterton Cumb 37 J5
Castle Acre Norfk 24 F4
Castlebay W Isls 62 b14
Castle Carrock Cumb 42 D6
Castle Cary Somset 13 G7
Castle Donington
  Leics 29 L6
Castle Douglas D & G 41 H5
Castleford Wakefd 34 B4
Castle Hedingham
  Essex 16 F4
Castlemartin Pembks 18 C6
Castle Rising Norfk 24 D4
Castleside Dur 43 H6
Castleton Derbys 29 H2
Castleton N York 39 G3
Castleton Newpt 12 D3
Castletown Highld 65 H2
Castletown IoM 36 b4
Caterham Surrey 10 C3
Catfield Norfk 25 K4
Caton Lancs 37 H6
Catrine E Ayrs 45 J5
Catsfield E Susx 10 F6
Catterick N York 38 C4
Caunton Notts 30 D4
Cawdor Highld 59 G4
Cawsand Cnwll 3 K5
Caxton Cambs 16 B2
Caythorpe Lincs 30 F5
Cayton N York 39 K5
Cemaes IoA 26 C1
Cemmaes Road
  Powys 20 C1
Ceres Fife 51 J5
Cerne Abbas Dorset 7 J2
Cerrigydrudion
  Conwy 27 H5
Chadderton Oldham 33 H6
Chadlington Oxon 14 B2
Chagford Devon 6 A3
Chale IoW 8 E7
Chalfont St Giles
  Bucks 15 G4
Chalfont St Peter
  Bucks 15 G5
Chalford Gloucs 13 J2
Challacombe Devon 4 F3
Challock Kent 11 H3
Chandler's Ford
  Hants 8 E4
Chapel-en-le-Frith
  Derbys 29 H2
Chapel St Leonards
  Lincs 31 L3
Chapeltown Sheff 34 A6
Chapmanslade Wilts 13 J6
Chard Somset 6 F2
Charing Kent 11 H4
Charlbury Oxon 14 B2
Charlecote Warwks 22 D5
Charlton Kings
  Gloucs 22 A7
Charlton Marshall
  Dorset 7 L2
Charlwood Surrey 10 B4
Charmouth Dorset 7 G3
Chartham Kent 11 J3
Chatburn Lancs 33 G3
Chatham Medway 10 F2
Chatteris Cambs 24 B7
Chatton Nthumb 47 K6
Chawleigh Devon 4 F6
Chawton Hants 9 G3
Cheadle Stockp 33 H7
Cheddar Somset 12 F6
Cheddleton Staffs 29 G5
Chelford Ches E 28 F3
Chelmsford Essex 16 F6
Cheltenham Gloucs 22 A7
Chepstow Mons 12 F3
Cheriton Hants 8 F3
Cheriton Fitzpaine
  Devon 5 H6
Chertsey Surrey 15 G6
Chesham Bucks 15 G4
Cheshunt Herts 15 K4
Chester Ches W 28 B3
Chesterfield Derbys 29 K3
Chester-le-Street Dur 43 L5
Chew Magna BaNES 13 G5
Chewton Mendip
  Somset 13 G6
Chicheley M Keyn 23 J5
Chichester W Susx 9 H5

Chickerell Dorset 7 J4
Chicklade Wilts 13 J7
Chiddingfold Surrey 9 J3
Chieveley W Berk 14 C6
Chigwell Essex 16 C7
Childer Thornton
  Ches W 28 B3
Chilham Kent 11 J3
Chillington Devon 6 B7
Chilmark Wilts 13 K7
Chilsworthy Devon 4 C6
Chilton Foliat Wilts 14 A6
Chineham Hants 14 D7
Chinnor Oxon 14 E4
Chippenham Cambs 16 E1
Chippenham Wilts 13 J4
Chipperfield Herts 15 G4
Chipping Lancs 32 F3
Chipping Campden
  Gloucs 22 C6
Chipping Norton
  Oxon 22 D7
Chipping Ongar
  Essex 16 D6
Chipping Sodbury
  S Glos 13 H3
Chipping Warden
  Nhants 22 F5
Chirbury Shrops 21 G1
Chirk Wrexhm 27 L6
Chirnside Border 47 J3
Chiseldon Swindn 13 M4
Chitterne Wilts 13 K6
Chittlehamholt
  Devon 4 F3
Chobham Surrey 15 G7
Cholderton Wilts 8 C2
Chorley Lancs 32 E5
Chorleywood Herts 15 G4
Christchurch Dorset 8 C6
Chudleigh Devon 6 C4
Chudleigh Knighton
  Devon 6 C4
Chulmleigh Devon 4 F6
Churchill Oxon 14 A2
Churchstoke Powys 21 G2
Church Stretton
  Shrops 21 H2
Churston Ferrers
  Torbay 6 C6
Churt Surrey 9 H3
Cinderford Gloucs 21 K8
Cirencester Gloucs 13 K2
Clachan Ag & B 44 B3
Clachan Highld 56 E5
Clackmannan Clacks 50 E7
Clacton-on-Sea Essex 17 J5
Clanfield Oxon 14 A4
Claonaig Ag & B 44 C3
Clapham Bed 23 K5
Clapham N York 37 K6
Clare Suffk 16 F3
Clatt Abers 60 C6
Claverdon Warwks 22 C4
Clavering Essex 16 D4
Clawton Devon 4 C7
Clay Cross Derbys 29 K4
Claydon Suffk 17 J3
Cleator Moor Cumb 36 D2
Cleethorpes NE Lin 35 J6
Cleeve N Som 12 F5
Cleeve Hill Gloucs 22 B7
Cleobury Mortimer
  Shrops 21 K3
Cleobury North
  Shrops 21 K2
Clevedon N Som 12 E4
Cleveleys Lancs 32 C3
Cley next the Sea
  Norfk 25 G2
Cliffe Medway 10 F2
Cliffe N York 34 D4
Cliffe Woods Medway 10 F2
Clifton Cumb 37 H2
Clifton upon Teme
  Worcs 21 L4
Climping W Susx 9 K5
Clitheroe Lancs 33 G3
Clola Abers 61 G5
Clophill C Beds 23 L6
Closworth Somset 7 H2
Cloughton N York 39 J4
Clova Angus 55 G6
Clovelly Devon 4 C5
Clovenfords Border 46 E6
Clowne Derbys 30 B3
Clows Top Worcs 21 L3
Clun Shrops 21 G2
Clydach Swans 19 J6
Clydebank W Duns 45 H2
Clynder Ag & B 49 K5

Clynnog-fawr Gwynd 26 D5
Clyro Powys 20 F6
Clyst St Mary Devon 6 D3
Coalport Wrekin 21 K1
Coalville Leics 29 L7
Coatbridge N Lans 45 K2
Cobham Kent 10 E2
Cockburnspath
  Border 47 H3
Cockermouth Cumb 41 L8
Cocking W Susx 9 J4
Coddenham Suffk 17 J2
Codford St Mary
  Wilts 13 K7
Codicote Herts 15 J3
Codnor Derbys 29 L5
Codsall Staffs 21 M1
Coedpoeth Wrexhm 27 L5
Coggeshall Essex 17 G5
Colchester Essex 17 H5
Cold Ash W Berk 14 C6
Cold Ashby Nhants 23 G3
Cold Ashton S Glos 13 H4
Coldingham Border 47 J3
Cold Norton Essex 17 G7
Coldstream Border 47 H5
Coleford Gloucs 13 G1
Colerne Wilts 13 J4
Coleshill Warwks 22 C2
Colintraive Ag & B 49 J6
Collier's End Herts 15 K2
Collieston Abers 61 G6
Collingbourne Ducis
  Wilts 13 M6
Collingham Leeds 34 B3
Colmonell S Ayrs 40 C3
Colne Lancs 33 H3
Colne Engaine Essex 17 G4
Coln St Aldwyns
  Gloucs 13 L2
Colpy Abers 60 D6
Colsterworth Lincs 30 F7
Coltishall Norfk 25 J4
Colwell Nthumb 43 G4
Colwyn Bay Conwy 27 G2
Colyford Devon 6 F3
Colyton Devon 6 F3
Combe Martin Devon 4 E3
Compton Surrey 9 J2
Compton W Berk 14 C5
Comrie P & K 50 D5
Congleton Ches E 28 F4
Congresbury N Som 12 E5
Coningsby Lincs 31 H4
Conington Cambs 23 M2
Conisbrough Donc 34 C6
Coniston Cumb 36 F4
Connah's Quay Flints 27 L3
Connel Ag & B 52 F7
Conon Bridge Highld 58 E4
Consett Dur 43 H6
Constantine Cnwll 2 D7
Contin Highld 58 D4
Conwy Conwy 27 G3
Cookham W & M 14 F5
Coolham W Susx 9 L4
Coombe Bissett Wilts 8 B3
Coombe Hill Gloucs 21 M7
Copdock Suffk 17 J3
Copford Green Essex 17 G5
Copley Dur 38 B2
Copplestone Devon 5 G6
Copthorne W Susx 10 B4
Corbiere Jersey 7 a2
Corbridge Nthumb 43 G5
Corby Nhants 23 J2
Corby Glen Lincs 30 F7
Corfe Somset 6 F1
Corfe Castle Dorset 7 M4
Corgarff Abers 55 G4
Cornhill-on-Tweed
  Nthumb 47 H5
Cornwood Devon 3 L5
Corpach Highld 53 H3
Corrie N Ayrs 44 D4
Corris Gwynd 26 F8
Corsham Wilts 13 J4
Corston Wilts 13 J3
Corton Suffk 25 M3
Corwen Denbgs 27 J5
Coryton Thurr 16 F8
Cosby Leics 22 F2
Cotebrook Ches W 28 D4
Cotherstone Dur 38 A2
Cottenham Cambs 16 C1
Cottered Herts 16 B4
Cottingham E R Yk 35 G4
Coulport Ag & B 49 K5
Coulter S Lans 46 B6
Countesthorpe Leics 23 G2
Coupar Angus P & K 51 G3

Cove Highld ... 62 D8
Coventry Covtry ... 22 E3
Coverack Cnwll ... 2 D8
Cowbit Lincs ... 31 H7
Cowbridge V Glam ... 12 B4
Cowden Kent ... 10 D4
Cowdenbeath Fife ... 51 G7
Cowes IoW ... 8 E6
Cowfold W Susx ... 9 L4
Cowling N York ... 33 J3
Coxheath Kent ... 10 F3
Coxwold N York ... 38 E5
Coylton S Ayrs ... 45 H6
Coylumbridge Highld ... 54 D3
Crackington Haven Cnwll ... 4 B7
Cracoe N York ... 37 M7
Crafthole Cnwll ... 3 J5
Craigellachie Moray ... 59 L5
Craighouse Ag & B ... 48 D6
Craignure Ag & B ... 52 E6
Craigrothie Fife ... 51 J5
Crail Fife ... 51 L4
Crailing Border ... 47 G7
Cramlington Nthumb ... 43 K4
Cranborne Dorset ... 8 B4
Cranbrook Kent ... 10 F5
Cranfield C Beds ... 23 K6
Cranham Gloucs ... 21 M8
Cranleigh Surrey ... 9 K2
Cranshaws Border ... 47 G4
Crarae Ag & B ... 49 H4
Craster Nthumb ... 47 M7
Crathie Abers ... 54 F5
Crathorne N York ... 38 E3
Craven Arms Shrops ... 21 H3
Crawford S Lans ... 46 A7
Crawfordjohn S Lans ... 45 M5
Crawley W Susx ... 10 B5
Crawley Down W Susx ... 10 B4
Creag Ghoraidh W Isls ... 62 c10
Creagorry W Isls ... 62 c10
Credenhill Herefs ... 21 H6
Crediton Devon ... 5 G7
Creetown D & G ... 40 F6
Cregneash IoM ... 36 a4
Cressage Shrops ... 21 K1
Crewe Ches E ... 28 E4
Crewkerne Somset ... 7 G2
Crianlarich Stirlg ... 53 K7
Criccieth Gwynd ... 26 D6
Crickhowell Powys ... 20 F7
Cricklade Wilts ... 13 L3
Crieff P & K ... 50 D5
Crimond Abers ... 61 H4
Crinan Ag & B ... 49 G4
Cringleford Norfk ... 25 J5
Crockernwell Devon ... 6 B3
Crocketford D & G ... 41 J4
Croglin Cumb ... 42 D6
Cromarty Highld ... 59 G3
Cromdale Highld ... 59 J6
Cromer Norfk ... 25 J2
Cromford Derbys ... 29 K4
Cromwell Notts ... 30 E4
Crook Dur ... 43 J7
Crooklands Cumb ... 37 H5
Cropredy Oxon ... 22 F5
Cropton N York ... 39 G4
Crosby IoM ... 36 b3
Crosby Sefton ... 32 C6
Crossford Fife ... 46 B2
Crossford S Lans ... 45 L3
Cross Hands Carmth ... 19 H5
Crosshill S Ayrs ... 45 G6
Cross in Hand E Susx ... 10 D6
Crosskeys Caerph ... 12 D3
Crossmichael D & G ... 41 H5
Crossway Green Worcs ... 21 M4
Crosthwaite Cumb ... 37 G4
Crowborough E Susx ... 10 D5
Crowcombe Somset ... 5 K4
Crowhurst E Susx ... 10 F6
Crowland Lincs ... 31 H8
Crowle N Linc ... 34 E5
Crowthorne Wokham ... 14 F7
Croxton Kerrial Leics ... 30 E6
Croy Highld ... 59 G4
Croyde Devon ... 4 D4
Croydon Gt Lon ... 15 K7
Cruden Bay Abers ... 61 H5
Crudgington Wrekin ... 28 D7
Crudwell Wilts ... 13 K3
Crynant Neath ... 19 K5
Cuckfield W Susx ... 10 B5
Cuckney Notts ... 30 C3
Cuddington Ches W ... 28 D3
Cudworth Barns ... 34 B6

Cuffley Herts ... 15 K4
Culgaith Cumb ... 37 J1
Cullen Moray ... 60 C3
Cullompton Devon ... 5 J6
Culmstock Devon ... 5 K6
Cumbernauld N Lans ... 45 L1
Cuminestown Abers ... 60 E4
Cummertrees D & G ... 41 L5
Cumnock E Ayrs ... 45 J5
Cumnor Oxon ... 14 C4
Cumrew Cumb ... 42 D6
Cupar Fife ... 51 J5
Curry Rivel Somset ... 12 E8
Cwmbran Torfn ... 12 D2
Cwmystwyth Cerdgn ... 20 C3
Cymer Neath ... 19 L6
Cynwyl Elfed Carmth ... 19 G4

D

Dailly S Ayrs ... 40 D2
Dairsie Fife ... 51 J5
Dalbeattie D & G ... 41 J5
Dalby IoM ... 36 a3
Dale Pembks ... 18 B5
Dalgety Bay Fife ... 46 C2
Dalhalvaig Highld ... 64 L3
Dalkeith Mdloth ... 46 D3
Dallas Moray ... 59 J4
Dalmally Ag & B ... 53 J7
Dalmellington E Ayrs ... 45 H7
Dalry N Ayrs ... 45 G3
Dalrymple E Ayrs ... 45 G6
Dalston Cumb ... 42 B6
Dalton D & G ... 41 L4
Dalton-in-Furness Cumb ... 36 F6
Dalwhinnie Highld ... 54 A5
Damerham Hants ... 8 B4
Danbury Essex ... 16 F6
Darlington Darltn ... 38 C2
Darras Hall Nthumb ... 43 J5
Darrington Wakefd ... 34 B5
Dartford Kent ... 10 D2
Dartington Devon ... 6 B5
Dartmouth Devon ... 6 C6
Darvel E Ayrs ... 45 J4
Darwen Bl w D ... 32 F5
Datchet W & M ... 15 G6
Dava Highld ... 59 H5
Davenham Ches W ... 28 D3
Daventry Nhants ... 23 G4
Daviot Highld ... 58 F5
Dawlish Devon ... 6 C4
Deal Kent ... 11 L3
Dearham Cumb ... 41 L7
Debenham Suffk ... 17 J2
Deddington Oxon ... 22 F6
Dedham Essex ... 17 H4
Deeping St James Lincs ... 31 H8
Deeping St Nicholas Lincs ... 31 H7
Deganwy Conwy ... 27 G2
Delabole Cnwll ... 3 G3
Denbigh Denbgs ... 27 J3
Denby Dale Kirk ... 33 L6
Denham Bucks ... 15 G5
Denholm Border ... 46 F7
Denmead Hants ... 9 G5
Dennington Suffk ... 17 K1
Denny Falk ... 50 D8
Densole Kent ... 11 K4
Dent Cumb ... 37 K5
Denton Tamesd ... 33 H7
Derby C Derb ... 29 K6
Derbyhaven IoM ... 36 b4
Dereham Norfk ... 25 G4
Dersingham Norfk ... 24 E3
Dervaig Ag & B ... 52 B5
Desborough Nhants ... 23 H3
Desford Leics ... 22 F1
Devil's Bridge Cerdgn ... 20 B3
Devizes Wilts ... 13 K5
Dewsbury Kirk ... 33 L5
Dial Post W Susx ... 9 L4
Didcot Oxon ... 14 C5
Didmarton Gloucs ... 13 J3
Digby Lincs ... 31 G4
Dilwyn Herefs ... 21 H5
Dinas-Mawddwy Gwynd ... 27 G2
Dingwall Highld ... 58 E4
Dinnington Rothm ... 30 B2
Dippen Ag & B ... 44 C4
Diseworth Leics ... 29 L7
Dishforth N York ... 38 D6
Disley Ches E ... 29 G2
Diss Norfk ... 25 H7

Ditchling E Susx ... 10 B6
Dittisham Devon ... 6 C6
Ditton Priors Shrops ... 21 K2
Dobwalls Cnwll ... 3 H4
Docking Norfk ... 24 E3
Doddington Cambs ... 24 B6
Doddington Kent ... 11 G3
Doddington Nthumb ... 47 K6
Dodworth Barns ... 33 L6
Dolgellau Gwynd ... 26 F7
Dollar Clacks ... 50 E6
Dolphinton S Lans ... 46 B5
Dolton Devon ... 4 E6
Dolwyddelan Conwy ... 26 F5
Doncaster Donc ... 34 C6
Donington Lincs ... 31 H6
Dorchester Dorset ... 7 K3
Dorchester Oxon ... 14 D4
Dordon Warwks ... 22 D1
Dores Highld ... 58 E5
Dorking Surrey ... 9 L2
Dornie Highld ... 57 H6
Dornoch Highld ... 59 G1
Dorrington Shrops ... 21 J1
Dorstone Herefs ... 21 G6
Douglas IoM ... 36 c3
Douglas S Lans ... 45 L5
Dounby Ork ... 65 b3
Doune Stirlg ... 50 C6
Dousland Devon ... 3 L4
Dover Kent ... 11 L4
Doveridge Derbys ... 29 H6
Dowally P & K ... 50 E3
Downderry Cnwll ... 3 J5
Downham Market Norfk ... 24 D5
Downton Wilts ... 8 C4
Drakes Broughton Worcs ... 22 A5
Draycott Somset ... 12 F6
Drayton Norfk ... 25 J4
Drayton Oxon ... 14 C4
Driffield E R Yk ... 39 J7
Drimnin Highld ... 52 C5
Droitwich Worcs ... 22 A4
Dronfield Derbys ... 29 K3
Droxford Hants ... 8 F4
Drumbeg Highld ... 63 G4
Drummore D & G ... 40 C7
Drumnadrochit Highld ... 58 D6
Drymen Stirlg ... 50 A7
Drynoch Highld ... 56 D6
Duddington Nhants ... 23 K1
Dudley Dudley ... 22 A2
Duffield Derbys ... 29 K5
Dufftown Moray ... 59 L5
Duffus Moray ... 59 K3
Dulnain Bridge Highld ... 59 H6
Dulverton Somset ... 5 H4
Dumbarton W Duns ... 49 M5
Dumfries D & G ... 41 K4
Dunbar E Loth ... 47 G2
Dunbeath Highld ... 65 H5
Dunblane Stirlg ... 50 D6
Dunchurch Warwks ... 22 F3
Dundee C Dund ... 51 J4
Dundonald S Ayrs ... 45 G4
Dundonnell Highld ... 57 K1
Dundrennan D & G ... 41 H6
Dunecht Abers ... 55 L4
Dunfermline Fife ... 50 F7
Dunkeld P & K ... 50 F3
Dunlop E Ayrs ... 45 H2
Dunnet Highld ... 65 H1
Dunning P & K ... 50 F5
Dunoon Ag & B ... 49 K5
Dunragit D & G ... 40 C6
Duns Border ... 47 H4
Dunscore D & G ... 41 J4
Dunsfold Surrey ... 9 K3
Dunsford Devon ... 6 B3
Dunsop Bridge Lancs ... 32 F2
Dunstable C Beds ... 15 G2
Dunster Somset ... 5 J3
Duntish Dorset ... 7 K2
Dunure S Ayrs ... 44 F6
Dunvant Swans ... 19 J6
Dunvegan Highld ... 56 C4
Dunwich Suffk ... 25 L8
Durham Dur ... 43 K7
Durness Highld ... 63 J2
Duror Highld ... 53 G5
Durrington Wilts ... 8 C2
Durris Abers ... 55 L5
Dursley Gloucs ... 13 H2
Duxford Cambs ... 16 D3
Dyce C Aber ... 55 M3
Dyffryn Ardudwy Gwynd ... 26 E7
Dymchurch Kent ... 11 J5
Dymock Gloucs ... 21 K7

E

Eaglesfield D & G ... 42 A4
Eaglesham E Rens ... 45 J3
Ealing Gt Lon ... 15 J5
Earby Lancs ... 33 H3
Eardisley Herefs ... 21 G5
Earith Cambs ... 24 B7
Earley Wokham ... 14 E6
Earls Barton Nhants ... 23 J4
Earls Colne Essex ... 17 G4
Earl Shilton Leics ... 22 F1
Earlston Border ... 46 F6
Earsham Norfk ... 25 K6
Easdale Ag & B ... 48 F2
Easebourne W Susx ... 9 J4
Easington Dur ... 43 L7
Easington E R Yk ... 35 K5
Easingwold N York ... 38 E6
East Ayton N York ... 39 J5
East Barkwith Lincs ... 31 H2
East Bergholt Suffk ... 17 J4
Eastbourne E Susx ... 10 E7
East Chinnock Somset ... 7 H1
Eastchurch Kent ... 11 H2
East Cowes IoW ... 8 E6
East Dean E Susx ... 10 D8
East Dean W Susx ... 9 J4
East Goscote Leics ... 30 C7
East Grinstead W Susx ... 10 C4
East Harling Norfk ... 25 G6
East Hoathly E Susx ... 10 D6
East Horsley Surrey ... 15 H8
East IIsley W Berk ... 14 C5
East Kilbride S Lans ... 45 J3
East Knoyle Wilts ... 13 J7
East Lavant W Susx ... 9 H5
Eastleigh Hants ... 8 E4
East Linton E Loth ... 46 F3
East Lulworth Dorset ... 7 L4
Easton Suffk ... 17 K2
East Prawle Devon ... 6 B7
East Preston W Susx ... 9 K5
Eastriggs D & G ... 42 A5
East Rudham Norfk ... 24 F3
Eastry Kent ... 11 L3
East Saltoun E Loth ... 46 E3
East Stoke Notts ... 30 D5
East Wittering W Susx ... 9 H6
East Witton N York ... 38 B5
Eastwood Notts ... 29 L5
Eaton Socon Cambs ... 23 L4
Ebbw Vale Blae G ... 12 C1
Ebchester Dur ... 43 H6
Ecclefechan D & G ... 41 M4
Eccles Border ... 47 H5
Eccleshall Staffs ... 28 F6
Echt Abers ... 55 K4
Eckington Derbys ... 29 L2
Eckington Worcs ... 22 A6
Edderton Highld ... 58 F2
Eddleston Border ... 46 C5
Edenbridge Kent ... 10 C4
Edinbane Highld ... 56 D4
Edinburgh C Edin ... 46 C3
Edlington Lincs ... 31 H3
Edmundbyers Dur ... 43 H6
Ednam Border ... 47 G6
Edwinstowe Notts ... 30 C3
Edzell Angus ... 55 J7
Effingham Surrey ... 15 H7
Eggesford Devon ... 4 F6
Eggleston Dur ... 37 M2
Egham Surrey ... 15 G6
Eglingham Nthumb ... 47 K7
Eglwyswrw Pembks ... 18 E3
Egremont Cumb ... 36 D3
Egton Bridge N York ... 39 H3
Elan Village Powys ... 20 C4
Elgin Moray ... 59 K3
Elgol Highld ... 56 E7
Elham Kent ... 11 J4
Elie Fife ... 51 K6
Eikseley Notts ... 30 D3
Elkstone Gloucs ... 13 K1
Elland Calder ... 33 K5
Ellesmere Shrops ... 28 B6
Ellesmere Port Ches W ... 28 B3
Ellingham Norfk ... 25 K6
Ellon Abers ... 61 G6
Elloughton E R Yk ... 34 F4
Elmstead Market Essex ... 17 H5
Elsdon Nthumb ... 43 G3
Elsrickle S Lans ... 46 B5
Elstead Surrey ... 9 J2

Elstree Herts 15 J4
Elterwater Cumb 37 G3
Eltisley Cambs 16 B2
Elton Cambs 23 L2
Elveden Suffk 24 F7
Elvetham Heath
Hants 14 E7
Elvington C York 34 D3
Elworthy Somset 5 J4
Ely Cambs 24 C7
Embleton Nthumb 47 M7
Embo Highld 64 E8
Empingham Rutlnd 30 F8
Emsworth Hants 9 H5
Enderby Leics 22 F1
Enfield Gt Lon 15 K4
Ennerdale Bridge
Cumb 36 D2
Enstone Oxon 14 B2
Epping Essex 16 C6
Epsom Surrey 15 J7
Epworth N Linc 34 E6
Errogie Highld 58 G6
Errol P & K 51 H4
Erwood Powys 20 E6
Esher Surrey 15 H7
Eskdale Green Cumb ... 36 E4
Eskdalemuir D & G 42 A3
Essendine Rutlnd 31 G8
Essendon Herts 15 J3
Eston R & Cl 38 E2
Etal Nthumb 47 J6
Etchingham E Susx 10 F5
Eton W & M 15 G6
Ettington Warwks 22 D5
Ettrick Border 46 D7
Ettrickbridge Border ... 46 E2
Evanton Highld 58 E3
Evercreech Somset 13 G2
Eversley Hants 14 E7
Evesham Worcs 22 B6
Ewen Gloucs 13 K2
Ewhurst Surrey 9 K2
Ewyas Harold Herefs .. 21 H7
Exebridge Somset 5 H5
Exeter Devon 6 C3
Exford Somset 5 H4
Exminster Devon 6 C3
Exmouth Devon 6 D4
Eye C Pete 23 M1
Eye Suffk 25 H7
Eyemouth Border 47 J4
Eynsford Kent 10 D2
Eynsham Oxon 14 B3

F

Failsworth Oldham 33 H6
Fairbourne Gwynd 26 E8
Fairford Gloucs 13 L2
Fairlie N Ayrs 44 F3
Fairlight E Susx 11 G6
Fakenham Norfk 24 F3
Fala Mdloth 46 E4
Faldingworth Lincs 31 G2
Falfield S Glos 13 G3
Falkirk Falk 50 E8
Falkland Fife 51 H6
Falmouth Cnwll 2 E7
Falstone Nthumb 42 E3
Fareham Hants 8 F5
Faringdon Oxon 14 A4
Farnborough Hants 14 F7
Farnell Angus 51 L2
Farnham Surrey 9 H2
Farnham Common
Bucks 15 G5
Farningham Kent 10 D2
Far Sawrey Cumb 37 G4
Fauldhouse W Loth 45 M2
Faversham Kent 11 H3
Fawley Hants 8 E5
Fazeley Staffs 22 C1
Fearnan P & K 50 C3
Felixstowe Suffk 17 K4
Felsted Essex 16 E5
Felton Nthumb 43 J2
Feltwell Norfk 24 E6
Fenny Bentley
Derbys 29 J5
Fenny Bridges Devon ... 6 E3
Fenny Compton
Warwks 22 E5
Fenny Drayton Leics .. 22 E1
Fenwick E Ayrs 45 H4
Ferndown Dorset 8 B5
Fernhill Heath Worcs .. 21 M4
Fernhurst W Susx 9 J3
Fernilee Derbys 29 G3

Ferring W Susx 9 K5
Ferryhill Dur 43 K8
Fettercairn Abers 55 K6
Ffestiniog Gwynd 26 F5
Filby Norfk 25 L4
Filey N York 39 K5
Fincham Norfk 24 E5
Finchingfield Essex 16 E4
Findhorn Moray 59 J3
Findochty Moray 60 C3
Findon W Susx 9 L5
Finedon Nhants 23 J3
Finningham Suffk 17 H1
Finningley Donc 34 D6
Finstown Ork 65 b4
Fintry Stirlg 50 B7
Fionnphort Ag & B 48 C2
Firle E Susx 10 D7
Fishbourne IoW 8 F4
Fishguard Pembks 18 C3
Fittleworth W Susx 9 K4
Fitzhead Somset 5 K4
Five Oaks Jersey 7 c2
Fladdabister Shet 61 c6
Flamborough E R Yk ... 39 L6
Flamstead Herts 15 H3
Fleet Hants 14 F7
Fleetwood Lancs 32 C3
Flimby Cumb 41 K7
Flint Flints 27 K3
Flitwick C Beds 23 K6
Flixton N York 39 K5
Flore Nhants 23 G4
Fochabers Moray 59 L4
Folkestone Kent 11 K5
Folkingham Lincs 31 G6
Fontmell Magna
Dorset 7 L1
Fontwell W Susx 9 J5
Ford Nthumb 47 J6
Fordcombe Kent 10 D4
Fordingbridge Hants 8 C4
Fordoun Abers 55 K6
Fordwich Kent 11 J3
Forest Guern 6 a2
Forest Row E Susx 10 C5
Forfar Angus 51 J2
Formby Sefton 32 C6
Forres Moray 59 J4
Fort Augustus Highld .. 58 C7
Fortevoit P & K 50 F5
Forth S Lans 45 M3
Fortingall P & K 50 C3
Forton Lancs 32 E2
Fortrose Highld 58 F4
Fortuneswell Dorset 7 J4
Fort William Highld 53 H4
Foston Lincs 30 E5
Four Crosses Powys ... 27 L7
Four Marks Hants 9 G3
Fowey Cnwll 3 G5
Fownhope Herefs 21 J6
Foxdale IoM 36 b3
Foyers Highld 58 D7
Framlingham Suffk 17 K2
Frampton Dorset 7 J3
Frant E Susx 10 E5
Fraserburgh Abers 61 G3
Freckenham Suffk 24 D8
Freckleton Lancs 32 D4
Frensham Surrey 9 H2
Freshwater IoW 8 D6
Fressingfield Suffk 25 J7
Freswick Highld 65 J2
Fridaythorpe E R Yk ... 39 H7
Frilford Oxon 14 B6
Frinton-on-Sea Essex . 17 K5
Friockheim Angus 51 K2
Fritton Norfk 25 L5
Frizington Cumb 36 D2
Frocester Gloucs 13 H2
Frodsham Ches W 28 C3
Frome Somset 13 H6
Froxfield Wilts 14 A6
Funtington W Susx 9 H5
Furnace Ag & B 49 J4
Furness Vale Derbys ... 29 G2
Fyfield Essex 16 D6
Fyfield Oxon 14 B4
Fyvie Abers 60 E5

G

Gailey Staffs 28 F8
Gainford Dur 38 B2
Gainsborough Lincs 34 K7
Gairloch Highld 57 H2
Gairlochy Highld 53 J3
Galashiels Border 46 E6

Galgate Lancs 37 H7
Galston E Ayrs 45 H4
Gamlingay Cambs 16 B3
Gamston Notts 30 D3
Ganllwyd Gwynd 26 F7
Garboldisham Norfk ... 25 G7
Gardenstown Abers 60 E3
Garelochhead Ag & B . 49 K4
Garforth Leeds 34 B4
Gargrave N York 33 H2
Garlieston D & G 40 F6
Garlogie Abers 55 L4
Garrigill Cumb 42 E7
Garstang Lancs 32 E3
Garth Powys 20 D5
Garvald E Loth 46 F3
Garve Highld 58 C3
Gatehouse of Fleet
D & G 41 G6
Gateshead Gatesd 43 K5
Gaydon Warwks 22 E5
Gayton Norfk 24 E4
Gedney Drove End
Lincs 31 K6
Gedney Hill Lincs 31 J8
Georgeham Devon 4 D4
Gerrards Cross Bucks . 15 G5
Gifford E Loth 46 F3
Giggleswick N York 37 L6
Gillingham Dorset 13 H8
Gillingham Medway 10 F2
Gillingham Norfk 25 L6
Gilling West N York 38 B3
Gills Highld 65 J1
Gilmerton P & K 50 E4
Gilsland Nthumb 42 E5
Gilwern Mons 21 G8
Girton Cambs 16 C2
Girvan S Ayrs 40 C3
Gisburn Lancs 33 G2
Glamis Angus 51 J3
Glanton Nthumb 47 K7
Glapwell Derbys 30 B3
Glasbury Powys 20 F6
Glasgow C Glas 45 J2
Glaston Rutlnd 23 J1
Glastonbury Somset ... 12 F7
Glemsford Suffk 17 G3
Glenbarr Ag & B 44 A4
Glenborrodale Highld . 52 D5
Glencaple D & G 41 K5
Glencoe Highld 53 H5
Glendaruel Ag & B 49 H5
Glendevon P & K 50 E6
Glenelg Highld 57 H7
Glenfarg P & K 51 G5
Glenfinnan Highld 52 F3
Glenkindie Abers 55 H3
Glenlivet Moray 59 K6
Glenluce D & G 40 C6
Glen Maye IoM 36 b3
Glenridding Cumb 37 G2
Glenrothes Fife 51 H6
Glentham Lincs 35 G7
Glossop Derbys 33 J7
Gloucester Gloucs 21 M7
Glyn Ceiriog Wrexhm .. 27 K6
Glyncorrwg Neath 19 L6
Glynde E Susx 10 C7
Glynneath Neath 19 L5
Glyntawe Powys 20 C8
Gnosall Staffs 28 F7
Goathland N York 39 H3
Goathurst Somset 12 D7
Gobowen Shrops 27 L6
Godalming Surrey 9 J2
Godmanchester
Cambs 23 M4
Godshill IoW 8 F7
Goginan Cerdgn 20 B3
Golborne Wigan 32 F6
Goldhanger Essex 17 G6
Golspie Highld 64 E7
Gomshall Surrey 9 K2
Goodwick Pembks 18 C3
Goole E R Yk 34 K4
Goostrey Ches E 28 E3
Gordon Border 47 G5
Gorebridge Mdloth 46 D4
Gorey Jersey 7 c1
Goring Oxon 14 D5
Gorran Haven Cnwll 2 F7
Gorseinon Swans 19 J6
Gosberton Lincs 31 H6
Gosforth Cumb 36 D3
Gosforth N u Ty 43 J5
Gosport Hants 8 F5
Goudhurst Kent 10 F4
Gourock Inver 49 K5
Gowerton Swans 19 J6
Goxhill N Linc 35 H5

Grain Medway 11 G2
Grainthorpe Lincs 35 K6
Grampound Cnwll 2 F6
Gramsdal W Isls 62 d9
Gramsdale W Isls 62 d9
Grandes Rocques
Guern 6 a1
Grange Cumb 36 F2
Grangemouth Falk 50 E8
Grange-over-Sands
Cumb 37 G5
Grantham Lincs 30 F6
Grantown-on-Spey
Highld 59 J6
Grantshouse Border ... 47 H4
Grasmere Cumb 37 G3
Grassington N York 38 A6
Graveley Herts 16 B4
Gravesend Kent 10 E2
Grays Thurr 10 E1
Great Ayton N York 38 F3
Great Badminton
S Glos 13 H3
Great Bardfield Essex . 16 E4
Great Barford Bed 23 L5
Great Bircham Norfk .. 24 E3
Great Blakenham
Suffk 17 J3
Great Casterton
Rutlnd 30 F8
Great Chesterford
Essex 16 D3
Great Dalby Leics 30 D7
Great Dunmow Essex . 16 E5
Great Durnford Wilts 8 B3
Great Gidding Cambs .. 23 L3
Great Gransden
Cambs 16 B2
Greatham Hants 9 H3
Great Harwood
Lancs 33 G4
Great Haywood
Staffs 29 G7
Great Hockham
Norfk 25 G6
Great Kimble Bucks ... 14 F3
Great Langdale
Cumb 36 F3
Great Malvern Worcs .. 21 L5
Great Massingham
Norfk 24 E4
Great Missenden
Bucks 14 F4
Great Notley Essex 16 F5
Great Ponton Lincs 30 F6
Great Sampford
Essex 16 E4
Great Saughall
Ches W 28 B3
Great Shefford
W Berk 14 B6
Great Shelford
Cambs 16 C3
Great Smeaton
N York 38 D3
Great Tew Oxon 22 E7
Great Torrington
Devon 4 E5
Great Wakering
Essex 17 G8
Great Waltham
Essex 16 E6
Great Witley Worcs 21 L4
Great Yarmouth
Norfk 25 L5
Great Yeldham Essex .. 16 F4
Greenfield Flints 27 K3
Green Hammerton
N York 38 E7
Greenhead Nthumb 42 E5
Greenhow Hill N York . 38 B6
Greenlaw Border 47 G5
Greenloaning P & K 50 D6
Greenock Inver 49 L5
Greenodd Cumb 36 F5
Greetham Rutlnd 30 F7
Gresford Wrexhm 27 L4
Greta Bridge Dur 38 B3
Gretna D & G 42 B5
Gretna Green D & G 42 B5
Greystoke Cumb 42 C8
Grimsby NE Lin 35 J5
Grimsthorpe Lincs 31 G5
Grindleford Derbys 29 J3
Gringley on the Hill
Notts 34 E7
Groby Leics 30 B8
Grosmont Mons 21 H7
Grouville Jersey 7 c2
Grove Oxon 14 B5
Guardbridge Fife 51 J5

Guestling Green
E Susx 11 G6
Guildford Surrey 9 K2
Guisborough R & Cl .. 38 F2
Guiseley Leeds 33 K3
Guist Norfk 25 G4
Gullane E Loth 46 E2
Gunness N Linc 34 E5
Gunnislake Cnwll 3 K4
Gunthorpe Notts 30 D5
Gurnard IoW 8 E6
Gussage All Saints
Dorset 8 A5
Gutcher Shet 61 d2
Guyhirn Cambs 24 B5
Gweek Cnwll 2 D7
Gwernymynydd
Flints 27 K4
Gwithian Cnwll 2 C6
Gwyddelwern
Denbgs 27 J5

H

Hackland Ork 65 b3
Hackness N York 39 J4
Hackney Gt Lon 15 K5
Haddenham Bucks 14 E3
Haddenham Cambs 24 C7
Haddington E Loth 46 F3
Haddiscoe Norfk 25 L6
Hadleigh Suffk 17 H3
Hadlow Kent 10 E4
Hagworthingham
Lincs 31 J3
Hailsham E Susx 10 E7
Halberton Devon 5 J6
Hales Norfk 25 K6
Halesowen Dudley 22 A3
Halesworth Suffk 25 K7
Halifax Calder 33 K4
Halkirk Highld 65 G2
Halstead Essex 16 F4
Halstead Kent 10 D3
Haltwhistle Nthumb ... 42 E5
Halwell Devon 6 B6
Halwill Junction
Devon 4 D7
Hambledon Hants 9 G4
Hamble-le-Rice
Hants 8 E5
Hambleton Lancs 32 D3
Hamilton S Lans 45 K3
Hammersmith Gt Lon .. 15 J6
Hampstead Norreys
W Berk 14 C6
Hampsthwaite
N York 38 C7
Hamstead Marshall
W Berk 14 B7
Hamstreet Kent 11 H5
Handcross W Susx 10 B8
Handley Ches W 28 C4
Hanley C Stke 28 F5
Happisburgh Norfk 25 K3
Harbertonford
Devon 6 B6
Hardwicke Gloucs 13 H1
Hare Street Herts 16 C4
Harewood Leeds 33 L3
Harewood End
Herefs 21 J7
Harlech Gwynd 26 E6
Harleston Norfk 25 J7
Harlosh Highld 56 C5
Harlow Essex 16 C6
Harlyn Cnwll 2 E4
Haroldswick Shet 61 d1
Harpenden Herts 15 H3
Harrogate N York 33 L2
Harrold Bed 23 K5
Harrow Gt Lon 15 H5
Harston Cambs 16 C3
Hartburn Nthumb 43 J4
Hartest Suffk 17 G3
Hartfield E Susx 10 D5
Hartington Derbys 29 H4
Hartland Devon 4 B4
Hartlepool Hartpl 43 M8
Hartley Wintney
Hants 14 E7
Hartpury Gloucs 21 L7
Harvington Worcs 22 B5
Harwich Essex 17 K4
Haseley Warwks 22 D4
Haslemere Surrey 9 J3
Hastings E Susx 10 F7
Hatch Beauchamp
Somset 12 D8

Hatfield Donc 34 D5
Hatfield Herts 15 J3
Hatfield Broad Oak
Essex 16 D5
Hatfield Heath Essex .. 16 D5
Hatfield Peverel
Essex 16 F6
Hatherleigh Devon 4 E6
Hathern Leics 36 B7
Hathersage Derbys 29 J2
Hatton Abers 61 H5
Havant Hants 9 G5
Havenstreet IoW 8 F6
Haverfordwest
Pembks 18 C5
Haverhill Suffk 16 E3
Hawarden Flints 27 L3
Hawes N York 37 L4
Hawick Border 46 F7
Hawkedon Suffk 16 F3
Hawkhurst Kent 10 F5
Hawkinge Kent 11 K4
Hawkshead Cumb 37 G4
Hawnby N York 38 E4
Haworth C Brad 33 J3
Haxby C York 38 F7
Haxey N Linc 34 E6
Haydon Bridge
Nthumb 42 F5
Hayle Cnwll 2 C6
Hay-on-Wye Powys ... 21 G6
Haywards Heath
W Susx 10 B6
Hazel Grove Stockp ... 28 F2
Heacham Norfk 24 D3
Headcorn Kent 11 G4
Heanor Derbys 29 L5
Heath Derbys 29 L3
Heathfield E Susx 10 E6
**Heath Hayes &
Wimblebury**
Staffs 29 G8
Hebden Bridge
Calder 33 J4
Heckington Lincs 31 G5
Hedge End Hants 8 E4
Hednesford Staffs 29 G8
Hedon E R Yk 35 H4
Helensburgh Ag & B .. 49 L5
Hellifield N York 37 L7
Helmingham Suffk 17 K2
Helmsdale Highld 65 G6
Helmsley N York 38 F5
Helpringham Lincs 31 G5
Helsby Ches W 28 C3
Helston Cnwll 2 C7
Hemel Hempstead
Herts 15 H3
Hempnall Norfk 25 J6
Hemsby Norfk 25 L4
Hemsworth Wakefd ... 34 B5
Hemyock Devon 5 K6
Hendy Carmth 19 J6
Henfield W Susx 9 L4
Henham Essex 16 D4
Henley-in-Arden
Warwks 22 C4
Henley-on-Thames
Oxon 14 E5
Henllan Denbgs 27 J3
Henlow C Beds 23 L6
Henstead Suffk 25 L7
Henstridge Somset 7 K1
Hereford Herefs 21 J6
Hermitage W Berk 14 C6
Herne Bay Kent 11 J2
Hersden Kent 11 K3
Herstmonceux
E Susx 10 E6
Hertford Herts 15 K3
Hessle E R Yk 35 G4
Heswall Wirral 27 L2
Hethersett Norfk 25 H5
Heversham Cumb 37 H5
Hexham Nthumb 43 G5
Hexworthy Devon 3 M4
Heybrook Bay Devon ... 3 K6
Heysham Lancs 37 G7
Heytesbury Wilts 13 J6
Hibaldstow N Linc 35 G6
Hickstead W Susx 10 B6
Higham Ferrers
Nhants 23 K4
Highampton Devon 4 E6
High Bentham N York .. 37 J6
Highbridge Somset 12 D6
Highclere Hants 14 B7
High Ercall Wrekin ... 28 D7
Higher Town IoS 2 b1
High Halden Kent 11 G5
High Hesket Cumb 42 C7

Highley Shrops 21 L3
High Roding Essex 16 E5
Highworth Swindn 13 M3
High Wycombe
Bucks 14 F4
Hildenborough Kent .. 10 D4
Hill Brow Hants 9 H3
Hill of Fearn Highld .. 59 G2
Hillswick Shet 61 b3
Hilmarton Wilts 13 K4
Hilton Derbys 29 J6
Hinckley Leics 22 E2
Hinderwell N York 39 G2
Hindhead Surrey 9 J3
Hindon Wilts 13 J7
Hingham Norfk 25 G5
Hipswell N York 38 B4
Hirwaun Rhondd 12 A2
Histon Cambs 16 C2
Hitcham Suffk 17 H3
Hitchin Herts 23 M7
Hockley Essex 17 G7
Hockliffe C Beds 23 K7
Hoddesdon Herts 15 K3
Hodnet Shrops 28 D6
Hogsthorpe Lincs 31 L3
Holbeach Lincs 31 J7
Holbeton Devon 3 L5
Holbrook Suffk 17 J4
Holbury Hants 8 E5
Holkham Norfk 24 F2
Hollingbourne Kent ... 11 G3
Holmbury St Mary
Surrey 9 L2
Holmes Chapel
Ches E 28 E3
**Holme upon
Spalding Moor**
E R Yk 34 E3
Holmfirth Kirk 33 K6
Holmrook Cumb 36 D4
Holne Devon 6 A5
Holsworthy Devon 4 C6
Holt Norfk 25 H3
Holt Wilts 13 J5
Holt Wrexhm 28 B4
Holt Heath Worcs 21 L4
Holton le Clay Lincs .. 35 J6
Holyhead IoA 26 B2
Holy Island Nthumb .. 47 L5
Holytown N Lans 45 L2
Holywell Dorset 7 J2
Holywell Flints 27 K3
Homersfield Suffk 25 J7
Honing Norfk 25 H5
Honington Suffk 24 F7
Honiton Devon 6 E2
Hook Hants 14 E7
Hoo St Werburgh
Medway 10 F2
Hope Derbys 29 J2
Hope Devon 6 A7
Hope Flints 27 L4
Hope Bowdler
Shrops 21 J2
Hopeman Moray 59 K3
**Hope under
Dinmore** Herefs 21 J5
Hopton on Sea
Norfk 25 M5
Horam E Susx 10 D6
Horley Surrey 10 B4
Hornby Lancs 37 J6
Horncastle Lincs 31 H3
Horndean Hants 9 G4
Horns Cross Devon 4 D5
Hornsea E R Yk 35 H3
Horrabridge Devon 3 L4
Horsey Norfk 25 L4
Horsham W Susx 9 L3
Horsley Nthumb 43 H5
Horton Dorset 8 B5
Horton Somset 6 F1
Horton-cum-Studley
Oxon 14 D3
**Horton-in-
Ribblesdale**
N York 37 L6
Horwich Bolton 32 F5
Hoton Leics 30 C7
Houghton-le-Spring
Sundld 43 K6
**Houghton on the
Hill** Leics 23 G1
Hounslow Gt Lon 15 H6
Houton Ork 65 b4
Hove Br & H. 10 B7
Hovingham N York ... 38 F5
Howden E R Yk 34 E4
Hoxne Suffk 25 J7
Hoylake Wirral 32 B7

Hoyland Nether
Barns 34 B6
Hucknall Notts 30 B5
Huddersfield Kirk 33 K5
Hugh Town IoS 2 a2
Hull, Kingston upon
C KuH 35 G4
Humberston NE Lin .. 35 J6
Humbie E Loth 46 E4
Hume Border 47 G5
Hungerford W Berk .. 14 B6
Hunmanby N York ... 39 K5
Hunstanton Norfk ... 24 D2
Huntingdon Cambs .. 23 M3
Huntley Gloucs 21 L7
Huntly Abers 60 C5
Hursley Hants 8 E4
Hurstbourne Priors
Hants 8 E2
Hurstbourne Tarrant
Hants 14 B7
Hurst Green E Susx .. 10 F5
Hurst Green Lancs ... 32 F3
Hurstpierpoint
W Susx 10 B6
Hurworth-on-Tees
Darltn 38 C3
Husbands Bosworth
Leics 23 G2
Husborne Crawley
C Beds 23 K6
Huttoft Lincs 31 L3
Hutton-le-Hole
N York 39 G4
Hyde Tamesd 33 H7
Hynish Ag & B 48 b3
Hythe Hants 8 E5
Hythe Kent 11 J5

I

Ibstock Leics 29 K8
Ideford Devon 6 C4
Ilchester Somset 12 F8
Ilfracombe Devon 4 E3
Ilkeston Derbys 29 L5
Ilkley C Brad 33 K3
Ilminster Somset 7 G1
Immingham NE Lin ... 35 H5
Immingham Dock
NE Lin 35 H5
Inchnadamph Highld .. 63 H5
Ingatestone Essex 16 E7
Ingham Lincs 30 F2
Ingleton N York 37 K6
Ingoldmells Lincs 31 L3
Inkberrow Worcs 22 B5
Innellan Ag & B 49 K6
Innerleithen Border .. 46 D6
Insch Abers 60 D6
Insh Highld 54 C4
Instow Devon 4 D4
Inverallochy Abers ... 61 G3
Inveran Highld 64 C7
Inveraray Ag & B 49 J3
Inverasdale Highld ... 57 H2
Inverbervie Abers 55 L6
Invergarry Highld 53 K2
Invergordon Highld .. 58 F3
Invergowrie P & K ... 51 H4
Inverinate Highld 57 J6
Inverkeilor Angus 51 L2
Inverkeithing Fife ... 46 B2
Inverkeithny Abers .. 60 D5
Inverkip Inver 49 K6
Invermoriston Highld .. 58 D7
Inverness Highld 58 F5
Inverurie Abers 55 L3
Ipplepen Devon 6 B5
Ipstones Staffs 29 G5
Ipswich Suffk 17 J3
Irchester Nhants 23 J4
Ireby Cumb 42 A7
Ironbridge Wrekin ... 21 K1
Irthlingborough
Nhants 23 K3
Irvine N Ayrs 45 G4
Isle of Whithorn
D & G. 40 F7
Isleornsay Highld 57 G7
Islington Gt Lon 15 K5
Itchen Abbas Hants 8 F3
Iver Bucks 15 G5
Ivinghoe Bucks 15 G3
Ivybridge Devon 3 M5
Iwade Kent 11 G2
Iwerne Minster
Dorset 7 L1
Ixworth Suffk 25 G8

J

Jarrow S Tyne 43 K5
Jedburgh Border 47 G7
Jerbourg Guern 6 b2
Jevington E Susx 10 D7
John o' Groats Highld ... 65 J1
Johnshaven Abers 55 L7
Johnston Pembks 18 C5
Johnstone Rens 49 M6
Jurby IoM 36 c1

K

Kames Ag & B 49 H6
Keelby Lincs 35 H5
Kegworth Leics 30 B6
Keighley C Brad 33 J3
Keiss Highld 65 J2
Keith Moray 60 B4
Keld N York 37 L3
Kelham Notts 30 D4
Kelso Border 47 G6
Kelvedon Essex 17 G5
Kemble Gloucs 13 K2
Kemnay Abers 55 K3
Kempsey Worcs 21 M5
Kempston Bed 23 K5
Kendal Cumb 37 H4
Kenilworth Warwks 22 D3
Kenmore P & K 50 D3
Kennacraig Ag & B 49 G6
Kennford Devon 6 C3
Kenninghall Norfk 25 G7
Kentallen Highld 53 G5
Kentford Suffk 16 F2
Kenton Devon 6 C4
Kerry Powys 20 F2
Kessingland Suffk 25 L6
Keswick Cumb 36 F2
Kettering Nhants 23 J3
Kettlewell N York 37 M6
Ketton Rutlnd 23 K1
Keymer W Susx 10 B6
Keynsham BaNES 13 G4
Keyston Cambs 23 K3
Keyworth Notts 30 C6
Kibworth Harcourt
  Leics 23 G2
Kidderminster
  Worcs 21 M3
Kidlington Oxon 14 C3
Kidsgrove Staffs 28 F4
Kidwelly Carmth 19 G5
Kielder Nthumb 42 D3
Kilberry Ag & B 48 F6
Kilbirnie N Ayrs 45 G3
Kilburn Derbys 29 K5
Kilburn N York 38 E5
Kilchattan Ag & B 44 E3
Kilchoan Highld 52 C4
Kilchrenan Ag & B 49 J2
Kilcreggan Ag & B 49 K5
Kildale N York 38 F3
Kildrummy Abers 55 H3
Kildwick N York 33 J3
Kilfinan Ag & B 49 H5
Kilgetty Pembks 18 E5
Kilham E R Yk 39 K6
Kilkenzie Ag & B 44 B5
Kilkhampton Cnwll 4 C6
Killearn Stirlg 50 B7
Killin Stirlg 50 B4
Kilmacolm Inver 49 L6
Kilmany Fife 51 J3
Kilmarnock E Ayrs 45 H4
Kilmartin Ag & B 49 G4
Kilmaurs E Ayrs 45 H4
Kilmelford Ag & B 49 G3
Kilmorack Highld 58 D5
Kilninver Ag & B 49 G2
Kilsyth N Lans 50 C8
Kilve Somset 5 K3
Kilwinning N Ayrs 45 G4
Kimberley Norfk 25 H5
Kimbolton Cambs 23 L4
Kinbrace Highld 64 E5
Kincardine Fife 50 E7
Kincardine O'Neil
  Abers 55 J4
Kincraig Highld 54 C4
Kineton Warwks 22 E5
Kingsbarns Fife 51 K5
Kingsbridge Devon 6 B7
Kingsbury Warwks 22 D2
Kingsclere Hants 14 C7
King's Cliffe Nhants ... 23 K1

Kingsdown Kent 11 L4
Kingsfold W Susx 9 L3
Kingskerswell Devon 6 C5
Kingsland Herefs 21 H4
Kings Langley Herts 15 H4
Kingsley Staffs 29 G5
King's Lynn Norfk 24 D4
King's Mills Guern 6 a2
Kingsnorth Kent 11 H4
King's Somborne
  Hants 8 D3
King's Stag Dorset 7 K2
King's Stanley Gloucs .. 13 H2
Kingsteignton
  Devon 6 C4
Kingstone Herefs 21 H6
Kingston on Spey
  Moray 59 L3
Kingston upon Hull
  C KuH 35 G4
Kingston upon
  Thames Gt Lon 15 J6
Kingswear Devon 6 C6
Kings Worthy Hants 8 E3
Kington Herefs 21 G5
Kingussie Highld 54 B4
Kinlochbervie Highld ... 63 H3
Kinlocheil Highld 53 G3
Kinlochewe Highld 57 J3
Kinlochleven Highld 53 J5
Kinloch Rannoch
  P & K 50 C2
Kinloss Moray 59 J3
Kinmel Bay Conwy 27 H2
Kinneff Abers 55 L6
Kinross P & K 50 F6
Kintbury W Berk 14 B6
Kintore Abers 55 L3
Kippen Stirlg 50 C7
Kirby Misperton
  N York 39 G5
Kirby Muxloe Leics 22 F1
Kirkabister Shet 61 c6
Kirkbean D & G 41 K6
Kirkbride Cumb 42 A6
Kirkburton Kirk 33 K5
Kirkby Knows 32 D6
Kirkby in Ashfield
  Notts 30 B4
Kirkby Lonsdale
  Cumb 37 J5
Kirkby Malzeard
  N York 38 C5
Kirkbymoorside
  N York 39 G5
Kirkby Stephen
  Cumb 37 K3
Kirkcaldy Fife 51 H7
Kirkcolm D & G 40 B5
Kirkconnel D & G 45 K6
Kirkcowan D & G 40 D5
Kirkcudbright
  D & G 41 G6
Kirkham Lancs 32 D4
Kirkhill Highld 58 E5
Kirkinner D & G 40 E6
Kirkintilloch E Duns ... 45 K1
Kirk Langley Derbys ... 29 K6
Kirk Michael IoM 36 b2
Kirkmichael P & K 50 F2
Kirkmichael S Ayrs 45 G6
Kirknewton Nthumb 47 J6
Kirkoswald Cumb 42 D7
Kirkoswald S Ayrs 44 F6
Kirkpatrick-Fleming
  D & G 42 B5
Kirkton of Skene
  Abers 55 L4
Kirkwall Ork 65 c4
Kirkwhelpington
  Nthumb 43 H4
Kirriemuir Angus 51 J2
Kirton Lincs 31 J6
Kirton in Lindsey
  N Linc 34 F6
Kislingbury Nhants 23 H4
Knaresborough
  N York 38 D7
Knarsdale Nthumb 42 E6
Knebworth Herts 15 J2
Knighton Powys 21 G3
Knightwick Powys 21 L5
Knockan Highld 63 H6
Knockin Shrops 27 L7
Knottingley Wakefd 34 C4
Knowl Hill W & M 14 E5
Knutsford Ches E 28 E3
Kyleakin Highld 57 G6
Kyle of Lochalsh
  Highld 57 G6
Kylerhea Highld 57 G7

L

Laceby NE Lin 35 H6
Ladock Cnwll 2 E5
Ladybank Fife 51 H5
Laggan Highld 54 A5
La Greve de Lecq
  Jersey 7 a1
Laide Highld 62 E8
Lairg Highld 64 C6
Lakenheath Suffk 24 E7
Lamberhurst Kent 10 E5
Lambourn W Berk 14 B6
Lamerton Devon 3 K3
Lamington S Lans 46 A6
Lamlash N Ayrs 44 D5
Lampeter Cerdgn 19 J2
Lamport Nhants 23 H3
Lanark S Lans 45 M4
Lancaster Lancs 37 H6
Lanchester Dur 43 J6
Lancing W Susx 9 L5
L'Ancresse Guern 6 b1
Landrake Cnwll 3 J5
Langham Rutlnd 30 E8
Langholm D & G 42 B4
Langport Somset 12 E8
Langthwaite N York 38 A3
Langtoft E R Yk 39 J6
Langton Matravers
  Dorset 8 A7
Langwathby Cumb 42 D7
Langworth Lincs 31 G3
Lanivet Cnwll 3 G4
Lapford Devon 5 G6
Largoward Fife 51 J6
Largs N Ayrs 44 F2
Larkhall S Lans 45 L3
Larkhill Wilts 8 B2
Lastingham N York 39 G4
Latchingdon Essex 17 G7
Latheron Highld 65 H4
Lauder Border 46 F5
Laugharne Carmth 18 F5
Launceston Cnwll 3 J3
Laurencekirk Abers 55 K6
Laurieston D & G 41 G5
Lavenham Suffk 17 G3
Lawers P & K 50 C3
Laxey IoM 36 c3
Laxfield Suffk 25 K8
Lazonby Cumb 42 D7
Leadenham Lincs 30 F5
Leaden Roding Essex .. 16 E6
Leadgate Dur 43 J6
Leadhills S Lans 45 M6
Leamington Spa
  Warwks 22 D4
Leatherhead Surrey ... 15 J7
Lechlade on Thames
  Gloucs 13 M2
Ledbury Herefs 21 L6
Lee Devon 4 E3
Leebotwood Shrops 21 J1
Leeds Leeds 33 L4
Leek Staffs 29 G4
Leeming Bar N York ... 38 C4
Lee-on-the-Solent
  Hants 8 F5
Legbourne Lincs 31 J2
Leicester C Leic 23 G1
Leigh Kent 10 D4
Leigh Wigan 32 F6
Leigh Sinton Worcs 21 L5
Leighton Buzzard
  C Beds 23 J7
Leintwardine Herefs ... 21 H3
Leiston Suffk 17 M2
Lelant Cnwll 2 C6
Lendalfoot S Ayrs 40 C3
Lenham Kent 11 G3
Lennoxtown E Duns 50 B8
Leominster Herefs 21 J4
L'Erée Guern 6 a2
Lerwick Shet 61 c6
Leslie Abers 60 D6
Leslie Fife 51 H6
Lesmahagow S Lans .. 45 L4
Leswalt D & G 40 B5
L'Etacq Jersey 7 a1
Letchworth Garden
  City Herts 16 B4
Letham Angus 51 K3
Letterston Pembks 18 C4
Leuchars Fife 51 J5
Leven E R Yk 35 H3
Leven Fife 51 J6
Levens Cumb 37 H5
Leverburgh W Isls 62 e7
Lewes E Susx 10 C7

Lewisham Gt Lon 10 C2
Leyburn N York 38 B4
Leyland Lancs 32 E5
Leysdown-on-Sea
  Kent 11 H2
Lhanbryde Moray 59 L3
Libberton S Lans 46 A5
Lichfield Staffs 29 H8
Lidgate Suffk 16 F2
Lifton Devon 3 J3
Lightwater Surrey 15 G7
Lilliesleaf Border 46 F7
Limpley Stoke Wilts ... 13 H5
Lincoln Lincs 30 F3
Lindale Cumb 37 G5
Lingfield Surrey 10 C4
Linlithgow W Loth 46 A3
Linton Cambs 16 D3
Linton Kent 10 F4
Liphook Hants 9 H3
Liskeard Cnwll 3 H4
Liss Hants 9 H3
Lissington Lincs 31 G2
Litcham Norfk 24 F4
Litchfield Hants 14 C7
Little Abington
  Cambs 16 D3
Little Berkhamsted
  Herts 15 K3
Littleborough Rochdl .. 33 H5
Little Brickhill M Keyn .. 23 J6
Little Bytham Lincs 30 F7
Little Clacton Essex ... 17 J5
Little Gaddesden
  Herts 15 G3
Littlehampton
  W Susx 9 K5
Littleport Cambs 24 D6
Little Stretton Shrops . 21 H2
Little Torrington
  Devon 4 E5
Little Walsingham
  Norfk 25 G3
Liverpool Lpool 32 C7
Livingston W Loth 46 B3
Lizard Cnwll 2 D8
Llanaelhaearn
  Gwynd 26 C5
Llanarmon Dyffryn
  Ceiriog Wrexhm 27 K6
Llanarthne Carmth 19 H4
Llanbedr Gwynd 26 E6
Llanbedr-Dyffryn-
  Clwyd Denbgs 27 K4
Llanberis Gwynd 26 C6
Llanbrynmair Powys ... 20 D1
Llandanwg Gwynd 26 E6
Llanddarog Carmth 19 H5
Llandderfel Gwynd 27 H6
Llanddulas Conwy 27 H3
Llandeilo Carmth 19 J4
Llandinam Powys 20 E2
Llandissilio Pembks ... 18 E4
Llandovery Carmth 19 K3
Llandre Cerdgn 20 B2
Llandrillo Denbgs 27 J6
Llandrindod Wells
  Powys 20 E4
Llandrinio Powys 27 L7
Llandudno Conwy 27 G2
Llandwrog Gwynd 26 D4
Llandybie Carmth 19 J5
Llandysul Cerdgn 19 G3
Llanelli Carmth 19 H6
Llanerchymedd IoA 26 D2
Llanerfyl Powys 27 J8
Llanfachraeth IoA 26 C2
Llanfair Caereinion
  Powys 27 J8
Llanfair Dyffryn
  Clwyd Denbgs 27 J4
Llanfairfechan
  Conwy 26 F3
Llanfair P G IoA 26 D3
Llanfair Talhaiarn
  Conwy 27 H3
Llanfair Waterdine
  Shrops 21 G3
Llanfarian Cerdgn 20 A3
Llanfyllin Powys 27 K7
Llangadfan Powys 27 H8
Llangadog Carmth 19 K4
Llangammarch Wells
  Powys 20 D5
Llangedwyn Powys 27 K7
Llangefni IoA 26 D3
Llangeinor Brdgnd 19 L7
Llangeler Carmth 19 G3
Llangennith Swans ... 19 G5
Llangernyw Conwy 27 G3

Llangoed IoA 26 E2
Llangollen Denbgs 27 K5
Llangors Powys 20 F7
Llangrannog Cerdgn ... 18 F2
Llangurig Powys 20 D3
Llangynidr Powys 20 F7
Llangynog Powys 27 J7
Llanhamlach Powys 20 E7
Llanharan Rhondd 12 B3
Llanidloes Powys 20 D2
Llanilar Cerdgn 20 B3
Llanllechid Gwynd 26 E3
Llannefydd Conwy 27 H3
Llanrhaeadr-ym-
  Mochnant Powys ... 27 J7
Llanrhidian Swans 19 H6
Llanrhystud Cerdgn ... 20 A4
Llanrug Gwynd 26 D3
Llanrwst Conwy 27 G4
Llansanffraid Glan
  Conwy Conwy 27 G2
Llansannan Conwy 27 H3
Llansantffraid
  Cerdgn 19 H1
Llansantffraid-ym-
  Mechain Powys 27 K7
Llansawel Carmth 19 J3
Llansteffan Carmth 19 G5
Llanthony Mons 21 G7
Llantrisant Rhondd 12 B3
Llantwit Major
  V Glam 5 J1
Llanuwchllyn Gwynd .. 27 G6
Llanvetherine Mons ... 21 H8
Llanvihangel
  Crucorney Mons ... 21 G7
Llanwddyn Powys 27 J2
Llanwnda Gwynd 26 D4
Llanwrda Carmth 19 K3
Llanwrtyd Wells
  Powys 27 H7
Llanybydder Carmth .. 19 H2
Llanymynech Powys ... 27 L7
Llanystumdwy
  Gwynd 26 D6
Llay Wrexhm 27 L4
Llechryd Cerdgn 18 F3
Llwyngwril Gwynd 26 E8
Llwynmawr Wrexhm ... 27 K6
Llynclys Shrops 27 L7
Llyswen Powys 20 F6
Lochailort Highld 52 E3
Lochaline Highld 52 D6
Locharbriggs D & G ... 41 K4
Lochawe Ag & B 53 H7
Loch Baghasdail
  W Isls 62 c12
Lochboisdale W Isls ... 62 c12
Lochbuie Ag & B 52 D5
Lochcarron Highld 57 H5
Lochdonhead Ag & B .. 52 E7
Lochearnhead Stirlg ... 50 B4
Lochgair Ag & B 49 H4
Lochgilphead Ag & B .. 49 G4
Lochgoilhead Ag & B .. 49 K3
Lochinver Highld 63 G5
Lochmaben D & G 41 L4
Lochmaddy W Isls 62 d8
Loch nam Madadh
  W Isls 62 d8
Lochranza N Ayrs 44 D3
Lochwinnoch Rens 45 G2
Lockerbie D & G 41 L4
Lockton N York 39 H4
Loddon Norfk 25 K6
Lofthouse N York 38 B6
Loftus R & Cl 39 G2
London Gt Lon 15 J5
London Colney Herts .. 15 J4
Long Ashton N Som ... 12 F4
Long Bennington
  Lincs 30 E5
Long Buckby Nhants .. 24 B8
Longburton Dorset 7 J1
Long Compton
  Warwks 22 D6
Long Crendon Bucks .. 14 E3
Long Eaton Derbys 30 B6
Longford Gloucs 21 M7
Longformacus
  Border 47 G4
Longframlington
  Nthumb 43 J2
Longham Dorset 8 B6
Longhorsley Nthumb .. 43 J3
Longhoughton
  Nthumb 47 M7
Long Itchington
  Warwks 22 E4
Long Lawford
  Warwks 22 F3

Long Marston N York .. 34 C2
Long Melford Suffk 17 G3
Longniddry E Loth 46 E3
Longnor Shrops 21 J1
Longnor Staffs 29 H4
Long Preston N York .. 37 L7
Longridge Lancs 32 F3
Longridge W Loth 45 M2
Longside Abers 61 G5
Long Stratton Norfk ... 25 J6
Long Sutton Lincs 31 K7
Long Sutton Somset ... 12 F8
Longtown Lancs 32 D4
Longtown Cumb 42 B5
Longville in the Dale
  Shrops 21 J2
Looe Cnwll 3 H5
Lossiemouth Moray ... 59 K3
Lostwithiel Cnwll 3 G5
Loughborough Leics ... 30 B7
Louth Lincs 31 J2
Lowdham Notts 30 D5
Lower Diabaig Highld . 57 H4
Lower Dicker E Susx ... 10 D6
Lower Peover Ches E .. 28 E3
Lower Swell Gloucs 22 C7
Lowestoft Suffk 25 M6
Loweswater Cumb 36 E2
Lowick Nhants 23 K3
Lowick Nthumb 47 K5
Low Row N York 37 M4
Lubenham Leics 23 H2
Ludborough Lincs 35 J7
Ludgershall Wilts 8 D2
Ludham Norfk 25 K4
Ludlow Shrops 21 J3
Lugton E Ayrs 45 H3
Lugwardine Herefs 21 J6
Lumphanan Abers 55 J4
Lumsden Abers 55 H3
Lunan Angus 51 L2
Lupton Cumb 37 H5
Luss Ag & B 49 L4
Lusta Highld 56 C4
Luton Luton 15 H2
Lutterworth Leics 22 F2
Lybster Highld 65 H4
Lydbury North
  Shrops 21 H2
Lydd Kent 11 H6
Lydford Devon 3 L3
Lydford on Fosse
  Somset 12 F7
Lydham Shrops 21 G2
Lydney Gloucs 13 G2
Lyme Regis Dorset 7 G3
Lyminge Kent 11 J4
Lymington Hants 8 D6
Lymm Warrtn 28 E2
Lympne Kent 11 J5
Lyndhurst Hants 8 D5
Lyneham Wilts 13 K4
Lyness Ork 65 b5
Lyng Somset 12 E7
Lynmouth Devon 5 G3
Lynton Devon 4 F3
Lyonshall Herefs 21 G5
Lytham St Anne's
  Lancs 32 C4
Lythe N York 39 H3

M

Mablethorpe Lincs 31 K2
Macclesfield Ches E ... 28 F3
Macduff Abers 60 E3
Machrihanish Ag & B .. 44 A5
Machynlleth Powys 20 C1
Macmerry E Loth 46 E3
Maentwrog Gwynd 26 F5
Maerdy Rhondd 12 B2
Maesteg Brdgnd 19 L7
Maghull Sefton 32 D6
Maiden Bradley Wilts .. 13 H7
Maidencombe Torbay .. 6 C5
Maidenhead W & M ... 14 F5
Maiden Newton
  Dorset 7 J3
Maidstone Kent 10 F3
Mainsriddle D & G 41 K6
Malborough Devon 6 A7
Maldon Essex 17 G6
Malham N York 37 L6
Mallaig Highld 52 D2
Mallwyd Gwynd 27 G8
Malmesbury Wilts 13 J3
Malpas Ches W 28 C5
Maltby Rothm 34 C7
Malton N York 39 G6

Malvern Wells Worcs .. 21 L6
Manaccan Cnwll 2 D7
Manchester Manch 33 G6
Manea Cambs 24 C6
Manningtree Essex 17 J4
Manorbier Pembks 18 D6
Mansfield Notts 30 B4
Marazanvose Cnwll 2 E5
Marazion Cnwll 2 B7
March Cambs 24 B6
Marchwiel Wrexhm 28 B5
Marden Kent 10 F4
Mareham le Fen
  Lincs 31 J4
Margaretting Essex 16 E6
Margate Kent 11 L2
Mark Somset 12 E6
Mark Cross E Susx 10 E5
Market Bosworth
  Leics 22 E1
Market Deeping
  Lincs 31 G8
Market Drayton
  Shrops 28 D6
Market Harborough
  Leics 23 H2
Market Lavington
  Wilts 13 K6
Market Rasen Lincs ... 35 H7
Market Warsop
  Notts 30 C3
Market Weighton
  E R Yk 34 F3
Markfield Leics 30 B8
Markham Moor
  Notts 30 D3
Marksbury BaNES 13 G5
Marks Tey Essex 17 G5
Marlborough Wilts 13 M4
Marloes Pembks 18 B5
Marlow Bucks 14 F5
Marnhull Dorset 7 K1
Marshfield S Glos 13 H4
Marsh Gibbon Bucks .. 14 D2
Marske-by-the-Sea
  R & Cl 38 F2
Martin Lincs 31 G4
Martinstown Dorset ... 7 J3
Martlesham Heath
  Suffk 17 K3
Martock Somset 7 H1
Marton Warwks 22 E4
Marykirk Abers 55 K7
Maryport Cumb 41 K7
Mary Tavy Devon 3 L3
Marywell Abers 55 J5
Masham N York 38 C5
Matfield Kent 10 E4
Matlock Derbys 29 K4
Mattingley Hants 14 E7
Mauchline E Ayrs 45 H5
Maud Abers 60 F4
Maughold IoM 36 d2
Maulden C Beds 23 K6
Mawgan Porth Cnwll .. 2 E4
Mawnan Smith Cnwll . 2 D7
Maybole S Ayrs 45 G6
Mayfield E Susx 10 E5
Mayfield Staffs 29 H5
Meare Somset 12 F6
Measham Leics 29 K8
Medstead Hants 9 G3
Meeth Devon 4 E6
Meifod Powys 27 K8
Meigle P & K 51 H3
Melbourn Cambs 16 C3
Melbourne Derbys 29 K7
Meliden Denbgs 27 J2
Melksham Wilts 13 J5
Melling Lancs 37 J6
Melmerby Cumb 42 D7
Melrose Border 46 F6
Meltham Kirk 33 K5
Melton E R Yk 34 F4
Melton Constable
  Norfk 25 H3
Melton Mowbray
  Leics 30 D7
Melvaig Highld 57 G2
Melvich Highld 64 E2
Memsie Abers 61 G3
Memus Angus 51 J2
Menai Bridge IoA 26 E3
Mentmore Bucks 14 F2
Meopham Kent 10 E2
Mere Wilts 13 H7
Meriden Solhll 22 D7
Merthyr Tydfil Myr Td. 12 B2
Merton Devon 4 E6
Messingham N Linc ... 34 F6
Metfield Suffk 25 K7

Methil Fife 51 J6
Methlick Abers 60 F5
Methven P & K 50 F4
Methwold Norfk 24 E6
Mevagissey Cnwll 2 F6
Mexborough Donc 34 B6
Miabhig W Isls 62 f3
Miavaig W Isls 62 f3
Micheldever Hants 8 F2
Mickleton Dur 37 M2
Mickleton Gloucs 22 C6
Midbea Ork 65 c2
Middleham N York 38 B4
Middle Rasen Lincs ... 35 G7
Middlesbrough
  Middsb 38 E2
Middleton Cheney
  Nhants 22 F6
Middleton-in-
  Teesdale Dur 37 M2
Middleton-on-Sea
  W Susx 9 J5
Middleton on the
  Wolds E R Yk 34 F2
Middleton Stoney
  Oxon 14 C2
Middle Town IoS 2 a2
Middle Wallop Hants .. 8 D3
Middlewich Ches E 28 E3
Middlezoy Somset 12 E7
Midhurst W Susx 9 J4
Midsomer Norton
  BaNES 13 G6
Mid Yell Shet 61 d2
Milborne Port
  Somset 7 J1
Mildenhall Suffk 24 E7
Milfield Nthumb 47 J6
Milford Haven
  Pembks 18 C5
Milford on Sea Hants .. 8 D6
Millbrook Cnwll 3 K5
Millbrook Jersey 7 b2
Millom Cumb 36 E5
Millport N Ayrs 44 F3
Milnathort P & K 50 F6
Milngavie E Duns 45 J1
Milton Abbas Dorset .. 7 K2
Milton Abbot Devon ... 3 K3
Milton Damerel
  Devon 4 D6
Milton Ernest Bed 23 K5
Milton Keynes
  M Keyn 23 J6
Milverton Somset 5 K5
Minchinhampton
  Gloucs 13 J2
Minehead Somset 5 J3
Minster Kent 11 H2
Minster Kent 11 L2
Minsterley Shrops 28 B8
Minster Lovell Oxon ... 14 A3
Mintlaw Abers 61 G4
Mirfield Kirk 33 K5
Misterton Notts 34 E7
Misterton Somset 7 H2
Mitcheldean Gloucs ... 21 K7
Mobberley Ches E 28 E2
Mochrum D & G 40 E6
Modbury Devon 3 M5
Moffat D & G 41 L2
Mold Flints 27 K4
Moniaive D & G 41 H3
Monifieth Angus 51 K4
Monkleigh Devon 4 D5
Monkton S Ayrs 45 G5
Monmouth Mons 21 J8
Montacute Somset 7 H1
Montford Bridge
  Shrops 28 B7
Montgomery Powys ... 20 F1
Montrose Angus 51 L2
Mont Saint Guern 6 a2
Monyash Derbys 29 H3
Monymusk Abers 55 K3
Morchard Bishop
  Devon 5 G6
Morcott Rutlnd 23 J1
Mordiford Herefs 21 J6
Morebattle Border 47 H7
Morecambe Lancs 37 G6
Moreton Dorset 7 K3
Moretonhampstead
  Devon 6 B3
Moreton-in-Marsh
  Gloucs 22 C6
Morfa Nefyn Gwynd .. 26 B5
Morley Leeds 33 L4
Morpeth Nthumb 43 J3
Morston Norfk 25 G2
Mortehoe Devon 4 D3

Mortimer W Berk............14 D7
Morville Shrops............21 K2
Morwenstow Cnwll.............4 B5
Mossat Abers...............55 H3
Mosstodloch Moray......59 L4
Mosterton Dorset.............7 H2
Mostyn Flints..............27 K2
Motherby Cumb............37 G5
Motherwell N Lans.......45 K3
Moulsford Oxon............14 D5
Moulton Nhants............23 H4
Mountain Ash
  Rhondd..................12 B2
Mountsorrel Leics.......30 D7
Mousehole Cnwll............2 B7
Moy Highld................58 F5
Muchalls Abers............55 M5
Much Birch Herefs........21 J7
Much Hadham Herts.........15 L4
Much Marcle Herefs.......21 K6
Much Wenlock
  Shrops...................21 K1
Muddiford Devon............4 E4
Muirdrum Angus............51 K3
Muirhead Angus............51 H4
Muirkirk E Ayrs...........45 K5
Muir of Ord Highld........58 D4
Muker N York.............37 L4
Mullion Cnwll..............2 D8
Mundesley Norfk..........25 K3
Mundford Norfk............24 E6
Mungrisdale Cumb.........42 B8
Munlochy Highld...........58 E4
Munslow Shrops...........21 J2
Musselburgh E Loth.......46 D3
Muthill P & K.............50 D5

N

Nacton Suffk................17 K4
Nailsea N Som.............12 F4
Nailsworth Gloucs........13 J2
Nairn Highld...............59 G4
Nantgaredig Carmth......19 H4
Nantwich Ches E..........28 D5
Narberth Pembks..........18 E5
Narborough Norfk.........24 E4
Naseby Nhants............23 G3
Navenby Lincs.............30 F4
Nayland Suffk.............17 H4
Nazeing Essex.............16 C6
Neath Neath...............19 K6
Necton Norfk..............24 F5
Needham Market
  Suffk....................17 J2
Nefyn Gwynd..............26 C5
Nelson Lancs..............33 H3
Nesscliffe Shrops.........28 B7
Neston Ches W............27 L3
Nether Stowey
  Somset..................12 C7
Nether Wasdale
  Cumb....................36 E3
Nethy Bridge Highld.....54 D3
Nettlebed Oxon............14 E5
Nevern Pembks............18 E3
New Abbey D & G..........41 K5
New Aberdour Abers......60 F3
New Alresford Hants.......8 F3
Newark-on-Trent
  Notts....................30 E4
Newarthill N Lans........45 L2
Newbiggin Dur............37 L1
Newbiggin N York.........38 A5
Newbiggin-by-the-
  Sea Nthumb.............43 K3
Newbigging S Lans........46 A5
Newbold on Stour
  Warwks..................22 D5
New Bolingbroke
  Lincs.....................31 J4
Newborough IoA...........26 D4
Newbridge Caerph........12 C2
Newbridge D & G..........41 K4
Newbridge on Wye
  Powys....................20 E4
New Buckenham
  Norfk....................25 H6
Newburgh Abers...........61 G6
Newburgh Fife............51 G5
Newbury W Berk...........14 C6
Newby Bridge Cumb.....37 G5
Newcastle Emlyn
  Carmth..................18 F3
Newcastleton Border....42 C3
Newcastle-under-
  Lyme Staffs.............28 F5
Newcastle upon
  Tyne N u Ty.............43 K5

New Cumnock E Ayrs....45 J6
New Deer Abers...........60 F5
Newent Gloucs............21 L7
Newgale Pembks..........18 C4
New Galloway D & G....41 G4
New Grimsby IoS...........2 a1
Newhaven E Susx.........10 C7
New Holland N Linc.......35 G4
Newick E Susx............10 C6
New Luce D & G...........40 C5
Newlyn Cnwll...............2 B7
Newmains N Lans.........45 L3
Newmarket Suffk.........16 E2
Newmill Moray............60 B4
New Milton Hants..........8 C6
Newnham Gloucs..........13 G1
Newnham Worcs..........21 K4
New Pitsligo Abers.......60 F4
Newport Essex............16 D4
Newport IoW................8 E6
Newport Newpt...........12 D3
Newport Pembks..........18 D3
Newport Wrekin..........28 E7
Newport-on-Tay Fife....51 J4
Newport Pagnell
  M Keyn...................23 J6
New Quay Cerdgn.........19 G1
Newquay Cnwll.............2 E5
New Radnor Powys........20 F4
New Romney Kent........11 H5
Newsham N York.........38 B3
Newton Abbot
  Devon....................6 C5
Newton Aycliffe Dur....38 C2
Newton Ferrers
  Devon....................3 L6
Newton Ferry W Isls....62 d8
Newtongrange
  Mdloth...................46 D4
Newton Mearns
  E Rens...................45 J3
Newtonmore Highld.....54 B4
Newton-on-the-
  Moor Nthumb...........43 J2
Newton on Trent
  Lincs....................30 E3
Newton St Cyres
  Devon....................6 C3
Newton Solney
  Derbys...................29 J7
Newton Stewart
  D & G....................40 E5
Newtown Herefs..........21 K5
Newtown Powys..........20 F2
New Tredegar
  Caerph...................12 C2
Newtyle Angus............51 H3
Neyland Pembks..........18 D5
Nigg Highld...............59 G3
Ninfield E Susx...........10 E6
Niton IoW...................8 E7
Nocton Lincs..............31 G4
Norham Nthumb..........47 J3
Normanton Wakefd......34 B4
Northall Bucks............15 G2
Northallerton N York...38 D4
Northam Devon.............4 D4
Northampton
  Nhants...................23 H4
North Berwick
  E Loth....................46 F2
North Cave E R Yk......34 F4
Northchapel W Susx......9 J3
North Chideock
  Dorset.....................7 G3
North Cotes Lincs........35 K6
North Creake Norfk......24 F3
North Curry Somset......12 D8
North Dalton E R Yk.....34 F2
North Elmham Norfk....25 G4
North Ferriby E R Yk....35 G4
Northfleet Kent...........10 E2
North Frodingham
  E R Yk...................35 H2
North Grimston
  N York....................39 H6
North Hayling Hants......9 G5
North Hykeham
  Lincs.....................30 F3
Northiam E Susx..........11 G6
North Kessock
  Highld....................58 F4
North Kilworth Leics....23 G3
North Kyme Lincs........31 H4
Northleach Gloucs.......22 C8
North Luffenham
  Rutlnd...................23 J1
North Molton Devon......5 H4
North Muskham
  Notts....................30 E4
Northop Flints............27 K3

North Petherton
  Somset..................12 D7
North Rigton N York....33 L2
North Shields
  N Tyne...................43 K5
North Somercotes
  Lincs....................35 K6
North Walsham
  Norfk....................25 J3
North Waltham
  Hants.....................8 F2
North Weald Bassett
  Essex....................16 D6
Northwich Ches W......28 D3
North Wingfield
  Derbys...................29 K4
Northwold Norfk.........24 E6
Norton-on-Derwent
  N York....................39 G6
Norton St Philip
  Somset..................13 H5
Norwich Norfk............25 J5
Nottingham C Nott......30 C5
Nuneaton Warwks........22 E2
Nunney Somset...........13 H6
Nutley E Susx............10 C5

O

Oadby Leics...............23 G1
Oakham Rutlnd...........30 E8
Oakhill Somset............13 G6
Oakley Bed................23 K5
Oakley Bucks.............14 D3
Oakley Hants...............8 F2
Oban Ag & B..............52 F7
Ochiltree E Ayrs..........45 H5
Ockbrook Derbys.........29 L6
Ockley Surrey.............9 L2
Odiham Hants..............9 G2
Offenham Worcs..........22 B5
Ogbourne St George
  Wilts....................13 M4
Ogmore-by-Sea
  V Glam...................19 L8
Okehampton Devon.......4 E7
Old Deer Abers...........61 G4
Old Grimsby IoS...........2 a1
Oldham Oldham...........31 H6
Old Hurst Cambs.........24 B7
Old Leake Lincs...........31 K5
Oldmeldrum Abers.......60 F6
Old Rayne Abers..........60 D6
Old Sodbury S Glos......13 H3
Old Stratford
  Nhants...................23 H6
Old Town IoS...............2 b2
Old Windsor W & M.....15 G6
Ollaberry Shet............61 b3
Ollerton Notts............30 C3
Olney M Keyn..............23 J5
Ombersley Worcs.........21 M4
Onchan IoM...............36 c3
Onich Highld..............53 G5
Orford Suffk..............17 L3
Ormesby St
  Margaret Norfk........25 L4
Ormiston E Loth..........46 C6
Ormskirk Lancs...........32 D6
Orpington Gt Lon........10 D2
Orsett Thurr..............10 E1
Orton Cumb...............37 J3
Osbournby Lincs.........31 G6
Osmington Dorset.........7 K4
Osmotherley N York....38 E4
Ospringe Kent............11 H3
Ossett Wakefd............33 L5
Oswaldkirk N York.......38 F5
Oswestry Shrops.........27 L6
Otford Kent...............10 D3
Othery Somset............12 E7
Otley Leeds...............33 K3
Otterbourne Hants........8 E4
Otterburn Nthumb........43 G3
Otter Ferry Ag & B.......49 H5
Ottershaw Surrey........15 G7
Otterton Devon.............6 E4
Ottery St Mary
  Devon....................6 E3
Oundle Nhants............23 K2
Outwell Norfk.............24 C5
Overseal Derbys.........29 K7
Overton Hants..............8 F2
Overton Wrexhm.........28 B5
Ower Hants.................8 D4
Oxford Oxon..............14 C3
Oxted Surrey.............10 C3
Oxton Notts..............30 C5
Oxwich Swans............19 H7

P

Padbury Bucks...........23 H7
Paddock Wood Kent....10 E4
Padiham Lancs...........33 G4
Padstow Cnwll.............2 F4
Paignton Torbay...........6 C5
Pailton Warwks..........22 F3
Painswick Gloucs........13 J1
Paisley Rens.............45 H2
Palnackie D & G..........41 J6
Pandy Mons..............21 G7
Pangbourne W Berk....14 D6
Pannal N York............33 L2
Pant-y-dwr Powys.......20 E3
Papworth Everard
  Cambs....................16 B2
Parracombe Devon.........4 F3
Pateley Bridge
  N York....................38 B6
Patna E Ayrs..............45 H6
Patrick IoM...............36 b3
Patrington E R Yk.......35 J4
Patterdale Cumb.........37 G2
Pattishall Nhants........23 G5
Peacehaven E Susx......10 C7
Peasedown St John
  BaNES....................13 H5
Peasmarsh E Susx.......11 G6
Peebles Border...........46 C5
Peel IoM...................36 b3
Pelynt Cnwll................3 H5
Pembrey Carmth.........19 G6
Pembridge Herefs........21 H4
Pembroke Pembks.......18 D6
Pembroke Dock
  Pembks...................18 D6
Pembury Kent.............10 E4
Penally Pembks..........18 E6
Penarth V Glam..........12 C4
Pencoed Brdgnd..........12 A3
Pencraig Herefs..........21 J7
Pendine Carmth..........18 F5
Pendock Worcs...........21 L6
Pendoggett Cnwll.........3 G3
Pengam Caerph..........12 C2
Penicuik Mdloth..........46 C4
Penistone Barns.........33 L6
Penkridge Staffs.........29 G7
Penmachno Conwy.....27 G5
Penmaenmawr
  Conwy....................26 F3
Pennal Gwynd............20 B1
Pennan Abers.............60 F3
Penpont D & G............41 J3
Penrhyndeudraeth
  Gwynd....................26 E6
Penrith Cumb.............42 D8
Penryn Cnwll...............2 E7
Pensford BaNES..........13 G5
Penshurst Kent...........10 D4
Pensilva Cnwll.............3 J4
Pentewan Cnwll............2 F6
Pentraeth IoA............26 D3
Pentrefoelas Conwy....27 G5
Penybont Powys..........20 F4
Pen-y-bont-fawr
  Powys....................27 J7
Penygroes Gwynd.......26 D4
Penzance Cnwll............2 B7
Perranporth Cnwll.........2 D5
Pershore Worcs..........22 A5
Perth P & K...............50 F4
Peterborough C Pete...24 M1
Peterchurch Herefs......21 H6
Peterculter C Aber.......55 L4
Peterhead Abers.........61 H5
Peterlee Dur..............43 L7
Petersfield Hants..........9 H4
Petton Devon...............5 J5
Petworth W Susx..........9 J4
Pevensey E Susx.........10 E7
Pewsey Wilts.............13 L5
Pickering N York.........39 G5
Piercebridge Darltn....38 C2
Pierowall Ork.............65 C1
Pillaton Cnwll..............3 J4
Pillerton Priors
  Warwks..................22 D5
Pilling Lancs..............32 D3
Pinchbeck Lincs.........31 H7
Pinwherry S Ayrs.......40 C3
Pinxton Derbys..........29 L4
Pirbright Surrey.........15 G7
Pitcaple Abers...........60 E6
Pitlochry P & K..........50 E2
Pitmedden Abers.........60 F6
Pittenweem Fife.........51 K6
Pleasley Derbys.........30 B4
Plockton Highld..........57 H6

Pluckley Kent......11 G4
Plumpton E Susx......10 C6
Plumtree Notts......30 C6
Plymouth C Plym......3 M5
Plympton C Plym......3 L5
Pocklington E R Yk......34 E2
Polbathic Cnwll......3 J5
Polegate E Susx......10 D7
Polmont Falk......50 E8
Polperro Cnwll......3 H5
Polruan Cnwll......3 G5
Polzeath Cnwll......2 F3
Pontardawe Neath......19 K6
Pontarddulais Swans......19 J6
Pontefract Wakefd......34 B5
Ponteland Nthumb......43 J4
Ponterwyd Cerdgn......20 C3
Pontesbury Shrops......28 B8
Pontllanfraith
  Caerph......12 C2
Pontrhydfendigaid
  Cerdgn......19 K1
Pontrilas Herefs......21 H7
Pontyates Carmth......19 H5
Pontyberem Carmth......19 H5
Pontypool Torfn......12 D2
Pontypridd Rhondd......12 B3
Pool Leeds......33 L3
Poole Poole......8 A6
Poolewe Highld......57 H2
Pooley Bridge Cumb......37 H2
Porlock Somset......5 H3
Porlock Weir Somset......5 H3
Port Appin Ag & B......52 F6
Port Askaig Ag & B......48 D6
Portavadie Ag & B......49 H6
Port Bannatyne
  Ag & B......49 J6
Port Carlisle Cumb......42 A5
Port Charlotte
  Ag & B......48 B7
Portchester Hants......8 F5
Port Ellen Ag & B......48 C8
Port Erin IoM......36 a4
Porteshan Dorset......7 J3
Port Eynon Swans......19 H7
Port Glasgow Inver......49 L5
Portgordon Moray......60 B3
Porth Rhondd......12 B3
Porthcawl Brdgnd......19 L8
Porthcothan Cnwll......2 E4
Porthcurno Cnwll......2 A8
Port Henderson
  Highld......57 H2
Porthleven Cnwll......2 C7
Porthmadog Gwynd......26 E6
Porthtowan Cnwll......2 D6
Portinscale Cumb......36 F2
Port Isaac Cnwll......2 F3
Portishead N Som......12 F4
Portknockie Moray......60 C3
Portlethen Abers......55 M5
Portloe Cnwll......2 F6
Port Logan D & G......40 C7
Portmahomack
  Highld......59 H2
Portnacroish Ag & B......53 G6
Portnahaven Ag & B......48 A7
Port nan Long W Isls......62 d8
Port Nis W Isls......62 i1
Port of Menteith
  Stirlg......50 B6
Port of Ness W Isls......62 i1
Portpatrick D & G......40 B6
Portreath Cnwll......2 C6
Portree Highld......56 E5
Port St Mary IoM......36 a4
Portscatho Cnwll......2 E7
Portskerra Highld......64 E2
Portslade-by-Sea
  Br & H......10 B7
Portsmouth C Port......9 G5
Portsoy Abers......60 D3
Port Talbot Neath......19 K7
Port William D & G......40 E7
Postbridge Devon......3 M3
Postcombe Oxon......14 E4
Potterne Wilts......13 K5
Potters Bar Herts......15 J4
Potton C Beds......16 B3
Poulton-le-Fylde
  Lancs......32 C3
Powburn Nthumb......47 K7
Powick Worcs......21 M5
Poynton Ches E......28 F2
Praa Sands Cnwll......2 C7
Prees Shrops......28 C6
Preesall Lancs......32 D3
Prees Green Shrops......28 C6
Prenteg Gwynd......26 E5
Prestatyn Denbgs......27 J2

Prestbury Ches E......28 F3
Presteigne Powys......21 G4
Preston Border......47 H4
Preston Lancs......32 E4
Preston Candover
  Hants......8 F2
Preston Capes
  Nhants......22 F5
Prestonpans E Loth......46 E3
Prestwich Bury......33 G6
Prestwick S Ayrs......45 G5
Prestwood Bucks......14 F4
Priddy Somset......12 F6
Princes Risborough
  Bucks......14 F4
Princethorpe Warwks......22 E3
Princetown Devon......3 L4
Prospect Cumb......41 L7
Prudhoe Nthumb......43 H5
Pucklechurch S Glos......13 H4
Puddletown Dorset......7 K3
Pudsey Leeds......33 L4
Pulborough W Susx......9 K4
Pulford Ches W......28 B4
Pulham St Mary
  Norfk......25 J7
Pumsaint Carmth......19 J3
Purfleet Thurr......10 D1
Purton Wilts......13 L3
Pwll Carmth......19 H6
Pwllheli Gwynd......26 C6
Pyecombe W Susx......10 B6
Pyle Brdgnd......19 L7

Q

Quatt Shrops......21 L2
Queensferry Flints......27 L3
Quendon Essex......16 D4

R

Rackenford Devon......5 H5
Rackheath Norfk......25 J4
Radcliffe on Trent
  Notts......30 C6
Radlett Herts......15 H4
Radstock BaNES......13 G5
Radwinter Essex......16 E4
Radyr Cardif......12 C4
Rafford Moray......59 J4
Raglan Mons......12 E1
Rainham Gt Lon......10 D1
Rampside Cumb......36 F6
Ramsbury Wilts......14 A6
Ramsey Cambs......24 A7
Ramsey IoM......36 C2
Ramsgate Kent......11 L2
Rannoch Station
  P & K......53 L5
Rapness Ork......65 C2
Rathen Abers......61 G3
Raunds Nhants......23 K3
Ravenglass Cumb......36 E4
Ravenscar N York......39 J3
Ravenstonedale
  Cumb......37 K3
Rawmarsh Rothm......34 B7
Rawtenstall Lancs......33 G4
Rayleigh Essex......16 F7
Reading Readg......14 E6
Reay Highld......64 F2
Reculver Kent......11 K2
Redbourn Herts......15 H3
Redbrook Gloucs......12 F1
Redbrook Wrexhm......28 C5
Redcar R & Cl......38 F2
Redditch Worcs......22 B4
Redgrave Suffk......25 G7
Redhill N Som......12 F5
Redhill Surrey......10 B4
Redmile Leics......30 E6
Rednal Shrops......28 B6
Red Roses Carmth......18 F5
Red Row Nthumb......43 K2
Red Wharf Bay IoA......26 D7
Redruth Cnwll......2 D6
Reedham Norfk......25 L5
Reepham Norfk......25 H4
Reigate Surrey......10 B4
Reighton N York......39 K5
Rempstone Notts......30 C7
Renfrew Rens......45 H2
Renwick Cumb......42 D7
Repton Derbys......29 K6
Resolven Neath......19 L6
Retford Notts......30 D2

Reynoldston Swans......19 H7
Rhayader Powys......20 D4
Rhiconich Highld......63 H3
Rhoose V Glam......5 J2
Rhoslanerchrugog
  Wrexhm......27 L5
Rhosneigr IoA......26 C3
Rhôs-on-Sea Conwy......27 G2
Rhossili Swans......19 G7
Rhu Ag & B......49 L5
Rhuddlan Denbgs......27 J3
Rhyd-Ddu Gwynd......26 E4
Rhydowen Cerdgn......19 G2
Rhyl Denbgs......27 H2
Rhymney Caerph......12 C1
Richards Castle
  Herefs......21 J4
Richmond Gt Lon......15 J6
Richmond N York......38 B3
Rickmansworth
  Herts......15 H4
Riding Mill Nthumb......43 H5
Ridsdale Nthumb......43 G4
Rillington N York......39 H5
Ringford D & G......41 G6
Ringmer E Susx......10 C6
Ringwood Hants......8 C5
Ripley Derbys......29 K5
Ripley N York......38 C7
Ripley Surrey......15 H7
Ripon N York......38 D6
Ripple Worcs......21 M6
Ripponden Calder......33 J5
Risca Caerph......12 D3
Risegate Lincs......31 H6
Riseley Bed......23 K4
Riseley Wokham......14 E7
Risley Derbys......29 L6
Risley Warrtn......32 F7
Roade Nhants......23 H5
Roberton Border......46 E7
Roberton S Lans......45 M5
Robertsbridge E Susx......10 F6
Robeston Wathen
  Pembks......18 E5
Robin Hood's Bay
  N York......39 J3
Rocester Staffs......29 H6
Roch Pembks......18 C4
Rochdale Rochdl......33 H5
Roche Cnwll......2 F5
Rochester Medway......10 F2
Rochester Nthumb......42 F3
Rochford Essex......17 G7
Rock Cnwll......2 F3
Rockcliffe Cumb......42 B5
Rockcliffe D & G......41 J6
Rockingham Nhants......23 J2
Rogate W Susx......9 H4
Rogerstone Newpt......12 D3
Rollesby Norfk......25 L4
Rolvenden Kent......11 G5
Romaldkirk Dur......37 M2
Romanno Bridge
  Border......46 C5
Romford Gt Lon......16 D7
Romsey Hants......8 D4
Rookhope Dur......43 G7
Ropley Hants......9 G3
Rosedale Abbey
  N York......39 G4
Rosehall Highld......63 G3
Rosehearty Abers......61 G3
Rosemarkie Highld......58 F4
Rosewell Mdloth......46 D4
Rossett Wrexhm......28 B4
Ross-on-Wye Herefs......21 K7
Rosyth Fife......46 B2
Rothbury Nthumb......43 H2
Rotherfield E Susx......10 D5
Rotherham Rothm......34 B7
Rothes Moray......59 L4
Rothesay Ag & B......49 M4
Rothwell Leeds......33 M4
Rothwell Nhants......23 H3
Rottingdean Br & H......10 C7
Roughton Norfk......25 J3
Rowland's Castle
  Hants......9 G5
Rowland's Gill Gatesd......43 J6
Rowsley Derbys......29 J3
Roxburgh Border......47 G6
Roxwell Essex......16 E6
Royal Leamington
  Spa Warwks......22 D4
Royal Sutton
  Coldfield Birm......22 C2
Royal Tunbridge
  Wells Kent......10 E4
Royal Wootton
  Bassett Wilts......13 L3

Royston Barns......34 A5
Royston Herts......16 C4
Rozel Jersey......7 c1
Ruabon Wrexhm......27 L5
Ruddington Notts......30 C6
Rudgwick W Susx......9 K3
Rudston E R Yk......39 K6
Rufford Lancs......32 D5
Rugby Warwks......22 F3
Rugeley Staffs......29 G7
Rumbling Bridge
  P & K......50 F6
Runcorn Halton......28 C2
Rushden Nhants......23 K4
Rushyford Dur......38 C1
Ruskington Lincs......31 G5
Rustington W Susx......9 K5
Ruswarp N York......39 H3
Rutherglen S Lans......45 J2
Ruthin Denbgs......27 J4
Ruyton-XI-Towns
  Shrops......28 B7
Rydal Cumb......37 G3
Ryde IoW......8 F6
Rye E Susx......11 G6

S

Saddell Ag & B......44 B5
Saffron Walden
  Essex......16 D4
St Abbs Border......47 J3
St Agnes Cnwll......2 D5
St Albans Herts......15 H3
St Andrew Guern......6 a2
St Andrews Fife......51 K5
St Arvans Mons......12 F2
St Asaph Denbgs......27 J3
St Athan V Glam......5 J1
St Aubin Jersey......7 b2
St Austell Cnwll......2 F5
St Bees Cumb......36 D3
St Blazey Cnwll......3 G5
St Boswells Border......46 F6
St Brelade Jersey......7 a2
St Brelade's Bay
  Jersey......7 a2
St Briavels Gloucs......12 F2
St Buryan Cnwll......2 A7
St Catherines Ag & B......49 J3
St Clears Carmth......18 F5
St Cleer Cnwll......3 H4
St Clement Jersey......7 c2
St Columb Major
  Cnwll......2 F4
St Combs Abers......61 H3
St Cyrus Abers......55 K7
St Davids Pembks......18 B4
St Day Cnwll......2 D6
St Dogmaels Pembks......18 E2
St Fergus Abers......61 H4
St Fillans P & K......50 C4
St Florence Pembks......18 E6
St Helens IoW......9 G6
St Helens St Hel......32 E7
St Helier Jersey......7 b2
St Ives Cambs......24 A8
St Ives Cnwll......2 B6
St John Jersey......7 b1
St John's IoM......36 b3
St John's Chapel Dur......43 G7
St John's Town of
  Dalry D & G......41 G4
St Jude's IoM......36 C2
St Just Cnwll......2 A7
St Just-in-Roseland
  Cnwll......2 E7
St Keverne Cnwll......2 E8
St Keyne Cnwll......3 H5
St Lawrence IoW......8 F7
St Lawrence Jersey......7 b1
St Margaret's at
  Cliffe Kent......11 L4
St Margaret's Hope
  Ork......65 C5
St Marks IoM......36 b3
St Martin Guern......6 b2
St Martin Jersey......7 c1
St Mary Jersey......7 b1
St Mary's Ork......65 c4
St Mary's Bay Kent......11 J5
St Mawes Cnwll......2 E7
St Mawgan Cnwll......2 E5
St Monans Fife......51 K6
St Neots Cambs......23 M4
St Osyth Essex......17 J5
St Ouen Jersey......7 a1
St Owens Cross
  Herefs......21 J7

St Peter Jersey....7 b1
St Peter Port Guern....6 b2
St Peter's Guern....6 a2
St Sampson Guern....6 b1
St Saviour Guern....6 a2
St Saviour Jersey....7 b2
St Stephen Cnwll....2 F5
St Tudy Cnwll....3 G3
Salcombe Devon....6 B7
Sale Traffd....33 G7
Salen Ag & B....52 D6
Salen Highld....52 D6
Salfords Surrey....10 B4
Saline Fife....50 F7
Salisbury Wilts....8 C3
Saltash Cnwll....3 K5
Saltburn-by-the-Sea R & Cl....38 F2
Saltcoats N Ayrs....44 F4
Saltfleet Lincs....35 K7
Sampford Arundel Somset....5 K5
Sampford Brett Somset....5 J3
Sanaigmore Ag & B....48 B6
Sandbach Ches E....28 E4
Sandbank Ag & B....49 K5
Sandford-on-Thames Oxon....14 C4
Sandhaven Abers....61 G3
Sandhead D & G....40 C6
Sandhurst Br For....14 F7
Sandness Shet....61 a5
Sandon Staffs....29 G6
Sandown IoW....8 F7
Sandridge Herts....15 J3
Sandsend N York....39 H3
Sandwich Kent....11 L3
Sandwick Shet....61 c7
Sandy C Beds....23 L5
Sanquhar D & G....45 L6
Sarn Gwynd....26 B6
Sarre Kent....11 K2
Saundby Notts....34 E7
Saundersfoot Pembks....18 E5
Saunton Devon....4 D4
Sawbridgeworth Herts....16 D5
Sawston Cambs....16 D3
Sawtry Cambs....23 L3
Saxby Leics....30 E7
Saxilby Lincs....30 E3
Saxmundham Suffk....17 L2
Saxthorpe Norfk....25 H3
Scalasaig Ag & B....48 C4
Scalby N York....39 J4
Scalloway Shet....61 c6
Scamblesby Lincs....31 J3
Scarborough N York....39 K4
Scarinish Ag & B....48 b2
Scawby N Linc....34 F6
Scole Norfk....25 H7
Scone P & K....51 G4
Sconser Highld....56 E6
Scotch Corner N York....38 C3
Scotter Lincs....34 F6
Scotton N York....38 B4
Scoulton Norfk....25 G5
Scourie Highld....63 G4
Scrabster Highld....65 G2
Scunthorpe N Linc....34 F5
Seaford E Susx....10 D7
Seaham Dur....43 L6
Seahouses Nthumb....47 L6
Seal Kent....10 D3
Seamer N York....39 J5
Sea Palling Norfk....25 L3
Seascale Cumb....36 D3
Seathwaite Cumb....36 F4
Seaton Devon....6 F3
Seaton Delaval Nthumb....43 K4
Seave Green N York....38 F4
Seaview IoW....9 G6
Sedbergh Cumb....37 J4
Sedgeberrow Worcs....22 B6
Sedgebrook Lincs....30 E6
Sedgefield Dur....38 D1
Sedlescombe E Susx....10 F4
Seend Wilts....13 K5
Selborne Hants....9 G3
Selby N York....34 D4
Selkirk Border....46 E6
Sellindge Kent....11 J4
Selsey W Susx....9 H6
Selston Notts....29 L4
Send Surrey....15 G7
Sennen Cnwll....2 A7
Sennybridge Powys....20 D7
Setchey Norfk....24 D4

Settle N York....37 L6
Sevenoaks Kent....10 D3
Seven Sisters Neath....19 L5
Shaftesbury Dorset....13 J8
Shalford Essex....16 F4
Shalford Surrey....9 K2
Shandon Ag & B....49 K5
Shanklin IoW....8 F7
Shap Cumb....37 H2
Shardlow Derbys....29 L6
Sharnbrook Bed....23 K4
Sharpness Gloucs....13 G2
Shaugh Prior Devon....3 L4
Shavington Ches E....28 E5
Shawbury Shrops....28 C7
Shebbear Devon....4 D6
Sheepwash Devon....4 E6
Sheerness Kent....11 G2
Sheffield Sheff....29 K2
Shefford C Beds....23 L6
Shepreth Cambs....16 C3
Shepshed Leics....30 B7
Shepton Mallet Somset....13 G6
Sherborne Dorset....7 J1
Sherburn N York....39 J5
Sherburn in Elmet N York....34 C4
Sherfield on Loddon Hants....14 D7
Sheriff Hutton N York....38 F6
Sheringham Norfk....25 H2
Shiel Bridge Highld....57 J7
Shieldaig Highld....57 H4
Shifnal Shrops....28 E8
Shildon Dur....38 C2
Shillingford Oxon....14 D4
Shillingstone Dorset....7 L2
Shinfield Wokham....14 E6
Shinness Highld....63 K6
Shipdham Norfk....25 G5
Shiplake Oxon....14 E6
Shipley C Brad....33 K3
Shipston-on-Stour Warwks....22 D6
Shipton N York....38 E7
Shiptonthorpe E R Yk....34 E3
Shirebrook Derbys....30 B3
Shoeburyness Sthend....17 G8
Shoreham-by-Sea W Susx....9 L5
Shorwell IoW....8 E7
Shotley Suffk....17 K4
Shottisham Suffk....17 L3
Shotts N Lans....45 L2
Shrewsbury Shrops....28 C8
Shrewton Wilts....13 L6
Shrivenham Oxon....13 M3
Shurdington Gloucs....22 A7
Shute Devon....6 F3
Sibsey Lincs....31 J5
Sibson Leics....22 E1
Sidmouth Devon....6 E3
Silchester Hants....14 D7
Sileby Leics....30 C7
Silk Willoughby Lincs....31 G5
Silloth Cumb....41 L6
Silsoe C Beds....23 L6
Silverdale Lancs....37 H5
Silver End Essex....16 F5
Silverstone Nhants....23 G6
Silverton Devon....5 H6
Simonburn Nthumb....42 F4
Simonsbath Somset....5 G4
Singleton W Susx....9 J4
Sissinghurst Kent....10 F4
Sittingbourne Kent....11 G3
Sixpenny Handley Dorset....8 A4
Skegness Lincs....31 L4
Skellingthorpe Lincs....30 F3
Skelmersdale Lancs....32 D6
Skelmorlie N Ayrs....49 K6
Skelton Cumb....42 C7
Skelton R & Cl....38 F2
Skenfrith Mons....21 H7
Skerray Highld....64 C2
Skipness Ag & B....48 C3
Skipsea E R Yk....35 H2
Skipton N York....32 J2
Skirling Border....46 B6
Skirwith Cumb....42 D8
Slaidburn Lancs....32 F2
Slaley Nthumb....43 G6
Slamannan Falk....45 L1
Slapton Devon....6 B7
Sleaford Lincs....31 G5
Sledmere E R Yk....39 J6
Sleights N York....39 H3

Slingsby N York....39 G5
Slough Slough....15 G5
Smailholm Border....47 G6
Smarden Kent....11 G4
Smithfield Cumb....42 C5
Snainton N York....39 J5
Snape Suffk....17 L2
Snettisham Norfk....24 E3
Snodland Kent....10 E3
Soham Cambs....24 D7
Solihull Solhll....22 C3
Solva Pembks....18 B4
Somersham Cambs....24 B7
Somerton Somset....12 F7
Sompting W Susx....9 L5
Sonning Wokham....14 E6
Sonning Common Oxon....14 E5
Sorbie D & G....40 E6
Souldby Cumb....37 K3
Souldern Oxon....22 F6
Souldrop Bed....23 K4
Sourton Devon....3 L2
Southam Warwks....22 E4
Southampton C Sotn....8 E5
South Benfleet Essex....16 F8
Southborough Kent....10 D4
South Brent Devon....6 A5
South Cave E R Yk....34 F4
South Elmsall Wakefd....34 B5
Southend Ag & B....44 B6
Southend-on-Sea Sthend....17 G8
Southery Norfk....24 D6
South Harting W Susx....9 H4
South Hayling Hants....9 G5
South Holmwood Surrey....9 L2
South Kyme Lincs....31 H5
South Mimms Herts....15 J4
Southminster Essex....17 H7
South Molton Devon....4 F5
Southmoor Oxon....14 B4
South Normanton Derbys....29 L4
South Ockendon Thurr....16 E8
South Petherton Somset....7 G1
Southport Sefton....32 C5
South Queensferry C Edin....46 B3
South Raynham Norfk....24 F4
Southrepps Norfk....25 J3
Southsea C Port....9 G6
South Shields S Tyne....43 L5
South Stainley N York....38 C6
South Walsham Norfk....25 K4
Southwell Notts....30 D4
Southwick Hants....9 G5
Southwick W Susx....10 B7
South Witham Lincs....30 F7
Southwold Suffk....25 L7
South Woodham Ferrers Essex....16 F7
South Zeal Devon....3 M2
Sowerby N York....38 D5
Sowerby Bridge Calder....33 J4
Spalding Lincs....31 H7
Sparkford Somset....13 G8
Sparsholt Hants....8 E3
Spean Bridge Highld....53 J3
Spennymoor Dur....43 K7
Spetisbury Dorset....7 L2
Spey Bay Moray....60 B3
Spilsby Lincs....31 K3
Spinningdale Highld....58 F1
Spittal Highld....65 H3
Spittal of Glenshee P & K....54 E7
Spixworth Norfk....25 J4
Spofforth N York....34 A2
Springholm D & G....41 H5
Sproatley E R Yk....35 H4
Stadhampton Oxon....14 D4
Stadhlaigearraidh W Isls....62 c11
Staffin Highld....56 E3
Stafford Staffs....28 F7
Staindrop Dur....38 B2
Staines-upon-Thames Surrey....15 G4
Stainforth N York....37 L6
Staithes N York....39 G2
Stalham Norfk....25 K4
Stamford Lincs....31 G8

Stamford Bridge E R Yk....39 G7
Stamfordham Nthumb....43 H5
Standingstone Cumb....41 K7
Standish Wigan....32 E5
Standon Herts....16 C5
Stanford in the Vale Oxon....14 B4
Stanford le Hope Thurr....10 E1
Stanhope Dur....43 G7
Stanley Dur....43 J6
Stanley P & K....50 F4
Stannington Nthumb....43 J4
Stansted Mountfitchet Essex....16 D5
Stanton Suffk....25 G7
Stanton St Quintin Wilts....13 J4
Stanway Gloucs....22 B6
Staple Fitzpaine Somset....6 F1
Stapleford Notts....30 B6
Staplehurst Kent....10 F4
Starbotton N York....37 M5
Staveley Cumb....37 H4
Staveley Derbys....29 L3
Staverton Nhants....22 F4
Staxton N York....39 J5
Steeple Essex....17 G6
Steeple Aston Oxon....22 F7
Steeple Bumpstead Essex....16 E3
Stenhousemuir Falk....50 D8
Steornabhagh W Isls....62 h3
Stevenage Herts....16 B5
Stevenston N Ayrs....44 F4
Steventon Oxon....14 C5
Stewarton E Ayrs....45 H3
Stewkley Bucks....23 J7
Steyning W Susx....9 L5
Stibb Cross Devon....4 D5
Stickford Lincs....31 J4
Stickney Lincs....31 J4
Stiffkey Norfk....25 G2
Stilligarry W Isls....62 c11
Stillington N York....38 F6
Stilton Cambs....23 L2
Stirling Stirlg....50 D7
Stock Essex....16 E7
Stockbridge Hants....8 D3
Stockport Stockp....33 H7
Stocksbridge Sheff....33 L6
Stockton-on-Tees S on T....38 E2
Stogursey Somset....12 C6
Stoke by Clare Suffk....16 F3
Stoke-by-Nayland Suffk....17 H4
Stoke Canon Devon....6 C3
Stoke Ferry Norfk....24 E5
Stoke Fleming Devon....6 C6
Stoke Gabriel Devon....6 C6
Stoke Goldington M Keyn....23 J5
Stoke Lacy Herefs....21 K5
Stoke Mandeville Bucks....14 F3
Stokenchurch Bucks....14 E4
Stoke-on-Trent C Stke....28 F5
Stoke Poges Bucks....15 G5
Stokesley N York....38 E3
Stone Staffs....28 F6
Stonehaven Abers....55 L5
Stonehouse Gloucs....13 H2
Stonehouse S Lans....45 K3
Stoneykirk D & G....40 B6
Stonor Oxon....14 E5
Stony Stratford M Keyn....23 H6
Stornoway W Isls....62 h3
Storrington W Susx....9 K5
Stotfold C Beds....16 A4
Stoulton Worcs....22 A5
Stourbridge Dudley....21 M3
Stourpaine Dorset....7 L2
Stourport-on-Severn Worcs....21 L3
Stourton Staffs....21 M2
Stow Border....46 E5
Stow-cum-Quy Cambs....16 D2
Stowmarket Suffk....17 H2
Stow-on-the-Wold Gloucs....22 C7
Strachan Abers....55 L5
Strachur Ag & B....49 J3
Stradbroke Suffk....25 J7

Stradishall Suffk............16 F3
Stradsett Norfk...........24 D5
Straiton S Ayrs.............45 G7
Stranraer D & G...........40 B5
Stratfield Turgis
  Hants......................14 E7
Stratford Gt Lon..........16 C8
Stratford St Andrew
  Suffk......................17 L2
Stratford-upon-
  Avon Warwks...........22 C5
Strathaven S Lans........45 K4
Strathblane Stirlg.........50 B8
Strathcanaird
  Highld.....................63 G7
Strathdon Abers..........55 G3
Strathpeffer Highld......58 D4
Strathy Highld............64 E2
Strathyre Stirlg...........50 B5
Stratton Cnwll................4 B6
Stratton-on-the-
  Fosse Somset........13 G6
Streatley W Berk..........14 D5
Street Somset.............12 F7
Strensall C York...........38 F7
Strete Devon................6 C6
Stretford Traffd...........33 G7
Stretham Cambs..........24 C7
Stretton Rutlnd...........30 F7
Strichen Abers............61 G4
Stromeferry Highld......57 H5
Stromness Ork...........65 b4
Stronachlachar
  Stirlg......................49 M3
Strone Ag & B.............49 K5
Strontian Highld..........52 F5
Strood Medway...........10 F2
Stroud Gloucs.............13 J2
Struy Highld...............58 C5
Stuartfield Abers.........61 G4
Studland Dorset............8 B7
Studley Warwks..........22 B4
Sturminster Newton
  Dorset......................7 K1
Sturry Kent................11 J3
Sturton by Stow
  Lincs......................30 E2
Sudbury Derbys..........29 H6
Sudbury Suffk............17 G3
Sulby IoM..................36 c2
Summercourt Cnwll......2 E5
Sunbury-on-Thames
  Surrey....................15 H6
Sunderland Sundld......43 L6
Surfleet Lincs.............31 H6
Sutterton Lincs...........31 J6
Sutton Cambs............24 C7
Sutton Gt Lon.............10 B2
Sutton Benger Wilts....13 K4
Sutton Bridge Lincs....24 C4
Sutton Coldfield
  Birm......................22 C2
Sutton Courtenay
  Oxon......................14 C4
Sutton on Sea Lincs....31 L2
Sutton-on-the-
  Forest N York.........38 F6
Sutton on Trent
  Notts.....................30 E3
Sutton Scotney
  Hants.......................8 E2
Sutton Valence
  Kent.......................10 F4
Swadlincote Derbys....29 K7
Swaffham Norfk..........24 F5
Swainswick BaNES.....13 H4
Swalcliffe Oxon...........22 E6
Swallow Lincs.............35 H6
Swallowfield
  Wokham..................14 E7
Swanage Dorset...........8 B7
Swanley Kent.............10 D2
Swansea Swans..........19 J6
Swanwick Derbys........29 K4
Swanwick Hants...........8 F5
Swaton Lincs..............31 G6
Swavesey Cambs........16 C1
Sway Hants..................8 D6
Swindon Swindn.........13 L3
Swineshead Bed.........23 K4
Swineshead Lincs........31 H5
Swinford Leics............22 F3
Swinton Border...........47 H5
Swinton Rothm...........34 B6
Syderstone Norfk........24 F3
Symbister Shet...........61 d4
Symington S Ayrs........45 G5
Symington S Lans........46 A6
Symonds Yat Herefs...21 J8
Syresham Nhants........23 G6
Syston Leics...............30 C8

T

Tadcaster N York.........34 B3
Tadley Hants...............14 D7
Tain Highld................59 G2
Tairbeart W Isls..........62 f6
Talgarreg Cerdgn.......19 G2
Talgarth Powys...........20 F6
Talladale Highld..........57 J3
Talley Carmth............19 J3
Talmine Highld...........64 C2
Talsarnau Gwynd........26 E6
Tal-y-bont Cerdgn.......20 B2
Tal-y-bont Conwy.......26 F3
Tal-y-bont Gwynd.......26 E7
Tal-y-Cafn Conwy.......27 G3
Tamworth Staffs........22 C1
Tannadice Angus........51 J2
Tan-y-groes Cerdgn....18 F2
Taplow Bucks.............14 F5
Tarbert Ag & B............49 G6
Tarbert W Isls............62 f6
Tarbet Ag & B.............49 L3
Tarbolton S Ayrs........45 H5
Tarland Abers............55 H4
Tarleton Lancs...........32 D5
Tarporley Ches W........28 C4
Tarrant Hinton
  Dorset......................7 M2
Tarskavaig Highld.......56 F7
Tarves Abers..............60 F6
Tarvin Ches W............28 C3
Tattershall Lincs.........31 H4
Taunton Somset.........12 D8
Taverham Norfk..........25 H4
Tavistock Devon...........3 K4
Tayinloan Ag & B........44 B3
Taynton Oxon.............22 D8
Taynuilt Ag & B...........53 G7
Tayport Fife...............51 J4
Tayvallich Ag & B........48 F5
Tebay Cumb...............37 J3
Tedburn St Mary
  Devon......................6 B3
Teddington Gloucs......22 A6
Teignmouth Devon.......6 C4
Telford Wrekin...........28 E8
Temple Mdloth...........46 D4
Temple Bar Cerdgn.....19 H2
Templecombe
  Somset...................13 H8
Temple Sowerby
  Cumb......................37 J1
Tempsford C Beds.......23 L5
Tenbury Wells Worcs...21 K4
Tenby Pembks............18 E6
Tenterden Kent...........11 G5
Ternhill Shrops...........28 D6
Terrington St
  Clement Norfk........24 C4
Tetbury Gloucs...........13 J3
Tetford Lincs..............31 J3
Tetney Lincs...............35 J6
Tetsworth Oxon..........14 E4
Teviothead Border.......42 C2
Tewkesbury Gloucs.....21 M6
Teynham Kent............11 H3
Thame Oxon...............14 E3
Thatcham W Berk........14 C6
Thaxted Essex............16 E4
Theale W Berk............14 D6
Theberton Suffk.........17 M2
The Bungalow IoM....36 C2
Thetford Norfk...........24 F7
Theydon Bois Essex....16 C7
Thirsk N York.............38 D5
Thornbury S Glos........13 G3
Thorne Donc..............34 D5
Thorney C Pete..........24 A5
Thornham Norfk.........24 E2
Thornhill D & G...........41 J3
Thornhill Stirlg..........50 C6
Thornley Dur.............43 L7
Thornton Fife............51 H6
Thornton-le-Dale
  N York....................39 H5
Thornton-le-Street
  N York....................38 D5
Thornton Watlass
  N York....................38 C5
Thorpe End Norfk........25 J5
Thorpe-le-Soken
  Essex......................17 J5
Thorpeness Suffk.......17 M2
Thorrington Essex.......17 J5
Thrapston Nhants........23 K3
Three Cocks Powys.....20 F6
Threekingham Lincs....31 G6
Threlkeld Cumb...........36 F2
Threshfield N York.......37 M6

Thropton Nthumb........43 H2
Thrumster Highld........65 J4
Thurcroft Rothm.........34 C7
Thurlestone Devon........6 A7
Thurnscoe Barns.........34 B6
Thursby Cumb............42 B6
Thurso Highld............65 G2
Thurstaston Wirral......27 K2
Thurston Suffk...........17 G2
Thwaite N York...........37 L4
Tibshelf Derbys...........29 L4
Ticehurst E Susx.........10 E5
Tickhill Donc..............34 C7
Ticknall Derbys...........29 K7
Tideswell Derbys.........29 H3
Tidworth Wilts.............8 C2
Tigh a Ghearraidh
  W Isls.....................62 c8
Tigharry W Isls...........62 c8
Tilbury Thurr..............10 E2
Tilford Surrey...............9 J2
Tillicoultry Clacks.......50 E6
Tilshead Wilts............13 K6
Tilstock Shrops..........28 C6
Tilton on the Hill
  Leics......................30 D8
Tintagel Cnwll..............3 G3
Tintern Parva Mons....12 F2
Tiptree Essex.............17 G5
Tisbury Wilts..............13 K7
Tissington Derbys.......29 J5
Tittensor Staffs..........28 F6
Tiverton Devon.............5 H6
Tobermory Ag & B.......52 C5
Toddington C Beds......23 K7
Todmorden Calder......33 H4
Toft Shet...................61 c3
Toft Hill Dur...............38 B1
Tolastadh W Isls.........62 i2
Tollard Royal Wilts.......7 M1
Tollesbury Essex........17 H6
Tolleshunt D'Arcy
  Essex......................17 G6
Tolpuddle Dorset..........7 K3
Tolsta W Isls..............62 i2
Tomatin Highld...........59 G6
Tomintoul Moray.........54 F3
Tomnavoulin Moray.....59 K6
Tonbridge Kent...........10 E4
Tongue Highld............64 C3
Tonypandy Rhondd.....12 B3
Tonyrefail Rhondd.......12 B3
Topcliffe N York..........38 D5
Topsham Devon............6 D3
Torbeg N Ayrs............44 C5
Torcross Devon............6 B7
Tore Highld................58 E4
Torksey Lincs.............30 E3
Torphichen W Loth......46 A3
Torphins Abers...........55 J4
Torpoint Cnwll..............3 K5
Torquay Torbay............6 C5
Torrance E Duns........45 J1
Torridon Highld..........57 H4
Torrin Highld..............56 F7
Torryburn Fife............46 B2
Torthorwald D & G.......41 K4
Torver Cumb..............36 F4
Totland IoW..................8 D6
Totnes Devon...............6 B5
Totton Hants................8 D4
Towcester Nhants.......23 G5
Tow Law Dur..............43 J7
Town Yetholm
  Border....................47 H6
Traquair Border..........46 D6
Trawden Lancs...........33 H3
Trawsfynydd Gwynd....26 F6
Trearddur Bay IoA.......26 B2
Trecastle Powys..........20 D7
Tredegar Blae G.........12 C1
Treen Cnwll..................2 A8
Trefriw Conwy............27 G4
Tregaron Cerdgn.........19 J1
Tregony Cnwll...............2 E6
Treherbert Rhondd......19 M6
Trellech Mons............12 F2
Tremadog Gwynd........26 E5
Trimdon Dur...............43 L7
Trimingham Norfk........25 J3
Tring Herts................14 F3
Trinity Jersey...............7 b1
Troon S Ayrs..............45 G5
Trotton W Susx.............9 H4
Troutbeck Cumb..........37 G3
Trowbridge Wilts.........13 J5
Truro Cnwll..................2 E6
Tugby Leics................23 H1
Tullibody Clacks.........50 E6
Tummel Bridge P & K...50 D2
Tunbridge Wells Kent..10 E4

Tunstall Suffk.............17 L2
Turnberry S Ayrs.........44 F7
Turnditch Derbys........29 K5
Turner's Hill W Susx....10 B5
Turriff Abers...............60 E4
Turvey Bed.................23 K5
Tutbury Staffs............29 J6
Tuxford Notts.............30 D3
Twycross Leics...........22 E1
Twyford Hants..............8 E4
Twyford Wokham........14 E6
Twynholm D & G..........41 G6
Tyndrum Stirlg............53 K7
Tynemouth N Tyne.....43 L5
Tytherleigh Devon........6 F2
Tywyn Gwynd.............20 A1

U

Uckfield E Susx...........10 D6
Uffculme Devon............5 J6
Uffington Oxon...........14 A5
Ugborough Devon.........6 A6
Uig Highld..................56 D3
Ulceby N Linc.............35 H5
Uldale Cumb...............42 A7
Ullapool Highld...........63 G7
Ullenhall Warwks........22 C4
Ulpha Cumb...............36 E4
Ulsta Shet.................61 c3
Ulverston Cumb..........36 F5
Umberleigh Devon........4 F5
Unapool Highld...........63 H4
Upavon Wilts..............13 L5
Uplyme Devon..............6 F3
Uppottery Devon..........6 E2
Upper Beeding
  W Susx.....................9 L5
Upper Benefield
  Nhants....................23 K2
Upper Broughton
  Notts......................30 D7
Upper Largo Fife........51 J6
Upper Lydbrook
  Gloucs....................21 K8
Upper Tean Staffs.......29 G5
Uppingham Rutlnd......23 J1
Upstreet Kent............11 K3
Upton Snodsbury
  Worcs.....................22 A5
Upton-upon-Severn
  Worcs.....................21 M6
Urchfont Wilts............13 K5
Usk Mons..................12 E2
Uttoxeter Staffs.........29 H6
Uxbridge Gt Lon.........15 H5
Uyeasound Shet.........61 d2

V

Vale Guern...................6 b1
Ventnor IoW.................8 F7
Verwood Dorset............8 B5
Vidlin Shet................61 c4
Virginia Water
  Surrey....................15 G6
Voe Shet...................61 c4

W

Waddesdon Bucks......14 E3
Waddington Lancs......33 G3
Waddington Lincs.......30 F4
Wadebridge Cnwll.........2 F4
Wadesmill Herts.........15 K3
Wadhurst E Susx........10 E5
Wainfleet All Saints
  Lincs......................31 K4
Wakefield Wakefd.......33 M5
Walberswick Suffk......25 L7
Walgherton Ches E.....28 E5
Walkerburn Border......46 D6
Walkern Herts............16 B5
Walkington E R Yk......35 G3
Wallasey Wirral..........32 C7
Wallingford Oxon........14 D5
Walls Shet.................61 b5
Walsall Wsall.............22 B1
Waltham NE Lin.........35 J6
Waltham Abbey
  Essex......................16 C7
Waltham on the
  Wolds Leics...........30 E7
Walton Powys............21 G4
Walton Somset...........12 F7

Walton-on-Thames
Surrey..............................15 H6
Walton on the Naze
Essex................................17 K5
Wanlockhead D & G........45 L6
Wansford C Pete...............23 L1
Wanstrow Somset.............13 H6
Wantage Oxon...................14 B5
Warboys Cambs................24 A7
Warcop Cumb....................37 K2
Wardlow Derbys................29 J3
Ware Herts.........................15 K3
Wareham Dorset.................7 L3
Warenford Nthumb...........47 L6
Wargrave Wokham............14 E6
Wark Nthumb.....................42 F4
Wark Nthumb.....................47 H6
Warkworth Nthumb...........43 K2
Warmington
Warwks...........................22 E5
Warminster Wilts..............13 J6
Warninglid W Susx...........10 B5
Warrington Warrtn............32 F7
Warsash Hants.....................8 E5
Warslow Staffs..................29 H4
Warton Lancs.....................32 D4
Warwick Warwks...............22 D4
Wasbister Ork....................65 b2
Wasdale Head Cumb........36 E3
Washingborough
Lincs...............................30 F3
Washington Sundld...........43 K6
Watchet Somset..................5 J3
Watchgate Cumb...............37 H4
Waterbeach Cambs............16 D2
Waterbeck D & G..............42 A4
Waterhouses Staffs...........29 H5
Waterlooville Hants.............9 G5
Watermillock Cumb...........37 G2
Watford Herts....................15 H4
Watford Nhants.................23 G4
Wath upon Dearne
Rothm..............................34 B6
Watlington Oxon................14 B4
Watten Highld....................65 H3
Watton Norfk.....................24 F5
Watton-at-Stone
Herts...............................15 K2
Wearhead Dur....................42 F7
Weasenham All
Saints Norfk....................24 F4
Weaverham Ches W...........28 D3
Wedmore Somset...............12 E6
Weedon Nhants..................23 G4
Week St Mary Cnwll............4 B7
Weem P & K.......................50 D2
Welburn Lincs....................30 F4
Wellesbourne
Warwks...........................22 D5
Wellingborough
Nhants.............................23 J4
Wellington Somset..............5 K5
Wellington Wrekin.............28 D8
Wells Somset......................12 F6
Wells-next-the-sea
Norfk...............................24 F2
Welney Norfk......................24 C6
Welshampton Shrops.........28 B6
Welshpool Powys...............27 K8
Welton Nhants....................23 G4
Welwyn Herts.....................15 J3
Welwyn Garden City
Herts...............................15 J3
Wem Shrops.......................28 C6
Wembley Gt Lon................15 J5
Wembury Devon..................3 L6
Wendover Bucks................14 F3
Wensley N York..................38 B4
Wentbridge Wakefd...........34 B5
Weobley Herefs.................21 H5
Wereham Norfk..................24 D5
West Auckland Dur............38 B2
West Bay Dorset...................7 H3
West Bexington
Dorset...............................7 H3
West Bilney Norfk.............24 E4
West Bridgford
Notts...............................30 C6
West Bromwich
Sandw.............................22 B2
Westbury Shrops...............28 B8
Westbury Wilts..................13 J6
West Calder W Loth..........46 A4
West Chiltington
W Susx...............................9 K4
Westcott Surrey..................9 L2
Westerham Kent.................10 C3
West Felton Shrops...........27 L7
Westfield E Susx.................10 F4
West Haddon Nhants.........23 G3
West Hoathly W Susx........10 C5

West Horsley Surrey..........15 H8
West Huntspill
Somset.............................12 D6
West Kilbride N Ayrs........44 F3
West Kirby Wirral...............27 K2
West Lavington Wilts........13 K6
West Linton Border............46 C5
West Lulworth
Dorset...............................7 L4
West Lynn Norfk................24 D4
West Malvern Worcs..........21 L5
West Meon Hants.................9 G4
West Mersea Essex............17 H6
West Moors Dorset..............8 B5
Westnewton Cumb.............41 L7
West Newton Norfk............24 E3
Weston Herts......................16 B4
Weston Staffs.....................29 G6
Westonbirt Gloucs.............13 J3
Weston Heath
Shrops.............................28 E7
Weston-on-the-
Green Oxon.....................14 C3
Weston-sub-Edge
Gloucs.............................22 C6
Weston-super-Mare
N Som.............................12 D5
Weston-under-
Redcastle Shrops...........28 D6
West Pennard
Somset.............................12 F7
West Pentire Cnwll..............2 D5
West Rounton N York.........38 D3
West Runton Norfk............25 J2
Westruther Border.............47 G5
West Sandwick Shet..........61 c3
Westward Ho! Devon..........4 D4
West Wittering
W Susx...............................9 H6
West Witton N York...........38 A4
West Woodburn
Nthumb............................43 G3
Wetheral Cumb..................42 C6
Wetherby Leeds.................34 B3
Wetwang E R Yk................39 J7
Weybourne Norfk...............25 H4
Weybridge Surrey..............15 H7
Weyhill Hants.......................8 D2
Weymouth Dorset................7 J4
Whaley Bridge
Derbys.............................29 G2
Whalley Lancs....................33 G3
Whaplode Lincs.................31 J7
Whaplode Drove
Lincs...............................31 J7
Whauphill D & G...............40 E6
Wheathampstead
Herts...............................15 J3
Wheatley Oxon...................14 D3
Wheddon Cross
Somset...............................5 H4
Whepstead Suffk................17 G2
Wherwell Hants....................8 E2
Whickham Gatesd..............43 J5
Whiddon Down
Devon................................6 A3
Whimple Devon....................6 D3
Whipsnade C Beds.............15 G3
Whitburn W Loth................46 A4
Whitby N York....................39 H3
Whitchurch Bucks.............14 E2
Whitchurch Hants................8 E2
Whitchurch Herefs.............21 J8
Whitchurch Shrops............28 C5
Whitebridge Highld...........58 D7
Whitehaven Cumb..............36 D2
Whitehill and
Bordon Hants....................9 H3
Whitehills Abers.................60 D3
Whitehouse Ag & B...........49 G6
Whitekirk E Loth...............46 F2
Whitewell Lancs.................32 F3
Whithorn D & G.................40 E7
Whiting Bay N Ayrs...........44 E5
Whitland Carmth...............18 E5
Whitley Bay N Tyne...........43 K5
Whitley Chapel
Nthumb............................43 G6
Whitminster Gloucs...........13 H1
Whitstable Kent.................11 J2
Whittington Shrops............27 L6
Whittlebury Nhants...........23 G6
Whittlesey Cambs..............24 A6
Whitton Powys...................21 G4
Whitwell Derbys.................30 B3
Whitwell Herts....................15 J2
Wick Highld........................65 J3
Wickford Essex..................16 F7
Wickham Hants....................8 F5
Wickham Market
Suffk................................17 K2

Wickwar S Glos.................13 H3
Widdrington
Nthumb............................43 K3
Widecombe in the
Moor Devon......................6 A4
Widegates Cnwll..................3 J5
Widemouth Bay
Cnwll.................................4 B6
Widford Herts.....................16 C5
Widmerpool Notts.............30 C6
Widnes Halton....................28 C2
Wigan Wigan......................32 E6
Wiggenhall St
Germans Norfk................24 D4
Wigston Leics....................23 G1
Wigton Cumb......................42 A6
Wigtown D & G..................40 E6
Wilberfoss E R Yk..............34 D2
Wilby Nhants......................23 J4
Willand Devon......................5 J6
Willingham Cambs.............24 B8
Wilmcote Warwks..............22 C4
Wilmington Devon...............6 F2
Wilmslow Ches E...............28 F2
Wilsontown S Lans............46 A4
Wilstead Bed......................23 L6
Wilton Wilts........................13 L7
Wimbledon Gt Lon.............15 J6
Wimblington Cambs...........24 B6
Wimborne Minster
Dorset...............................8 A5
Wincanton Somset.............13 H7
Winchcombe Gloucs...........22 B7
Winchelsea E Susx.............11 G6
Winchester Hants.................8 E3
Windermere Cumb.............37 G4
Windsor W & M..................15 G6
Wing Bucks.........................14 F2
Wingate Dur.......................43 L7
Wingham Kent....................11 K3
Winkfield Br For.................14 F6
Winkleigh Devon..................4 F6
Winscombe N Som............12 E5
Winsford Ches W...............28 D3
Winsford Somset..................5 H4
Winsham Somset..................7 G2
Winslow Bucks...................23 H7
Winster Derbys...................29 J4
Winterborne
Monkton Dorset...............7 J3
Winterborne
Stickland Dorset..............7 L2
Winterborne
Whitechurch
Dorset...............................7 L2
Winterbourne
Abbas Dorset....................7 J3
Winterbourne Stoke
Wilts...............................13 L7
Winteringham
N Linc.............................34 F5
Winterslow Wilts..................8 C3
Winterton N Linc................34 F5
Winwick Cambs..................23 L3
Wirksworth Derbys............29 J4
Wisbech Cambs..................31 K8
Wisborough Green
W Susx...............................9 K3
Wishaw N Lans..................45 L3
Witham Essex......................16 F5
Witheridge Devon................5 G6
Withern Lincs......................31 K2
Withernsea E R Yk.............35 K4
Withington Gloucs.............22 B8
Withington Herefs.............21 J7
Withyham E Susx................10 D5
Withypool Somset................5 H4
Witnesham Suffk................17 J3
Witney Oxon.......................14 B3
Wittersham Kent................11 G5
Witton le Wear Dur............43 J8
Wiveliscombe
Somset...............................5 J4
Wivelsfield E Susx.............10 C6
Wivenhoe Essex.................17 H5
Wix Essex...........................17 J4
Woburn C Beds...................23 K6
Woking Surrey....................15 G7
Wokingham Wokham..........14 F6
Wolf's Castle
Pembks.............................18 C4
Wollaston Nhants...............23 J4
Wollaston Shrops...............27 L8
Wolsingham Dur.................43 H7
Wolverhampton
Wolves.............................21 M3
Wolvey Warwks..................22 E2
Wolviston S on T................38 E2
Wombourne Staffs.............21 M2
Wombwell Barns.................34 B6
Wooburn Bucks..................14 F5

Woodbridge Suffk..............17 K3
Woodchurch Kent...............11 G5
Woodford Gloucs...............13 G2
Woodhall Spa Lincs...........31 H4
Woodland Dur....................38 B2
Woodstock Oxon................14 C3
Woofferton Shrops.............21 J4
Wookey Hole Somset........12 F6
Wool Dorset..........................7 L3
Woolacombe Devon.............4 D3
Wooler Nthumb...................47 K6
Woolhampton
W Berk..............................14 D6
Woolpit Suffk.....................17 H2
Woolwich Gt Lon................10 C1
Woore Shrops......................28 E5
Wootton N Linc...................35 G5
Wootton Oxon.....................14 B2
Wootton Bassett
Wilts...............................13 L3
Wootton Courtenay
Somset...............................5 H3
Wootton Wawen
Warwks...........................22 C4
Worcester Worcs................21 M5
Workington Cumb...............36 D1
Worksop Notts....................30 C2
Worlingworth Suffk............17 K1
Wormit Fife.........................51 J4
Worplesdon Surrey............15 G7
Worthen Shrops..................21 G1
Worthing W Susx..................9 L5
Worth Matravers
Dorset...............................7 M4
Wotton-under-Edge
Gloucs.............................13 H3
Wragby Lincs......................31 G3
Wrangaton Devon.................6 A6
Wrangle Lincs.....................31 K5
Wrawby N Linc....................35 G6
Wrelton N York....................39 G5
Wrentham Suffk..................25 L7
Wrestlingworth
C Beds..............................16 B3
Wrexham Wrexhm..............27 L5
Wroughton Swindn............13 L4
Wroxall IoW..........................8 F7
Wroxeter Shrops.................28 D8
Wroxham Norfk...................25 K4
Wroxton Oxon.....................22 E6
Wyboston Bed....................23 L5
Wye Kent............................11 H4
Wylye Wilts.........................13 K7
Wymondham Leics.............30 E7
Wymondham Norfk.............25 H5

Yarcombe Devon..................6 F2
Yardley Gobion
Nhants.............................23 H5
Yardley Hastings
Nhants.............................23 J5
Yarm S on T........................38 D3
Yarmouth IoW......................8 D6
Yarrowford Border.............46 E6
Yateley Hants......................14 F7
Yatton N Som......................12 E5
Yatton Keynell Wilts..........13 J4
Yaxley Cambs......................23 M2
Yeadon Leeds.....................33 K3
Yealmpton Devon.................3 L5
Yelverton Devon...................3 L4
Yelverton Norfk...................25 K5
Yeovil Somset.......................7 H1
Yeovilton Somset................12 F8
Yetts o'Muckhart
Clacks.............................50 E6
Y Felinheli Gwynd..............26 D3
Y Maerdy Conwy.................27 J5
York C York.........................34 C2
Youlgreave Derbys.............29 J4
Yoxall Staffs.......................29 H7
Yoxford Suffk......................17 L1
Y Rhiw Gwynd.....................26 B6
Ysbyty Ystwyth
Cerdgn.............................20 B3
Ystalyfera Neath.................19 K5
Ystradgynlais
Powys...............................19 K3
Ystrad Mynach
Caerph.............................12 C2

Zeals Wilts..........................13 H7
Zennor Cnwll........................2 B6

This chart shows distances in miles between two towns along AA-recommended routes. Using motorways and other main roads this is normally the fastest route, though not necessarily the shortest.

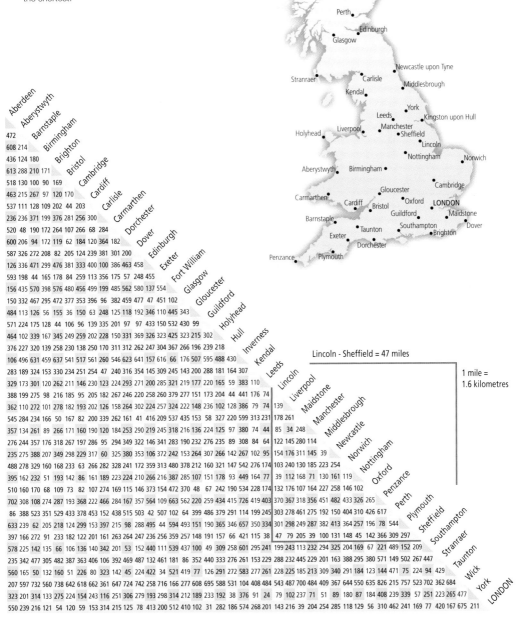

Lincoln - Sheffield = 47 miles

1 mile = 1.6 kilometres

Aberdeen
472 — Aberystwyth
608 214 — Barnstaple
436 124 180 — Birmingham
613 288 210 171 — Brighton
518 130 100 90 169 — Bristol
463 215 267 97 120 170 — Cambridge
537 111 128 109 202 44 203 — Cardiff
236 236 371 199 376 281 256 300 — Carlisle
520 48 190 172 264 107 266 68 284 — Carmarthen
600 206 94 172 119 62 184 120 364 182 — Dorchester
587 326 272 208 82 205 124 239 381 301 200 — Dover
126 336 471 299 476 381 400 100 386 463 458 — Edinburgh
593 198 44 165 178 84 259 113 356 175 57 248 455 — Exeter
156 435 570 398 576 480 456 499 199 485 562 580 137 554 — Fort William
150 332 467 295 472 377 353 396 96 382 459 477 47 451 102 — Glasgow
484 113 126 56 155 36 150 63 248 125 118 192 346 110 445 343 — Gloucester
571 224 175 128 44 106 96 139 335 201 97 97 433 150 532 430 99 — Guildford
464 102 339 167 345 249 259 202 228 150 331 369 326 323 425 323 215 302 — Holyhead
376 227 320 139 258 230 138 250 170 311 312 262 247 304 367 266 196 239 218 — Hull
106 496 631 459 637 541 517 561 260 546 623 641 157 616 66 176 507 595 488 430 — Inverness
283 189 324 153 330 234 251 254 47 240 316 354 145 309 245 143 200 288 181 164 307 — Kendal
329 173 301 120 262 211 146 230 123 224 293 271 200 285 321 219 177 220 165 59 383 110 — Leeds
388 199 275 98 216 185 95 205 182 267 246 220 258 260 379 277 173 204 44 441 176 74 139 — Lincoln
362 110 272 101 278 182 193 202 126 158 264 302 224 257 324 222 148 236 102 128 386 79 74 139 — Liverpool
545 284 234 166 50 167 82 200 339 262 161 41 416 209 537 435 153 58 327 220 599 313 231 178 261 — Maidstone
357 134 261 89 266 171 160 190 120 184 253 290 219 245 318 216 136 224 125 97 380 74 44 85 34 248 — Manchester
276 244 357 176 318 267 197 286 95 294 349 322 146 341 283 190 232 276 235 89 308 84 64 122 145 280 114 — Middlesbrough
235 275 388 207 349 298 229 317 60 325 380 353 106 372 242 153 264 307 266 142 267 102 95 154 176 311 145 39 — Newcastle
488 278 329 160 168 233 63 266 282 328 241 172 359 433 480 378 212 160 321 147 542 276 174 303 278 461 275 192 150 — Norwich
395 162 232 51 193 142 86 161 189 223 224 210 266 216 387 285 107 151 178 93 449 164 77 39 112 168 71 130 161 119 — Nottingham
510 160 170 68 109 73 82 107 274 169 115 146 373 154 472 370 48 67 242 190 534 228 174 132 176 107 164 227 258 146 102 — Oxford
702 308 108 274 287 193 368 222 466 284 167 357 564 109 663 562 220 259 434 415 726 419 403 370 367 318 356 451 482 433 326 265 — Penzance
86 388 523 351 529 433 378 453 152 438 515 503 42 507 102 64 399 486 379 291 114 199 245 303 278 461 275 192 150 404 310 426 617 — Perth
633 239 62 205 218 124 299 153 397 215 98 288 495 44 594 493 151 190 365 346 657 350 334 301 298 249 287 382 413 364 257 196 78 544 — Plymouth
397 166 272 91 233 182 122 201 161 263 264 247 236 256 359 257 148 191 157 66 421 115 38 47 79 205 39 100 131 148 45 142 366 309 297 — Sheffield
578 225 142 135 66 106 136 140 342 201 53 152 440 111 539 437 100 49 309 258 601 295 241 199 243 113 232 294 325 204 169 67 221 489 152 209 — Southampton
235 342 477 305 482 387 363 406 106 392 469 487 132 461 181 86 352 440 333 276 261 153 229 288 232 445 229 201 163 388 295 380 571 149 502 267 447 — Stranraer
560 165 50 132 160 51 226 80 323 142 45 224 422 34 521 419 77 126 291 272 583 277 261 228 225 185 213 309 340 291 184 123 144 471 75 224 94 429 — Taunton
207 597 732 560 738 642 618 662 361 647 724 742 716 166 277 608 695 588 531 104 408 484 543 487 700 484 409 367 644 550 635 826 215 757 523 702 362 684 — Wick
323 201 314 133 275 224 154 243 116 251 306 279 193 298 314 212 189 233 192 38 376 91 24 79 102 237 71 51 89 180 87 184 408 239 339 57 251 223 265 477 — York
565 239 216 121 54 120 59 153 314 215 125 78 413 200 512 410 102 31 282 186 574 268 201 143 216 39 204 254 285 118 129 56 310 462 241 169 77 420 167 675 211 — LONDON

1

2

3

4

Lisdo
Doolin   R478 R481 Kil
Inishere Sound
Liscannor R478   Ennisty
Hags Head Lahinch   N85
Mal Bay   N67 6
Milltown Malbay
Spanish Point
31   R460
Doo Lough   R4
31
Donegal Point Doonbeg   N6
Cooraclare R483 N68
Kilkee N67 13 R473   Killady
Kilrush N67 57 R4
Killimer R486 33
Ⓥ Loghill
Tarbert
Loop Head Mouth of the R551 26 Glin
Shannon   R524
R553 Ballylongford
Ballybunion 18
Ballyduff Athea R523
Kerry Head Causeway 30 **Listowel** 17 R523 **Nev**
Ballyheige R551 R556 24 Duagh **(An**
Ballyheige 42 Abbeydorney N69 **Abbeyfeale** N21 20
Bay
Rough Point Ardfert 321 Kilkinlea R576
Brandon R558 Lower
Castlegregory 950 Camp 24
CNOC 824 R560 851 **Tralee** N21 R578
BRÉANAINN BEENOSKEE 32 BAURTREGAUN 18 **Castleisland**   Billy
Ceann Sibéal Castlemaine N70 16 R577 Scartaglin R582
Sybil Point R549 Anascaul N86 27 Castlemaine Farranfore 21 Bo 11
An Inch R561 Milltown N22 Kerry R582
Blascaod 17 R561 R561 25 **Killarney** N72 R58
Mór Ceann **Killorglin** 10 N72 24
Great Sléibhe N70 R563 21 N71
Blasket Slea Head Glenbeigh Beaufort
Island Dingle Bay 41 Lough Muckross
Doulus Head 9 Killarney 837 Poulgorm
Valencia Island 1038 National MANGERTON Bridge
Dairbhre **Cahersiveen** 781 **CARRAUNTOOHIL** Park MTN R569 47
13 MULLAGHANATTIN 32 Kilgarvan Baile Mhic Íre
N70 R586 **Kenmare** 53 Ballymakeery
R565 An Coireán Sneem N70 27 Béal Átha an
R566 Waterville 40 N71 Ghaorthaidh Ballingeary
Ceann Parknasilla Tahilla 52 705 Inchigeela
Bhólais R573 Lauragh KNOCKBOY 48 R585
Bolus Head Cathair Dónall Kenmare River R571
An Scairbh Caherdaniel Glengarriff 12 Ballylickey
Scariff Island Ardgroom R574 R572 **Bantry** 6 **Dunmanway**
Cod's Head Adrigole 34 N71 R586
685 30 Drimolea
Allihies R575 R572 Durrus R59A Leap
Castletownbere R591 16 R593
Dursey Island R572 Bear Island Bantry Bay Glandor
Oileán Mór N71 33 Ballydehob Castlet
Muntervary or Dunmanus Bay R591 R592 Schull **Skibbereen**
Sheep's Head Goleen Toormore **Baltimore** Toe Head
Mizen Head Crookhaven
Oileán Cléire
Clear Island

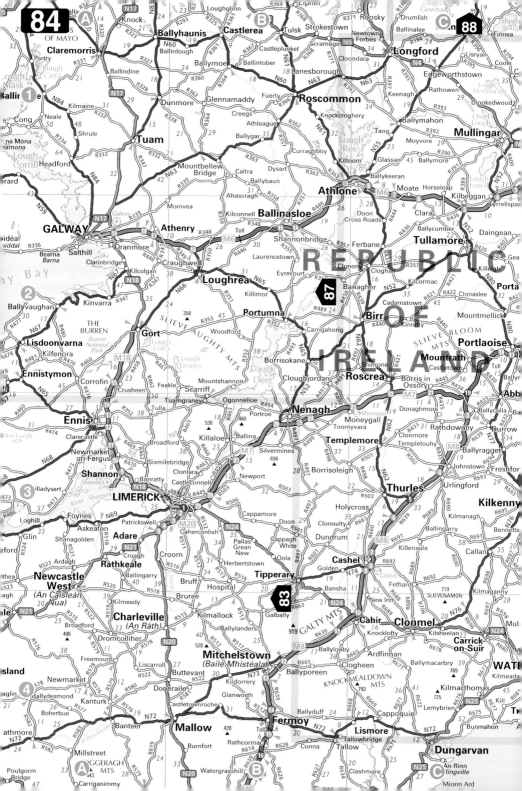

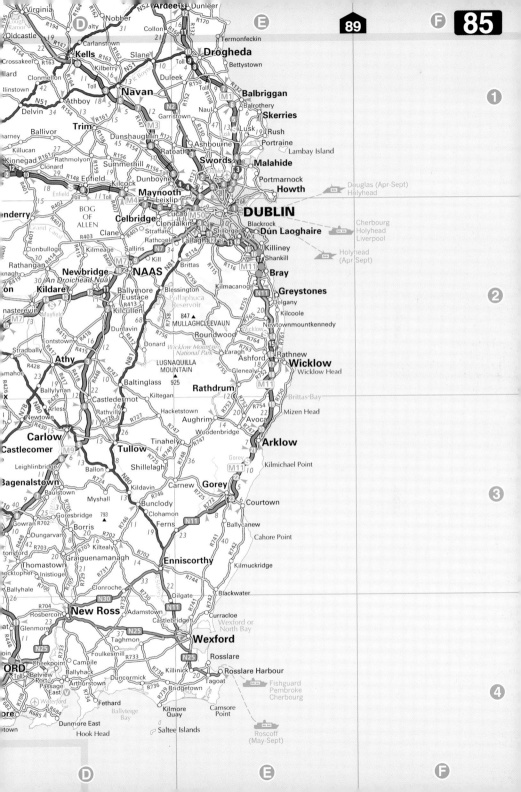

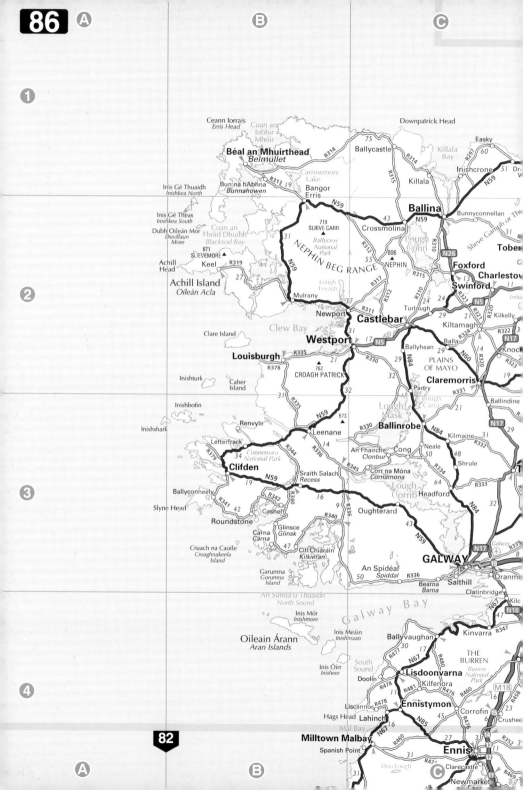

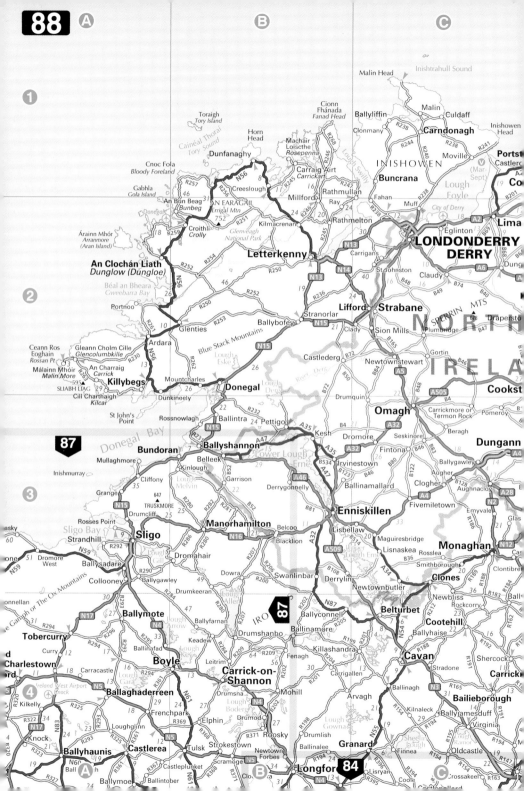

Distance chart - Ireland

Portrush
Donegal
An Clochán
Liath
Dunglow
City of Derry
Londonderry
Derry
Larne
NI
Donegal
Omagh
Belfast
International
BELFAST
George Best
Belfast City
Enniskillen
Armagh
Downpatrick
Béal an Mhuirthead
Belmullet
Sligo
Cavan
Dundalk
Ireland West
Airport Knock
Roscommon
Clifden
Athlone
Galway
DUBLIN
Dún Laoghaire
Tullamore
IRL
Portlaoise
Wicklow
Ennis
Shannon
Kilkee
Limerick
Kilkenny
Tipperary
Wexford
Tralee
Waterford
Killarney
Mallow
An Coireán
Waterville
Cork

This chart shows distances, in both miles and kilometres, between two towns along AA-recommended routes. Using motorways and other main roads this is normally the fastest route, though not necessarily the shortest.

For example, the distance between Cork and Omagh is 435 kilometres or 270 miles (8 kilometres is approximately 5 miles).

Distances in miles

	Athlone	Belfast	Béal an Mhuirthead Belmullet	Cavan	Clifden	Cork	Donegal	Downpatrick	Dublin	Dundalk	An Clochán Liath Dunglow	Dún Laoghaire	Ennis	Enniskillen	Galway	Kilkee	Kilkenny	Killarney	Larne	Limerick	Londonderry Derry	Mallow	Omagh	Portlaoise	Portrush	Roscommon	Sligo	Tipperary	Tralee	Tullamore	Waterford	An Coireán Waterville	Wexford	Wicklow
Armagh	99	41	168	83	196	246	84	53	86	33	96	93	167	50	150	299	164	274	62	208	71	233	37	138	68	101	92	197	268	145	186	313	180	123
Athlone		148	123	95	101	136	113	144	78	93	150	89	68	84	57	189	76	142	170	74	145	115	111	45	160	20	74	89	138	28	114	182	116	111
Belfast			202	117	230	264	116	22	105	51	129	111	251	84	231	319	182	294	22	228	72	252	70	156	63	142	126	215	288	165	205	333	200	143
Béal an Mhuirthead Belmullet				98	91	231	116	212	189	195	153	201	144	118	111	274	199	236	223	167	161	210	144	169	199	103	76	191	232	147	236	277	239	216
Cavan					153	187	69	100	68	61	106	84	121	132	103	239	143	193	109	125	93	166	59	90	109	55	70	139	189	68	168	233	161	104
Clifden						170	144	240	177	196	181	187	91	146	50	215	179	178	251	113	189	150	172	148	227	98	104	138	171	125	189	216	218	207
Cork							248	257	157	213	285	167	87	214	122	57	92	56	286	64	304	22	270	108	308	156	208	64	76	129	80	99	112	185
Donegal								127	143	111	36	156	161	42	128	285	215	248	120	184	46	220	47	159	84	93	40	209	242	138	240	287	229	172
Downpatrick									98	44	144	104	246	95	226	314	175	289	44	223	93	245	80	155	85	146	136	214	282	160	198	327	194	138
Dublin										53	176	8	147	99	129	214	80	192	126	124	151	150	112	54	150	96	133	114	182	66	103	227	92	35
Dundalk											131	59	168	64	152	266	130	241	73	175	99	200	65	105	98	102	105	164	235	81	153	280	147	90
An Clochán Liath Dunglow												178	198	74	165	322	251	284	136	221	61	256	59	196	91	130	77	246	278	175	276	323	269	212
Dún Laoghaire													152	114	139	221	85	197	133	129	153	155	119	59	160	107	139	119	193	71	110	238	83	26
Ennis														153	42	130	122	92	273	23	207	66	186	91	229	86	122	47	88	101	101	133	139	174
Enniskillen															136	270	173	225	106	157	61	198	27	122	98	86	41	170	221	100	198	265	192	135
Galway																172	131	134	223	64	173	102	165	101	210	49	88	89	124	80	142	169	171	159
Kilkee																	155	63	306	57	241	97	222	125	263	127	156	82	43	137	135	96	173	208
Kilkenny																		121	200	75	224	80	189	31	228	96	150	51	139	51	30	172	65	87
Killarney																			315	70	285	42	251	136	339	162	208	92	20	137	119	50	157	216
Larne																				250	75	273	75	178	55	164	147	241	310	187	226	355	222	165
Limerick																					219	43	183	68	273	94	145	25	65	69	78	110	116	151
Londonderry Derry																						296	34	202	40	137	85	261	280	161	250	325	242	185
Mallow																							260	95	298	136	181	51	63	116	78	92	116	175
Omagh																								168	71	114	68	227	247	127	215	292	203	147
Portlaoise																									205	66	120	59	132	21	66	177	70	82
Portrush																										163	122	278	347	224	267	392	259	202
Roscommon																											53	109	158	44	134	203	136	129
Sligo																												169	202	98	186	247	190	159
Tipperary																													88	80	53	133	91	141
Tralee																														133	139	53	177	215
Tullamore																															87	178	91	93
Waterford																																170	38	80
An Coireán Waterville																																	208	256
Wexford																																		59

Distances in kilometres

	Armagh	Athlone	Belfast	Béal an Mhuirthead Belmullet	Cavan	Clifden	Cork	Donegal	Downpatrick	Dublin	Dundalk	An Clochán Liath Dunglow	Dún Laoghaire	Ennis	Enniskillen	Galway	Kilkee	Kilkenny	Killarney	Larne	Limerick	Londonderry Derry	Mallow	Omagh	Portlaoise	Portrush	Roscommon	Sligo	Tipperary	Tralee	Tullamore	Waterford	An Coireán Waterville	Wexford
Athlone	159																																	
Belfast	66	238																																
Béal an Mhuirthead Belmullet	270	198	324																															
Cavan	144	84	141	238																														
Clifden	315	163	370	147	246																													
Cork	396	218	425	371	300	274																												
Donegal	135	182	187	187	111	232	399																											
Downpatrick	85	232	35	342	161	387	414	204																										
Dublin	139	125	169	305	109	285	253	230	157																									
Dundalk	53	150	83	314	99	316	342	179	71	85																								
An Clochán Liath Dunglow	155	242	207	246	171	291	459	58	232	283	211																							
Dún Laoghaire	150	143	179	324	135	301	269	251	167	13	95	287																						
Ennis	269	110	404	232	194	146	139	260	396	236	271	319	245																					
Enniskillen	81	135	135	189	52	235	345	68	152	159	102	119	184	245																				
Galway	241	91	372	179	166	80	196	205	364	208	244	265	224	67	219																			
Kilkee	324	176	259	287	261	202	188	315	449	291	329	375	300	55	309	123																		
Kilkenny	257	122	287	321	230	288	148	346	282	123	204	404	137	196	279	211	250																	
Killarney	441	228	473	380	310	287	90	399	465	309	388	457	317	149	363	216	101	195																
Larne	100	274	36	359	175	404	460	193	71	203	117	219	214	440	170	359	493	322	507															
Limerick	335	119	367	268	201	184	103	296	359	199	282	356	208	37	252	104	92	121	112	403														
Londonderry Derry	114	233	115	259	149	305	490	74	150	242	159	98	246	333	98	278	388	361	481	120	353													
Mallow	376	185	405	338	268	242	35	354	394	241	322	412	250	106	319	164	156	129	67	440	69	477												
Omagh	60	178	112	232	95	277	435	75	129	180	104	95	192	300	43	266	357	304	405	120	295	55	419											
Portlaoise	222	73	251	272	145	238	173	256	250	87	168	315	95	146	197	163	202	49	219	286	110	325	153	271										
Portrush	109	258	101	319	175	365	496	135	136	242	158	147	258	369	158	338	424	367	546	89	440	64	480	115	330									
Roscommon	163	32	299	166	88	157	251	150	235	155	164	209	172	139	138	78	205	155	261	263	152	221	219	184	106	262								
Sligo	147	118	202	123	112	168	335	64	219	214	169	123	224	196	67	141	252	241	335	236	233	137	291	110	192	193	86							
Tipperary	317	143	347	308	224	223	102	336	345	183	263	396	192	76	274	144	132	82	148	388	40	420	82	366	95	447	176	272						
Tralee	432	221	464	374	303	275	122	390	454	293	378	448	311	142	355	200	69	223	33	499	105	451	99	398	212	559	254	325	141					
Tullamore	233	45	266	237	109	201	207	221	258	106	131	281	113	163	161	129	221	83	221	301	111	259	189	204	34	361	71	158	128	214				
Waterford	301	184	330	380	271	304	129	386	320	167	248	444	177	162	319	229	218	48	192	366	126	403	125	346	106	431	216	300	86	224	140			
An Coireán Waterville	504	294	536	446	376	348	159	462	527	366	451	520	383	214	427	272	154	277	82	572	177	523	148	470	285	631	327	398	214	85	286	273		
Wexford	290	186	322	385	260	351	180	370	312	148	237	433	134	223	310	275	278	105	253	357	186	390	187	327	113	417	219	305	147	285	147	61	334	
Wicklow	198	178	230	348	166	333	298	276	222	56	145	341	42	280	217	256	335	140	348	266	243	298	282	236	131	325	207	256	227	346	150	129	412	95

Index to places in Ireland

This index lists places appearing in the main-map section of the atlas in alphabetical order. The reference following each name gives the atlas page number and grid reference of the square in which the place appears. The map shows counties, unitary authorities and administrative areas, together with a list of the abbreviated name forms used in the index.

Northern Ireland

Antrim	**Antrim**
Armagh	**Armagh**
Belfst	**Belfast**
Down	**Down**
Ferman	**Fermanagh**
Lderry	**Londonderry Derry**
Tyrone	**Tyrone**

Republic of Ireland

Carlow	**Carlow**
Cavan	**Cavan**
Clare	**Clare**
Cork	**Cork**
Donegl	**Donegal**
Dublin	**Dublin**
Dublin	**Dublin City (1)**
Dublin	**Dún Laoghaire-Rathdown (2)**
Dublin	**Fingal (3)**
Dublin	**South Dublin (4)**
Galway	**Galway**
Kerry	**Kerry**
Kildre	**Kildare**
Kilken	**Kilkenny**
Laois	**Laois**
Leitrm	**Leitrim**
Limrck	**Limerick**
Longfd	**Longford**
Louth	**Louth**
Mayo	**Mayo**
Meath	**Meath**
Monhan	**Monaghan**
Offaly	**Offaly**
Roscom	**Roscommon**
Sligo	**Sligo**
Tippry	**Tipperary North**
Tippry	**Tipperary South**
Watfd	**Waterford**
Wmeath	**Westmeath**
Wexfd	**Wexford**
Wicklw	**Wicklow**

A

Place	Page	Grid
Abbeydorney Kerry	82	C2
Abbeyfeale Limrck	82	C2
Abbeyleix Laois	84	C3
Adamstown Wexfd	85	D4
Adare Limrck	83	D2
Adrigole Cork	82	C3
Aghadowey Lderry	89	D2
Ahascragh Galway	87	D3
Aghoghill Antrim	89	D2
Allihies Cork	82	B3
Anascaul Kerry	82	B2
An Bun Beag Donegl	88	B2
An Charraig Donegl	88	A2
An Clochán Liath Donegl	88	A2
An Coireán Kerry	82	B3
An Daingean Kerry	82	B2
An Fhairche Galway	86	C3

Place	Page	Grid
Annalong Down	89	E4
Annestown Watfd	84	C4
An Rinn Watfd	83	F3
An Spidéal Galway	86	C3
Antrim Antrim	89	D2
Ardagh Limrck	83	D2
Ardara Donegl	88	A2
Ardee Louth	89	D4
Ardfert Kerry	82	C2
Ardfinnan Tippry	84	C4
Ardglass Down	89	E3
Ardgroom Cork	82	B3
Ardmore Watfd	83	E3
Arklow Wicklw	85	E3
Arless Laois	85	D3
Armagh Armagh	89	D3
Armoy Antrim	89	D1
Arthurstown Wexfd	85	D4
Arvagh Cavan	88	B4
Ashbourne Meath	85	E1

Place	Page	Grid
Ashford Wicklw	85	E2
Askeaton Limrck	83	D1
Athboy Meath	85	D1
Athea Limrck	82	C2
Athenry Galway	87	D3
Athleague Roscom	87	D3
Athlone Wmeath	84	C1
Athy Kildre	85	D2
Augher Tyrone	88	C3
Aughnacloy Tyrone	88	C3
Aughrim Wicklw	85	E3
Avoca Wicklw	85	E3

B

Place	Page	Grid
Bagenalstown Carlow	85	D3
Baile Mhic Íre Cork	82	C3
Bailieborough Cavan	88	C4
Balbriggan Dublin	85	E1
Balla Mayo	86	C2

Place	Page	Grid
Ballaghaderreen Roscom	87	D2
Ballina Mayo	86	C2
Ballina Tippry	83	D1
Ballinafad Sligo	87	D2
Ballinagh Cavan	88	C4
Ballinakill Laois	84	C3
Ballinalee Longfd	88	B4
Ballinamallard Ferman	88	B3
Ballinamore Leitrm	88	B4
Ballinascarty Cork	83	D3
Ballinasloe Galway	87	D3
Ballindine Mayo	86	C3
Ballineen Cork	83	D3
Ballingarry Limrck	83	D2
Ballingarry Tippry	84	C3
Ballingeary Cork	82	C3
Ballinhassig Cork	83	D3
Ballinlough Roscom	87	D2
Ballinrobe Mayo	86	C3

Ballinspittle Cork 83 D3
Ballintober Roscom 87 D2
Ballintra Donegl 88 B3
Ballivor Meath 85 D1
Ballon Carlow 85 D3
Ballybaun Galway 87 D3
Ballybay Monhan 88 C4
Ballybofey Donegl 88 B2
Ballybunion Kerry 82 C2
Ballycanew Wexfd 85 E3
Ballycarry Antrim.............89 E2
Ballycastle Antrim............89 D1
Ballycastle Mayo 86 C1
Ballyclare Antrim 89 E2
Ballycolla Laois 84 C3
Ballyconneely Galway......86 B3
Ballyconnell Cavan..........88 B4
Ballycotton Cork 83 E3
Ballycumber Offaly 84 C2
Ballydehob Cork 82 C4
Ballydesmond Cork 82 C2
Ballyduff Kerry 82 C2
Ballyduff Watfd 84 B4
Ballyfarnan Roscom.........87 D2
Ballygalley Antrim 89 E2
Ballygar Galway 87 D3
Ballygawley Sligo............87 D1
Ballygawley Tyrone..........88 C3
Ballygowan Down 89 E3
Ballyhack Wexfd 85 D4
Ballyhaise Cavan 88 C4
Ballyhale Kilken 85 D3
Ballyhaunis Mayo.............87 D2
Ballyhean Mayo................86 C2
Ballyheige Kerry 82 B2
Ballyjamesduff Cavan......88 C4
Ballykeeran Wmeath........84 C1
Ballylanders Limrck 83 E2
Ballylickey Cork................82 C3
Ballyliffin Donegl..............88 C1
Ballylongford Kerry 82 C2
Ballylooby Tippry 84 B4
Ballylynan Laois...............85 D2
Ballymacarbry Watfd........84 C4
Ballymahon Longfd..........84 C1
Ballymakeery Cork...........82 C3
Ballymena Antrim.............89 D2
Ballymoe Galway 87 D3
Ballymoney Antrim...........89 D2
Ballymore Wmeath...........84 C1
Ballymore Eustace
　Kildre 85 D2
Ballymote Sligo 87 D2
Ballynahinch Down 89 E3
Ballynure Antrim...............89 E2
Ballyporeen Tippry...........84 B4
Ballyragget Kilken............84 C3
Ballyroan Laois 84 C2
Ballyronan Lderry 89 D2
Ballysadare Sligo.............87 D1
Ballyshannon Donegl.......87 D1
Ballyvaughan Clare 86 C4
Ballywalter Down 89 E3
Balrothery Dublin 85 E1
Baltimore Cork.................82 C4
Baltinglass Wicklw...........85 D2
Banagher Offaly 84 B2
Banbridge Down 89 D3
Bandon Cork....................83 D3
Bangor Down....................89 E2
Bangor Erris Mayo 86 B2
Bansha Tippry 84 B3
Banteer Cork 83 D2
Bantry Cork.......................82 C3
Barna Galway 86 C3

Béal an Mhuirthead
　Mayo 86 B1
Béal Átha an
　Ghaorthaidh Cork........82 C3
Bearna Galway 86 C3
Beaufort Kerry...................82 C3
Belcoo Ferman 87 E1
Belfast Belfst 89 E3
Belgooly Cork 83 D3
Bellaghy Lderry..................89 D2
Belleek Ferman 87 D1
Bellmullet Mayo 86 B1
Belturbet Cavan 88 C4
Belview Port Kilken............85 D4
Benburb Tyrone 89 D3
Bennettsbridge Kilken 85 D3
Beragh Tyrone 88 C3
Bettystown Meath..............85 E1
Birr Offaly..........................84 C2
Blacklion Cavan 87 E1
Blackrock Dublin 85 E2
Blackwater Wexfd 85 E3
Blarney Cork 83 D3
Blessington Wicklw 85 D2
Boherbue Cork...................83 D2
Borris Carlow.....................85 D3
Borris-in-Ossory Laois 84 C2
Borrisokane Tippry 87 D4
Borrisoleigh Tippry 84 C3
Boyle Roscom....................87 D2
Bracknagh Offaly...............85 D2
Bray Wicklw 85 E2
Bridgetown Wexfd 85 D4
Brittas Dublin.....................85 E2
Broadford Clare 83 D1
Broadford Limrck 83 D2
Broughshane Antrim..........89 D2
Bruff Limrck 83 D2
Bruree Limrck 83 D2
Bunbeg Donegl..................88 B2
Bunclody Wexfd 85 D3
Buncrana Donegl 88 C1
Bundoran Donegl 87 D1
Bunmahon Watfd 84 C4
Bun na hAbhna Mayo........86 B1
Bunnahowen Mayo 86 B1
Bunnyconnellan Mayo.......86 C2
Bunratty Clare....................83 D1
Burnfort Cork 83 D3
Bushmills Antrim................89 D1
Buttevant Cork 83 D2

Carraig Airt Donegl 88 B1
Carrick Donegl 88 A2
Carrickart Donegl...............88 B1
Carrickfergus Antrim 89 E2
Carrickmacross
　Monhan 89 D4
Carrickmore or
　Termon Rock
　Tyrone 88 C3
Carrick-on-Shannon
　Leitrm.............................87 D2
Carrick-on-Suir Tippry 84 C4
Carrigahorig Tippry............87 D4
Carrigaline Cork 83 D3
Carrigallen Leitrm 88 B4
Carriganimmy Cork............83 D3
Carrigans Donegl 88 C2
Carrigtohill Cork 83 E3
Carryduff Down 89 E3
Cashel Galway 86 B3
Cashel Tippry.....................84 C3
Castlebar Mayo 86 C2
Castlebellingham
　Louth.............................89 D4
Castleblayney
　Monhan 89 D4
Castlebridge Wexfd 85 E4
Castlecomer Kilken 85 D3
Castleconnell Limrck 83 D1
Castlederg Tyrone 88 B2
Castledermot Kildre 85 D2
Castlegregory Kerry 82 B2
Castleisland Kerry 82 C2
Castlemaine Kerry.............82 C2
Castlemartyr Cork 83 E3
Castleplunket Roscom.......87 D2
Castlepollard Wmeath.......84 C1
Castlerea Roscom 87 D2
Castlerock Lderry 88 C1
Castleshane Monhan.........88 C3
Castletown Laois...............84 C2
Castletownbere Cork 82 B3
Castletownroche
　Cork 83 D2
Castletownshend
　Cork 82 C4
Castlewellan Down.............89 E3
Cathair Dónall Kerry..........82 B3
Causeway Kerry.................82 C2
Cavan Cavan......................88 C4
Celbridge Kildre.................85 D2
Charlestown Mayo.............86 C2
Charleville Cork 83 D2
Cheekpoint Watfd..............85 D4
Cill Charthaigh
　Donegl...........................88 A2
Cill Chiaráin Galway..........86 B3
Clady Tyrone 88 C2
Clane Kildre 85 D2
Clara Offaly 84 C2
Clarecastle Clare 83 D1
Claremorris Mayo..............86 C2
Clarinbridge Galway..........86 C3
Clashmore Watfd 83 E3
Claudy Lderry....................88 C2
Clifden Galway...................86 B3
Cliffony Sligo.....................87 D1
Clogh Kilken......................85 D3
Cloghan Offaly...................84 C2
Clogheen Tippry 84 B4
Clogher Tyrone..................88 C3
Clohamon Wexfd 85 D3
Clonakilty Cork 83 D4
Clonard Meath 85 D1
Clonaslee Laois 84 C2

Clonbulloge Offaly 85 D2
Clonbur Galway 86 C3
Clondalkin Dublin 85 E2
Clones Monhan 88 C3
Clonlara Clare 83 D1
Clonmany Donegl 88 C1
Clonmel Tippry 84 C4
Clonmellon Wmeath..........85 D1
Clonmore Tippry 84 C3
Clonony Offaly 84 C2
Clonoulty Tippry 84 B3
Clonroche Wexfd 85 D3
Clontibret Monhan.............88 C3
Cloondara Longfd 84 C1
Clough Down 89 E3
Cloughjordan Tippry 87 D4
Cloyne Cork 83 E3
Coagh Tyrone 89 D2
Coalisland Tyrone 89 D3
Cobh Cork 83 E3
Coleraine Lderry 89 D1
Collinstown Wmeath..........85 D1
Collon Louth.......................89 D4
Collooney Sligo 87 D1
Comber Down 89 E3
Cong Mayo 86 C3
Conna Cork 83 E3
Cookstown Tyrone 89 D2
Coole Wmeath....................84 C1
Cooraclare Clare................82 C1
Cootehill Cavan..................88 C4
Cork Cork 83 D3
Cornamona Galway............86 C3
Corr na Móna Galway.........86 C3
Corrofin Clare 86 C4
Courtmacsherry
　Cork 83 D4
Courtown Wexfd.................85 E3
Craigavon Armagh.............89 D3
Craughwell Galway............87 D3
Crawfordsburn Down 89 E2
Creegs Galway 87 D3
Creeslough Donegl 88 B1
Croagh Limrck....................83 D2
Croithli Donegl...................88 B2
Crolly Donegl 88 B2
Crookedwood
　Wmeath.........................84 C1
Crookhaven Cork 82 C4
Crookstown Cork 83 D3
Croom Limrck.....................83 D2
Crossakeel Meath..............85 D1
Cross Barry Cork................83 D3
Crosshaven Cork 83 E3
Crossmaglen Armagh.........89 D4
Crossmolina Mayo..............86 C2
Crumlin Antrim...................89 D2
Crusheen Clare 86 C4
Culdaff Donegl...................88 C1
Cullybackey Antrim............89 D2
Curracloe Wexfd 85 E4
Curraghboy Roscom 87 D3
Curry Sligo.........................87 D2
Cushendall Antrim..............89 D1
Cushendun Antrim..............89 D1

Daingean Offaly..................84 C2
Delgany Wicklw 85 E2
Delvin Wmeath 85 D1
Derry Lderry 88 C2
Derrygonnelly Ferman....87 E1
Derrylin Ferman 88 B3
Dervock Antrim...................89 D1

Dingle Kerry 82 B2
Doagh Antrim 89 D2
Donaghadee Down 89 E2
Donaghmore Laois 84 C3
Donard Wicklw 85 D2
Donegal Donegl..................88 B2
Doneraile Cork 83 D2
Doolin Clare......................86 C4
Doon Limrck 83 E1
Doonbeg Clare...................82 C1
Doon Cross Roads
  Offaly 84 C2
Douglas Cork 83 D3
Downpatrick Down 89 E3
Dowra Cavan.....................87 E1
Draperstown
  Lderry 89 D2
Drimoleague Cork 82 C3
Dripsey Cork 83 D3
Drogheda Louth..................85 E1
Dromahair Leitrm 87 D1
Dromcolliher Limrck 83 D2
Dromore Down...................89 D3
Dromore Tyrone 88 C3
Dromore West Sligo 86 C1
Drumcliff Sligo 87 D1
Drumcondra Meath 89 D4
Drumkeeran Leitrm 87 D1
Drumlish Longfd 88 B4
Drumod Leitrm 87 E2
Drumquin Tyrone 88 C3
Drumshanbo Leitrm 87 D2
Drumsna Leitrm 87 E2
Duagh Kerry 82 C2
Dublin Dublin 85 E2
Duleek Meath.....................85 E1
Dunboyne Meath 85 D1
Duncormick Wexfd..............85 D4
Dundalk Louth 89 D4
Dunderrow Cork 83 D3
Dundonald Down.................89 E3
Dundrum Down...................89 E3
Dundrum Tippry 84 B3
Dunfanaghy Donegl.............88 B1
Dungannon Tyrone 89 D3
Dungarvan Kildre.................85 D3
Dungarvan Watfd 83 F3
Dungiven Lderry 88 C2
Dunglow Donegl.................88 A2
Dungourney Cork 83 E3
Dunkineely Donegl..............88 A2
Dun Laoghaire
  Dublin 85 E2
Dunlavin Wicklw 85 D2
Dunleer Louth 89 D4
Dunloy Antrim 89 D2
Dunmanway Cork................82 C3
Dunmore Galway 87 D3
Dunmore East Watfd............85 D4
Dunmurry Antrim 89 E3
Dunshaughlin Meath............85 D1
Durrow Laois......................84 C3
Durrus Cork 82 C4
Dysart Roscom 87 D3

E

Easky Sligo 86 C1
Edenderry Offaly 85 D2
Edgeworthstown
  Longfd 84 C1
Eglinton Lderry 88 C2
Elphin Roscom 87 D2
Emyvale Monhan 88 C3
Enfield Meath 85 D1

Ennis Clare........................83 D1
Enniscorthy Wexfd 85 D3
Enniskean Cork 83 D3
Enniskillen Ferman 88 B3
Ennistymon Clare 86 C4
Eyrecourt Galway 87 D4

F

Fahan Donegl 88 C2
Farranfore Kerry 82 C2
Feakle Clare 87 D4
Fenagh Leitrm 87 E2
Ferbane Offaly 84 C2
Fermoy Cork 83 E2
Ferns Wexfd 85 E3
Fethard Tippry 84 C3
Fethard Wexfd 85 D4
Finnea Wmeath 88 C4
Fintona Tyrone 88 C3
Fivemiletown Tyrone 88 C3
Fontstown Kildre 85 D2
Foulkesmill Wexfd 85 D4
Foxford Mayo 86 C2
Foynes Limrck 83 D1
Freemount Cork 83 D2
Frenchpark Roscom 87 D2
Freshford Kilken 84 C3
Fuerty Roscom 87 D3

G

Galbally Limrck 83 E2
Galway Galway 86 C3
Garrison Ferman 87 D1
Garristown Dublin................85 E1
Garryvoe Cork 83 E3
Garvagh Lderry 89 D2
Geashill Offaly 84 C2
Gilford Down......................89 D3
Glandore Cork 82 C4
Glanmire Cork 83 D3
Glanworth Cork 83 E2
Glaslough Monhan 88 C3
Glassan Wmeath 84 C1
Gleann Cholm Cille
  Donegl 88 A2
Glenarm Antrim 89 E2
Glenavy Antrim...................89 D3
Glenbeigh Kerry..................82 B3
Glencolumbkille
  Donegl 88 A2
Glenealy Wicklw 85 E2
Glengarriff Cork 82 C3
Glenmore Kilken 85 D4
Glennamaddy Galway...........87 D3
Glenties Donegl 88 B2
Glin Limrck 82 C2
Glinsce Galway 86 B3
Glinsk Galway 86 B3
Golden Tippry.....................84 B3
Goleen Cork 82 C4
Goresbridge Kilken 85 D3
Gorey Wexfd 85 E3
Gort Galway 86 C4
Gortin Tyrone 88 C2
Gowran Kilken....................85 D3
Graiguenamanagh
  Kilken 85 D3
Granard Longfd 88 C4
Grange Sligo......................87 D1
Greenore Louth 89 D4
Greyabbey Down 89 E3
Greystones Wicklw 85 E2
Gulladuff Lderry 89 D2

H

Hacketstown Carlow 85 D3
Headford Galway 86 C3
Herbertstown Limrck 83 D2
Hillsborough Down...............89 D3
Hilltown Down....................89 D3
Holycross Tippry..................84 C3
Holywood Down 89 E2
Horseleap Wmeath 84 C1
Hospital Limrck 83 D2
Howth Dublin 85 E1

I

Inch Kerry 82 B2
Inchigeelagh Cork 82 C3
Inishannon Cork 83 D3
Inishcrone Sligo 86 C1
Inistioge Kilken 85 D3
Irvinestown Ferman..............88 B3

J

Johnstown Kilken................84 C3

K

Kanturk Cork 83 D2
Keadew Roscom 87 D2
Keady Armagh 89 D3
Keel Mayo 86 B2
Keenagh Longfd 84 C1
Kells Antrim 89 D2
Kells Meath 85 D1
Kenmare Kerry 82 C3
Kesh Ferman 88 B3
Kilbeggan Wmeath 84 C2
Kilberry Meath 85 D1
Kilbrittain Cork 83 D3
Kilcar Donegl.....................88 A2
Kilcock Kildre 85 D1
Kilcolgan Galway.................86 C4
Kilconnell Galway................87 D3
Kilcoole Wicklw 85 E2
Kilcormac Offaly 84 C2
Kilcullen Kildre 85 D2
Kilcurry Louth 89 D4
Kildare Kildre.....................85 D2
Kildavin Carlow 85 D3
Kildorrery Cork 83 D2
Kilfenora Clare....................86 C4
Kilgarvan Kerry...................82 C3
Kilkee Clare 82 C1
Kilkeel Down 89 E4
Kilkelly Mayo......................86 C2
Kilkenny Kilken 84 C3
Kilkieran Galway 86 B3
Kilkinlea Lower Limrck 82 C2
Kill Kildre 85 D2
Kill Watfd 84 C4
Killadysert Clare 83 D1
Killala Mayo 86 C1
Killaloe Clare 83 D1
Killarney Kerry 82 C3
Killashandra Cavan..............88 C4
Killeagh Cork 83 E3
Killeigh Offaly 84 C2
Killenaule Tippry..................84 C3
Killimer Clare......................82 C1
Killimor Galway 87 D4
Killiney Dublin 85 E2
Killinick Wexfd 85 E4
Killorglin Kerry....................82 C2
Killough Down 89 E3

Killucan Wmeath 85 D1
Killybegs Donegl.................88 A2
Killyleagh Down 89 E3
Kilmacanoge Wicklw............85 E2
Kilmacrenan Donegl.............88 B2
Kilmacthomas Watfd 84 C4
Kilmaganny Kilken 84 C3
Kilmaine Mayo 86 C3
Kilmallock Limrck 83 D2
Kilmanagh Kilken 84 C3
Kilmeadan Watfd 84 C4
Kilmeage Kildre 85 D2
Kilmeedy Limrck..................83 D2
Kilmichael Cork 83 D3
Kilmore Quay Wexfd 85 D4
Kilmuckridge Wexfd.............85 E3
Kilnaleck Cavan 88 C4
Kilrea Lderry 89 D2
Kilrush Clare.......................82 C1
Kilsheelan Tippry 84 C4
Kiltamagh Mayo 86 C2
Kiltealy Wexfd 85 D3
Kiltegan Wicklw 85 D3
Kiltoom Roscom 87 E3
Kingscourt Cavan.................89 D4
Kinlough Leitrm...................87 D1
Kinnegad Wmeath 85 D1
Kinnitty Offaly 84 C2
Kinsale Cork 83 D3
Kinvarra Galway 86 C4
Kircubbin Down 89 E3
Knock Mayo 86 C2
Knockcroghery Roscom........87 D3
Knocklofty Tippry 84 C4
Knocktopher Kilken 85 D3

L

Lahinch Clare 86 C4
Lanesborough Roscom..........84 B1
Laragh Wicklw 85 E2
Larne Antrim 89 E2
Lauragh Kerry 82 C3
Laurencetown Galway 87 D3
Leap Cork 82 C4
Leenane Galway 86 B3
Leighlinbridge Carlow 85 D3
Leitrim Leitrm 87 D2
Leixlip Kildre 85 D2
Lemybrien Watfd 84 C4
Letterfrack Galway 86 B3
Letterkenny Donegl 88 B2
Lifford Donegl.....................88 C2
Limavady Lderry 88 C2
Limerick Limrck 83 D1
Lisbellaw Ferman 88 C3
Lisburn Antrim 89 D3
Liscannor Clare 86 C4
Liscarroll Cork 83 D2
Lisdoonvarna Clare...............86 C4
Lismore Watfd 84 C4
Lisnaskea Ferman 88 C3
Lisryan Longfd 84 C1
Listowel Kerry 82 C2
Loghill Limrck 82 C1
Londonderry Lderry 88 C2
Longford Longfd 84 C1
Loughbrickland Down 89 D3
Loughgall Armagh 89 D3
Loughglinn Roscom..............87 D2
Loughrea Galway 87 D4
Louisburgh Mayo 86 B2
Lucan Dublin 85 E2
Lurgan Armagh 89 D3
Lusk Dublin........................85 E1

M

Machair Loiscthe
Donegl................88 B1
Macroom Cork................83 D3
Maghera Down................89 E3
Maghera Lderry................89 D2
Magherafelt Lderry................89 D2
Maguiresbridge
Ferman................88 C3
Malahide Dublin................85 E1
Malin Donegl................88 C1
Malin More Donegl................88 A2
Mallow Cork................83 D2
Manorhamilton Leitrm..87 D1
Markethill Armagh................89 D3
Martinstown Antrim...........89 D2
Maynooth Kildre................85 D1
Mazetown Antrim................89 D3
Middletown Armagh........88 C3
Midleton Cork................83 E3
Milford Donegl................88 B2
Millstreet Cork................83 D3
Milltown Kerry................82 C2
Milltown Malbay
Clare................82 C1
Min an Aoire Donegl........88 A2
Mitchelstown Cork........83 E2
Moate Wmeath................84 C1
Mohill Leitrm................87 E2
Monaghan Monhan................88 C3
Monasterevin Kildre........85 D2
Moneygall Offaly................84 C3
Moneymore Lderry........89 D2
Monivea Galway................87 D3
Mooncoin Kilken................84 C4
Moorfields Antrim................89 D2
Mountbellew Bridge
Galway................87 D3
Mountcharles Donegl........88 B2
Mountmellick Laois........84 C2
Mountrath Laois................84 C2
Mountshannon Clare...87 D4
Moville Donegl................88 C1
Moy Tyrone................89 D3
Moynalty Meath................88 C4
Moyvore Wmeath................84 C1
Muckross Kerry................82 C3
Muff Donegl................88 C2
Mullaghmore Sligo........87 D1
Mullinavat Kilken................85 D4
Mullingar Wmeath................84 C1
Mulrany Mayo................86 B2
Myshall Carlow................85 D3

N

Naas Kildre................85 D2
Naul Dublin................85 E1
Navan Meath................85 D1
Neale Mayo................86 C3
Nenagh Tippry................83 E1
Newbliss Monhan................88 C3
Newbridge Kildre................85 D2
Newcastle Down................89 E3
Newcastle West Limrck..83 D2
New Inn Tippry................84 C4
Newmarket Cork................83 D2
Newmarket-on-
Fergus Clare................83 D1
Newport Mayo................86 B2
Newport Tippry................83 D1
New Ross Wexfd................85 D4
Newry Down................89 D3
Newtown Laois................85 D3

Newtownabbey
Antrim................89 E2
Newtownards Down.....89 E3
Newtownbutler
Ferman................88 C3
Newtown Forbes
Longfd................84 C1
Newtownhamilton
Armagh................89 D3
Newtownmountkennedy
Wicklw................85 E2
Newtownstewart
Tyrone................88 C2
Nobber Meath................89 D4

O

Ogonnelloe Clare................83 D1
Oilgate Wexfd................85 D4
Oldcastle Meath................88 C4
Omagh Tyrone................88 C3
Omeath Louth................89 D4
Oola Limrck................83 E2
Oranmore Galway................86 C3
Oughterard Galway........86 C3
Ovens Cork................83 D3

P

Pallas Green New
Limrck................83 E2
Parknasilla Kerry................82 B3
Partry Mayo................86 C2
Passage East Watfd......85 D4
Passage West Cork........83 E3
Patrickswell Limrck........83 D1
Paulstown Kilken................85 D3
Pettigo Donegl................88 B3
Plumbridge Tyrone........88 C2
Pomeroy Tyrone................88 C3
Portadown Armagh........89 D3
Portaferry Down................89 E3
Portarlington Laois........85 D2
Portavogie Down................89 E3
Portballintrae Antrim....89 D1
Portglenone Antrim........89 D2
Portlaoise Laois................84 C2
Portmarnock Dublin......85 E1
Portnoo Donegl................88 A2
Portraine Dublin................85 E1
Portroe Tippry................83 E1
Portrush Antrim................89 D1
Portstewart Lderry........89 D1
Portumna Galway................87 D4
Poulgorm Bridge Kerry..82 C3
Poyntz Pass Armagh......89 D3

R

Raharney Wmeath................85 D1
Randalstown Antrim......89 D2
Rasharkin Antrim................89 D2
Rathangan Kildre................85 D2
Rathcoole Dublin................85 E2
Rathcormack Cork........83 E3
Rathdowney Laois........84 C3
Rathdrum Wicklw................85 E2
Rathfriland Down................89 D3
Rathkeale Limrck................83 D2
Rathmelton Donegl........88 B2
Rathmolyon Meath........85 D1
Rathmore Kerry................82 C3
Rathmullan Donegl........88 C2
Rathnew Wicklw................85 E2
Rathowen Wmeath........84 C1

Rathvilly Carlow................85 D3
Ratoath Meath................85 E1
Ray Donegl................88 B2
Recess Galway................86 B3
Renvyle Galway................86 B3
Ringaskiddy Cork........83 E3
Ringville Watfd................83 F3
Rockcorry Monhan........88 C4
Roosky Roscom................87 E2
Rosbercon Wexfd................85 D4
Roscommon Roscom......87 D3
Roscrea Tippry................84 C2
Rosepenna Donegl........88 B1
Ross Carbery Cork........83 D4
Rosses Point Sligo........87 D1
Rosslare Wexfd................85 E4
Rosslare Harbour
Wexfd................85 E4
Rosslea Ferman................88 C3
Rossnowlagh Donegl....88 B3
Rostrevor Down................89 D4
Roundstone Galway......86 B3
Roundwood Wicklw........85 E2
Rush Dublin................85 E1

S

Saintfield Down................89 E3
St Johnston Donegl......88 C2
Sallins Kildre................85 D2
Salthill Galway................86 C3
Scarriff Clare................87 D4
Scartaglin Kerry................82 C2
Scarva Down................89 D3
Schull Cork................82 C4
Scramoge Roscom........87 D2
Seskinore Tyrone................88 C3
Shanagarry Cork................83 E3
Shanagolden Limrck......83 D2
Shankill Dublin................85 E2
Shannon Clare................83 D1
Shannonbridge Offaly....87 D3
Shercock Cavan................88 C4
Shillelagh Wicklw................85 D3
Shinrone Offaly................84 C2
Shrule Mayo................86 C3
Silvermines Tippry........83 E1
Sion Mills Tyrone................88 C2
Sixmilebridge Clare........83 D1
Skerries Dublin................85 E1
Skibbereen Cork................82 C4
Slane Meath................85 D1
Sligo Sligo................87 D1
Smithborough
Monhan................88 C3
Sneem Kerry................82 B3
Spanish Point Clare........82 C1
Spiddal Galway................86 C3
Sraith Salach Galway......86 B3
Stewartstown Tyrone......89 D3
Stillorgan Dublin................85 E2
Stonyford Kilken................85 D3
Strabane Tyrone................88 C2
Stradbally Laois................85 D2
Stradone Cavan................88 C4
Straffan Kildre................85 D2
Strandhill Sligo................87 D1
Strangford Down................89 E3
Stranorlar Donegl........88 B2
Strokestown Roscom....87 D2
Summerhill Meath........85 D1
Swanlinbar Cavan................88 B3
Swatragh Lderry................89 D2
Swinford Mayo................86 C2
Swords Dublin................85 E1

T

Taghmon Wexfd................85 D4
Tagoat Wexfd................85 E4
Tahilla Kerry................82 B3
Tallaght Dublin................85 E2
Tallow Watfd................83 E3
Tallowbridge Watfd........84 B4
Tandragee Armagh........89 D3
Tang Wmeath................84 C1
Tarbert Kerry................82 C2
Templemore Tippry........84 C3
Templetouhy Tippry........84 C3
Termonfeckin Louth........89 D4
Thomastown Kilken........85 D3
Thurles Tippry................84 C3
Timahoe Laois................85 D3
Timoleague Cork................83 D3
Tinahely Wicklw................85 E3
Tipperary Tippry................84 B3
Tobercurry Sligo................87 D2
Tobermore Lderry................89 D2
Toomyvara Tippry................84 B3
Toormore Cork................82 C4
Tralee Kerry................82 C2
Tramore Watfd................85 D4
Trim Meath................85 D1
Tuam Galway................86 C3
Tuamgraney Clare........83 D1
Tulla Clare................83 D1
Tullamore Offaly................84 C2
Tullow Carlow................85 D3
Tulsk Roscom................87 D2
Turlough Mayo................86 C2
Tyrrellspass Wmeath......84 C1

U

Urlingford Kilken................84 C3

V

Virginia Cavan................88 C4

W

Warrenpoint Down........89 D4
Waterford Watfd................85 D4
Watergrasshill Cork........83 E3
Waterville Kerry................82 B3
Westport Mayo................86 C2
Wexford Wexfd................85 E4
Whitegate Cork................83 E3
Whitehead Antrim................89 E2
Wicklow Wicklw................85 E2
Woodenbridge Wicklw....85 E3
Woodford Galway................87 D4

Y

Youghal Cork................83 E3

GLOVEBOX ATLAS
TOWN PLANS

Atlas contents

Key to town plans	96
Town plans	97–191
Major airports	192–197
Channel Tunnel	198

Index to town plans

Aberdeen	108	Edinburgh	133	Newquay	157	Swansea	182
Aberystwyth	109	Exeter	134	Northampton	158	Swindon	183
Basingstoke	110	Glasgow	135	Norwich	159	Taunton	184
Bath	111	Gloucester	136	Nottingham	160	Torquay	185
Birmingham	112	Great Yarmouth	137	Oldham	161	Warwick	186
Blackpool	113	Guildford	138	Oxford	162	Watford	187
Bournemouth	114	Harrogate	139	Perth	163	Winchester	188
Bradford	115	Huddersfield	140	Peterborough	164	Wolverhampton	189
Brighton	116	Inverness	141	Plymouth	165	Worcester	190
Bristol	117	Ipswich	142	Portsmouth	166	York	191
Cambridge	118	Kingston upon Hull	143	Preston	167		
Canterbury	119	Lancaster	144	Reading	168	**Airports**	
Cardiff	120	Leeds	145	Royal Tunbridge Wells	169		
Carlisle	121	Leicester	146	St Andrews	170	London Heathrow	192
Cheltenham	122	Lincoln	147	Salisbury	171	London Gatwick	192
Chester	123	Liverpool	148	Scarborough	172	London Stansted	193
Colchester	124	Llandudno	149	Sheffield	173	London Luton	193
Coventry	125	London	97–107	Shrewsbury	174	London City	194
Darlington	126	Luton	150	Southampton	175	Birmingham Int'l	194
Derby	127	Maidstone	151	Southend-on-Sea	176	East Midlands	195
Doncaster	128	Manchester	152	Stirling	177	Manchester	195
Dover	129	Middlesbrough	153	Stockton-on-Tees	178	Leeds Bradford	196
Dundee	130	Milton Keynes	154	Stoke-on-Trent	179	Aberdeen	196
Durham	131	Newcastle upon Tyne	155	Stratford-upon-Avon	180	Edinburgh	197
Eastbourne	132	Newport	156	Sunderland	181	Glasgow	197

Key to town plans

Town plan legend

M8	Motorway with number
	Primary Road
	A Road
	B Road
	Local / other road
	Restricted access road
	Pedestrian area
– – – –	Footpath
College ■	Building of interest
†	Church
✡	Synagogue
☾	Mosque
	Park and open space
P	Car park
P+R	Park and Ride
	Bus / coach station
	Toilet
→	One-way, gated/closed road
	Shopmobility
✉	Post Office
◉	World Heritage Site (UNESCO)
H	24-hour Accident & Emergency hospital
H	Hospital
i	Tourist Information Centre
•——•	Light rapid transit system
	Central London Congestion Charging Zone

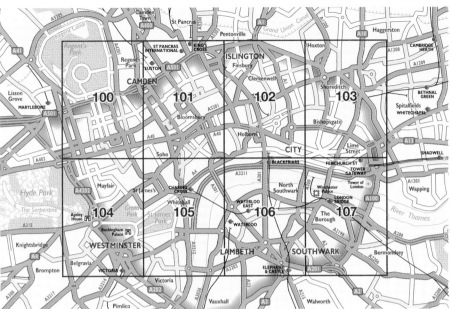

Abbey Orchard Street... 105 F6
Abbey Street... 107 K6
Abchurch Lane... 107 G1
Aberdour Street... 107 H7
Abingdon Street... 105 H6
Acton Street... 101 J2
Adam's Row... 104 B2
Adam Street... 105 J2
Addington Street... 105 K5
Adeline Place... 101 G5
Agdon Street... 102 C3
Air Street... 104 E2
Alaska Street... 106 B4
Albany Street... 100 C1
Albemarle Street... 104 D2
Albion Place... 102 D4
Aldenham Street... 101 F1
Aldermanbury... 103 F6
Aldersgate Street... 102 E4
Aldford Street... 104 B3
Aldgate... 103 J7
Aldgate High Street... 103 K6
Aldwych... 101 K7
Alfred Place... 101 F5
Alice Street... 107 H7
Alie Street... 103 K7
Allhallows Lane... 107 F2
Allington Street... 104 D6
Alscot Road... 107 K7
Ambrosden Avenue... 104 E7
America Street... 106 E4
Ampton Street... 101 J2
Amwell Street... 102 B1
Angel Lane... 107 G2
Angel Street... 102 E6
Ann's Close... 104 A5
Apple Tree Yard... 105 F3
Appold Street... 103 H4
Aquinas Street... 106 B3
Arch Street... 106 E7
Argyle Square... 101 H2
Argyle Street... 101 H2
Argyll Street... 100 E7
Arlington Street... 104 E3
Arlington Way... 102 C1
Arne Street... 101 H6
Arnold Circus... 103 K2
Arthur Street... 107 G2
Artillery Lane... 103 J5
Artillery Row... 105 F6
Arundel Street... 106 A1
Ashby Street... 102 D2
Ashford Street... 103 H2
Ashley Place... 104 E7
Augustus Street... 100 D1
Austin Street... 103 J2
Austral Street... 106 C7
Ave Maria Lane... 102 D6
Avery Row... 104 C1
Aybrook Street... 100 B5
Aylesbury Street... 102 C3
Ayres Street... 106 E4
Babmaes Street... 105 F3
Bache's Street... 103 G2
Back Hill... 102 B4
Bacon Grove... 107 J7
Bainbridge Street... 101 G6
Baker's Row... 102 B3
Baker Street... 100 A4
Balderton Street... 104 B1
Baldwin's Gardens... 101 B1

Balfour Place... 104 B2
Baltic Street East... 102 E3
Baltic Street West... 102 E4
Bank End... 107 F3
Bankside... 106 E2
Banner Street... 103 F3
Barge House Street... 106 C3
Barlow Place... 104 D2
Barnby Street... 100 E1
Barnham Street... 107 J4
Baron's Place... 106 C5
Barrett Street... 100 B7
Barter Street... 101 H6
Bartholomew Close... 102 E5
Bartholomew Lane... 103 G6
Bartholomew Street... 107 G7
Bartlett Court... 102 C6
Basinghall Lane... 103 F6
Basinghall Street... 103 F6
Bastwick Street... 102 E3
Bateman's Buildings... 101 F6
Bateman's Yard... 103 J3
Bateman Street... 101 F7
Bath Street... 103 F2
Bath Terrace... 106 E6
Battle Bridge Lane... 107 H3
Bayley Street... 101 F5
Baylis Road... 106 B5
Beak Street... 104 E1
Bear Lane... 106 D3
Beaumont Place... 100 E3
Beaumont Street... 100 B4
Beckett Street... 107 G6
Bedale Street... 107 G3
Bedford Avenue... 101 G6
Bedfordbury... 105 H2
Bedford Place... 101 H5
Bedford Square... 101 G5
Bedford Street... 105 H2
Bedford Way... 101 G3
Beech Street... 102 E4
Beeston Place... 104 D6
Belgrave Place... 104 B6
Belgrave Square... 104 B6
Belgrove Street... 101 H1
Bell Lane... 103 J5
Bell Yard... 102 B6
Belvedere Road... 105 K5
Benjamin Street... 102 C4
Bentinck Street... 100 B6
Berkeley Square... 104 C2
Berkeley Street... 104 D3
Bermondsey Street... 107 H5
Bernard Street... 101 H4
Berners Place... 101 F6
Berners Street... 100 E6
Berry Street... 102 D3
Berwick Street... 101 F7
Bethnal Green Road... 103 K3
Betterton Street... 101 H6
Bevenden Street... 103 G1
Bevis Marks... 103 J6
Bickenhall Street... 100 A4
Bidborough Street... 101 G2
Billiter Street... 103 J7
Bingham Place... 100 B4
Binney Street... 100 B7
Birchin Lane... 103 G7
Birdcage Walk... 105 F5
Birde Lane... 102 C7
Bird Street... 100 B7

Birkenhead Street... 101 H1
Bishopsgate... 103 H5
Bittern Street... 106 E5
Blackall Street... 103 H3
Blackburne's Mews... 104 B2
Black Friars Lane... 106 D1
Blackfriars Road... 106 C5
Blackhorse Court... 107 G6
Blandford Street... 100 A6
Blenheim Street... 100 C7
Bletchley Street... 103 F1
Blomfield Street... 103 G5
Bloomsbury Square... 101 H5
Bloomsbury Street... 101 G5
Bloomsbury Way... 101 H6
Blue Ball Yard... 104 E3
Bolsover Street... 100 D4
Bolton Street... 104 D3
Bonhill Street... 103 G4
Boot Street... 103 H2
Borough High Street... 106 E5
Borough Road... 106 D6
Boscobel Place... 104 B7
Botolph Lane... 107 H2
Boundary Row... 106 C4
Boundary Street... 103 J2
Bourdon Street... 104 C2
Bouverie Street... 102 C7
Bow Lane... 103 F7
Bowling Green Lane... 102 B3
Bowsell Street... 101 J4
Bow Street... 101 J7
Boyfield Street... 106 D5
Braham Street... 103 K6
Bread Street... 102 E7
Bream's Buildings... 102 B6
Bressenden Place... 104 D6
Brewer Street... 104 E2
Brick Lane... 103 K3
Bricklayer's Arms... 107 G7
Brick Street... 104 C4
Bridewell Place... 102 C7
Bridge Street... 105 H5
Bridge Street... 106 E1
Brill Place... 101 G1
Briset Street... 102 C4
Britannia Street... 101 J1
Britannia Walk... 103 F1
Britannia Way... 103 F1
Britton Street... 102 C4
Broadbent Street... 104 C2
Broad Sanctuary... 105 G5
Broadstone Place... 100 A5
Broad Walk... 100 B1
Broad Walk... 104 B3
Broadwall... 106 C3
Broadway... 105 F6
Broadwick Street... 101 F7
Brockham Street... 107 F6
Brook Drive... 106 C7
Brook Street... 102 B5
Brook Street... 104 C1
Brown Heart Gardens... 104 B1
Brownlow Mews... 101 K3
Brownlow Street... 101 K5
Brune Street... 103 K5
Brunswick Close... 107 J5
Brunswick Place... 103 G2
Brunswick Square... 101 H3
Brushfield Street... 103 J5

Bruton Lane... 104 D2
Bruton Place... 104 D2
Bruton Street... 104 D2
Bryanston Street... 100 A7
Buckingham Gate... 104 D6
Buckingham Palace Road... 104 C7
Buckingham Place... 104 E6
Bulstrode Street... 100 B6
Bunhill Row... 103 F3
Burdett Street... 106 B6
Burge Street... 107 G6
Burleigh Street... 101 J7
Burlington Arcade... 104 E2
Burlington Gardens... 104 D2
Burrell Street... 106 D3
Burton Street... 101 G2
Bury Place... 101 H5
Bury Street... 103 J6
Bury Street... 104 E3
Bush Lane... 107 G2
Butteland Street... 103 G2
Byng Place... 101 F4
Byward Street... 107 J2
Cadogan Gate... 104 A7
Cadogan Lane... 104 A7
Cadogan Place... 104 A6
Caledonian Road... 101 J1
Caledonia Street... 101 H1
Calthorpe Street... 101 K3
Calvert Avenue... 103 J2
Calvin Street... 103 K4
Cambridge Gate... 100 C3
Cambridge Gate Mews... 100 D3
Cambridge Terrace... 100 C2
Camlet Street... 103 K3
Camomile Street... 103 H6
Cannon Street... 107 F1
Canon Row... 105 H5
Capper Street... 101 F4
Carburton Street... 100 D4
Cardington Street... 100 E2
Carey Street... 102 A6
Carlisle Lane... 106 A6
Carlisle Place... 104 E7
Carlisle Street... 101 F6
Carlos Place... 104 C2
Carlton Gardens... 105 F4
Carlton House Terrace... 105 F3
Carmelite Street... 106 C1
Carnaby Street... 100 E7
Carpenter Street... 104 C2
Carrington Street... 104 C3
Carteret Street... 105 F5
Carter Lane... 102 D7
Carting Lane... 105 J2
Cartwright Gardens... 101 G2
Castle Lane... 104 E6
Catherine Place... 104 E6
Catherine Street... 105 J1
Cavendish Place... 100 D6
Cavendish Square... 100 C6
Caxton Street... 105 F6
Cayton Street... 103 F2
Centaur Street... 106 A6
Central Street... 102 E2
Chadwell Street... 102 C1
Chadwick Street... 105 F6
Chalton Street... 101 G1
Chambord Street... 103 K2
Chancel Street... 106 D3
Chancery Lane... 102 B6
Chance Street... 103 K3

Chandos Place... 105 H2
Chandos Street... 100 D5
Chapel Street... 104 B6
Chaplin Close... 106 C5
Charing Cross Road... 101 G6
Charles II Street... 105 F2
Charles Square... 103 H2
Charles Street... 104 C3
Charlotte Road... 103 H2
Charlotte Street... 100 E5
Charterhouse Square... 102 D4
Charterhouse Street... 102 C4
Chart Street... 103 G2
Cheapside... 102 E6
Chenies Street... 101 F5
Chequer Street... 103 F3
Chequer Street... 103 F4
Chesham Close... 104 B7
Chesham Place... 104 A7
Chesham Street... 104 A7
Chester Close North... 100 C1
Chester Close South... 100 D2
Chesterfield Gardens... 104 C3
Chesterfield Hill... 104 C3
Chesterfield Street... 104 C3
Chester Gate... 100 C2
Chester Mews... 104 C6
Chester Road... 100 C1
Chester Row... 104 C2
Chester Square... 104 C7
Chester Street... 104 C6
Chester Terrace... 100 C2
Chichester Street... 105 K4
Chiltern Street... 100 A5
Chiswell Street... 103 F4
Chitty Street... 100 E4
Christina Street... 103 H3
Christopher Street... 103 G4
Church Way... 101 G2
City Garden Row... 102 D1
City Road... 102 D1
City Road... 103 G3
Claremont Square... 102 B1
Clarence Gardens... 100 D3
Clarges Street... 104 D3
Clay Street... 100 A5
Clements Lane... 107 G1
Clere Street... 103 G3
Clerkenwell Close... 102 C3
Clerkenwell Green... 102 C3
Clerkenwell Road... 102 C4
Cleveland Place... 104 E3
Cleveland Row... 104 E4
Cleveland Street... 100 D4
Clifford Street... 104 D2
Clink Street... 107 F3
Clipstone Street... 100 D4
Cloak Lane... 107 F1
Cloth Fair... 102 D5
Cloth Street... 102 E5
Club Row... 103 K3
Cluny Place... 107 H6
Cobb Street... 103 J6
Cobourg Street... 100 E2
Cock Lane... 102 D5
Cockspur Street... 105 G3
Coin Street... 106 B3
Coleman Street... 103 F6
Cole Street... 107 F5
College Street... 107 F1
Colnbrook Street... 106 C6

Colombo Street......106 C3
Colonnade......101 H4
Columbia Road......103 K2
Commercial Street......103 J4
Compton Street......102 D3
Concert Hall Approach......105 K4
Conduit Street......104 D2
Cons Street......106 C4
Constitution Hill......104 C5
Conway Street......100 D3
Conway Street......100 E4
Coombs Street......102 D1
Copperfield Street......106 E4
Copthall Avenue......103 G6
Coptic Street......101 H5
Coral Street......106 B5
Coram Street......101 G3
Corbet Street......103 K4
Cork Street......104 D2
Cornhill......103 G7
Cornwall Road......106 B3
Cornwall Terrace Mews......100 A4
Coronet Street......103 H2
Corporation Row......102 C3
Corsham Street......103 G2
Cosser Street......106 B6
County Street......107 G7
Cousin Lane......107 F2
Covent Garden......105 H1
Coventry Street......105 F2
Cowcross Street......102 C5
Cowper Street......103 G3
Cramer Street......100 B5
Cranbourn Street......105 G2
Cranwood Street......103 G2
Craven Street......105 H3
Crawford Passage......102 B3
Creechurch Lane......103 J7
Cremer Street......103 J1
Crestfield Street......101 H1
Crimscott Street......107 J7
Crispin Street......103 J5
Cromer Street......101 H2
Crondall Street......103 G1
Crondall Street......103 H1
Crosby Row......107 G5
Cross Lane......107 H2
Crosswall......107 J1
Crucifix Lane......107 H4
Cruikshank Street......102 B1
Crutched Friars......107 J1
Cubitt Street......101 K2
Culross Street......104 A2
Cumberland Market......100 D2
Cumberland Terrace......100 C1
Cumming Street......101 K1
Curlew Street......107 K4
Cursitor Street......102 B6
Curtain Road......103 H2
Curtis Street......107 J7
Curzon Gate......104 B4
Curzon Street......104 C4
Cutler Street......103 J6
Cynthia Street......102 A1
Cypress Place......100 E4
Cyrus Street......102 D3
D'Arblay Street......100 E7
Dacre Street......105 F6
Dallington Street......102 D3
Dane Street......101 J5
Dansey Place......105 F2
Dartmouth Street......105 F5
Davies Street......104 C1
Deacon Way......106 E7
Dean Bradley Street......105 H7
Deanery Street......104 B3
Dean Farrar Street......105 G6
Dean Ryle Street......105 G4
Dean Stanley Street......105 H7
Dean Street......101 F7
Dean's Yard......105 G6
Decima Street......107 H6
Denman Street......105 F2
Denmark Street......101 G6
Derby Gate......105 H5
Derby Street......104 C3
Dering Street......100 C7
Deverell Street......107 G7
Devonshire Close......100 C4
Devonshire Mews South......100 C4
Devonshire Mews West......100 C4
Devonshire Place......100 B4
Devonshire Square......103 J6
Devonshire Street......100 C4
Dickens Square......107 F6
Dingley Place......102 E2
Dingley Road......102 E2
Disney Place......107 F5
Diss Street......103 K1
Dodson Street......106 C5
Dolben Street......106 D4
Dombey Street......101 J4
Donegal Street......102 A1
Doon Street......106 B3
Doric Way......101 F2
Dorset Rise......102 C7
Dorset Street......100 A5
Doughty Mews......101 J3
Doughty Street......101 J3
Dover Street......104 D3
Dowgate Hill......107 F2
Downing Street......105 G4
Down Street......104 C4
Druid Street......107 J4
Druid Street......107 K4
Drummond Crescent......101 F1
Drummond Street......100 E3
Drury Lane......101 H6
Drysdale Street......103 J2
Duchess Street......100 C5
Duchy Street......106 B3
Duck Lane......101 F7
Dufferin Street......103 F4
Duke's Place......103 J6
Duke's Road......101 G2
Duke of Wellington Place......104 B5
Duke of York Street......105 F3
Duke Street......100 B6

Duke Street Hill......107 G3
Duke Street St James's......104 E3
Duncannon Street......105 H3
Dunraven Street......104 A1
Dunster Court......107 H1
Dyott Street......101 G6
Eagle Street......101 J5
Earlham Street......101 G7
Earl Street......103 H4
Earnshaw Street......101 G6
Eastcastle Street......101 F6
Eastcheap......107 H2
Easton Street......102 B3
East Road......103 G2
Eaton Lane......104 D6
Eaton Mews North......104 B7
Eaton Mews South......104 C7
Eaton Place......104 B7
Eaton Row......104 C6
Eaton Square......104 B7
Ebor Street......103 J3
Ebury Street......104 C7
Eccleston Mews......104 B6
Eccleston Place......104 C7
Edwards Mews......100 B6
Elder Street......103 J4
Eldon Place......103 G5
Elephant & Castle......106 D7
Elephant Road......106 E7
Elim Street......107 G6
Elliott's Row......106 D7
Elm Street......102 A4
Everton Street......105 F7
Embankment Place......105 H3
Emerald Street......101 J4
Emerson Street......106 E3
Emery Hill Street......104 E7
Endell Street......101 H6
Endsleigh Gardens......101 F3
Endsleigh Place......101 G3
Endsleigh Street......101 G3
Epworth Street......103 G3
Errol Street......103 F4
Essex Street......106 B1
Euston Road......101 F3
Euston Square......101 F2
Euston Street......101 F3
Eversholt Street......101 E1
Everton Buildings......100 D2
Ewer Street......106 E3
Exeter Street......105 J2
Exmouth Market......102 B3
Exton Street......106 B4
Eyre Street Hill......102 B4
Fairchild Street......103 J3
Fair Street......107 J4
Falkirk Street......103 J1
Falmouth Road......107 F7
Fann Street......102 E4
Fanshaw Street......103 H1
Fareham Street......101 F6
Farringdon Lane......102 B4
Farringdon Road......102 B3
Farringdon Street......102 C4
Fashion Street......103 K5
Featherstone Street......103 F3
Fenchurch Avenue......103 J7
Fenchurch Buildings......103 J7
Fenchurch Street......107 H1
Fenning Street......107 H4
Fernsbury Street......102 B2
Fetter Lane......102 B6
Finch Lane......103 G7
Finsbury Circus......103 G5
Finsbury Square......103 G4
Finsbury Street......103 F5
Fisher Street......101 J5
Fish Hill......107 G2
Fitzhardinge Street......100 B6
Fitzroy Square......100 D4
Fitzroy Street......100 E4
Flaxman Terrace......101 G2
Fleet Street......102 C7
Fleur de lis Street......103 J4
Flitcroft Street......101 G6
Floral Street......105 H1
Foley Street......100 E5
Folgate Street......103 J4
Fore Street......103 F5
Fortune Street......102 E4
Foster Lane......102 E6
Fournier Street......103 K5
Francis Street......104 E7
Frazier Street......106 B5
Frederick Street......101 J2
Friend Street......102 C2
Frith Street......101 F7
Furnival Street......102 B6
Gainsford Street......107 K4
Galway Street......103 F2
Gambia Street......106 D3
Garden Row......106 C6
Garnault Place......102 C2
Garrett Street......103 F4
Garrick Street......105 H1
Gaunt Street......106 D6
Gayfere Street......105 G6
Gaywood Street......106 D6
Gedling Place......107 K6
Gee Street......102 E3
George Street......100 B6
Geraldine Street......106 C7
Gerrard Street......105 F2
Gerridge Street......106 C5
Gilbert Street......100 C7
Gildea Street......100 D5
Giltspur Street......102 D6
Gladstone Street......106 C6
Glasshill Street......106 D5
Glasshouse Street......105 F2
Globe Street......107 F6
Gloucester Place......100 A5
Gloucester Place Mews......100 A5
Gloucester Way......102 C2
Godliman Street......102 D7

Golden Lane......102 E4
Golden Square......104 E2
Goldsmith Street......102 E6
Goodge Place......100 E5
Goodge Street......100 E5
Gordon Square......101 F3
Gordon Street......101 F3
Gorsuch Street......103 J1
Gosfield Street......100 D5
Goswell Road......102 D1
Gough Street......102 A3
Goulston Street......103 K6
Gower Place......101 F3
Gower Street......101 F3
Gracechurch Street......107 G1
Grafton Place......101 F2
Grafton Street......104 D2
Grafton Way......100 E4
Graham Street......102 D1
Granby Terrace......100 D1
Grand Avenue......102 D5
Grange Road......107 J7
Grange Walk......107 J6
Grange Yard......107 J6
Granville Place......100 B6
Granville Square......102 A2
Grape Street......101 H6
Gravel Lane......103 J6
Gray's Inn Road......101 J1
Gray's Inn Square......102 A5
Gray Street......106 C5
Great Castle Street......100 D6
Great Chapel Street......101 F6
Great College Street......105 G6
Great Dover Street......107 F6
Great Eastern Street......103 H3
Great George Street......105 G5
Great Guildford Street......106 E3
Great James Street......101 J4
Great Marlborough Street......100 E7
Great Maze Pond......107 G4
Great New Newport Street......105 G1
Great Ormond Street......101 J4
Great Percy Street......102 A2
Great Peter Street......105 G6
Great Portland Street......100 D4
Great Pulteney Street......104 E1
Great Queen Street......101 J6
Great Russell Street......101 G6
Great Scotland Yard......105 H3
Great Smith Street......105 G6
Great Suffolk Street......106 D4
Great Sutton Street......102 D4
Great Titchfield Street......100 D5
Great Tower Street......107 H2
Great Winchester Street......103 G6
Great Windmill Street......105 F2
Greek Street......101 G6
Greencoat Place......104 A7
Greenham Close......106 B5
Green Street......104 A1
Greenwell Street......100 D4
Greet Street......106 C4
Gresham Street......102 E6
Gresse Street......101 F6
Greville Street......102 B5
Greycoat Place......105 F7
Greycoat Street......105 F7
Grey Eagle Street......103 K4
Grosvenor Crescent......104 B5
Grosvenor Gardens......104 C6
Grosvenor Hill......104 C2
Grosvenor Place......104 C5
Grosvenor Square......104 B2
Grosvenor Street......104 C2
Guilford Street......101 J4
Gunthorpe Street......103 K5
Guy Street......107 G5
Haberdasher Street......103 G1
Hackney Road......103 K1
Half Moon Street......104 C3
Halkin Street......104 B6
Hallam Street......100 D5
Hall Street......102 D1
Hamilton Place......104 C4
Hamlet Way......107 G5
Hampstead Road......100 E1
Hanbury Street......103 K4
Handel Street......101 H3
Hankey Place......107 G5
Hanover Square......100 D7
Hanover Street......100 D7
Hanson Street......100 D4
Hanway Place......101 F6
Hanway Street......101 F6
Harbour Street......101 H3
Hardwick Street......102 B2
Hardwidge Street......107 H5
Harley Street......100 C5
Harper Road......107 F6
Harriet Street......104 A5
Harriet Walk......104 A5
Harrington Street......100 E1
Harrison Street......101 H2
Harrow Place......103 J6
Hart Street......107 J1
Hastings Street......101 H2
Hatfields......106 C3
Hatton Garden......102 B4
Hatton Wall......102 B4
Haverstock Street......102 D1
Hay's Lane......107 H3
Hay's Mews......104 C2
Haydon Street......107 K1
Hay Hill......104 D2
Hayles Street......106 D7
Haymarket......105 F2
Haywood Place......102 C3
Headfort Place......104 B5
Hearn Street......103 H4
Heathcote Street......101 J3
Helmet Row......102 E3
Henley Drive......107 K7
Henrietta Place......100 C6
Henrietta Street......105 H2
Herbal Hill......102 B4

Herbrand Street......101 H3
Hercules Road......106 A6
Hermit Street......102 C1
Hertford Street......104 C4
Hewett Street......103 H3
High Holborn......101 H6
Hills Place......100 E6
Hill Street......104 C3
Hinde Street......100 B6
Hobart Place......104 C6
Hocker Street......103 K2
Holborn......102 B5
Holborn Circus......102 B6
Holborn Viaduct......102 C5
Holford Street......102 A1
Holland Street......106 D3
Hollen Street......101 F6
Holles Street......100 D6
Holyrood Street......107 H4
Holywell Lane......103 J3
Holywell Row......103 H4
Hopkins Street......101 F7
Hopton Street......106 D3
Horseferry Road......105 F7
Horse Guards Avenue......105 H4
Horse Guards Road......105 G4
Horselydown Lane......107 J4
Hosier Lane......102 D5
Houndsditch......103 J6
Howick Place......104 E7
Howland Street......100 E4
Hoxton Square......103 H2
Hunter Street......101 H3
Huntley Street......101 F4
Hutton Street......102 C7
Hyde Park Corner......104 B4
India Street......103 J7
Ingestre Place......105 F1
Inglebert Street......102 B1
Inner Circle......100 B2
Invicta Plaza......106 C3
Ironmonger Lane......103 F7
Ironmonger Row......102 E2
Irving Street......105 G2
James Street......100 B6
James Street......105 H1
Jermyn Street......104 E3
Jewery Street......103 J7
Joan Street......106 C3
Jockey's Fields......101 K4
John Adam Street......105 H2
John Carpenter Street......106 C1
John Prince's Street......100 D6
John Street......101 K4
Joiner Street......107 G3
Judd Street......101 H2
Juxon Street......106 A7
Keeley Street......101 J6
Keel Street......106 D6
Kemble Street......101 J7
Kendall Place......100 A5
Kennington Road......106 B6
Kenrick Place......100 A5
Kenton Street......101 H3
Keyworth Street......106 D6
King Arms Yard......103 F6
King's Bench Street......106 D5
King's Cross Road......101 K1
King's Mews......102 A4
King's Scholars Passage......104 E7
King Charles Street......105 G5
King Edward Street......102 E6
King Edward Walk......106 B6
King James Street......106 D5
Kingly Street......104 E1
King's Head Yard......107 G4
Kingsland Road......103 J1
King Square......102 E2
King Street......103 F7
King Street......104 E3
King Street......105 H2
Kingsway......101 J6
King William Street......107 G2
Kinnerton Street......104 A5
Kipling Street......107 G5
Kirby Grove......107 H5
Kirby Street......102 B4
Knightrider Street......106 D1
Knightsbridge......104 A4
Lackington Street......103 G5
Lafone Street......107 K4
Lamb's Conduit Street......101 J4
Lamb's Passage......103 F4
Lambeth Hill......102 E7
Lambeth Palace Road......105 J6
Lambeth Road......106 A7
Lambeth Walk......106 A7
Lamb Street......103 J4
Lamb Way......107 H5
Lancaster Place......105 J2
Lancaster Street......106 D5
Lancing Street......101 F2
Langham Place......100 D5
Langham Street......100 D5
Langley Street......101 H6
Langton Close......101 K3
Lansdowne Place......107 G6
Lant Street......106 E5
Launcelot Street......106 B5
Lavington Street......106 D4
Law Street......107 H6
Laystall Street......102 B4
Leadenhall Street......103 H7
Leake Street......106 A5
Leather Lane......102 B4
Leathermarket Street......107 H5
Leeke Street......101 J1
Lees Place......104 B1
Leicester Street......105 G2
Leigh Street......101 H3
Leonard Street......103 G3
Leroy Street......107 H6
Lever Street......102 E2
Lewisham Street......105 G5
Lexington Street......104 E1
Library Street......106 D5
Limeburner Lane......102 C6
Lime Street......107 H1

Lincoln's Inn Fields......101 K6
Lindsey Street......102 D5
Lisle Street......105 G2
Little Argyll Street......100 D7
Little Britain......102 D5
Little Britain......102 E6
Little Chester Street......104 C6
Little Marlborough Street......100 E7
Little New Street......102 C6
Little Portland Street......100 D6
Little Russell Street......101 H6
Little St James's Street......104 E4
Little Sanctuary......105 G6
Little Titchfield Street......100 D5
Liverpool Street......103 H5
Lloyd Baker Street......102 A2
Lloyd's Avenue......107 J1
Lloyd Square......102 B2
Lloyd's Street......102 B1
Lockyer Street......107 G5
Lollard Street......106 A7
Loman Street......106 D4
Lombard Lane......102 B7
Lombard Street......107 G1
London Bridge Street......107 G3
London Road......107 D6
London Street......107 J1
London Wall......102 E6
Long Acre......101 H7
Longford Street......100 D3
Long Lane......102 D5
Long Lane......107 G5
Longmoore Street......104 E7
Lorenzo Street......101 J1
Lothbury......103 G6
Lovat Lane......107 H2
Lower Belgrave Street......104 C7
Lower Grosvenor Place......104 C6
Lower James Street......104 E2
Lower John Street......104 E2
Lower Marsh......106 B5
Lower Thames Street......107 H2
Lowndes Place......104 A6
Lowndes Square......104 A5
Lowndes Street......104 A5
Ludgate Hill......102 D7
Luke Street......103 H3
Lumley Street......100 B7
Luxborough Street......100 A4
Lyall Street......104 B7
Macclesfield Road......102 E2
Macklin Street......101 H6
Maddox Street......104 D1
Magdalen Street......107 H4
Maguire Street......107 K4
Maiden Lane......105 H2
Maiden Lane......107 F3
Malet Street......101 G4
Maltby Street......107 J5
Maltby Street......107 K5
Manchester Square......100 B6
Manchester Street......100 B5
Manciple Street......107 G5
Mandeville Place......100 B6
Manette Street......101 G6
Mansell Street......103 K7
Mansfield Street......100 C5
Maple Street......100 D4
Marchmont Street......101 H3
Margaret Street......100 D6
Margery Street......102 B2
Market Place......100 D6
Mark Lane......107 J2
Marlborough Road......104 E4
Marlborough Street......104 E7
Marshalsea Road......106 E4
Marsham Street......105 G7
Martin Lane......107 G2
Marylebone High Street......100 B5
Marylebone Lane......100 B6
Marylebone Road......100 C4
Matthew Parker Street......105 G5
Maunsel Street......105 F7
Mayfair Place......104 D3
McAuley Close......106 B6
Meadow Row......106 E7
Mead Row......106 B6
Mecklenburgh Square......101 J3
Medway Street......105 F7
Melior Street......107 H4
Melton Street......101 F2
Mepham Street......106 A4
Mercer Street......101 H7
Meredith Street......102 C2
Merrick Square......107 F6
Meymott Street......106 C4
Middlesex Street......103 J5
Middlesex Street......103 J6
Middle Street......102 E5
Middle Temple Lane......102 B7
Midland Road......101 G1
Milcote Street......106 D5
Milford Lane......106 A1
Milk Street......103 F6
Millbank......105 H7
Millman Street......101 J3
Millstream Road......107 K5
Milton Street......103 F5
Milton Street......103 G5
Mincing Lane......107 H2
Minories......107 K7
Mitchell Street......102 E3
Mitre Road......106 C5
Mitre Street......103 J7
Monck Street......105 G7
Monkwell Square......102 E5
Monmouth Street......101 H7
Montague Close......107 F3
Montague Place......101 G4
Montague Street......101 H5
Montagu Place......100 A5
Montagu Square......100 A5
Montclare Street......103 J3
Montrose Place......104 B5
Monument Street......107 G2
Monument Street......107 H2
Moorfields......103 G5
Moorgate......103 G5

Moor Lane....103 F5
Mora Street....103 F2
Moreland Street....102 D2
Morgan's Lane....107 H4
Morley Street....106 B6
Morocco Street....107 H4
Morpeth Terrace....104 E7
Mortimer Street....100 E5
Morwell Street....101 F5
Motcomb Street....104 A6
Mount Pleasant....102 A4
Mount Row....104 C2
Mount Street....104 B2
Moxon Street....100 B5
Mundy Street....103 H2
Munster Square....100 D3
Munton Road....107 F7
Murphy Street....106 B5
Murray Grove....103 F1
Museum Street....101 H5
Muredown Passage....102 B1
Myddelton Square....102 B2
Myddelton Street....102 C2
Naoroji Street....102 B2
Nash Street....100 D2
Nassau Street....100 E5
Navarre Street....103 J3
Neal Street....101 H6
Neckinger....107 K6
Nelson Place....102 D1
Nelson Square....106 D4
Nelson Terrace....100 D1
Netley Street....100 E2
New Bond Street....100 C7
New Bridge Street....102 C7
New Broad Street....103 G5
New Burlington Street....104 E2
Newbury Street....102 E5
New Cavendish Street....100 C5
New Change....107 F4
Newcomen Street....107 F4
New Fetter Lane....102 D6
Newgate Street....102 D6
New Goulston Street....103 K6
Newham's Row....107 J6
Newington Causeway....106 E6
New Inn Street....103 J3
New Inn Yard....103 J3
New Kent Road....107 F7
Newman Street....101 F5
New North Place....103 H3
New North Road....103 G1
New North Street....101 J4
New Oxford Street....101 G6
New Row....105 H6
New Square....102 A6
New Street....102 C6
New Street Square....102 C6
Newton Street....101 J6
New Union Street....103 F5
Nicholas Lane....107 G1
Nicholson Street....106 C4
Nile Street....103 F1
Noble Street....102 E6
Noel Street....100 E6
Norman Street....102 E2
Northampton Road....102 B3
Northampton Square....102 D2
North Audley Street....104 B1
Northburgh Street....102 D3
North Gower Street....100 E2
Northington Street....101 K4
North Mews....102 A4
North Row....104 A1
Northumberland Alley....103 J7
Northumberland Avenue....105 H3
Northumberland Street....105 H3
Norton Fulgate....103 J4
Norwich Street....102 B6
Nottingham Place....100 B3
Nottingham Street....100 B4
O'Meara Street....107 F4
Ogle Street....100 E5
Old Bailey....102 D6
Old Barrack Yard....104 A5
Old Bond Street....104 D2
Old Broad Street....103 G6
Old Burlington Street....104 D2
Oldbury Place....100 B4
Old Castle Street....103 K6
Old Cavendish Street....100 C6
Old Compton Street....105 F1
Old Gloucester Street....101 H4
Old Jewry....103 F6
Old Nichol Street....103 J3
Old North Street....101 J5
Old Paradise Street....105 J7
Old Park Lane....104 C4
Old Pye Street....105 F6
Old Queen Street....105 G5
Old Square....102 A6
Old Street....102 E3
Omega Place....101 J1
Ontario Street....106 D6
Orange Street....105 G2
Orchard Street....100 B6
Ordehall Street....101 J4
Orient Street....106 C7
Osnaburgh Street....100 D3
Osnaburgh Terrace....100 D3
Ossington Street....101 G1
Ossulston Street....101 G1
Oswin Street....106 D7
Outer Circle....100 B3
Outer Circle....102 C1
Owen Street....102 C1
Oxendon Street....105 F2
Oxford Street....100 B7
Paddington Street....100 A5
Page's Walk....107 J7
Page Street....105 G7
Pakenham Street....102 A2
Palace Street....104 E6
Pall Mall....105 F3
Pall Mall East....105 G2
Palmer Street....105 F6
Panton Street....105 F2
Pardoner Street....107 G6
Paris Garden....106 C3

Park Crescent....100 C4
Parker Street....101 H6
Park Lane....104 A2
Park Place....104 E3
Park Square East....100 C3
Park Square West....100 C3
Park Street....104 A1
Park Street....106 E3
Parliament Square....105 H5
Parliament Street....105 H5
Paul Street....103 H3
Pavilion Road....104 A7
Pavilion Street....104 A7
Pearman Street....106 B6
Pear Tree Court....102 C3
Pear Tree Street....102 F1
Peerless Street....103 F2
Pelter Street....103 K2
Pemberton Row....102 B6
Pembroke Close....104 B5
Penton Rise....102 A1
Pentonville Road....101 J1
Pepper Street....106 E4
Pepys Street....107 J2
Percival Street....102 D3
Percy Circus....102 A2
Percy Street....101 F5
Peter Street....105 F1
Peto Place....100 D3
Petticoat Lane....103 J5
Petty France....105 F6
Petty Wales....107 J2
Philpot Lane....107 H2
Phoenix Place....102 A3
Phoenix Road....101 F1
Phoenix Street....101 G1
Piccadilly....104 D4
Piccadilly Arcade....104 E2
Piccadilly Circus....105 F2
Pickard Street....102 D1
Pilgrimage Street....107 F5
Pinder Street....103 H4
Pine Street....102 B3
Pitfield Street....103 H1
Pitfield Street....103 H2
Plough Yard....103 J4
Pocock Street....106 D5
Poland Street....100 E7
Polygon Road....101 F1
Pont Street....104 A6
Pope Street....107 J5
Porlock Street....107 G5
Porter Street....100 A4
Porter Street....107 F4
Portland Place....100 C4
Portman Close....100 A6
Portman Square....100 A7
Portman Street....100 A7
Portpool Lane....102 B4
Portsmouth Street....101 K6
Portsoken Street....107 K1
Portugal Street....101 K6
Potier Street....107 G6
Poultry....103 F7
Prescot Street....107 K1
Primrose Street....103 H4
Prince's Street....103 G6
Princelet Street....103 K5
Princess Street....106 D7
Princes Street....100 D7
Princeton Street....101 J5
Priory Street....107 G7
Proctor Street....101 J5
Provident Court....104 B1
Provost Street....103 G2
Pudding Lane....107 G2
Purbrook Street....107 J6
Quaker Street....103 K4
Queen's Walk....104 E4
Queen's Walk....104 E4
Queen Anne's Gate....105 F5
Queen Anne Street....100 C6
Queen Elizabeth Street....107 K4
Queen Square....101 H4
Queen Street....103 F7
Queen Street....104 C3
Queen Street Place....107 F2
Queen Victoria Street....107 F7
Queen Victoria Street....106 E1
Radcliffe Road....107 J6
Radnor Street....102 F2
Railway Approach....107 G3
Ramillies Place....100 E6
Ramillies Street....100 E6
Rathbone Place....101 F6
Rathbone Street....101 F6
Ravenscroft Street....103 K1
Rawstone Street....102 C2
Redchurch Street....103 J3
Redcross Way....106 E4
Redhill Street....100 D1
Red Lion Square....101 J5
Red Lion Street....101 K5
Regent Place....104 E2
Regent Square....101 H2
Regent Street....100 D7
Regent Street....105 F2
Remington Street....102 D1
Remnant Street....101 J6
Rennie Street....106 C3
Rhoda Street....103 K3
Richmond Terrace....105 H4
Ridgemount Gardens....101 F4
Ridgemount Street....101 F4
Riding House Street....100 D5
Riley Road....107 J6
Risborough Street....106 D5
River Street....102 B2
Rivington Street....103 H2
Robert Adam Street....100 A6
Robert Street....100 D2
Rochelle Street....103 K2
Rochester Row....105 F7
Rochester Street....105 F7
Rockingham Street....106 E7
Rodmarton Street....100 A5
Rodney Place....107 F7

Roger Street....101 K4
Romilly Street....105 G1
Romney Street....105 G7
Rood Lane....107 H2
Ropemaker Street....103 F5
Roper Lane....107 J5
Roscoe Street....103 F3
Rose Alley....106 E3
Rosebery Avenue....102 B3
Rotary Street....106 D6
Rothsay Street....107 H6
Roupell Street....106 C4
Royal Oak Yard....107 H5
Royal Street....105 K6
Rugby Street....101 J4
Rupert Street....105 F1
Rushworth Street....106 D5
Russell Square....101 H4
Russell Street....105 J1
Ryder Street....104 E3
Sackville Street....104 E2
Saffron Hill....102 C4
Saffron Street....102 C4
Sail Street....106 A7
St Alban's Street....105 F2
St Andrew's Place....100 C3
St Andrews Hill....106 D1
St Andrew Street....102 C6
St Ann's Street....105 G6
St Anselm's Place....104 C1
St Botolph Street....103 J6
St Bride Street....102 C6
St Chad's Street....101 H1
St Clements Lane....101 K6
St Cross Street....102 B4
St Dunstan's Hill....107 H2
St George's Circus....106 C6
St George's Road....106 C6
St George Street....104 D1
St Giles High Street....101 G6
St James's Place....104 E4
St James's Square....105 F3
St James's Street....104 E3
St James Walk....102 C3
St John's Lane....102 D4
St John's Square....102 C4
St John Street....102 D1
St James's Lane....105 G2
St Martin's Le Grand....102 E6
St Martin's Place....105 G2
St Mary at Hill....107 H2
St Mary Axe....103 H6
St Matthew Street....105 F6
St Paul's Churchyard....102 D7
St Swithin's Lane....107 G1
St Thomas Street....107 G4
St Vincent Street....100 B5
Salisbury Court....102 C7
Sandland Street....101 K5
Sandwich Street....101 H1
Sans Walk....102 C3
Sardinia Street....101 K6
Savile Row....104 D1
Savoy Hill....105 J2
Savoy Place....105 J2
Savoy Street....105 J2
Sawyer Street....106 E4
Sclater Street....103 K3
Scoresby Street....106 D4
Scrutton Street....103 H3
Searles Road....107 G7
Sebastian Street....102 D2
Secker Street....106 B4
Seddon Street....101 K2
Seething Lane....107 J2
Sekforde Street....102 C3
Serle Street....101 K6
Serpentine Road....104 A4
Seven Dials....101 G7
Seville Street....104 A5
Seward Street....102 E2
Seymour Mews....100 B6
Seymour Street....100 A7
Shad Thames....107 K4
Shaftesbury Avenue....101 G7
Shand Street....107 H4
Shenfield Street....103 J1
Shepherdess Walk....103 F1
Shepherd Street....104 C3
Ship and Mermaid Row....107 H5
Shoe Lane....102 C6
Shoreditch High Street....103 J2
Shorter Street....107 K2
Shorts Gardens....101 H7
Short Street....106 C4
Sidmouth Street....101 J2
Silex Street....106 D5
Silk Street....103 F5
Silvester Street....107 F5
Singer Street....103 G2
Skinner Street....102 C3
Sloane Street....104 A6
Smithfield Street....102 D5
Smith Square....105 H7
Snow Hill....102 D5
Snowsfields....107 G4
Soho Square....101 F6
Soho Street....101 F6
Southall Place....107 F5
Southampton Buildings....102 A5
Southampton Place....101 H5
Southampton Row....101 H5
Southampton Street....105 H2
South Audley Street....104 B2
South Molton Lane....100 C7
South Molton Street....100 C7
South Place....103 G5
South Square....102 A5
South Street....104 B3
Southwark Bridge Road....106 E5
Southwark Street....106 E3
Spa Road....107 K6
Spencer Street....102 C2
Spenser Street....104 E6
Spital Square....103 J4
Spring Gardens....105 G3
Spurgeon Street....107 F6

Spur Road....106 B5
Stable Yard Road....104 E4
Stacey Street....101 G7
Stafford Place....104 D6
Stafford Street....104 D3
Stainer Street....107 G4
Stamford Street....106 B3
Stanhope Gate....104 B3
Stanhope Row....104 C4
Stanhope Street....100 D1
Staple Street....107 G5
Starcross Street....100 E2
Station Approach Road....106 A4
Stephenson Way....100 E3
Stephen Street....101 F6
Stevens Street....107 J6
Stew Lane....106 E2
Stone Buildings....102 A5
Stonecutter Street....102 C6
Stoney Lane....103 J6
Stoney Street....107 F3
Store Street....101 F5
Storey's Gate....105 G5
Strand....105 H2
Stratford Place....100 C6
Stratton Street....104 D3
Strype Street....103 J5
Stukeley Street....101 H6
Sudrey Street....106 E5
Suffolk Lane....107 G2
Sumner Street....106 D3
Sun Street....103 H4
Surrey Row....106 D4
Surrey Street....105 K2
Sutton Row....101 F6
Suttons Way....103 F4
Swallow Street....104 E2
Swanfield Street....103 K2
Swan Lane....107 G2
Swan Mead....107 H7
Swan Street....107 F6
Sweeney Crescent....107 K5
Swinton Street....101 J2
Tabard Street....107 G6
Tabernacle Street....103 G4
Tanner Street....107 J5
Taplow Street....103 F1
Tavistock Place....101 H3
Tavistock Square....101 G3
Tavistock Street....105 J2
Taviton Street....101 F3
Temple Avenue....106 C1
Temple Lane....102 B7
Temple Place....106 A2
Tennis Street....107 F4
Tenterden Street....100 C7
Terminus Place....104 D7
Thanet Street....101 H2
Thayer Street....100 B6
The Cut....106 C4
Theed Street....106 B4
The Grange....107 J6
The Mall....105 F4
Theobald's Road....101 J5
Theobald Street....107 G7
Thirleby Road....104 E7
Thoresby Street....102 E1
Thrale Street....106 E4
Thrawl Street....103 K5
Threadneedle Street....103 G6
Throgmorton Avenue....103 G6
Throgmorton Street....103 G6
Tilverton Street....106 E6
Tonbridge Street....101 H2
Tooley Street....107 G3
Tooley Street....107 J4
Torrington Place....101 F4
Torrington Square....101 G3
Tothill Street....105 G6
Tottenham Court Road....100 E4
Tottenham Street....100 E5
Toulmin Street....106 E5
Tower Bridge Approach....107 K2
Tower Bridge Road....107 H7
Tower Hill....107 J2
Tower Place....107 J2
Tower Street....101 G7
Toynbee Street....103 K5
Trafalgar Square....105 G3
Trebeck Street....104 C3
Trinity Church Square....107 F6
Trinity Square....107 J2
Trinity Street....107 F6
Trump Street....103 F6
Tudor Street....106 C1
Tufton Street....105 G6
Turnmill Street....102 C4
Tyers Gate....107 H5
Tyers Street....105 K7
Ufford Street....106 C5
Ulster Place....100 C4
Undershaft....103 H6
Underwood Street....103 F1
Union Street....106 D4
Union Walk....103 J1
University Street....100 E4
Upper Belgrave Street....104 B6
Upper Brook Street....104 A2
Upper Grosvenor Street....104 B2
Upper Ground....106 B3
Upper Harley Street....100 C3
Upper James Street....104 E1
Upper John Street....104 E1
Upper March....105 K6
Upper St Martin's....105 G1
Upper Thames Street....106 E2
Upper Wimpole Street....100 C4
Upper Woburn Place....101 G2
Valentine Place....106 C5
Vandon Passage....104 E6
Vandon Street....104 E6
Vandy Street....103 H4
Vauban Street....107 K7
Vauxhall Bridge Road....104 E7
Vere Street....100 C6
Vernon Place....101 H5
Vernon Rise....102 A1
Verulam Street....102 B4

Vestry Street....103 G2
Victoria Embankment....105 H4
Victoria Square....104 D6
Victoria Street....104 D7
Vigo Street....104 E2
Villiers Street....105 H3
Vincent Square....105 F7
Vince Street....103 G2
Vine Street....103 J7
Virginia Road....103 K2
Viscount Street....102 E4
Wakefield Street....101 H2
Wakley Street....102 D1
Walbrook....103 F7
Walcot Square....106 B7
Walnut Tree Walk....106 A7
Warden's Grove....106 E4
Wardour Street....101 F7
Warner Street....102 B4
Warren Street....100 D4
Warwick House Street....105 G3
Warwick Lane....102 D6
Warwick Row....104 D6
Warwick Street....104 E2
Waterloo Place....105 F3
Waterloo Road....106 B5
Waterloo Street....103 J2
Watling Street....102 E7
Waverton Street....104 C3
Weavers Lane....107 J4
Webber Row....106 C5
Webber Street....106 C5
Webb Street....107 H7
Weigh House Street....104 B1
Welbeck Street....100 C5
Welbeck Way....100 C6
Wellesley Terrace....103 F1
Wellington Street....105 J1
Wells Street....100 E6
Wenlock Road....103 F1
Wenlock Street....103 F1
Wentworth Street....103 K5
Werrington Street....101 F1
Western Street....107 F4
West Halkin Street....104 A6
Westland Place....103 F1
Westminster Bridge Road....106 B5
Westmoreland Street....100 B5
Weston Street....107 G6
Weston Street....107 H4
West Poultry Avenue....102 C5
West Smithfield....102 D5
West Square....106 C7
West Street....105 G1
West Tenter Street....103 K7
Weymouth Street....100 C4
Wharf Road....102 E1
Wharton Street....102 A2
Wheatley Street....100 B5
Wheler Street....103 K4
Whetstone Park....101 J6
Whidborne Street....101 H2
Whiskin Street....102 C2
Whitby Street....103 K3
Whitcomb Street....105 G2
White's Grounds....107 H5
White's Row....103 K5
Whitechapel High Street....103 K6
Whitecross Street....103 F3
Whitefriars Street....102 C7
Whitehall....105 H4
Whitehall Court....105 H4
Whitehall Place....105 H3
White Hart Yard....107 G4
White Horse Street....104 C3
White Lion Hill....106 D2
White Lion Street....102 B1
Whitfield Street....100 E4
Whittlesey Street....106 B4
Wicklow Street....101 J1
Widegate Street....103 J5
Wigmore Place....100 C6
Wigmore Street....100 B6
Wild's Rents....107 H6
Wild Street....101 J6
Wilfred Street....104 E6
Wilkes Street....103 K5
William IV Street....105 H2
William Road....100 E2
Willow Street....103 H3
Willow Walk....107 J7
Wilmington Square....102 B2
Wilmington Street....102 B2
Wilson Street....103 G5
Wilton Crescent....104 A5
Wilton Place....104 A5
Wilton Row....104 A5
Wilton Street....104 C6
Wimpole Mews....100 C5
Wimpole Street....100 C5
Winchester Street....101 F5
Windmill Street....101 F5
Windsor Terrace....102 E1
Winnett Street....105 F1
Winsley Street....100 E6
Woburn Place....101 G3
Woburn Square....101 G3
Woodbridge Street....102 C3
Wood Street....102 E6
Wood Street....100 B4
Wooton Street....106 B4
Wormwood Street....103 H6
Wren Street....101 K3
Wyclif Street....102 C2
Wyndham Street....100 A4
Yardley Street....102 B2
York Boulevard....105 H2
York Bridge....100 B4
York Gate....100 B4
York Road....105 K4
York Street....100 A5
York Terrace East....100 C4
York Terrace West....100 B4
York Way....101 H1
Zoar Street....106 E3

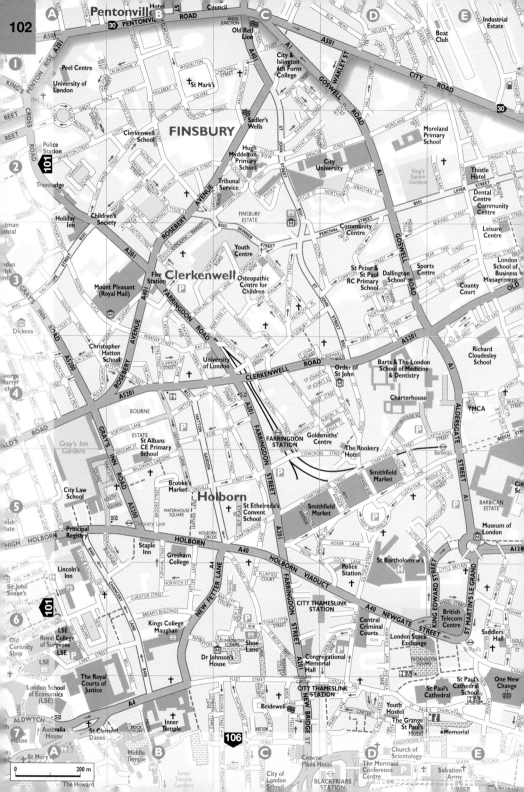

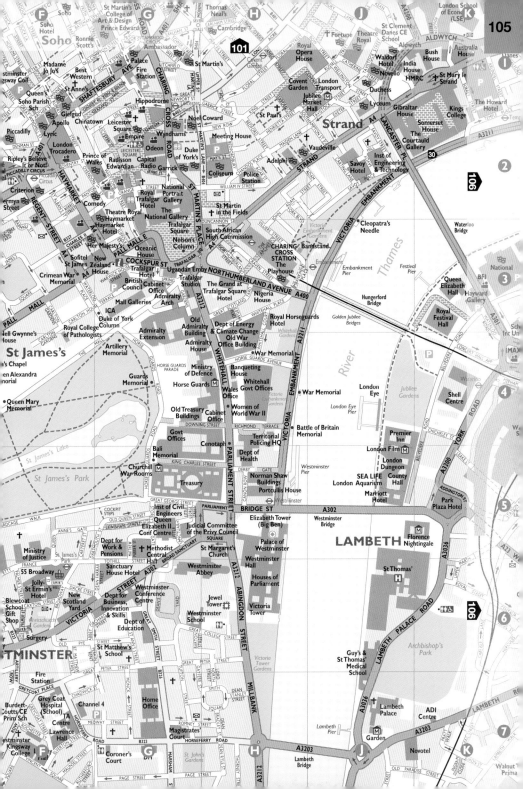

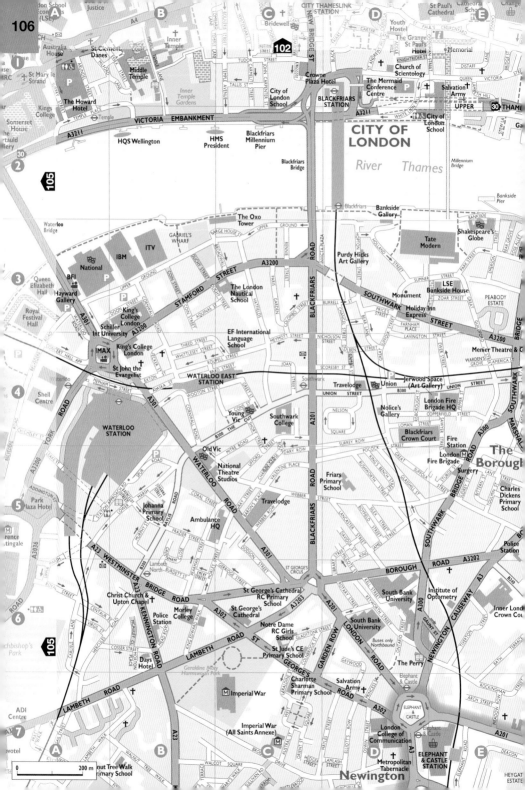

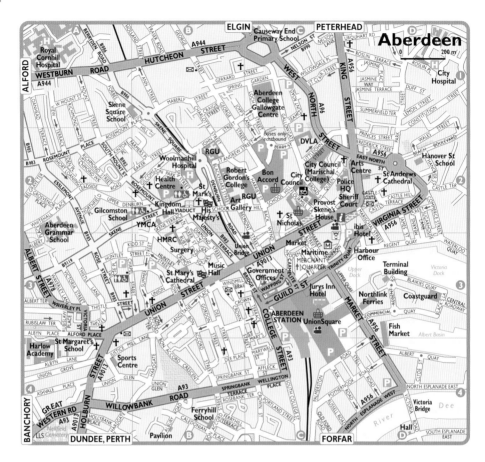

Affleck Street	C4	
Albert Place	A3	
Albert Quay	D4	
Albert Street	A3	
Albury Road	B4	
Albyn Lane	A4	
Albyn Place	A3	
Alford Place	A3	
Ann Street	B1	
Ashvale Place	A4	
Back Wynd	C2	
Baker Street	B2	
Beach Boulevard	D2	
Belgrave Terrace	A2	
Belmont Street	B2	
Berry Street	C2	
Berryden Road	A1	
Blackfriars Street	B2	
Black's Lane	D3	
Blaikies Quay	D3	
Bon Accord Crescent	B4	
Bon Accord Street	B3	
Bon Accord Terrace	B3	
Bridge Street	C3	
Broad Street	C2	
Caledonian Place	B4	
Carmelite Street	C3	
Castle Hill	D2	
Castle Terrace	D2	
Castlegate	D2	
Central Roadway	D3	
Chapel Street	A3	
Charlotte Street	B1	
Clyde Street	D4	
College Street	C3	
Commerce Street	D2	

Commercial Quay	D3	
Constitution Street	D1	
Craigie Street	B1	
Crimon Place	B3	
Crown Street	B3	
Crown Terrace	C3	
Dee Place	B4	
Dee Street	B3	
Denburn Road	B2	
Diamond Street	B3	
Duff Street	D1	
East North Street	D2	
Eden Place	A2	
Esslemont Avenue	A2	
Farmers Place	B2	
Ferryhill Terrace	B4	
Flourmill Lane	C2	
Forbes Street	A1	
Fraser Road	B1	
Frederick Street	D1	
Gallowgate	C1	
George Street	B1	
Gerrard Street	B1	
Gilcomston Park	B2	
Golden Square	B3	
Gordon Street	B3	
Great Western Road	A4	
Grosvenor Place	A2	
Guild Street	C3	
Hadden Street	C3	
Hanover Street	D2	
Hardgate	A4	
Hardgate	B4	
Harriet Street	C2	
Hill Street	B2	
Holburn Street	A4	

Holland Street	A1	
Hollybank Place	A4	
Howburn Place	A4	
Huntley Street	A3	
Hutcheon Street	B1	
James Street	D2	
Jasmine Place	D1	
Jasmine Terrace	D1	
Jasmine Way	D1	
John Street	B2	
Jopp's Lane	B1	
Justice Mill Lane	A4	
Kidd Street	A3	
King Street	C1	
Kintore Place	A2	
Langstane Place	B3	
Leadside Road	A2	
Lemon Street	D1	
Littlejohn Street	C2	
Loanhead Terrace	A1	
Loch Street	B1	
Maberly Street	B1	
Marischal Street	D2	
Market Street	C3	
Marywell Street	C4	
Mearns Street	D2	
Mount Street	A1	
Nelson Street	C1	
North Esplanade East	D4	
North Esplanade West	D4	
North Silver Street	B2	
Northfield Place	A2	
Old Ford Road	C4	
Palmerston Road	C4	
Park Street	D1	
Portland Street	C4	

Poynernook Road	C4	
Princes Street	D2	
Queen Street	C2	
Raik Road	C4	
Regent Quay	D3	
Regent Road	D3	
Richmond Street	A2	
Richmond Terrace	A1	
Richmond Walk	A1	
Rose Place	A3	
Rose Street	A3	
Rosebank Terrace	B4	
Rosemount Place	A2	
Rosemount Viaduct	A2	
Roslin Place	D1	
Roslin Terrace	D1	
Rubislaw Place	A3	
Rubislaw Terrace	A3	
Ruby Lane	B3	
Russell Road	C4	
St Andrew Street	B2	
St Clair Street	C1	
St Mary's	C4	
School Hill	C2	
Seamount Road	C1	
Shiprow	C3	
Short Loanings	A2	
Skene Square	B2	
Skene Street	A3	
Skene Terrace	B2	
South College Street	C4	
South Esplanade East	D4	
South Mount Street	A2	
Spa Street	B2	
Spring Garden	B1	
Springbank Street	B4	

Springbank Terrace	B4	
Stell Road	C4	
Sugarhouse Lane	D2	
Summer Street	B3	
Summerfield Terrace	D1	
Thistle Lane	A3	
Thistle Place	A3	
Thistle Street	A3	
Trinity Quay	C3	
Union Bridge	B3	
Union Glen	A4	
Union Grove	A4	
Union Row	B3	
Union Street	B3	
Union Terrace	B2	
Upper Denburn	A2	
Upper Quay	C3	
Urquhart Road	D1	
Victoria Bridge	D4	
Victoria Road	D4	
Victoria Street	A3	
View Terrace	A1	
Virginia Street	D2	
Wales Street	C3	
Wapping Street	C3	
Waterloo Quay	D2	
Waverley Lane	A3	
Waverley Place	A3	
Wellington Place	C4	
West Mount Street	A1	
West North Street	C1	
Westburn Road	A1	
Whitehall Place	A2	
Willowbank Road	A4	
Willowdale Place	C1	
Windmill Brae	B3	

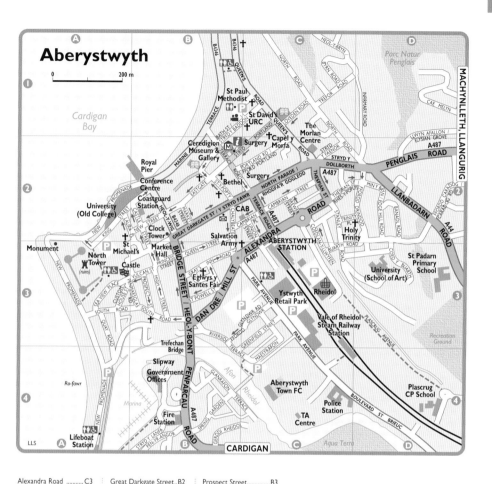

Alexandra Road C3	Great Darkgate Street..B2	Prospect Street..............B3
Banadl Road................D2	Greenfield Street...........C3	Quay Road...................A3
Bath Street..................B1	Heol-Y-Bont.................B3	Queen's Road................B1
Boulevard St Brieuc.....C4	Heol-Y-Bryn..................C1	Queen Street................B3
Brewer Street...............C2	Heol-Y-Wig..................B2	Rhes-Y-Poplys..............C2
Bridge Street................B3	High Street...................B3	Rhodfa'r Gogledd..........C2
Buarth Road.................C3	Infirmary Road..............D1	Riverside Terrace...........B3
Byrn Road....................C1	King Street...................A2	St Powell Street.............B3
Cae Melyn...................D1	Laura Place..................A1	Sea View Place.............A3
Cambrian Place............B2	Llanbadarn Road...........D2	South Road..................A3
Cambrian Street...........C2	Llwyn Afallon...............D1	Spring Gardens.............B4
Caradog Road..............D2	Loveden Road..............C1	Stanley Road.................C2
Castle Street................B2	Maesyrafon C4	Stryd Portland...............B2
Chalybeate Street.........B2	Marine Terrace.............B2	Stryd Y Baddon............B2
Coedlan-Y-Llwyfen.......C2	Market Street................B2	Stryd Y Dollborth C2
Coed Y Buarth.............D3	Mill Street B3	Stryd Y Faenor.............C2
Custom House	Min Y Bryn..................D2	Stryd Y Lanfa................B4
Street.........................A3	New Promenade A2	St-Y-Popty B2
Dan Dre B3	New Street...................B2	Terrace Road................B2
Eastgate B2	North Parade................C2	Thespian Street C2
Edge Hill Road............D2	North Road..................C1	Trefor Road..................C1
Elysian Grove D1	Park Avenue C3	Trinity Place..................C2
Ffordd Caradog............D2	Penglais Road...............C2	Union Street..................C2
Ffordd Drindod D2	Penmaesglas Road........A3	Vulcan Street................B3
Ffordd Glyndwr............B3	Penparcau Road............B4	Y Stryd Fawr................B2
Fford Portland.............B2	Pen-Yr-Angor..............B4	
Gerddi Rheidol............B4	Plascrug Avenue............D3	
Glanrafon Terrace.........B4	Pont Aberystwth...........B3	
Glyndwr Road..............C3	Portland Road C2	
Gray's Inn Road............B3	Princess Street..............B3	

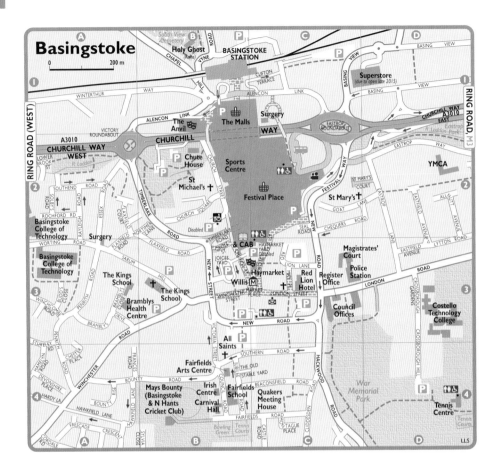

Alencon Link C1
Allnutt Avenue D2
Basing View C1
Beaconsfield Road........ C4
Bounty Rise A4
Bounty Road A4
Bramblys Close............ A3
Bramblys Drive............. A3
Budd's Close................. A3
Castle Road................... C4
Chapel Hill.....................B1
Chequers Road.............. C2
Chester Place................ A4
Churchill Way................B2
Churchill Way East........D1
Churchill Way West..... A2
Church Square...............B2
Church Street................B2
Church Street B3
Cliddesden Road C4
Clifton Terrace............. C1
Cordale Road................ A4
Council Road.................B4
Crossborough
  Gardens......................D3
Crossborough Hill D3
Cross Street...................B3
Devonshire Place.......... A4
Eastfield Avenue...........D2
Eastrop Lane..................D2

Eastrop Roundabout C1
Eastrop Way D2
Essex Road A2
Fairfields Road B4
Festival Way...................C2
Flaxfield Court.............. A2
Flaxfield Road................ A3
Flaxfield Road................B3
Frances Road................. A4
Frescade Crescent........ A4
Goat Lane C2
Hackwood Road............ C4
Hamelyn Road A4
Hardy Lane A4
Hawkfield Lane A4
Haymarket Yard............ C3
Joices Yard.....................B3
Jubilee Road..................B4
London Road.................D3
London Street............... C3
Lower Brook Street...... A2
Lytton Road...................D3
Market Place.................B3
May Place C3
Montague Place C4
Mortimer Lane.............. A2
New Road.......................B3
New Road.......................C2
New Street.....................B3
Penrith Road A3

Rayleigh Road................ A2
Red Lion Lane............... C3
Rochford Road.............. A2
St Mary's Court............. C2
Sarum Hill A3
Seal Road C2
Solby's Road.................. A2
Southend Road............. A2
Southern Road..............B4
Stukeley Road A3
Sylvia Close B4
Timberlake Road...........B2
Victoria Street B3
Victory Roundabout..... A1
Vyne Road B1
Winchcombe Road....... A3
Winchester Road.......... A4
Winchester Street.........B3
Winterthur Way............ A1
Worting Road................ A3
Wote Street C3

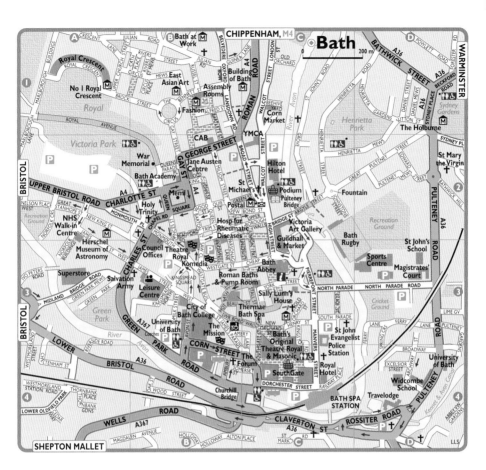

Abbey View Gardens	D4	Daniel Mews	D1
Alfred Street	B1	Daniel Street	D1
Alton Place	B4	Dorchester Street	C4
Ambury	B4	Duke Street	C3
Amery Lane	B3	Edward Street	D2
Archway Street	D4	Excelsior Street	D4
Argyle Street	C2	Ferry Lane	D3
Avon Street	B3	Forester Road	D1
Bartlett Street	B1	Gay Street	B1
Barton Street	B2	George Street	B2
Bathwick Hill	D2	Great Pulteney Street	C2
Bathwick Street	D1	Great Stanhope Street	A2
Beauford Square	B2	Green Park	A3
Beau Street	B3	Green Park Mews	A3
Beckford Road	D1	Green Park Road	A3
Beehive Yard	C1	Green Street	B2
Belvedere	B1	Grove Street	C2
Bennett Street	B1	Guinea Lane	B1
Bridewell Lane	B3	Henrietta Gardens	D1
Bridge Street	C2	Henrietta Mews	C2
Broad Street	C2	Henrietta Road	C1
Broadway	D4	Henrietta Street	C2
Brock Street	A1	Henry Street	C3
Cath Street	B1	High Street	C2
Cedar Way	A4	Holloway	B4
Chapel Road	B2	Hot Bath Street	B3
Charles Street	A3	Ivo Peters Road	A3
Charlotte Street	A2	James Street West	B3
Cheap Street	C3	Johnstone Street	C2
Cheltenham Street	A4	John Street	B2
Churchill Bridge	B4	Julian Road	A1
Circus Mews	B1	Kingsmead North	B3
Circus Place	B1	Kingsmead Square	B3
Claverton Street	C4	Kingston Road	C3
Corn Street	B4	Lansdown Road	B1
Crescent Lane	A1	Lime Grove	D3

London Street	C1	Queen Street	B2
Lower Borough Walls	B3	Quiet Street	B2
Lower Bristol Road	A3	Railway Place	C4
Lower Oldfield Park	A4	Riverside Road	A4
Magdalen Avenue	A4	Rivers Street	B1
Manvers Street	C3	Rivers Street Mews	B1
Marlborough Buildings	A1	Roman Road	C1
Marlborough Lane	A2	Rossiter Road	C4
Midland Bridge Road	A3	Royal Avenue	A1
Milk Street	B3	Royal Crescent	A1
Milsom Street	B2	Russel Street	B1
Monmouth Place	A2	St James's Parade	B3
Monmouth Street	B2	St John's Road	C1
Nelson Place West	A2	St Mark's Road	C4
New Bond Street	B2	Saw Close	B3
New King Street	A2	Somerset Street	B4
New Orchard Street	C3	Southgate Street	C4
Norfolk Buildings	A3	South Parade	C3
Norfolk Crescent	A2	Spring Crescent	D4
North Parade	C3	Stall Street	C3
North Parade Road	D3	Sutton Street	D1
Oak Street	B4	Sydney Place	D1
Old Orchard	C1	Sydney Place	D2
Old Orchard Street	C3	The Circus	B1
Oxford Row	B1	Thornbank Gardens	A4
Parsonage Lane	B3	Thornbank Place	A4
Pierrepont Street	C3	Trim Street	B2
Powlett Road	D1	Union Passage	C2
Princes Street	B2	Union Street	B2
Pulteney Bridge	C2	Upper Borough Walls	B2
Pulteney Gardens	D3	Upper Bristol Road	A2
Pulteney Mews	D2	Upper Church Street	A1
Pulteney Road	D2	Walcot Street	C2
Queens Parade Place	B2	Wells Road	A4
Queen Square	B2	Westgate Buildings	B3
		Westgate Street	B3

Westmoreland Station Road	A4
Westmoreland Street	A4
Wood Street	B2
Wood Street	B4
York Street	C3

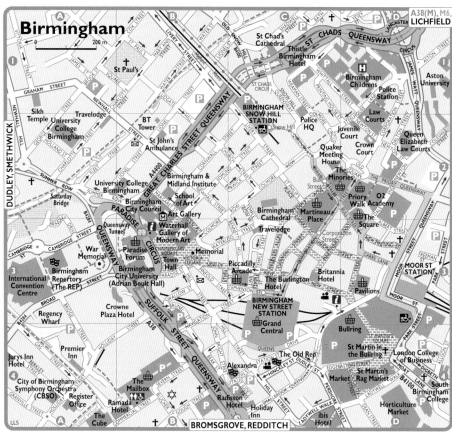

Albert Street D3
Allison Street D4
Aston Street D1
Barwick Street C2
Bath Street C1
Beak Street B4
Bennetts Hill C3
Berkley Street A4
Blucher Street B4
Bridge Street A3
Brindley Drive A3
Broad Street A3
Brook Street A1
Brunel Street B3
Bull Street C2
Cambridge Street A3
Cannon Street C3
Carrs Lane D3
Chamberlain Square B3
Charlotte Street A2
Cherry Street C2
Church Street B2
Colmore Circus
  Queensway C2
Colmore Row B3
Commercial Street B4
Cornwall Street B2
Corporation Street C3
Cox Street B1
Dale End D2

Dalton Street D2
Dean Street D4
Digbeth D4
Dudley Street C4
Eden Place B3
Edgbaston Street C4
Edmund Street B2
Ethel Street B3
Fleet Street A2
Freeman Street D3
Gas Street A4
George Street A2
Gloucester Street D4
Gough Street B4
Graham Street A1
Granville Street A4
Great Charles Street
  Queensway B2
High Street D3
Hill Street B3
Hinckley Street C4
Holland Street A2
Holliday Street A4
James Street A1
James Watt
  Queensway D1
John Bright Street B4
Ladywell Walk C4
Ladywell Walk D4
Lancaster Circus D1

Lionel Street B2
Livery Street B1
Lower Temple
  Street C3
Ludgate Hill B1
Margaret Street B2
Martineau Way C3
Mary Ann Street B1
Moat Lane D4
Moor Street D3
Moor Street
  Queensway D3
Navigation Street B4
Needless Lane C3
Newhall Hill A1
Newhall Street A1
Newhall Street B2
New Meeting Street D3
New Street B3
Newton Street D2
Old Snow Hill B1
Old Square D2
Paradise Circus A2
Paradise Street B3
Park Street D3
Park Street D4
Pershore Street C4
Pinfold Street B3
Printing House
  Street C1

Queens Drive C4
Queensway A3
Queensway Tunnel A3
St Chads Circus C1
St Chads
  Queensway C1
St Jude's Passage C4
St Martin's Square D4
St Philip's Place C2
Saturday Bridge A2
Severn Street B4
Shadwell Street C1
Smallbrook
  Queensway C4
Snow Hill
  Queensway C1
Station Street C4
Steelhouse Lane D2
Stephenson Street C3
Suffolk Street
  Queensway B3
Summer Row A2
Swallow Street B3
Temple Row C2
Temple Row West C2
Temple Street C3
The Priory
  Queensway D2
Union Street C3
Vesey Street D1

Victoria Square B3
Vittoria Street A1
Waterloo Street B3
Water Street B1
Weaman Street C1
Whittall Street C1

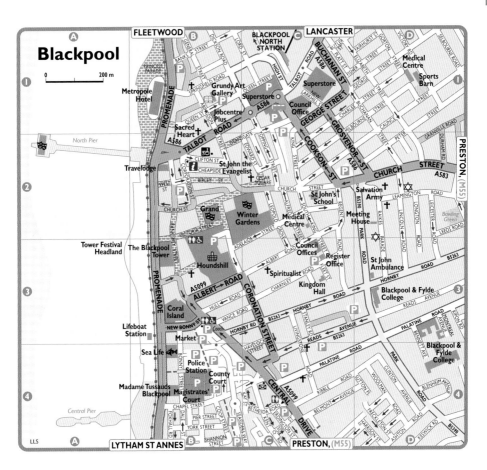

Abingdon Street B1
Adelaide Street..............B3
Albert Road....................B3
Albert Road....................C3
Alfred Street..................C2
Ashton Road D4
Bank Hey Street............B2
Banks Street B1
Belmont Avenue C4
Bennett Avenue D3
Bethesda Road..............C4
Birley Street B2
Blenheim Avenue..........D4
Bonny Street B4
Buchanan Street C1
Butler Street..................C1
Caunce Street................D1
Cedar Square................C2
Central Drive................C4
Chapel Street................C4
Charles Street...............C1
Charnley Road..............C3
Cheapside......................B2
Church Street...............B2
Church Street...............C2
Church Street...............D2
Clifton Street................B2
Clinton Avenue............D4
Cookson Street.............C2
Coop Street B4

Coronation Street C3
Corporation Street........B2
Dale Street B4
Deansgate B2
Dickson Road...............B1
Durham Road................D2
Edward Street...............C2
Elizabeth Street............D1
Fairhurst Street.............D1
Fisher Street..................C1
Fleet Street C3
Foxhall Road B4
Freckleton Street...........D4
General Street................B1
George Street................D1
Gorton Street................D1
Granville Road..............D2
Grosvenor Street..........C1
Harrison Street.............D4
Havelock Street.............C4
High Street C1
Hornby Road B3
Hornby Road D3
Hull Road......................B3
Kay Street C4
Kent Road C4
Keswick Road................D4
King Street.....................C2
Larkhill Street C1
Leamington Road..........D2

Leeds Road....................D2
Leicester Road..............D2
Leopold Grove C2
Lincoln Road................D2
Livingstone Road..........C3
Longton Road................D2
Lord Street....................B1
Louise Street.................C4
Milbourne Street...........C1
Montreal Avenue..........D3
New Bonny Street.........B3
New Larkhill Street.......C1
Palatine Road C4
Palatine Road D3
Park Road D2
Park Road D4
Peter Street...................D2
Pier Street.....................B4
Princess Parade.............B1
Promenade....................B1
Queen Street B1
Raikes Parade................D2
Reads Avenue................C3
Reads Avenue................D3
Regent Road C2
Ribble Road C4
Ripon Road...................D3
Seasiders Way B4
Seed Street C1
Selbourne Road.............D1

Shannon Street B4
South King Street.........C2
Springfield Road............B1
Stanley Road..................C3
Talbot Road B2
Talbot Road C1
Topping Street...............C2
Vance Road....................B3
Victoria Street...............B2
Victory Road..................D1
West Street....................B2
Woolman Road D4
York Street B4

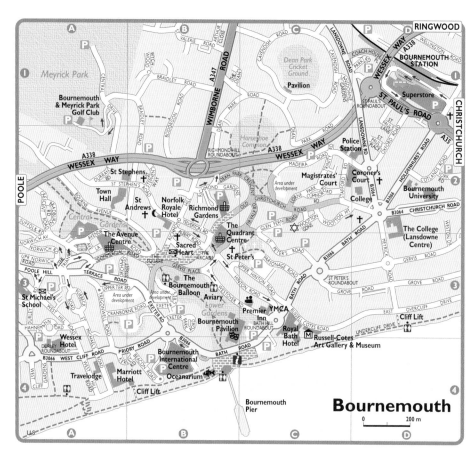

Bournemouth

0   200 m

Albert Road.................B3
Arthur Close................B1
Avenue Lane...............A3
Avenue Road...............A3
Bath Hill
  Roundabout C3
Bath Road B4
Beacon Road..............B4
Bodorgon Road..........B2
Bourne Avenue A2
Bradburne Road..........A2
Braidley Road..............B1
Cavendish Road..........C1
Central Drive...............A1
Christchurch Road D2
Coach House Place.....D1
Commercial Road........A3
Cotlands Road............D2
Cranborne Road.........A3
Crescent Road............A2
Cumnor Road.............C2
Dean Park Crescent.....B2
Dean Park Road..........B2
Durley Road................A3
Durley Roundabout......A4
Durrant Road..............A2
East Overcliff Drive.....D3
Exeter Crescent..........B3
Exeter Park Road........B3
Exeter Road B3

Fir Vale Road C2
Gervis Place B3
Gervis Road D3
Glen Fern Road..........C2
Grove Road C3
Hahnemann Road........A3
Hinton Road................B3
Holdenhurst Road.......D2
Kerley Road................A4
Lansdowne Gardens.....C1
Lansdowne Road..........C1
Lorne Park Road.........C2
Madeira Road.............C2
Meyrick Road..............D3
Norwich Avenue A3
Norwich Road A3
Old Christchurch
  Road C2
Orchard Street A3
Oxford Road...............D2
Park Road D1
Parsonage Road..........C3
Poole Hill A3
Priory Road A4
Purbeck Road.............A3
Richmond Gardens......B2
Richmond Hill.............B3
Richmond Hill
  Roundabout B2
Russell Cotes Road......C3

St Michael's Road A3
St Paul's Lane............D1
St Paul's Place............D2
St Paul's Road............D1
St Paul's Roundabout ..D1
St Peter's Road C3
St Peter's
  Roundabout C3
St Stephen's Road A2
St Stephen's Way B2
St Valerie Road............B1
Stafford Road C2
Suffolk Road A2
Terrace Road..............A3
The Arcade B3
The Deans..................B1
The Square B3
The Triangle A3
Tregonwell Road A3
Trinity Road................C2
Undercliff Drive...........D3
Upper Hinton Road......C3
Upper Norwich
  Road A3
Upper Terrace Road....A3
Wellington Road..........D1
Wessex Way A2
West Cliff Gardens......A4
West Cliff Road...........A4
West Hill Road............A3

Weston Drive D2
Westover Road............B3
Wimborne Road B1
Wootton Gardens C2
Wootton Mount...........C2
Wychwood Close.........B1
Yelverton Road............B2
York Road...................D2

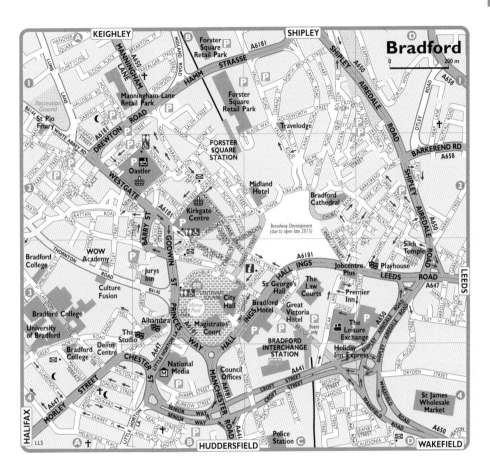

Aldermanbury	B3	Dale Street	B2	Hick Street	D2
Anne Gate	D2	Darfield Street	A1	Holdsworth Street	C1
Ann Place	B4	Darley Street	B2	Houghton Place	A1
Balme Street	C2	Drake Street	C3	Howard Street	A4
Bank Street	B2	Drewton Road	A2	Hustlergate	B3
Baptist Place	A2	Dryden Street	D4	Infirmary Street	A1
Barkerend Road	D2	Duke Street	B2	James Street	B2
Barry Street	B2	Dyson Street	A2	John Street	B2
Bedford Street	C4	East Parade	D3	Joseph Street	D3
Bolling Road	C4	East Place	C4	Kirkgate	B3
Bolton Road	C2	Edmund Street	A4	Komla Close	D2
Brearton Street	B1	Edward Street	C4	Lansdowne Place	A4
Bridge Street	C3	Eldon Place	A1	Leeds Road	D3
Britannia Street	C4	Field Street	C2	Leeming Street	C1
Broadway	C3	Filey Street	D3	Little Horton Lane	A4
Burnett Street	D2	Fulton Street	A2	Longcroft Link	A2
Burrow Street	B4	Garnett Street	D3	Lower Kirkgate	C2
Caledonia Street	D4	George Street	C3	Lumb Lane	A1
Canal Road	C1	Godwin Street	B2	Manchester Road	B4
Captain Street	C2	Goit Side	B3	Manningham Lane	A1
Carlton Street	A3	Granby Street	C4	Mannville Terrace	A4
Carroll Street	D3	Grattan Road	A2	Manor Row	B1
Carter Street	D4	Great Horton Road	A4	Market Street	B3
Cater Street	D2	Green Street	D3	Melbourne Place	A4
Centenary Square	B3	Grove Terrace	A4	Midland Road	B1
Chain Street	A2	Guy Street	C4	Mill Street	C1
Chandos Street	C3	Halfield Road	A1	Morley Street	B4
Chapel Street	D3	Hall Ings	B4	Neal Street	B4
Cheapside	B2	Hall Lane	D3	Nelson Street	B4
Chester Street	A4	Hamerton Street	D3	New Augustus Street	D4
Church Bank	C2	Hamm Strasse	B1	New John Street	A2
City Park	B3	Hanover Square	A1	Norfolk Gardens	B3
Claremont	A4	Hardy Street	C4	North Brook Street	C1
Croft Street	C4	Harris Street	D2	Northgate	B2
Cross Sun Street	C1	Heap Lane	D2	North Parade	B1
Currer Street	C2	Heaton Street	D4	North Street	C2

North Wing	D1	Thornton Road	A3
Nuttall Road	D2	Trafalgar Street	B1
Otley Road	D1	Tyrell Street	B3
Paradise Street	A2	Tyson Street	A1
Park Gate	D2	Upper Miller Gate	B3
Peckover Street	D2	Upper Park Gate	D2
Piccadilly	B2	Upper Piccadilly	B2
Pine Street	C2	Valley Road	C1
Portland Street	C4	Vaughan Street	A2
Priestley Street	C1	Vicar Lane	C3
Princes Way	B3	Vincent Street	A3
Quebec Street	B3	Wakefield Road	D4
Queen's Gate	B2	Wapping Road	D1
Radwell Drive	B4	Water Lane	A2
Randall Well Street	A3	Wellington Street	C2
Rawson Road	A2	Well Street	C2
Rawson Square	B2	Wenlock Street	D3
Rebecca Street	A2	Westend Street	A2
Sackville Street	B3	Westgate	A2
St Blaise Way	C1	West Street	C3
Salem Street	B1	Wharf Street	C1
Sawrey Place	B4	White Abbey Road	A1
Scoresby Street	D2	Wigan Street	A2
Senior Way	B4	Wilton Street	A4
Sharpe Street	B4		
Shipley Airedale Road	C1		
Simes Street	A2		
Snowden Street	B1		
Stone Street	B2		
Stott Hill	C2		
Sunbridge Road	A2		
Sunbridge Street	B3		
Sun Street	D1		
Swan Street	B4		
Sylhet Close	A1		
Tetley Street	A3		

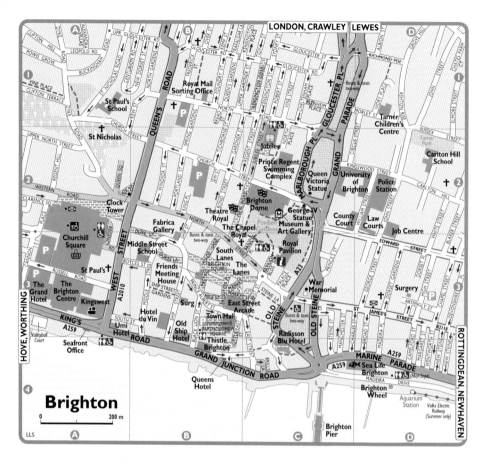

Brighton

0   200 m

Air Street A2
Albion Street D1
Alexandra Villas A1
Ardingly Street D3
Ashton Rise D1
Bartholomew
Square B3
Black Lion Street B3
Blaker Street D3
Blenheim Place C1
Bond Street B2
Boyces Street A3
Bread Street B1
Brighton Place B3
Brighton Square B3
Brills Lane C4
Broad Street D4
Buckingham Road A1
Camelford Street D4
Cannon Place A3
Carlton Hill D2
Centurion Road A1
Chapel Street D3
Charles Street C4
Chates Farm Court D1
Cheltenham Place C1
Church Street A1
Circus Street C2
Clifton Hill A1
Clifton Terrace A1

Devonshire Place D3
Dorset Place D3
Dukes Lane B3
Duke Street B2
Dyke Road A1
East Street C3
Edward Street C2
Elmore Street D1
Foundry Street B1
Frederick Street B1
Gardner Street B2
George Street D3
Gloucester Place C1
Gloucester Road B1
Gloucester Street C1
Grand Junction
Road B4
Grand Parade C2
Grove Hill D1
High Street D3
Ivory Place D1
Jew Street B2
John Street D2
Jubilee Street C2
Kemp Street B1
Kensington Gardens C1
Kensington Place C1
Kensington Street C1
Kew Street B1
King Place B2

King's Road A3
Kingswood Street C2
Leopold Road A1
Little East Street B4
Madeira Drive D4
Madeira Place D4
Manchester Street C4
Margaret Street D4
Marine Parade D4
Market Street B3
Market Street B3
Marlborough Place C2
Meeting House Lane B3
Middle Street B3
Morley Street D1
New Dorset Street B1
New Road B2
New Steine D4
Nile Street B3
North Gardens B1
North Place C2
North Road B1
North Street B2
Old Steine C3
Over Street B1
Palace Place C3
Pavilion Buildings C3
Portland Street B2
Powis Grove A1
Prince Albert Street B3

Princes Place C3
Prince's Street C3
Queen's Gardens B1
Queen Square A2
Queen's Road B2
Regency Road A2
Regent Hill A2
Regent Street C2
Robert Street C1
St George's Mews C1
St James's Street D3
St Nicholas Road A1
Ship Street B3
South Street A3
Spring Gardens B1
Steine Lane C3
Steine Street C4
Sussex Street D2
Sydney Street C1
Trafalgar Lane B1
Tichborne Street B2
Tidy Street C1
Upper Gardner
Street B1
Upper Gloucester
Road A1
Upper North Street A2
Vine Place A1
Vine Street C1
Wentworth Street D4

Western Road A2
West Street A3
White Street D3
William Street D2
Windsor Street B2

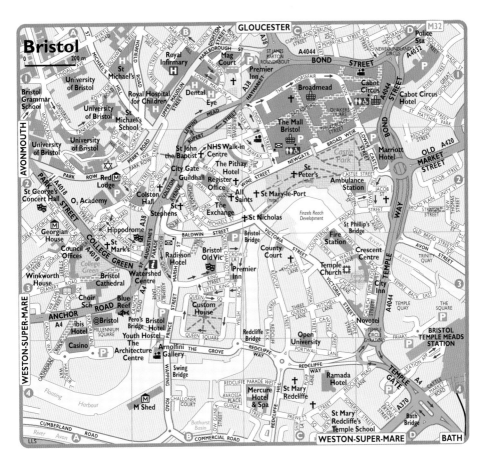

Alfred Hill B1
Anchor Road A3
Assembly Rooms Lane B3
Avon Street D3
Baldwin Street B2
Barossa Place B4
Bath Bridge D4
Bond Court C1
Bond Street D2
Brandon Steep A3
Bridewell Street B1
Bristol Bridge C3
Broadmead C1
Broad Plain D2
Broad Quay B3
Broad Street B2
Broad Weir C2
Brunswick Square C1
Canon's Road B3
Canons Way A3
Canynge Street C2
Castle Street C2
Cathedral Walk A4
Cattle Market Road D4
Challoner Court B4
Chatterton Street C4
Cheese Lane D2
Church Lane C3
Church Street D3
Clare Street B2
College Green A3
College Square A3
College Street A3
Colston Avenue B2
Colston Street B2
Commercial Road B4

Corn Street B2
Cottage Place B1
Counterslip C3
Crow Lane B3
Culver Street A4
Cumberland Road A4
Cumberland Street C1
Deanery Road A3
Denmark Street A3
Dighton Street B1
Eugene Street B1
Explore Lane A3
Fairfax Street C2
Ferry Street C3
Friary D3
Frog Lane A3
Frogmore Street A2
Great George Street A3
Great George Street D1
Guinea Street B4
Harbour Way A4
Haymarket C1
Hill Street A2
Horfield Road B1
Horton Street D1
Host Street B2
Houlton Street D1
Jacob Street D2
King Street B3
Leonard Lane B2
Lewins Mead B2
Little King Street B3
Lodge Street A2
Lower Castle Street D2
Lower Church Lane A2
Lower Lamb Street A3

Lower Maudlin Street B1
Lower Park Row B2
Low Guinea Street B4
Marlborough Hill B1
Marlborough Street B1
Marsh Street B3
Millennium Square A3
Mitchell Lane C3
Montague Street B1
Myrtle Road A1
Newfoundland Circus D1
Newgate C2
New Street D1
New Thomas Street D2
Old Bread Street D2
Old Market Street D2
Old Park Hill A2
Orange Street D1
Orchard Street A2
Park Row A2
Park Street A2
Passage Street C2
Pembroke Street C1
Penn Street C1
Pero's Bridge B3
Perry Road A2
Philadelphia Street C2
Pipe Lane B2
Portwall Lane C4
Prewett Street C4
Prince Street B3
Pump Lane C4
Quakers Friars C1
Queen Charlotte Street B3
Queen Square B3
Queen Street C2

Redcliff Back C3
Redcliffe Bridge C3
Redcliffe Hill C4
Redcliffe Parade West B4
Redcliffe Way C4
Redcliff Mead Lane C4
Redcliff Street C3
Redcross Street D2
River Street D2
Royal Fort Road A1
Rupert Street B2
Russ Street D2
St Augustine's Parade B1
St George's Road B2
St James Barton
   Roundabout C4
St Matthias Park C4
St Michael's Hill A1
St Michaels Street B3
St Phillip's Bridge A3
St Stephen's Street C1
St Thomas Street C3
Silver Street A1
Small Street B2
Somerset Square C2
Somerset Street D2
Southwell Street C3
Station Approach D2
Straight Street D2
Swing Bridge B4
Tankards Close A1
Telephone Avenue B2
Temple Back C3
Temple Back East D3
Temple Circle Gyratory D3
Temple Gate D4

Temple Quay D3
Temple Rose D3
Temple Street C3
Temple Way D3
Terrell Street B1
The Grove B4
The Horsefair C1
The Pithay C2
The Square D3
Thomas Lane C3
Three Queens Lane C3
Tower Hill D2
Trenchard Street A2
Trinity Quay D3
Tyndall Avenue A1
Union Street C1
Unity Street A3
Unity Street D2
University Walk A1
Upper Maudlin Street B1
Victoria Street C2
Wade Street D1
Wapping Road B4
Water Lane C3
Welsh Back B3
Whitson Street B1
Wine Street C2
Woodland Road A1

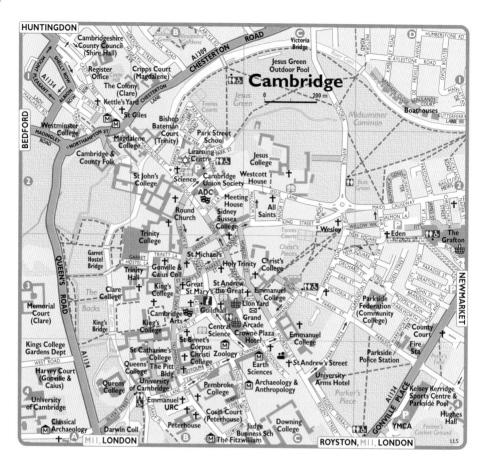

Adam and Eve Street ... D3
Albion Row A1
Auckland Road D2
Aylestone Road D1
Bailey Mews D2
Banhams Close D1
Beaulands Court D1
Belmont Place C2
Belvoir Road D1
Bene't Street B3
Botolph Lane B4
Brandon Place D3
Bridge Street B2
Brunswick Gardens D2
Brunswick Terrace D2
Burleigh Place D3
Carlyle Road B1
Castle Row A1
Castle Street A1
Chesterton Lane B1
Chesterton Road D2
Christchurch Street D3
City Road D3
Clarendon Street C3
Cutterferry Lane D1
De Freville Avenue D1
Downing Place C4
Downing Street B4
Drummer Street C3
Earl Street C3

Eden Street D3
Elm Street D3
Emmanuel Road C3
Fair Street D2
Fitzroy Lane D2
Fitzroy Street D3
Fitzwilliam Street B4
Garret Hostel Bridge ... A3
Garret Hostel Lane A3
Gonville Place D4
Grafton Street D3
Grant Place B4
Green Street B3
Hobson Street B3
Humberstone Road D1
James Street D3
Jesus Lane B2
Jesus Terrace D3
John Street D3
Kimberley Road D1
King's Bridge A3
King's Parade B3
King Street C2
Lady Margaret Road ... A1
Lower Park Street B2
Madingley Road A2
Magdalene Street B2
Magrath Avenue A1
Maids Causeway D2
Malcolm Street C2

Manhattan Drive D1
Manor Street C2
Market Street B3
Mill Lane B4
Mortimer Road D4
Mount Pleasant A1
Napier Street D2
New Park Street B2
New Square C2
Northampton Street A2
Orchard Street C3
Paradise Street D3
Parker Street C3
Park Parade B1
Parkside D3
Park Street B2
Park Terrace C4
Parsonage Street D2
Peas Hill B3
Pembroke Street B4
Pound Hill A1
Pretoria Road D1
Prospect Row D3
Queen's Road A3
Regent Street C4
Regent Terrace C4
Rose Crescent B3
St Andrew's Street C3
St John's Road B2
St Mary's Street B3

St Peter's Street A1
Salmon Lane D2
Shelly Row A1
Shop Street C2
Sidney Street B2
Silver Street A4
Sussex Street B3
Tennis Court Road B4
Tennis Court Terrace ... B4
Thompson's Lane B2
Trinity Lane B3
Trinity Street B2
Trumpington Street B4
Victoria Avenue C1
Victoria Bridge C1
Victoria Street C3
Warkworth Street D3
Warkworth Terrace D3
West Road A4
Willow Walk C2

University Colleges

Christ's College C3
Clare College A3
Corpus Christi
College B4
Darwin College A4
Downing College C4
Emmanuel College C3
Gonville &
Caius College B3
Jesus College C2
King's College B3
Magdalene College A2
Pembroke College B4
Peterhouse B4
Queens' College B4
St Catharine's College .. B4
St John's College B2
Sidney Sussex College .. B2
Trinity College B3
Westminster College ... A2

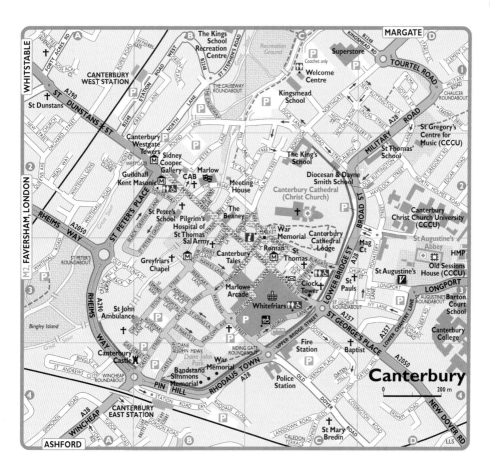

Adelaide Place...............B3	Edgar Road.....................D2	Monastery Street..........D3	St Augustine's	Tower Way.....................B2
Albert Road...................D3	Edward Road..................D3	New Dover Road...........D4	Roundabout...............D3	Tudor Road....................A4
Albion Place..................C2	Elgar Bretts Court.........B4	New Ruttington	St Dunstans Street.......A1	Union Street..................D1
All Saints Lane..............B2	Ersham Road..................D4	Lane..........................D1	St Edmunds Road........B3	Upper Bridge Street......C4
Alma Street...................D1	Gas Street......................A4	North Lane.....................B1	St Georges Lane...........C3	Vernon Place.................C4
Artillery Street.............C1	Gordon Road.................B4	Northgate......................C1	St George's Place.........C3	Victoria Row.................C1
Back Lane......................A3	Guildhall Street.............B2	Notley Street.................D1	St George's	Watling Street...............B3
Beercart Lane................B3	Havelock Street.............D2	Nunnery Fields..............C4	Roundabout...............C3	Westgate.......................A2
Best Lane......................B2	Hawks Lane...................B3	Oaten Hill......................C4	St George's Street........C3	White Horse Lane.........B3
Bingley Court................A4	Henry Court..................B4	Oaten Hill Place.............C4	St Gregory's Road.........D2	Whitefriars....................C2
Black Griffin Lane..........A3	High Street.....................B2	Old Dover Road............C4	St Johns Lane................B3	Whitehall Gardens.........A2
Borough........................C2	Hospital Lane................B3	Old Ruttington Lane D2	St Margaret's Street......B3	Whitehall Road.............A2
Broad Street..................D2	Ivy Lane.........................C3	Old Watling Street.........A3	St Marys Street.............B3	Wincheap......................A4
Burgate.........................C3	Jewry Lane....................B3	Orchard Street..............A2	St Peter's Grove............B3	Wincheap
Butter Market................C2	King Street.....................C2	Orient Place...................B1	St Peter's Lane..............B2	Roundabout...............A4
Caledon Terrace............C4	Kirby's Lane..................B1	Palace Street..................C2	St Peter's Place.............A3	York Road.....................A4
Canterbury Lane............C3	Lansdown Road.............C4	Parade...........................C2	St Peter's	
Castle Row....................B4	Linden Close..................A2	Pin Hill..........................B4	Roundabout...............A3	
Castle Street..................B3	Linden Grove.................A2	Pound Lane...................B2	St Peters Street.............B2	
Chaucer	Link Lane......................C3	Queens Avenue.............A2	Shepherdsgate...............B1	
Roundabout...............D1	Longport........................D3	Rheims Way...................A3	Station Road East...........B4	
Church Lane..................B3	Love Lane......................D3	Rhodaus Close...............B4	Station Road West.........A1	
Church Street................A1	Lower Bridge Street......C3	Rhodaus Town...............B4	Stour Street...................B3	
Cossington Road...........C4	Lower Chantry	Riding Gate	Sturry Road...................D1	
Craddock Drive..............D1	Lane..........................D4	Roundabout...............C4	Sun Street......................C2	
Creine Mill Lane	Marlowe Avenue...........B3	Rose Acre Close.............A1	The Causeway................B1	
North.........................A3	Mead Way......................A2	Rose Lane......................B3	The Causeway	
Dane John Mews............B4	Mercery Lane.................C3	Rosemary Lane..............B3	Roundabout...............B1	
Dover Street..................C3	Military Road.................D2	St Alphege Lane.............B2	The Friars.....................B2	
Duck Lane......................C1	Mill Lane.......................B1	St Andrews Close..........A4	Tourtel Road..................D1	

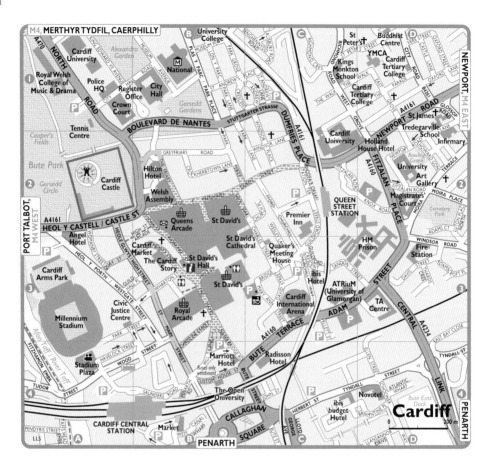

Adam Street................D3	Fitzalan Place................D2	Mill Lane........................B4	Salisbury Road..............C1
Adams Court................D2	Fitzalan Road................D2	Moira Place....................D2	Sandon Street................C3
Adamscroft Place........D3	Fitzhamon	Moira Terrace................D2	Saunders Road..............B4
Atlantic Wharf..............D4	Embankment..............A4	Museum Avenue............B1	Schooner Way................D4
Boulevard de Nantes....B2	Glossop Road................D1	Museum Place................B1	Senghennydd Road........C1
Bridge Street................C3	Greyfriars Road..............B2	Newport Road Lane....D2	Station Terrace..............C2
Brigantine Place............C3	Guildford Crescent......C3	North Luton Place........D2	Stuttgarter Strasse........B1
Bute Street....................C4	Guildford Street............C3	North Road....................A1	Taffs Mead
Bute Terrace................C3	Guildhall Place..............A3	Oxford Lane..................D1	Embankment..............A4
Callaghan Square..........B4	Havelock Street..............A4	Oxford Street................D1	Tharsis Crescent............D3
Caroline Street..............B3	Hayes Bridge Road......B3	Park Grove....................B1	The Friary......................B2
Castle Lane....................D1	Heol Siarl......................B2	Park Lane......................B1	The Hayes......................B3
Castle Street..................A2	Heol Y Castell..............A2	Park Place......................B1	The Parade....................D1
Central Link..................D2	Heol Y Frenhines..........B2	Park Street....................A3	The Walk........................C1
Charles Street................B2	Heol Y Porth................A3	Pellett Street................C3	Trinity Street................B3
Church Place................C2	Heole Glwys..................B3	Penarth Road................B4	Tudor Street..................A4
Churchill Way................C2	Herbert Street..............C4	Pendyris Street..............A4	Tyndall Street................D4
City Hall Road..............A1	High Street....................B3	Plas Y Parc....................B1	Vere Street....................D1
City Road......................D1	High Street Arcade......B2	Quay Street....................A3	Wesley Lane..................C2
Crockherbtown	Hills Street....................B3	Queen Street..................B2	West Canal Wharf........B4
Lane..........................B2	Howard Gardens..........D2	Rhodfa'r Orsaf..............C2	West Grove....................C1
Custom House	John Street....................C4	Richmond Crescent......C1	Westgate Street............A3
Street........................B4	King Edward VII	Richmond Road............C1	Wharton Street..............B3
David Street..................C3	Avenue......................A1	St Andrew's	Windsor Lane................C2
Davis Street..................D3	Knox Road....................D2	Crescent..................B1	Windsor Place................C1
Dumfries Place..............C2	Llansannor Drive..........D4	St Andrew's Lane..........C1	Windsor Road................D3
East Bay Close..............D3	Lloyd George	St Andrew's Place........B1	Womanby Street............A3
East Grove....................D1	Avenue......................C4	St John Street................B2	Wood Street..................A4
Ellen Street..................D4	Lon Y Parc....................B1	St Mary Street..............B3	Working Street..............B3
Fford Churchill..............C2	Mary Ann Street..........C3	St Peter's Street............C1	

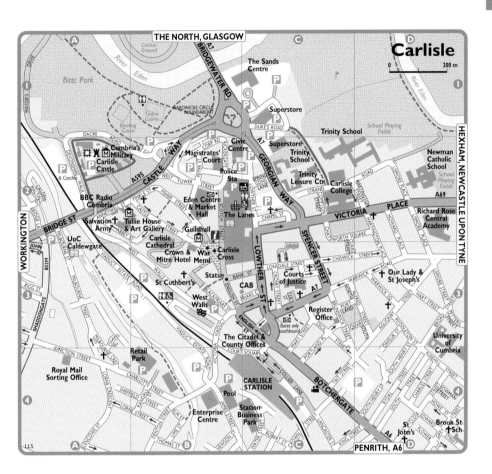

Abbey Street A2	Currie Street C3	Lorne Crescent A4	Viaduct Estate Road A3
Aglionby Street D3	Dacre Road A1	Lorne Street A4	Victoria Place C2
Annetwell Street A2	Denton Street B4	Lowther Street C2	Victoria Viaduct B4
Bank Street B3	Devonshire Walk A2	Mary Street C3	Warwick Road D3
Blackfriars Street B3	Duke's Road C1	Mayor's Drive A1	Warwick Square D3
Blencowe Street A4	Edward Street D4	Milbourne Crescent A3	Water Street C4
Botchergate C4	Elm Street B4	Milbourne Street A3	West Tower Street B2
Bowman Street D4	English Street B3	Myddleton Street D3	West Walls B3
Bridge Lane A2	Finkle Street B2	North Alfred Street D3	
Bridge Street A2	Fisher Street B2	Orfeur Street D3	
Bridgewater Road B1	Flower Street D4	Peter Street B2	
Broad Street D3	Friars Court C3	Petteril Street D3	
Brunswick Street C3	Fusehill Street D4	Portland Place C4	
Caldew Maltings A2	Georgian Way C2	Portland Square C3	
Castle Street B2	Grey Street D4	Randall Street B4	
Castle Way B2	Hartington Place D2	Rickergate B2	
Cecil Street C3	Hartington Street D2	Rigg Street A3	
Chapel Place A3	Hart Street D3	Robert Street C4	
Chapel Street C2	Hewson Street B4	Rydal Street D4	
Charles Street D4	Howard Place D2	Scotch Street B2	
Charlotte Street A4	Howe Street D4	Sheffield Street A4	
Chatsworth Square C2	James Street B4	South Alfred Street D3	
Chiswick Street C3	John Street A3	South Henry Street D4	
Close Street D4	Junction Street A4	Spencer Street C2	
Collier Lane C4	King Street C4	Spring Gardens	
Compton Street C2	Lancaster Street C4	Lane............................. C2	
Corporation Road B2	Lime Street B4	Strand Road C2	
Court Square B4	Lismore Place D2	Tait Street C4	
Crosby Street C3	Lismore Street D3	Thomas Street B4	
Crown Street C4	Lonsdale Street C3		

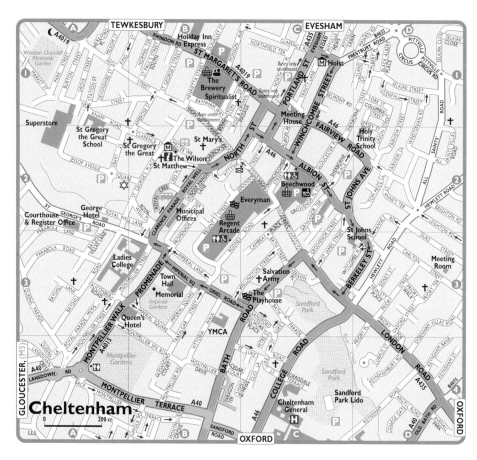

Albert Place	D1
Albion Place	C2
Albion Street	C2
All Saints' Road	D2
All Saints' Villas Road	D2
Ambrose Street	B1
Argyll Road	D4
Avenal Park	D4
Back Montpellier Terrace	A4
Bath Parade	C3
Bath Road	B4
Bath Street	C3
Bathville Mews	C4
Baynham Way	B1
Bayshill Lane	A3
Bayshill Road	A3
Bayshill Villas Lane	A3
Belmont Road	C1
Belmore Place	C3
Bennington Street	B1
Berkeley Street	C3
Black Albert Place	D1
Brighton Road	D2
Burton Street	A1
Cambray Place	C3
Carlton Street	D3
Cedar Court	B4
Chester Walk	B2
Church Street	B2
Clarence Parade	B2
Clarence Road	C1
Clarence Street	B2
College Gate	D4
College Road	C4
Columbia Street	D1

Corpus Street	D4
Crescent Place	B2
Crescent Terrace	B2
Devonshire Street	A1
Duke Street	D3
Dunalley Street	B1
Evesham Road	C1
Fairview Close	D2
Fairview Road	C2
Fairview Street	D2
Fauconberg Road	A3
Glenfall Street	D1
Glesanda Court	B4
Gloucester Place	C2
Grosvenor Place South	C3
Grosvenor Street	C3
Grosvenor Terrace	C3
Grove Street	A1
Henrietta Street	B1
Hereford Place	A1
Hewlett Place	D3
Hewlett Road	D3
High Street	A1
High Street	C2
Imperial Lane	B3
Imperial Square	B3
Jersey Street	D1
Jessop Avenue	A2
Keynsham Bank	D4
Keynshambury Road	D4
Keynsham Road	D4
Keynsham Street	D4
King Street	A1
Knapp Road	A1
Lansdown Crescent	A4
Lansdown Road	A4

Leighton Road	D2
London Road	D3
Malden Road	D1
Market Street	A1
Milsom Street	A1
Mitre Street	C4
Monson Avenue	B1
Montpellier Drive	B4
Montpellier Grove	B4
Montpellier Parade	B4
Montpellier Spa Road	B4
Montpellier Street	A4
Montpellier Terrace	A4
Montpellier Walk	A4
New Street	A1
Normal Terrace	B1
Northfield Terrace	C1
North Place	C1
North Street	B2
Old Bath Road	D4
Olio Lane	C4
Oriel Road	B3
Orrisdale Terrace	C4
Oxford Street	D3
Parabola Lane	A3
Parabola Road	A3
Paragon Terrace	B4
Park Street	C2
Pittville Circus	D1
Pittville Circus Road	D1
Pittville Lawn	C1
Pittville Mews	C1
Pittville Street	B2
Portland Square	D1
Portland Street	C1
Post Office Lane	B2

Prestbury Road	C1
Priory Parade	D3
Priory Place	D4
Priory Street	D3
Priory Terrace	D3
Priory Walk	D3
Promenade	B3
Queens Lane	A4
Queens Parade	A3
Regent Street	B2
Rodney Road	B3
Rose & Crown Passage	B1
Royal Crescent	B2
Royal Parade Mews	A4
Royal Well	B2
Royal Well Lane	A2
Royal Well Place	B2
St Anne's Road	D2
St Anne's Terrace	D2
St George's Place	B2
St George's Road	A2
St George's Street	B1
St James' Square	A2
St James Street	C3
St Johns Avenue	C2
St Luke's	C4
St Luke's Place	C3
St Luke's Road	C4
St Margaret's Road	B1
St Paul's Street South	B1
Sandford Road	B4
Sandford Street	C3
Selkirk Close	D1
Selkirk Street	D1
Sherborne Place	C2
Sherborne Street	C2

Sidney Street	D3
Station Street	A1
Suffolk Parade	B4
Swindon Road	B1
Sydenham Villas Road	D3
Tom Price Close	D2
Trafalgar Street	B4
Trinity Lane	C1
Union Street	D2
Vernon Place	C3
Vittoria Walk	B4
Wellington Street	C3
Winchcombe Street	C2
Winstonian Road	D2
Witcombe Place	C3
York Street	D1

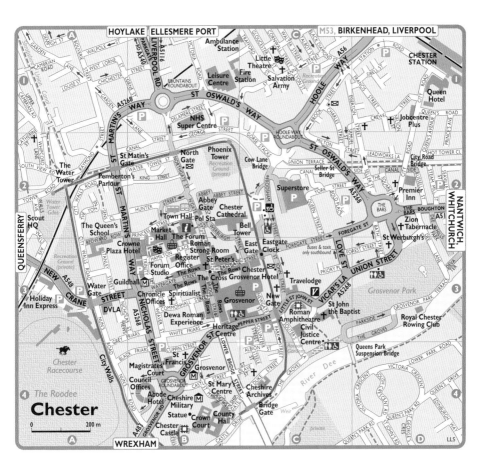

Chester

Abbey Square	B2	Delamere Street	B1	Little St John Street	C3	Raymond Street A2	The Square D2
Abbey Street	B2	Denbigh Street	A1	Liverpool Road	B1	Russell Street D2	The Yonne A2
Albion Street	C4	Deva Terrace	D3	Lorne Street	A1	St Anne Street C1	Tower Road A2
Bath Street	D2	Duke Street	C4	Louise Street	A1	St George's Crescent .. D4	Trafford Street C1
Bedward Row	A3	Eastgate Street	B3	Love Street	C3	St John's Road D4	Trinity Street B3
Black Diamond		Edinburgh Way	D4	Lower Bridge Street	B4	St John Street C3	Union Street D3
Street	C1	Egerton Street	C1	Lower Park Road	D4	St Martin's Way A2	Union Terrace C2
Black Friars	A4	Foregate Street	C2	Lyon Street	C1	St Mary's Hill B4	Upper Cambrian
Bold Place	C2	Forest Street	C3	Milton Street	C2	St Olave Street C4	Road A1
Boughton	D2	Fountains Roundabout	B1	Nelson Street	D1	St Oswald's Way B1	Vicar's Lane C3
Bouverie Street	A1	Francis Street	D1	New Crane Street	A3	St Werburgh Street B2	Victoria Crescent D4
Bridge Street	B3	Frodsham Street	C2	Newgate Street	C3	Samuel Street C2	Victoria Road B1
Brook Street	C1	Garden Lane	A1	Nicholas St Mews	A3	Seaville Street D2	Volunteer Street C3
Cambrian Road	A1	George Street	B2	Nicholas Street	B3	Seller Street D2	Walls Avenue A2
Canal Side	C2	Gloucester Street	C1	Northgate Street	B2	Seller Street Bridge C2	Walpole Street A1
Canal Street	B2	Gorse Stacks	C2	Nun's Road	A3	Sens Close A2	Walter Street C1
Castle Drive	B4	Grey Friars	A4	Parkside	D3	Shipgate Street B4	Watergate Street B3
Castle Street	B4	Grosvenor Park		Park Street	C3	Shot Tower Close...... D2	Water Tower Street .. B2
Catherine Street	A2	Terrace	D3	Pepper Street	C3	Sibell Street D1	Weaver Street B3
Charles Street	C1	Grosvenor Road	B4	Prince's Avenue	D2	Souter's Lane C3	West Lorne Street A1
Chichester Street	A1	Grosvenor		Princess Street	C3	South Crescent		White Friars B3
City Road	D2	Roundabout	B4	Priory Place	C3	Road D4	York Street C2
City Walls Road	A2	Grosvenor Street	B4	Queen's Avenue	D2	South View Road A2	
Commonhall Street	B3	Hamilton Place	B3	Queen's Drive	D1	Stanley Street A3	
Cornwall Street	C1	Hoole Way	C1	Queen's Park Road	C4	Station Road D1	
Cow Lane Bridge	C2	Hoole Way		Queens Park		Steam Mill Street D2	
Crewel Street	D1	Roundabout	C2	Suspension Bridge	D4	Steele Street C4	
Cuppin Street	B4	Hunter Street	B2	Queen's Road	D1	Talbot Street C1	
Dee Hills Park	D2	King Street	B2	Queen Street	C2	The Bars D2	
Dee Lane	D2	Leadworks Lane	D2	The Groves	C4		

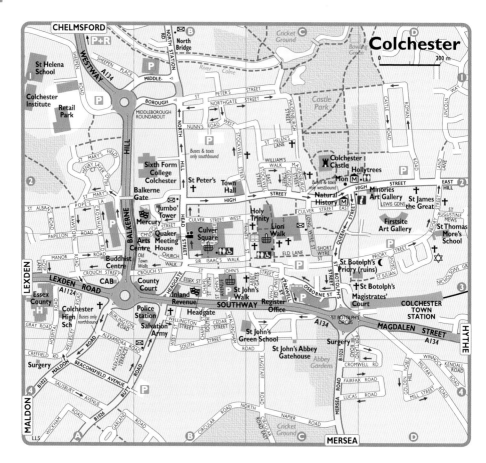

Abbey Gates C3
Alexandra Road............. A3
Alexandra Terrace.......... A4
Balkerne Hill................. A3
Beaconsfield Avenue...... A4
Burlington Road............. A3
Butt Road..................... A4
Castle Road.................. D1
Cedar Street................. B3
Chapel Street
  North........................ B3
Chapel Street South B3
Church Street................ B3
Church Walk B3
Circular Road East........ C4
Circular Road
  North........................ B4
Creffield Road............... A4
Cromwell Road C4
Crouch Street................ A3
Crouch Street................ B3
Crowhurst Road A2
Culver Street East........ C2
Culver Street West....... B2
East Hill D2
East Stockwell Street ... C2
Eld Lane C3
Essex Street................. B3
Fairfax Road C4
Flagstaff Road............... C4

Garland Road................ A4
George Street............... C2
Golden Noble Hill......... D4
Gray Road.................... A3
Headgate B3
Head Street.................. B2
Henry Laver Court........ A2
High Street................... B2
Hospital Road A4
Hospital Lane A3
Kendall Road D4
Land Lane.................... D2
Lewis Gardens D2
Lexden Road................. A3
Lincoln Way D1
Long Wyre Street.......... C2
Lucas Road C4
Magdalen Street........... D3
Maidenburgh
  Street....................... C1
Maldon Road................ A4
Manor Road.................. A3
Mersea Road................ C4
Middleborough.............. B1
Middleborough
  Roundabout A1
Military Road................ D4
Mill Street D4
Napier Road................. C4
Nicholsons Green......... D3

North Bridge................. B1
Northgate Street........... B1
North Hill..................... B1
North Station Road....... B1
Nunn's Road................ B1
Osborne Street C3
Papillon Road............... A3
Pope's Lane................. A2
Portland Road............... C4
Priory Street D3
Queen Street C3
Rawstorn Road............. A2
Roman Road................. D1
St Alban's Road............ A2
St Augustine Mews....... D2
St Botolph's Circus....... C3
St Botolph's Street....... C3
St Helen's Lane............ C2
St John's Avenue.......... B3
St John's Street............ B3
St Julian Grove............. D3
St Mary's Fields........... A2
St Peter's Street........... B1
Salisbury Avenue.......... A4
Sheepen Place A1
Sheepen Road.............. A1
Short Wyre Street C3
Sir Isaac's Walk........... B3
South Street B4
Southway...................... B3

Stanwell Street............. C3
Trinity Street................. B2
Walsingham Road......... B3
Wellesley Road............. A4
Wellington Street.......... B3
West Stockwell
  Street....................... B1
West Street.................. B4
Westway....................... A1
Whitewell Road............. C3
Wickham Road.............. A4
William's Walk.............. C2
Winnock Road.............. D4

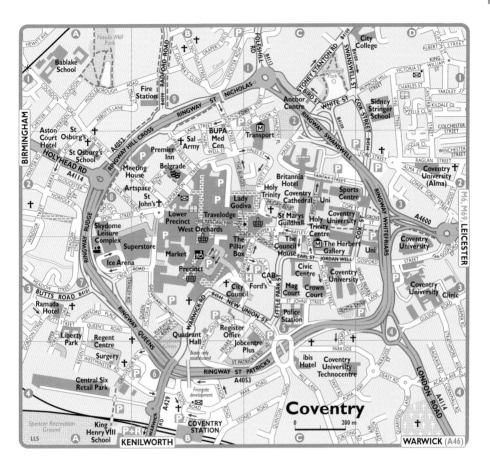

Abbotts Lane	A1	Draper's Field	B1	Lamb Street	B2	Queen Victoria
Acacia Avenue	D4	Earl Street	C3	Leicester Row	B1	Road	B3
Albert Street	D1	Eaton Road	B4	Little Park Street	C3	Quinton Road	C4
Alma Street	D2	Fairfax Street	C2	London Road	D4	Radford Road	B1
Barras Lane	A2	Far Gosford Street	D3	Lower Ford Street	D2	Raglan Street	D2
Bayley Lane	C2	Foleshill Road	C1	Lower Holyhead		Regent Street	A4
Bird Street	C1	Ford Street	D2	Road	A2	Ringway Hill Cross	A2
Bishop Street	B1	Friars Road	B4	Manor House Road	B4	Ringway Queens	A3
Bond Street	B2	Furlong Road	C4	Manor Road	B4	Ringway Rudge	A3
Broadgate	B2	Gazelle Close	D1	Meadow Street	A3	Ringway St Nicholas	B1
Butts Road	A3	Gloucester Street	A2	Meriden Street	A1	Ringway St Patricks	B4
Butts Street	A3	Gordon Street	A4	Middleborough		Ringway Swanswell	C1
Canterbury Street	D1	Gosford Street	D3	Road	A1	Ringway Whitefriars	D2
Chapel Street	B2	Greyfriars Lane	B3	Mile Lane	C4	Rodyard Way	D4
Charles Street	D1	Greyfriars Road	B3	Mill Street	A1	St Columba's Close	B1
Chauntry Place	C1	Grosvenor Road	A4	Minster Road	C4	St Johns Street	C3
Chester Street	A2	Grove Street	D2	Much Park Street	C3	St Nicholas Street	B1
Cheylesmore	C3	Gulson Road	D3	New Union Street	B3	St Patrick's Road	B3
Clifton Street	D1	Hales Street	C2	Norfolk Street	A2	Salt Lane	C3
Colchester Street	D1	Harper Road	D3	Paradise Street	A2	Seagrave Road	D4
Cook Street	C1	Hay Lane	C3	Park Road	B4	Short Street	C4
Cope Street	C2	Hertford Place	A3	Parkside	C4	Silver Street	C2
Cornwall Road	D4	Hewitt Avenue	A1	Pepper Lane	C2	Spon Street	A2
Corporation Street	B2	High Street	C3	Percy Street	A2	Stanley Road	A3
Coundon Road	A1	Hill Street	B2	Primrose Hill Street	D1	Stoney Road	B4
Coundon Street	A1	Hodd Street	D2	Priory Row	C2	Stoney Stanton
Cox Street	D1	Holyhead Road	A2	Priory Street	C2	Road	C1
Cox Street	D2	Jordan Well	C3	Puma Way	C4	Strathmore Avenue	D3
Croft Road	A3	Kildale Close	D1	Quarfield Lane	D4	Swanswell Street	C1
Deasy Road	D4	King William Street	D1	Queen's Road	A3	Swift Road	C4
The Burges	B2
The Precinct	B2
Tower Street	B1
Trinity Street	C2
Upper Hill Street	B2
Upper Wells Street	A4
Upper York Street	A2
Victoria Street	D1
Vine Street	D1
Vogue Close	D2
Warwick Road	B3
Warwick Road	B4
Warwick Row	B3
Watch Close	A2
Well Street	B2
Westminster Road	A4
White Friars Lane	C3
White Friars Street	D3
White Street	C1
Winchester Street	D2
Windsor Street	A3
Yardley Street	D1
York Street	A3

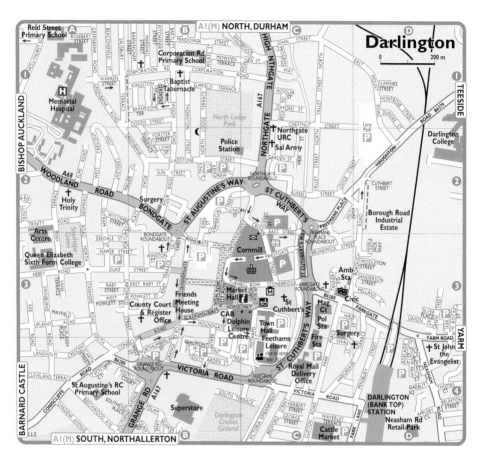

Abbey Road	A3	East Raby Street	B3	King Street	B2	Progress Way	C1	Union Street	B2
Adelaide Street	D4	East Street	C3	Kitchener Street	B1	Quaker Lane	B4	Uplands Road	A3
Albert Street	D4	Elmfield Terrace	B1	Langholm Crescent	A4	Quebec Street	C2	Valley Street North	C2
Appleby Close	D4	Elms Road	A2	Larchfield Street	A3	Raby Street	A3	Vane Terrace	A2
Barningham Street	B1	Eskdale Street	A3	Lodge Street	C2	Raby Terrace	B3	Victoria Embankment	C4
Bartlett Street	B1	Feethams	C4	Lowe Street	B2	Rocket Street	D3	Victoria Road	B4
Beaconsfield Street	A1	Feethams Roundabout	C4	Marshall Street	B1	Rockingham Street	C4	Warren Street	A1
Beaumont Street	B2	Fife Road	A3	Maude Street	A2	Rosebery Street	A1	Waverley Terrace	C4
Beaumont Street West	B1	Forster Street	B2	Mayfield	A3	Russell Street	C2	Weir Street	C2
Beck Road	C1	Four Riggs	B2	Melland Street	D3	St Augustine's Way	B2	Westbrook Way	C1
Bedford Street	B2	Freemans Place	C2	Middleton Street	D3	St Cuthbert's Way	C2	Westcliffe Court	A4
Beechwood Avenue	A4	Freemans Place		Montrose Street	D1	St James Place	D4	West Crescent	A2
Blackwellgate	B3	Roundabout	C3	Mowden Street	C1	Salisbury Terrace	A1	West Powlett Street	A3
Bondgate	B3	Garbutt Square	D4	Mowden Terrace	B1	Salt Yard	B3	West Row	B3
Bondgate Roundabout	B3	Garden Street	C2	Napier Street	A3	Sanderson Street	D3	West Street	B4
Borough Road	D3	George Street	C2	Neasham Road	D4	Scarth Street	A4	Wilkes Street	B1
Branksome Terrace	B1	Gladstone Street	B2	Northgate	C2	Selbourne Terrace	B2	Winston Street	B3
Brunswick Street	C3	Grange Road	B4	Northgate Roundabout	C2	Silver Place	D2	Woodland Road	A2
Brunton Street	D4	Grange Road		North Lodge Terrace	B2	Skinnergate	B3	Wooler Street	C1
Burleigh Place	A3	Roundabout	B4	Northumberland Street	B4	South Arden Street	B4	Wycombe Street	A2
Chestnut Street	C1	Greenbank Road	A1	Oakdene Avenue	A4	Southend Avenue	A4	Yarm Road	D3
Church Row	C2	Green Street	D3	Outram Street	A2	Southend Place	A4		
Cleveland Terrace	A4	Hargreave Terrace	C4	Oxford Street	C1	South Terrace	B4		
Clifton Road	C4	Haughton Road	C2	Parkgate	D3	Stanhope Road North	A2		
Commercial Street	B2	Herbert Street	C4	Parkgate Roundabout	C3	Stanhope Road South	A3		
Coniscliffe Road	A4	High Northgate	C1	Park Lane	D4	Stonebridge	C3		
Corporation Road	B1	High Row	B3	Park Place	C4	Sun Street	B2		
Crown Street	C2	Hilda Street	C2	Peel Street	D3	Swan Street	C4		
Cuthbert Street	D2	Hird Street	C3	Pendower Street	B1	Swinburne Road	A3		
Derwent Street	B1	Hollyhurst Road	A1	Pensbury Street	D4	Tannery Yard	C3		
Dodds Street	B1	Horse Market	B3	Polam Lane	B4	Thomas Court	D4		
Duke Street	A3	Houndgate	B3	Polam Road	B4	Thornton Street	B1		
Dumfries Street	D1	Jack Way Steeple	D3	Portland Place	A3	Trinity Mews	A2		
Dundee Street	D1	John Street	C1	Powlett Street	B3	Trinity Road	A2		
Easson Road	B1	Kendrew Street	B2	Priestgate	C3	Tubwell Row	B3		
East Mount Road	D1	Kingston Street	B1	Princes Street	D4	Union Place	D3		

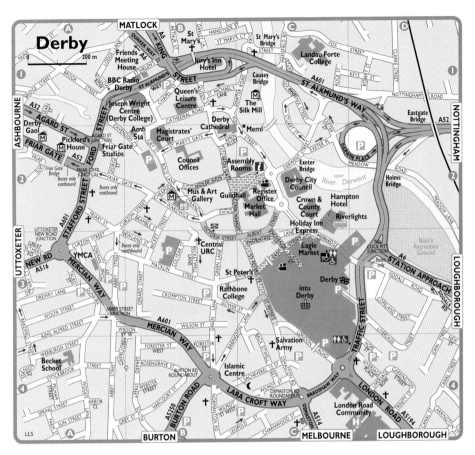

Derby

Abbey Street	A4	Cheapside	B2
Abbotsbarn Close	A4	Clarke Street	D1
Agard Street	A3	Colyear Street	B3
Agard Street Junction	A2	Copeland Street	D3
Albert Street	C3	Corn Market	B2
Albion Street	C3	Crompton Street	B3
Alice Street	C1	Curzon Street	A2
Amen Alley	B2	Darley Lane	B1
Arbor Close	A4	Darwin Place	C2
Arthur Street	B1	Derwent Street	C2
Babington Lane	B4	Drewry Court	A3
Back Sitwell Street	C4	Drewry Lane	A3
Bakewell Street	A3	Duke Street	C1
Becket Street	B3	Dunkirk	A3
Becketwell Lane	B3	East Street	C3
Bold Lane	B2	Eastgate Bridge	D1
Bradshaw Way	C4	Edensor Square	A4
Bramble Street	B2	Exchange Street	C3
Bridge Street	B1	Exeter Bridge	C2
Brook Street	A1	Exeter Place	C2
Burton Road	B4	Exeter Street	C2
Burton Road		Farm Street	A4
Roundabout	B4	Ford Street	A2
Canal Street	D4	Forester Street	
Carrington Street	D4	West	B4
Cathedral Road	B2	Forester Street	B4
Causey Bridge	C1	Forman Street	A3
Cavendish Court	A2	Fox Street	C1
Chapel Street	B1	Friar Gate	A2
Charnwood Street	C4	Friar Gate Junction	A2
Friary Street	A2	Mercian Way	B3
Full Street	B1	Monk Street	A3
George Street	A2	Morledge	C3
Gerard Street	B3	Newland Street	A3
Gower Street	B3	New Road	A3
Great Northern		New Street	D4
Road	A3	Nottingham Road	D1
Green Lane	B3	Nuns Street	A1
Grey Street	A4	Osmaston Road	C4
Handyside Street	B1	Osmaston Road	
Harcourt Street	B4	Roundabout	C4
Holms Bridge	D2	Pelham Street	A4
Hope Street	D4	Phoenix Street	C1
Iron Gate	B2	Quaker Way	B1
John Street	D4	Queen Street	B1
Jury Street	B2	Robert Street	D1
Keys Street	D1	Rosengrave Street	B4
King Alfred Street	A3	Sacheverel Street	C4
King Street	B1	Sadler Gate	B2
Lara Croft Way	B4	St Alkmund's Way	C1
Leopold Street	B4	St Helen's Street	A1
Liversage Place	D4	St Mary's Bridge	C1
Liversage Row	D4	St Mary's Court	B1
Liversage Street	D3	St Mary's Gate	B2
Lodge Lane	A1	St Michael's Lane	B1
London Road	C3	St Peter's Street	C3
Macklin Street	B3	Searl Street	A1
Mansfield Road	C1	Siddals Road	D3
Meadow Lane	D2	Sowter Road	C1
Meadow Road	D2	Spring Street	A4
Stafford Street	A3		
Station Approach	D3		
Stockbrook Street	A4		
Strand	B2		
Stuart Street	C1		
Sun Street	A4		
Talbot Street	A3		
The Cock Pitt			
Junction	D3		
Thorntree Lane	C3		
Traffic Street	D4		
Trinity Street	D4		
Uttoxeter New Road			
Junction	A3		
Victoria Street	B2		
Wardwick	B2		
Webster Street	B4		
Werburgh Street	A4		
West Wilmot Street	B4		
Willow Row	A1		
Wilmot Street	C4		
Wilson Street	B3		
Wilson Street West	A3		
Wolfa Street	A3		
Woods Lane	A4		

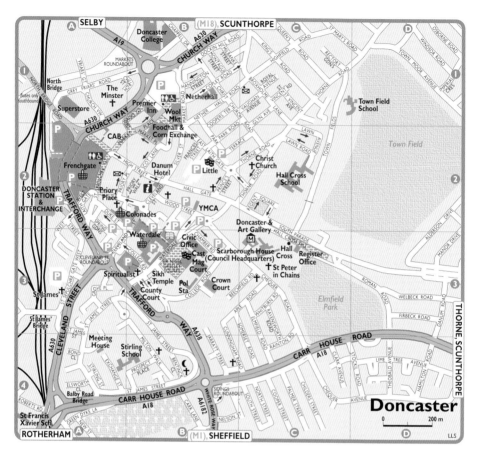

Doncaster

0   200 m

Alderson Drive D3
Apley Road B3
Balby Road Bridge.......... A4
Beechfield Road............. B3
Bentinck Close B4
Bond Close..................... A4
Broxholme Lane............. C1
Carr House Road C4
Carr Lane....................... B4
Chamber Road B3
Chappell Drive................ B1
Chequer Avenue............. C4
Chequer Road C3
Childers Street C4
Christ Church Road........ B1
Church Street A1
Church View A1
Church Way................... B1
Clark Avenue................. C4
Cleveland Street............ A4
Cleveland Street
  Roundabout A3
College Road................. B3
Cooper Street C4
Coopers Terrace B2
Copley Road B1
Cunningham Road........... B3
Danum Road C2
Dockin Hill Road B1
Duke Street................... A2

East Laith Gate B2
Elmfield Road C3
Elsworth Close A4
Exchange Street............. A4
Firbeck Road D3
Frances Street............... B2
Friars' Gate.................... A1
Georges Gate B2
Glyn Avenue C2
Green Dyke Lane........... A4
Grey Friars' Road.......... A1
Grove Place A3
Hall Cross Hill............... C2
Hall Gate....................... B2
Hamilton Road............... D4
Hannington Street.......... B1
High Street A2
Highfield Road C1
Imperial Crescent D1
Jarratt Street B4
King's Road C1
Lawn Avenue C2
Lawn Road C2
Lime Tree Avenue.......... D4
Manor Drive.................. D3
Market Place................. A2
Market Road................. B1
Markets
  Roundabout B1
Milbanke Street............. B1

Milton Walk B4
Montague Street............ B1
Nelson Street................ B4
Nether Hall Road B1
New Street A4
North Bridge................. A1
North Bridge Road........ A1
North Street C4
Osborne Road D1
Palmer Street................ C4
Park Road B2
Park Terrace................. B2
Prince's Street............... B2
Priory Place A2
Priory Walk................... B2
Prospect Place B4
Queen's Road C1
Rainton Road C4
Ravensworth Road......... C3
Rectory Gardens........... C1
Regent Square C2
Roberts Road................ A4
Roman Road D3
Royal Avenue................ C1
St James Street B4
St James's Bridge A3
St Mary's Road.............. C1
St Sepulchre Gate A2
St Sepulchre Gate
  West A3

St Vincent Avenue......... C1
St Vincent Road C1
Scot Lane B2
Sidings Roundabout....... B4
Silver Street.................. B2
Somerset Road B3
South Parade................ C2
South Street C4
Spring Gardens A2
Stirling Street A4
Stockil Road C4
Theobald Avenue.......... D4
Thorne Road................. C1
Thorne Road................. C2
Town Fields.................. C2
Town Moor Avenue D1
Trafford Way................ A2
Vaughan Avenue............ C1
Waterdale..................... B3
Welbeck Road D3
West Laith Gate A2
West Street A3
Whitburn Road C3
White Rose Way B4
Windsor Road D1
Wood Street................. B2

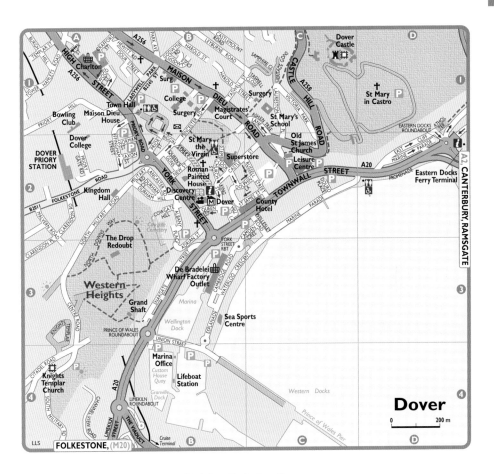

Dover

0 _____ 200 m

Adrian Street...................B3
Albany Place B2
Ashen Tree Lane............C1
Athol Terrace..................D1
Biggin Street...................B2
Burgh Hill.......................A1
Cambridge Road B3
Camden Crescent.........C2
Castle Hill Road C1
Castlemount Road.........B1
Castle Street..................B2
Centre Road..................A3
Channel View Road.......A4
Church Street................B2
Citadel Road..................A4
Clarendon Place............A3
Clarendon Road.............A2
Cowgate Hill..................B2
Crafford Street..............A1
Dolphin Lane..................B2
Douro Place..................C2
Dour Street...................A1
Durham Close.................B2
Durham Hill....................B2
East Cliff........................D2
Eastern Docks
  Roundabout.................D2
Effingham Street A2
Esplanade........................B3
Folkestone Road............A2

Godwyne Close..............B1
Godwyne Road...............B1
Harold Street.................B1
Heritage Gardens...........C1
Hewitt Road..................A1
High Street.....................A1
King Street......................B2
Knights Templar A3
Ladywell.........................A1
Lancaster Road...............B2
Laureston Place C1
Leyburne Road B1
Limekiln Roundabout.... A4
Limekiln Street A4
Maison Dieu Road B1
Malvern Road.................A2
Marine Parade................C2
Marine Parade................D2
Military Road..................B2
Mill Lane.........................B2
New Street......................B2
Norman Street................A2
North Downs Way A3
North Military Road A3
Park Avenue...................B1
Park Street......................B1
Pencester Road..............B2
Peter Street....................A1
Prince of Wales
  Roundabout.................B3

Priory Gate Road..........A2
Priory Hill A1
Priory Road....................A1
Priory Street B2
Promenade......................D2
Queen's Gardens............B2
Queen Street..................B2
Russell Street..................B2
St James Street B2
Samphire Close...............C1
Saxon Street...................A2
Snargate Street...............B3
South Military Road.......A4
Stembrook......................B2
Taswell Close.................C1
Taswell Street.................B1
Templar Street................A1
The Viaduct....................A4
Tower Hamlets
  Road............................A1
Townwall Street.............C2
Union Street....................B3
Victoria Park C1
Waterloo Crescent.......B3
Wellesley Road...............C2
Wood Street...................A1
York Street.....................B2
York Street
  Roundabout.................B3

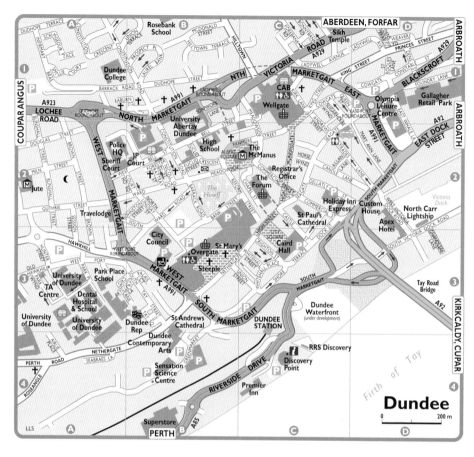

Airlie Place...................A4
Albert Square..............B2
Allan Lane...................C2
Artillery Lane...............A3
Bank Street..................B2
Barrack Road...............A1
Barrack Road...............B2
Bell Street....................B2
Blackscroft..................D1
Blinshall Street............A2
Bonnybank Road.........C1
Brown Street................A2
Candle Lane.................C2
Castle Street................C2
Chandlers Lane...........D3
City Square..................C3
Commercial Street.......C2
Constitution
  Crescent...................A1
Constitution Road........A1
Constitution Road........B2
Court House
  Square......................A2
Cowgate......................C1
Cowgate......................D1
Crighton Street...........C3
Cross Lane..................A3
Dens Brae...................D1
Dens Street.................D1

Dock Street.................C3
Douglas Street............A2
Dudhope
  Roundabout..............A1
Dudhope Street...........B1
Dudhope Terrace.........A1
East Dock Street..........D2
East Marketgait...........D1
East Port
  Roundabout..............D1
East Whale Lane..........D1
Euclid Crescent..........B2
Euclid Street...............B2
Forebank Road...........C1
Forester Street............B2
Foundry Lane..............D1
Gellatly Street.............C2
Greenmarket...............B4
Guthrie Street.............A2
Hawkhill......................A3
High Street..................C3
Hilltown......................B1
Hilltown Terrace..........B1
Horse Wynd.................C2
Hunter Street..............A3
Infirmary Brae.............A1
Johnston Street...........C1
King Street..................C1
Kirk Lane....................C1
Laburn Street..............A1

Ladywell Avenue..........C1
Ladywell
  Roundabout..............D1
Laurel Bank.................B1
Lochee Road...............A2
Mary Ann Lane............D2
McDonald Street..........B1
Meadowside.................B2
Miln Street..................A2
Murraygate..................C2
Nethergate..................A4
New Inn Entry.............C2
Nicoll Street................B2
North Lindsay
  Street........................B2
North Marketgait..........A1
North Victoria
  Road..........................C1
Old Hawkhill...............A3
Palais Court.................B3
Panmure Street...........B2
Park Place...................A3
Park Wynd...................A3
Perth Road..................A4
Princes Street..............D1
Prospect Place............B1
Queen Street...............A3
Rattray Street..............B2
Reform Street..............B2
Riverside Drive............B4

Roseangle....................A4
St Andrews Street.........C2
St Roques Lane............D1
Scrimgeour Place........A1
Seabraes Lane.............A4
Seagate.......................C2
Session Street..............A2
Shore Terrace..............C3
Smillie Court................A1
Soapwork Lane............B1
South Marketgait.........C3
South Tay Street..........B3
South Victoria
  Dock Road.................D3
South Ward Road.........B2
Sugarhouse
  Wynd.........................C1
Tay Road Bridge..........D3
Tay Square..................B3
Trades Lane.................C2
Union Street................B3
Union Terrace..............B1
Victoria Road...............C1
Ward Road...................B2
Weavers Yard...............D1
West Bell Street...........A2
West Marketgait...........A2
West Port....................A3
West Port
  Roundabout..............A3

West Victoria Dock
  Road..........................D2
Whitehall Place............C3
Whitehall Street...........C3

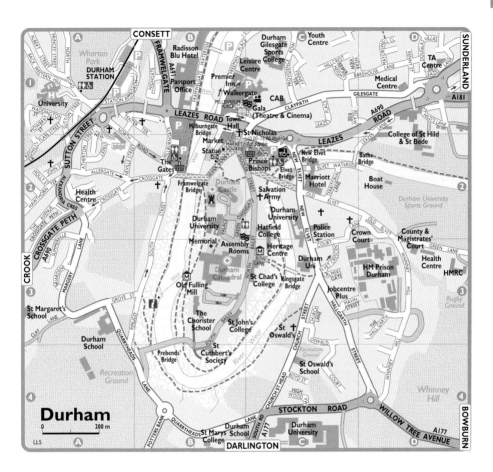

Albert Street................ A1	Green Lane.................... D3	Old Elvet......................... C2	Whinney Hill................ D3
Alexandria Crescent A2	Grove Street.................. A3	Oswald Court................ C3	Willow Tree Avenue D4
Allergate......................... A2	Hallgarth Street............. C3	Owengate........................ B2	
Atherton Street............. A2	Hawthorn Terrace......... A2	Palace Green.................. B2	
Back Western Hill......... A1	Highgate.......................... B1	Palmers Gate................. C3	
Bakehouse Lane............. C1	High Road View............ C4	Pelaw Rise...................... C1	
Baths Bridge................... C2	High Street..................... C2	Pimlico........................... A3	
Bow Lane........................ C3	Hillcrest.......................... C1	Potters Bank.................. B4	
Boyd Street.................... C4	Holly Street.................... A2	Prebends' Bridge B4	
Briardene....................... A3	John Street..................... A2	Princes' Street............... A1	
Church Lane................... C3	Keiper Heights............... C1	Providence Row............ C1	
Church Street................ C4	Kingsgate Bridge........... C3	Quarryheads Lane A3	
Church Street Head..... C4	Leazes Lane.................... D1	Redhills Lane.................. A2	
Clay Lane........................ A3	Leazes Lane.................... D2	Renny Street.................. D1	
Claypath.......................... C1	Leazes Place.................. C1	Saddler Street................ B2	
Court Lane...................... C3	Leazes Road B1	St Hild's Lane D1	
Crossgate....................... A2	Margery Lane................. A3	Silver Street................... B2	
Crossgate Peth A3	Market Square............... B2	South Bailey................... B3	
Douglas Villas................ D1	Mavin Street................... C3	South Road.................... C4	
Elvet Bridge C2	Mayorswell Close.......... D1	South Street................... B3	
Elvet Crescent C3	Milburngate Bridge........ B1	Station Approach........... A1	
Elvet Waterside............ C2	Millburngate................... B2	Stockton Road.............. C4	
Finney Terrace............... C1	Millennium Place............ B1	Summerville................... A3	
Flass Street.................... A2	Mowbray Street............. A1	Sutton Street................. A2	
Framwelgate................... B1	Neville Street................. A2	Tenter Terrace.............. A1	
Framwelgate Bridge...... B2	New Elvet...................... C2	Territorial Lane............. C2	
Framwelgate	New Elvet Bridge C2	The Avenue.................... A2	
Waterside.................. B1	New Street...................... A2	The Hall Garth.............. D3	
Freeman Place............... B1	North Bailey................... C3	Waddington Street A1	
Gilesgate......................... C1	North Road.................... A1	Wear View C1	

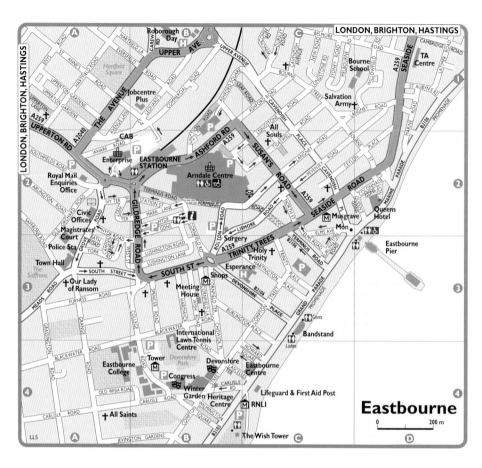

Arlington Road A2	Enys Road A1	Meads Road A3	Upperton Gardens A1
Ashford Road B2	Eversfield Road A1	Melbourne Road C1	Upperton Lane A1
Ashford Square B1	Furness Road A3	New Road C1	Upperton Road A1
Avenue Lane A1	Gildredge Road............. B2	North Street C2	West Street A3
Bath Road A3	Grand Parade C3	Old Orchard Road A2	West Terrace A2
Belmore Road C1	Grange Road A3	Old Wish Road A4	Wharf Road A2
Blackwater Road A4	Grassington Road A3	Pevensey Road C2	Willowfield Road D1
Bolton Road B3	Grove Road A3	Promenade C3	Wilmington Square B4
Bourne Street C1	Hardwick Road B3	Queen's Gardens D2	Winchcombe Road....... C1
Burlington Place............. B3	Hartfield Lane A1	Saffrons Road A2	Wish Road B3
Burlington Road C3	Hartfield Road A1	St Anne's Road A1	York Road A3
Cambridge Road D1	Hartington Place C3	St Aubyn's Road D1	
Camden Road A3	Howard Square C4	St Leonard's Road B1	
Carew Road B1	Hyde Gardens................ B2	Seaside D1	
Carlisle Road A4	Hyde Road A2	Seaside Road C2	
Cavendish Avenue C1	Ivy Terrace A2	Southfields Road........... A2	
Cavendish Place C1	Jevington Gardens A4	South Street A3	
Ceylon Place................. C2	Junction Road B2	South Street B3	
Chiswick Place B3	Langney Road C2	Spencer Road B3	
College Road................. B3	Lascelles Terrace B4	Station Street B2	
Colonnade Gardens D2	Latimer Road D1	Susan's Road C2	
Commercial Road........... B1	Leaf Road B1	Sutton Road B2	
Compton Street............. B4	Lion Lane D2	Sydney Road C1	
Cornfield Lane B3	Lismore Road B2	Terminus Road B2	
Cornfield Road B2	Longstone Road C1	Terminus Road C3	
Cornfield Terrace B3	Lushington Lane B3	The Avenue A1	
Devonshire Place........... B3	Lushington Road............ B3	Tidswell Road C2	
Dursley Road C1	Marine Parade D2	Trinity Place C3	
Elms Avenue C2	Marine Road D1	Trinity Trees B3	
Elms Road C3	Mark Lane B2	Upper Avenue B1	

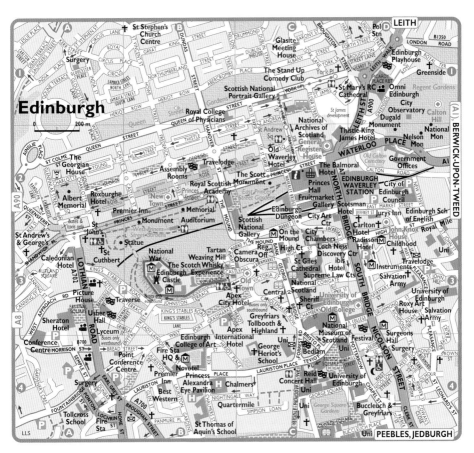

Abercromby Place	B1	Cowgate	C3	Heriot Bridge	B3
Adam Street East	D3	Davie Street	D4	Heriot Place	B4
Adam Street West	D3	Dean Terrace	A1	Heriot Row	A1
Ainslie Place	A2	Doune Terrace	A1	High Street	C3
Albany Street	C1	Drummond Place	C1	Hill Street	B2
Alva Street	A3	Drummond Street	D3	Home Street	A4
Bank Street	C3	Dublin Meuse	C1	Hope Street	A2
Barony Street	C1	Dublin Street	C1	Howden Street	D4
Bread Street	A4	Dunbar Street	A4	Howe Street	B1
Briery Bauks	D4	Dundas Street	B1	India Place	A1
Bristo Place	C4	Earl Grey Street	A4	India Street	A1
Bristo Square	C4	East Market Street	D2	Infirmary Street	D3
Brougham Street	B4	Elder Street	C1	Jamaica Street	
Broughton Street	C1	Esplanade	B3	North Lane	A1
Broughton Street Lane	D1	Festival Square	A3	Jamaica Street	
Brown Street	D4	Forrest Road	C4	South Lane	A1
Buccleuch Place	C4	Forth Street	C1	Jeffrey Street	D2
Calton Road	D2	Fountainbridge	A4	Johnston Terrace	B3
Cambridge Street	A3	Frederick Street	B2	Keir Street	B4
Candlemaker Row	C3	Gardener's Crescent	A4	Kerr Street	A1
Canning Street	A3	George IV Bridge	C3	King's Stables Lane	B3
Carlton Street	A1	George Square	C4	King's Stables Road	A3
Castlehill	B3	George Street	A2	Lady Lawson Street	B3
Castle Street	B2	Gilmour Street	D4	Lauriston Gardens	B4
Castle Terrace	A3	Glenfinlas Street	A2	Lauriston Place	B4
Chalmers Street	B4	Glen Street	B4	Lauriston Street	B4
Chambers Street	C3	Gloucester Lane	A1	Lawnmarket	C3
Chapel Street	D4	Gloucester Place	A1	Leith Street	D2
Charlotte Lane	A2	Grassmarket	B3	Leith Walk	D1
Charlotte Square	A2	Great King Street	B1	Leslie Place	A1
Circus Lane	A1	Greenside Row	D1	Lochrin Street	A4
Circus Place	A1	Grindlay Street	A3	London Road	D1
Clerk Street	D4	Guthrie Street	C3	Lothian Road	A3
Cockburn Street	C3	Haddon's Court	D4	Market Street	C3
Cornwall Street	A3	Hanover Street	B2	Middle Meadow Walk	C4
Cowan's Close	D4	Hart Street	C1	Morrison Street	A3

Mound Place	B3	St Stephen Street	A1
Nelson Street	B1	St Vincent Street	B1
New Street	D2	Saunders Street	A1
Nicolson Square	D4	Semple Street	A4
Nicolson Street	D3	Shandwick Place	A3
Nightingale Way	B4	Simpson Loan	C4
North Bridge	C2	South Bridge	D3
North Castle Street	A2	South Charlotte Street	A2
North St Andrew Street	C1	South College Street	D3
North St David Street	C1	South Colme Street	A2
Northumberland Street	B1	South St Andrew Street	C2
Panmure Place	B4	South St David Street	C2
Picardy Place	D1	Spittal Street	B4
Picardy Place		The Mound	B2
Roundabout	D1	Thistle Street	B2
Pleasance	C4	Union Street	D1
Ponton Street	A4	Victoria Street	C3
Potterrow	D4	Waterloo Place	C2
Princes Street	A2	Waverley Bridge	C2
Queensferry Street	A2	Wemyss Place	A2
Queen Street	A2	West Approach Road	A3
Ramsay Lane	B3	West Nicolson Street	D4
Randolph Lane	A2	West Port	B3
Richmond Lane	D4	West Richmond Street	D4
Richmond Place	D3	Windmill Street	C4
Rose Street	A2	York Lane	C1
Royal Circus	A1	York Place	C1
Royal Terrace	D1	Young Street	A2
Rutland Square	A3		
St Andrew Square	C2		
St James Place	C1		
St John's Hill	D3		
St John Street	D3		
St Leonard's Street	D4		
St Mary's Street	D3		
St Patrick Street	D4		

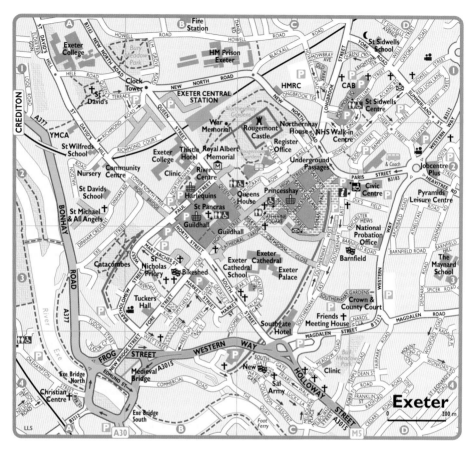

Acland Road.................D1
Archibald Road...........D3
Athelstan Road............D3
Bailey Street.................C2
Bampfylde Lane............C2
Bampfylde Street..........D2
Barnfield Hill................D3
Barnfield Road.............D3
Bartholomew Street
 West..........................B3
Bear Street..................C3
Bedford Street..............C2
Belgrave Road..............D2
Blackall Road................C1
Bonhay Road................A2
Bude Street..................D2
Bull Meadow Road.......C4
Castle Street.................C2
Cathedral Close............C3
Cathedral Yard............B3
Catherine Square.........C2
Cedars Road.................D4
Cheeke Street...............D1
Chichester Mews.........C3
Colleton Crescent........C4
Commercial Road.........B4
Coombe Street.............B3
Danes Road..................B1
Deanery Place..............C3
Dean Street..................D4

Denmark Road.............D3
Dinham Crescent.........A3
Dinham Road................A2
Dix's Field....................D2
Eastgate.......................C2
Edmund Street.............A4
Eldertree Garden..........A1
Elm Grove Road............B1
Exe Bridge North..........A4
Exe Bridge South..........B4
Exe Street......................A3
Fairpark Road...............D4
Fore Street....................B3
Franklin Street..............D4
Friars Gate....................C4
Friars' Walk..................C4
Friern Hay Street..........B3
Frog Street....................A4
George Street................B3
Guinea Street................B3
Haldon Road................A2
Heavitree Road.............D2
Hele Road.....................A1
High Street....................C2
Holloway Street............C4
Howell Road.................B1
Iron Bridge...................B2
King Street....................B3
King William Street.......D1
Longbrook Street..........C1

Longbrook Terrace........C1
Looe Road.....................A1
Lower North Street........B2
Lucky Lane....................C4
Magdalen Road.............D3
Magdalen Street............C4
Market Street................B3
Martins Lane.................C2
Mary Arches Street........B3
Melbourne Place...........C4
Melbourne Street..........C4
Mount Radford
 Close...........................D4
Mowbray Avenue...........C1
Musgrave Row...............C2
Nelson Road..................A4
New Bridge Street..........A4
New North Road...........A1
Northernhay Street.......B2
North Street..................B3
Okehampton Street........A4
Old Park Road...............C1
Oxford Road.................D1
Palace Gate...................C3
Paris Street....................D2
Paul Street.....................B2
Poltimore Square..........D2
Preston Street...............B4
Princesshay...................C2
Queens Crescent...........C1

Queen's Terrace............A1
Queen Street.................B1
Radford Road................D4
Radnor Place................D3
Red Lion Lane...............D1
Richmond Court............B2
Richmond Road............A2
Roberts Road.................C4
Roman Walk..................C2
Russell Street.................D2
St David's Hill...............A1
St Sidwells Avenue........D1
Sidwell Street................C2
Sidwell Street................D1
Smythen Street..............B3
Southernhay East...........C3
Southernhay
 Gardens......................C3
Southernhay West.........C3
Southgate......................B3
South Street..................B3
Spicer Road...................D3
Summerland Street........D1
Temple Road.................D4
The Quay......................C4
Tudor Court..................A4
Tudor Street..................A3
Verney Street.................D1
Vine Close.....................D3
Watergate......................C4

Wells Street...................D1
Western Way..................B4
West Street....................B4
Wonford Road...............D4
Wynards Lane................D3
York Road......................D1

Albion Street	D4	Dobbie's Loan	C1	Lister Street	D1
Argyle Arcade	B3	Douglas Street	A3	London Road	D4
Argyle Street	A3	Drury Street	B3	Maitland Street	B1
Baird Street	D1	Dundas Street	C2	Martha Street	C2
Bath Lane	A1	Dunlop Street	C4	Mart Street	C4
Bath Street	A1	Dyer's Lane	D4	Maxwell Street	B4
Bell Street	D3	Elmbank Street	A1	McAlpine Street	A3
Bishop Lane	A2	Fox Street	B4	McPhater Street	B1
Blackfriars Street	D3	Gallowgate	D4	Merchant Square	D3
Black Street	D1	Garnet Street	A1	Miller Street	C3
Blythswood Square	A2	Garth Street	C3	Milton Street	B1
Blythswood Street	A3	George Square	C2	Mitchell Street	B3
Bothwell Lane	A3	George Street	C2	Moir Street	D4
Bothwell Street	A2	George V Bridge	B4	Molendinar Street	D4
Bridgegate	C4	Glasgow Bridge	B4	Montrose Street	D3
Bridge Street	B4	Glassford Street	C3	Morrison Street	A4
Broomielaw	A4	Gordon Street	B3	New Wynd	C4
Brown Street	A3	Grafton Place	C2	North Frederick Street	C2
Brunswick Street	C3	Hanover Street	C2	North Hanover Street	C2
Buccleuch Street	A1	High Street	D4	North Portland Street	D2
Buchanan Street	B3	Hill Street	A1	North Wallace Street	D1
Cadogan Street	A3	Holland Street	A2	Oak Street	A3
Calgary Street	C1	Holm Street	A3	Osborne Street	C4
Cambridge Street	B1	Hope Street	B3	Oswald Street	A4
Candleriggs	D3	Howard Street	B4	Paisley Road	A4
Carlton Place	B4	Hutcheson Street	C3	Parnie Street	C4
Cathedral Street	C2	Ingram Street	C3	Parsonage Square	D3
Centre Street	A4	Jamaica Street	B4	Pitt Street	A2
Clyde Place	B4	James Watt Street	A3	Port Dundas Road	B1
Clyde Street	B4	John Street	C3	Portland Street	
Cochrane Street	C3	Kennedy Street	C1	Suspension Bridge	B4
Commerce Street	B4	Killermont Street	C1	Queen Street	C3
Couper Street	D1	Kingston Street	A4	Renfield Lane	B2
Cowcaddens Road	B1	King Street	C4	Renfield Street	B2
Dalhousie Lane	A1	Kyle Street	C1	Renfrew Lane	B1
Dixon Street	B4	Larbert Street	B1	Renfrew Street	A1

Richmond Street	D2	Wellington Street	B3
Riverview Gardens	A4	West Campbell Street	A3
Riverview Place	A4	West George Lane	A2
Robertson Street	A4	West George Street	A2
Rose Street	A1	West Nile Street	B2
Rottenrow	D2	West Regent Lane	B2
Royal Exchange Square	B3	West Regent Street	A2
St Andrew's Square	C4	West Street	A4
St Andrew's Street	D4	Wilson Street	C3
St James Road	D2	York Street	A3
St Mungo Avenue	C2		
St Vincent Lane	A2		
St Vincent Place	B2		
St Vincent Street	A2		
Saltmarket	C4		
Sauchiehall Lane	A1		
Sauchiehall Street	A1		
Scott Street	A1		
Shipbank Lane	C4		
Shuttle Street	D3		
South Frederick Street	C3		
Stafford Street	C1		
Steel Street	C4		
Stockwell Place	C4		
Stockwell Street	C4		
Taylor Place	D2		
Taylor Street	D2		
Tradeston Bridge	A4		
Trongate	C4		
Turnbull Street	D4		
Union Lane	B3		
Union Street	B3		
Virginia Street	C3		
Walls Street	D3		
Waterloo Street	A3		
Wellington Lane	A3		

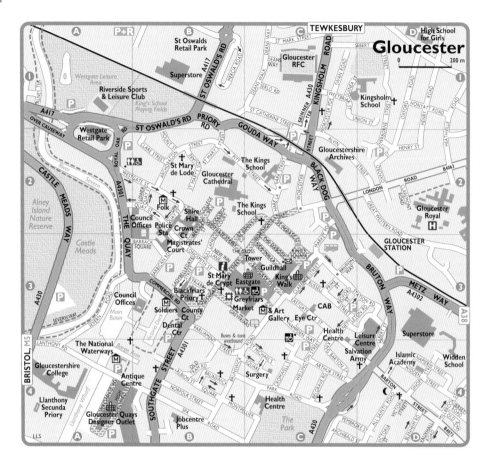

Albert Street D4	Deans Walk C1	Mount Street B2	Sebert Street C1
Albion Street B4	Deans Way C1	Napier Street D4	Serlo Road C1
All Saints' Road D4	Eastgate Street C3	Nettleton Road C3	Severn Road A3
Alney Terrace A1	Gouda Way B1	New Inn Lane B3	Severn Way A3
Alvin Street C2	Great Western	New Inn Lane C3	Sherborne Street D2
Archdeacon Street B2	Road D2	Norfolk Street B4	Sinope Street D4
Archibald Street C4	Greyfriars B3	Northgate Street C3	Skinner Terrace C1
Arthur Street C4	Guinea Street C1	Old Row D4	Southgate Street B3
Barbican Road B3	Hampden Way C3	Old Tram Road B4	Southgate Street B4
Barrack Square B3	Hare Lane C2	Over Causeway A1	Spa Road B4
Barton Street D4	Heathville Road D2	Oxford Road D1	Station Road C3
Bedford Street C3	Henry Road D1	Oxford Street D2	Swan Road C1
Belgrave Road C4	Henry Street D2	Park Road C4	Sweetbriar Street C1
Berkeley Street B3	High Orchard Street A4	Park Street C2	The Cross B3
Black Dog Way C2	Honyatt Road D1	Parliament Street B3	The Oxbode C3
Blackfriars B3	Jersey Road D4	Pembroke Street C4	The Quay A2
Blenheim Road D4	King Barton Street......C4	Pitt Street B2	Union Street C1
Brunswick Road B4	Kingsholm Road C1	Prime Street C3	Upper Quay Street B2
Brunswick Square B4	King's Square C3	Priory Road B1	Vauxhall Road D4
Bruton Way C3	Ladybellegate Street B3	Quay Street B2	Victoria Street D4
Bruton Way D3	Llanthony Road A4	Royal Oak Road A2	Wellington Street C4
Bull Lane B3	London Road D2	Russell Street C3	Westgate Street A2
Castle Meads Way........A2	Longsmith Street B3	St Aldate Street C2	Westgate Street B2
Claremont Road D2	Lower Quay Street B2	St Catherine Street C1	Widden Street D4
Clarence Street C3	Market Parade C3	St John's Lane B3	Worcester Parade C2
Clare Street B2	Merchants' Road A4	St Mark Street C1	Worcester Street C2
College Court B2	Mercia Road B1	St Mary's Square B2	
College Street B2	Metz Way D3	St Mary's Street B2	
Commercial Road B3	Millbrook Street D4	St Michael's Square C4	
Cromwell Street C4	Montpellier B4	St Oswald's Road B1	

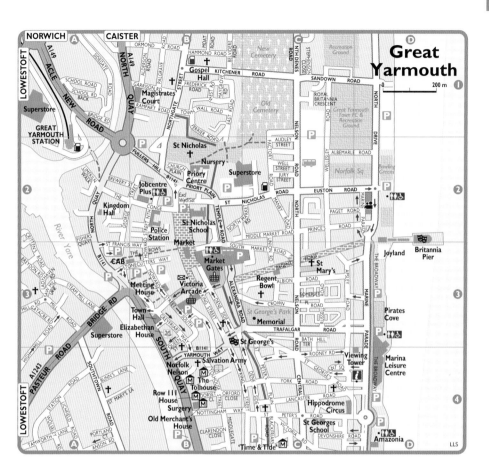

Acle New Road............A1	Garrison Road................B1	North Market Road.....C2	Somerset Place.............C3
Albemarle Road............C2	Gatacre Road................A3	North Quay..................A2	South Market Road......C3
Albion Road................C3	George Street...............A2	Northgate Street...........B1	South Quay..................B3
Alderson Road..............B1	Greyfriars Way..............B3	Nottingham Way............B4	Southtown Road............A4
Alexandra Road............B3	Hammond Road.............B1	Orford Close................B4	Station Road.................A4
Anson Road.................A4	High Mill Road..............A3	Ormond Road................B1	Steam Mill Lane............A3
Apsley Road.................C3	Howard Street	Paget Road...................C2	Stephenson Close..........C1
Audley Street................C2	North.......................B2	Palgrave Road...............B1	Stonecutters Way..........B3
Bath Hill Terrace...........C3	Howard Street	Pasteur Road................A4	Tamworth Lane.............A4
Belvidere Road.............B1	South.......................B3	Portland Court..............A4	Temple Road.................B2
Blackfriars Road............C4	Jury Street....................C2	Prince's Road................C2	The Broadway..............D3
Brewery Street..............A2	Kent Square..................C4	Priory Plain...................B2	The Conge...................A2
Breydon Road...............A3	King Street....................B3	Queen Street.................B4	The Rows....................B3
Bridge Road.................A1	Kitchener Road..............B1	Rampart Road...............B1	Tolhouse Street.............B4
Bridge Road.................A3	Ladyhaven Road............A3	Regent Road.................C3	Town Wall Road...........B1
Bunn's Lane.................A4	Lancaster Road..............C4	Rodney Road.................C4	Trafalgar Road..............C3
Church Plain.................B2	Lichfield Road................A4	Royal Britannia	Union Road...................C3
Clarendon Close...........B4	Limekiln Walk................A2	Crescent...................C1	Victoria Road................C4
Critten's Road...............A3	Manby Road..................C2	Russell Road.................C3	Well Street...................C2
Crown Road.................C3	Marine Parade...............D3	St Francis Way...............A3	Wellesley Road..............C2
Dene Side...................B3	Maygrove Road.............B1	St George's Road...........C4	West Road...................B1
Devonshire Road...........C4	Middle Market Road........C2	St Mary's Lane..............A4	Wolseley Road..............A4
Dorset Close.................B4	Middlegate...................B4	St Nicholas Road............B2	Yarmouth Way..............B4
East Road....................B1	Mill Road.....................A3	St Peter's Plain..............C4	York Road...................C4
Euston Road.................C2	Moat Road...................B1	St Peter's Road..............C4	
Factory Road................C2	Nelson Road	Sandown Road..............C1	
Ferrier Road.................B1	Central.....................C3	Saw Mill Lane...............A3	
Fishers Quay.................A2	Nelson Road North.........C1	School Road..................A1	
Frederick Road..............B1	North Denes Road..........C1	School Road Back...........A1	
Fullers Hill..................B2	North Drive...................D1	Sidegate Road...............A1	

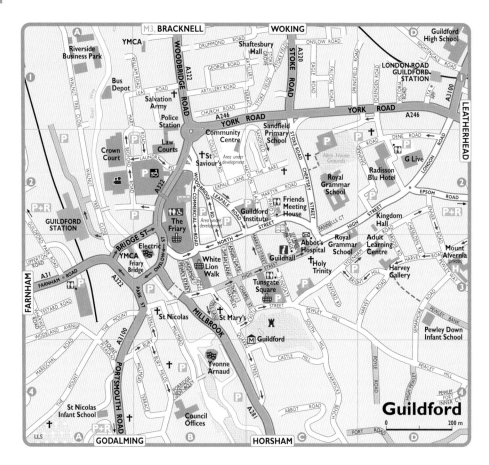

Abbot Road	C4	Harvey Road	D3
Angel Gate	B3	Haydon Place	C2
Artillery Road	B1	High Pewley	D4
Artillery Terrace	C1	High Street	B3
Bedford Road	A2	Jeffries Passage	C2
Bridge Street	A3	Jenner Road	D2
Bright Hill	C3	Laundry Road	B2
Brodie Road	D3	Leapale Lane	B2
Bury Fields	B4	Leapale Road	B2
Bury Street	B4	Leas Road	B1
Castle Hill	C4	London Road	D2
Castle Street	C3	Mareschal Road	A4
Chapel Street	B3	Market Street	C3
Chertsey Street	C2	Martyr Road	C2
Cheselden Road	D2	Mary Road	A1
Church Road	B1	Millbrook	B3
College Road	B2	Mill Lane	B3
Commercial Road	B2	Millmead	B3
Dene Road	D2	Millmead Terrace	B4
Denmark Road	D2	Mount Pleasant	A4
Drummond Road	B1	Nightingale Road	D1
Eagle Road	C1	North Street	B2
Epsom Road	D2	Onslow Road	C1
Falcon Road	C1	Onslow Street	B3
Fort Road	C4	Oxford Road	C3
Foxenden Road	D1	Pannells Court	C2
Friary Bridge	A3	Park Street	B3
Friary Street	B3	Pewley Bank	D3
George Road	B1	Pewley Fort Inner	
Guildford Park Road	A2	Court	D4

Pewley Hill	C3	Woodbridge Road	B1
Pewley Way	D3	York Road	B1
Phoenix Court	B3		
Porridge Pot Alley	B4		
Portsmouth Road	A4		
Poyle Road	D4		
Quarry Street	B3		
Sandfield Terrace	C2		
Semaphore Road	D3		
South Hill	C3		
Springfield Road	C1		
Station Approach	D1		
Stoke Fields	C1		
Stoke Grove	C1		
Stoke Road	C1		
Swan Lane	B3		
Sydenham Road	C3		
Testard Road	A3		
The Bars	C2		
The Mount	A4		
The Shambles	B3		
Tunsgate	C3		
Upperton Road	A3		
Victoria Road	D1		
Walnut Tree Close	A1		
Ward Street	C2		
Warwicks Bench	C4		
Wherwell Road	A3		
William Road	B1		
Wodeland Avenue	A3		

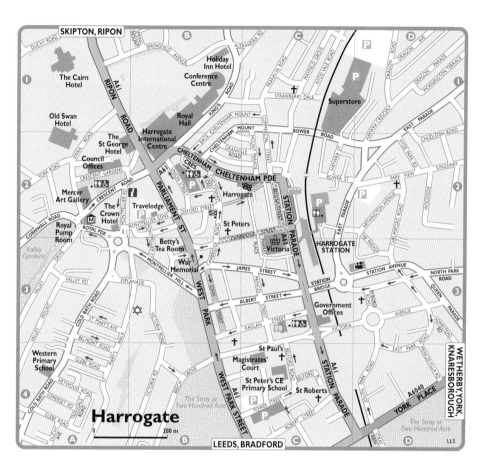

Albert Street.............. C3
Alexandra Road.........B1
Arthington Avenue.... D2
Back Cheltenham
  Mount......................B2
Beech Grove B4
Belford Place C4
Belford Road C4
Belmont Road............. A3
Beulah Street.............. C2
Bower Road C1
Bower Street.............. C2
Cambridge Road.........B3
Cambridge Street......... C2
Chelmsford Road........ D3
Cheltenham
  Crescent..................B2
Cheltenham Mount....... B2
Cheltenham Parade B2
Chudleigh Road........... D2
Cold Bath Road........... A3
Commercial Street C1
Cornwall Road............. A2
Crescent Gardens.........A2
Crescent Road............. A2
Dragon Avenue D1
Dragon Parade............ D1
Dragon Road............... D1
Duchy Avenue............. A4
Duchy Road.................. A1

East Parade.................. C2
East Park Road D4
Esplanade...................... A3
Franklin Road............... C1
Glebe Road.................. A4
Granville Road.............. B2
Haywra Street............... C2
Heywood Road............. A4
Homestead Road D3
Hyde Park Road......... D2
Hywra Crescent........... D2
James Street B3
John Street.................... B3
King's Road.................. B1
Kingsway...................... D2
Market Place................. C3
Marlborough Road........ D3
Mayfield Grove............. C1
Montpellier Gardens.....B2
Montpellier Hill............. B3
Montpellier Road A2
Montpellier Street......... B2
Mornington Terrace..... D1
Mount Parade C2
North Park Road......... D3
Nydd Vale Road........... C1
Oxford Street............... B2
Park View..................... D2
Parliament Street B2
Princes Street............... C3

Princes Villa Road.........D4
Queen Parade.............. D3
Raglan Street C3
Ripon Road................... A1
Robert Street................ C4
Royal Parade A2
St Mary's Avenue.......... A3
St Mary's Walk A4
Somerset Road............. A4
South Park Road.......... D4
Springfield Avenue........B1
Spring Mount............... B1
Station Avenue............. D3
Station Bridge............. C3
Station Parade.............. C2
Strawberry Dale........... C1
Stray Rein.................... D4
Swan Road................... A2
The Parade D2
Tower Street C4
Treesdale Road............ A4
Union Street................. B2
Valley Drive A3
Valley Mount A3
Valley Road.................. A3
Victoria Avenue C3
Victoria Road................ B3
West Park.................... B3
West Park Street.......... B4
Woodside..................... D2

York Place D4
York Road..................... A2

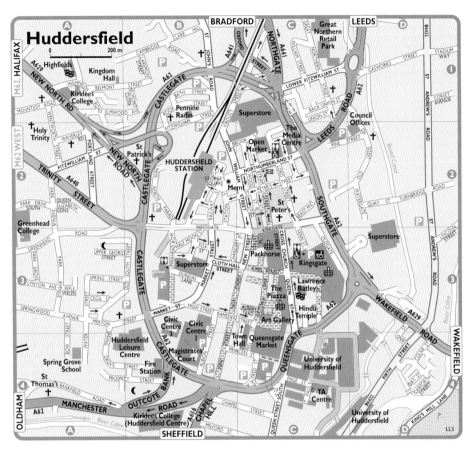

Albert Yard......................C3
Albion Street..................B4
Alfred Street..................C4
Back Union
  Street..........................C1
Bankfield Road..............A4
Bath Street....................B1
Beast Market..................C2
Belmont Close................B1
Belmont Street..............A1
Bow Street.....................A4
Brook Street...................C2
Byram Street..................C2
Cambridge Road............B1
Carforth Street..............D4
Castlegate......................B1
Cecil Street....................A3
Chancery Lane...............B3
Chapel Hill.....................B4
Chapel Street..................B4
Church Street.................C2
Clare Hill.......................B1
Claremont Street............B1
Cloth Hall Street............B3
Colne Street...................D4
Corset Avenue................D1
Cross Church
  Street..........................C3
Day Street......................D4
Dundas Lane..................B3

Elizabeth Queen
  Gardens......................A2
Elmwood Avenue...........A1
Firth Street....................D4
Fitzwilliam Street...........A2
Fitzwilliam Street...........B2
Fox Street.......................B3
Gasworks Street.............D1
Great Northern
  Street..........................C1
Greenhead Road............A3
Half Moon Street...........B3
High Street.....................B3
Highfields Road..............A1
John William Street........B2
King Street......................C3
King's Mill Lane.............D4
Kirkgate.........................C3
Leeds Road.....................C2
Lincoln Street.................D3
Lord Street.....................C2
Lower Fitzwilliam
  Street..........................C1
Lynton Avenue...............A3
Manchester Road...........A4
Market Place...................C3
Market Street..................B3
Merton Street.................A3
Milford Street.................B4
Mountjoy Road...............A1

New North Parade........B2
New North Road...........A1
New Street......................B4
Northgate.......................C1
Northumberland
  Street..........................C2
Old Leeds Road.............D2
Old South Street............B3
Oldgate..........................C3
Outcote Bank.................B4
Oxford Street..................C1
Page Street.....................C4
Park Avenue...................A2
Park Drive South............A2
Park Grove.....................A3
Peel Street......................C4
Pine Street......................C2
Portland Street...............A2
Princess Street................B4
Prospect Street...............A4
Quay Street....................D2
Queen Elizabeth
  Gardens......................A2
Queen Street...................C3
Queen Street South......C4
Queensgate....................C4
Railway Street................B2
Ramsden Street..............B3
Rifle Fields.....................A3
Rook Street....................B1

St Andrew's Road..........D2
St George's Square........B2
St John's Road................B1
St Paul's Street...............C4
St Peter's Street..............C2
Sand Street.....................D4
Southgate.......................C2
Spring Grove Street........A4
Spring Street...................A3
Springwood Avenue.......A3
Stadium Way..................D1
Station Street.................B2
Trinity Street..................A2
Turnbridge Road............D2
Union Street...................C1
Upper George
  Street..........................A3
Upperhead Row.............B3
Venn Street.....................C3
Viaduct Street.................B2
Victoria Lane..................C3
Wakefield Road..............D3
Water Street....................A3
Watergate.......................D2
Waverley Road...............A2
Wentworth Street...........A2
Westgate.........................B3
William Street.................C1
Wood Street...................C2
Zetland Street.................C3

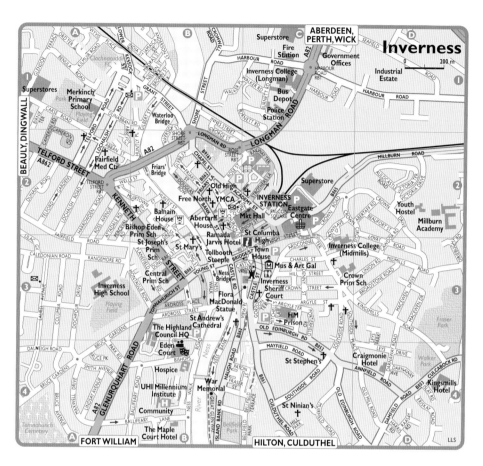

Abban Street	A2	Castle Wynd	B3
Abbey Court	A1	Cawdor Road	D3
Abertaff Road	D2	Celt Street	B2
Academy Street	B2	Chapel Street	B2
Anderson Street	B1	Charles Street	C3
Annfield Road	D4	Church Street	B2
Ardconnel Terrace	C3	Columba Road	A3
Ardross Place	B3	Cromwell Road	B1
Ardross Street	B3	Crown Avenue	C3
Argyle Street	C3	Crown Circus	C2
Argyle Terrace	C3	Crown Drive	D2
Attadale Road	A2	Crown Road	C2
Auldcastle Road	D2	Crown Street	C3
Ballifeary Lane	A4	Culcabock Road	D4
Ballifeary Road	B4	Culduthel Road	D4
Bank Street	B2	Dalneigh Road	A4
Beaufort Street	D2	Damfield Road	A4
Bellfield Park	C4	Darnaway Avenue	D4
Bellfield Terrace	C4	Darnaway Road	D4
Benula Road	A1	Denny Street	C3
Bernett Road	B1	Diriebught Road	D3
Birnie Terrace	A1	Dochfour Drive	A3
Bishops Road	B4	Douglas Row	B2
Bridge Street	B3	Dunabban Road	A1
Broadstone Road	D3	Dunain Road	A2
Brown Street	B1	Duncraig Street	B3
Bruce Avenue	A4	Eriskay Road	D4
Bruce Gardens	A4	Fairfield Road	A3
Bruce Park	A4	Falcon Square	C2
Burnett Road	C1	Fraser Street	B4
Caledonian Road	A3	Friars' Bridge	B2
Cameron Road	A2	Friars' Lane	B2
Cameron Square	A2	Friars' Street	B2
Carse Road	A1	George Street	B2
Castle Road	B3	Gilbert Street	B2
Castle Street	C3	Glebe Street	B2

Glendoe Terrace	A1	Madras Street	B1
Glenurquhart Road	A4	Maxwell Drive	A4
Gordon Terrace	C3	Mayfield Road	C4
Grant Street	B1	Midmills Road	D3
Great Glen Way	B4	Millburn Road	D2
Greig Street	B2	Mitchell's Lane	C3
Harbour Road	C1	Montague Row	B3
Harbour Road Roundabout	C1	Muirfield Road	C4
Harris Road	D4	Muirtown Street	A2
Harrowden Road	A2	Nelson Street	B1
Haugh Road	B4	Ness Bank	B4
High Street	C3	Ness Bridge	B3
Hill Park	C3	Ness Walk	B3
Hill Street	C3	Old Edinburgh Road	C3
Huntly Place	B2	Old Mill Road	D4
Huntly Street	B2	Ord Terrace	A1
India Street	B1	Park Road	A4
Innes Street	B1	Paton Street	B4
Island Bank Road	B4	Perceval Road	A2
Islay Road	D4	Planefield Road	B3
Jamaica Street	B1	Porterfield Road	C3
Kenneth Street	A2	Queensgate	B2
Kilmuir Road	A1	Raasay Road	D4
Kingsmills Road	D3	Railway Terrace	C2
King Street	B3	Rangemore Road	A3
Laurel Avenue	A3	Riverside Street	B2
Leys Drive	D4	Rose Street	B2
Leys Park	D4	Rose Street Roundabout	B2
Lilac Grove	A3	Ross Avenue	A2
Lindsay Avenue	A4	Seafield Road	D1
Lochalsh Road	A2	Shore Street	B2
Longman Road	C2	Shore Street Roundabout	B2
Lovat Road	D3	Smith Avenue	A4
Lower Kessock Street	A1	Southside Place	C3
MacEwen Drive	D3	Southside Road	C4

Strothers Lane	C2		
Telford Gardens	A2		
Telford Road	A2		
Telford Street	A2		
Telford Street Roundabout	A2		
Tomnahurich Street	B3		
Union Road	D3		
Union Street	C2		
Victoria Drive	D2		
Victoria Terrace	D2		
View Place	C3		
Walker Place	B1		
Walker Road	C1		
Waterloo Bridge	B1		
Wells Street	A2		
Wyvis Place	A1		
Young Street	B3		

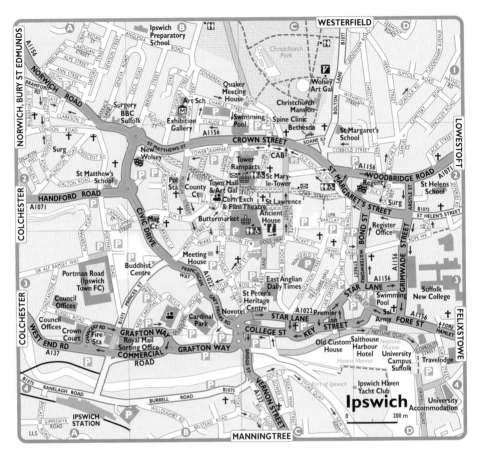

Ipswich

Alderman Road............A3
Alpe Street A1
Ancaster Road.............A4
Anglesea Road.............A1
Ann Street A1
Argyle Street...............D2
Austin Street...............C4
Barrack Lane...............A1
Bedford Street............B2
Bell Close...................C4
Belstead Road.............B4
Benezet Street............A1
Berners Street............B1
Black Horse Lane........B2
Blanche Street............D2
Bolton Lane................C1
Bond Street................D3
Bramford Road...........A1
Bridge Street..............C4
Burlington Road..........A2
Burrell Road...............B4
Canham Street............A2
Cardigan Street...........A1
Carr Street.................C2
Cecilia Street..............B3
Cecil Road.................B1
Cemetery Road...........D1
Chalon Street.............B3
Chancery Road...........A4
Chapman Lane............B2

Charles Street.............B1
Christchurch Street.....D1
Civic Drive.................B2
Clarkson Street...........A1
Claude Street..............B1
Cobbold Street...........C2
College Street.............C3
Commercial Road........A4
Constantine Road........A3
Coprolite Street..........D4
Crescent Road............A2
Crown Street..............B2
Cumberland Street......A1
Curriers' Lane.............B2
Cutler Street..............B3
Dalton Road...............A2
Dillwyn Street West A2
Dock Street................C4
Dogs Head Street........C3
Dove Street................D2
Duke Street................D4
Dyke Street................B1
Eagle Street................C3
Elm Street..................B2
Emlen Street...............A2
Falcon Street..............B3
Felaw Street...............C4
Finchley Road.............D2
Fonnereau Road.........B1
Fore Hamlet...............D3

Fore Street D3
Foundation Street C3
Franciscan Way B3
Friars Street B3
Gaye Street.................A1
Geneva Road...............A1
Gippeswyk Road..........A4
Gower Street...............C4
Grafton Way................B4
Great Gipping Street....A2
Great Whip Street........C4
Grey Friars Road.........B3
Grimwade Street..........D3
Handford Road............A2
Hayhill Road................D1
Hervey Street..............D1
High Street.................B1
Jefferies Road.............D2
Key Street..................C4
King Street.................B2
Lacey Street................D2
Lloyds Avenue.............B2
London Road A2
Lower Brook Street.....C3
Lower Orwell Street.....C3
Museum Street............B2
Neale Street................C1
Neptune Quay.............C4
New Cardinal Street.....B3
New Cut West.............C4

Newson Street A1
Norfolk Road..............D1
Northgate Street.........C2
Norwich Road.............A1
Oban Street................A1
Old Foundry Road.......C2
Orchard Street............D2
Orford Street..............A1
Orwell Place...............C3
Orwell Quay...............D4
Portman Road.............A4
Princes Street..............A3
Princes Street..............B3
Quadling Street...........A3
Quadling Street...........B3
Queen Street..............B3
Ranelagh Road............A4
Redan Street...............A1
Road Vermont............D1
Rope Walk.................D3
Rose Lane..................C3
Russell Road...............A3
St George's Street........B1
St Helen's Street..........D2
St Margaret's Street.....C2
St Matthews Street......B2
St Nicholas Street........B3
St Peter's Street..........B3
Samuel Close..............D2
Shire Hall Yard............C3

Silent Street................B3
Silk Street..................D2
Sir Alf Ramsey Way A3
Smart Street................C3
Soane Street...............C2
South Street...............A1
Star Lane...................C3
Stevenson Road..........A2
Stoke Quay................C4
Stoke Street...............B4
Suffolk Road...............D1
Tacket Street..............C3
Tavern Street..............C2
Tower Ramparts..........B2
Tower Street...............C2
Tuddenham Avenue.....D1
Tuddenham Road........C1
Turret Lane................C2
Upper Barclay Street....C2
Upper Orwell Street....C3
Vermont Street...........D1
Vernon Street.............C4
West End Road............A3
Westgate Street...........B2
Wilberforce Street A1
Willoughby Road..........B4
Wingfield Street...........C3
Withipoll Street...........C1
Wolsey Street..............B3
Woodbridge Road.......D2

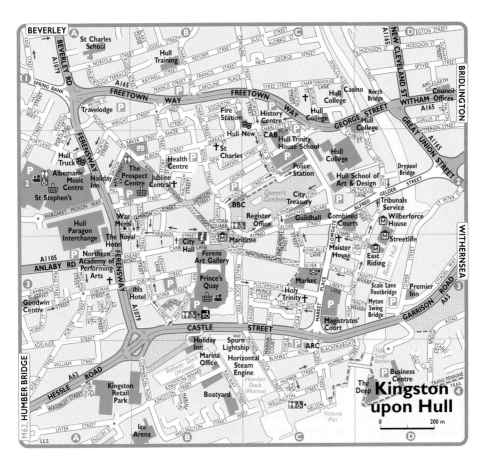

Kingston upon Hull

0 200 m

Adelaide Street	A4	English Street	A4
Albion Street	B2	Ferensway	A2
Aldborough Street	C1	Finkle Street	C4
Alfred Gelder Street	D3	Fish Street	C3
Anlaby Road	A3	Francis Street	B1
Applegarth Road	D1	Freetown Way	A1
Baker Street	A2	Gandhi Way	D2
Beverley Road	A1	Garrison Road	D3
Blackfriargate	C4	George Street	B2
Blake Close	B1	George Street	C1
Blanket Row	C4	Great Union Street	D1
Bond Street	B2	Grimston Street	C2
Bourne Street	C1	Guildhall Road	C2
Bowlalley Lane	C3	Hall Street	A1
Brook Street	A2	Hanover Court	A3
Cambridge Street	A3	Hanover Square	C2
Caroline Place	B1	Hessle Road	A4
Caroline Street	B1	High Street	C3
Carr Lane	B3	Hobart Street	A3
Castle Street	B3	Hodgson Street	D1
Chapel Lane	C2	Humber Dock Street	C3
Charles Street	B1	Humber Street	C4
Charlotte Street	C2	Hyperion Street	D2
Charlotte Street Mews	C2	Idas Close	D4
Charterhouse Lane	C1	Jameson Street	B2
Citadel Way	D3	Jarratt Street	B2
Coelus Street	D1	John Street	B1
Commercial Road	B4	King Edward Street	B2
Dagger Lane	C3	Kingston Street	B4
Dock Office Row	D2	Kingston Wharf	B4
Dock Street	B2	Lenham Lane	B3
Drypool Bridge	D2	Liberty Lane	C3
Durham Street	D1	Liddell Street	B1
Egginton Street	B1	Lime Street	D1
Egton Street	D1	Lister Street	A4
		Lowgate	C3

Malton Street	D1	Queen Street	C4
Manor Street	C2	Railway Street	B4
Margaret Moxon Way	A2	Raywell Street	B1
Marina Court	C4	Reed Street	B1
Marine Wharf	B4	Reform Street	B1
Market Place	C3	Roper Street	B3
Marlborough Terrace	A1	Russell Street	A1
Melville Street	A3	St Luke's Street	A3
Midland Street	A3	St Peter Street	D2
Milky Way	A1	Salthouse Lane	C2
Mill Street	A2	Saville Street	B2
Myton Street	B3	Scale Lane	C3
Myton Swing Bridge	D3	Scott Street	C1
Nelson Street	C4	Silver Street	C3
New Cleveland Street	D1	South Bridge Road	D4
New Garden Street	B2	South Church Side	C3
New George Street	C1	South Street	B2
Norfolk Street	A1	Spring Bank	A1
North Bridge	D1	Spring Street	A2
North Street	A2	Spruce Road	A4
Osborne Street	A3	Spyvee Street	D1
Paragon Street	B2	Stabbs Close	D4
Parliament Street	C3	Story Street	B2
Pearson Street	A2	Sykes Street	C1
Pease Street	A3	Tower Street	D3
Percy Street	B1	Trans Pennine Trail	D4
Pier Street	C4	Trinity Wharf	D3
Porter Street	A3	Trundle Street	B3
Portland Place	A2	Upper Union Street	A3
Portland Street	C3	Vane Street	A1
Postergate	C3	Vicar Lane	C3
Prince Street	C3	Victoria Square	B2
Princes Dock Street	B3	Waltham Street	B2
Princess Street	C1	Waterhouse Lane	B3
Prospect Street	A1	Waverley Street	A4
Pryme Street	A1	Wellington Street	C4

Wellington Street West	B4
West Street	A2
Whitefriargate	C3
William Street	A4
Wincolmlee	C1
Witham	D1
Worship Street	C1
Wright Street	A1

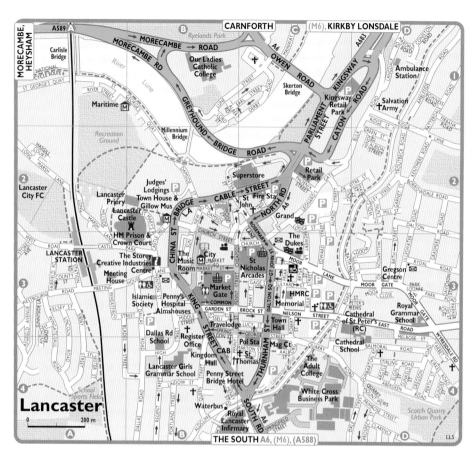

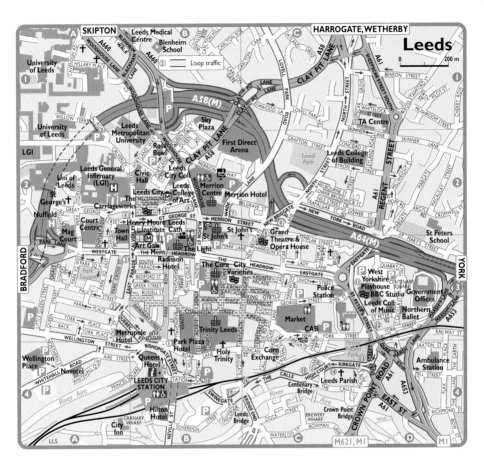

Aire Street........................A4
Albion Place.....................B3
Albion Street....................B2
Argyle Road......................D2
Back York Place................A3
Bedford Street..................B3
Belgrave Street.................B2
Benson Street...................D1
Bishopgate Street..............B4
Blackman Lane..................A1
Blenheim Walk..................A1
Boar Lane........................B4
Bowman Lane...................C4
Bow Street.......................C4
Bridge End.......................C3
Bridge Street....................C3
Briggate..........................B3
Butts Court......................B3
Byron Street.....................C2
Calverley Street.................A2
Call Lane.........................C4
Carlton Carr.....................B1
Carlton Gate.....................B1
Carlton Hill......................B1
Carlton Rise.....................B1
Cavendish Road................A1
Central Road.....................C3
Cherry Row......................D1
City Square......................B3
Clay Pit Lane....................B2
Commercial Street.............B4
Concordia Street...............B4
Concord Street..................C2
County Arcade..................C3

Cromwell Street................D2
Cross Arcade....................B3
Cross Stamford Street.........D1
Crown Point Bridge............C4
Crown Point Road..............D4
Crown Street.....................C4
Dock Street......................C4
Duke Street......................D4
Duncan Street...................C4
Dyer Street.......................C3
Eastgate..........................C3
East Parade......................A3
East Street........................D4
Elmwood Lane..................C1
Firth Street.......................D1
Flax Place........................D4
George Street....................C3
Gower Street....................C2
Grace Street.....................A3
Grafton Street...................C2
Great George Street...........A2
Greek Street.....................B3
Harewood Street...............C3
Harper Street....................C4
Harrison Street..................C3
High Court.......................C4
Hillary Place.....................A1
Hope Road.......................D2
Infirmary Street.................B3
King Edward Street.............B3
King Street.......................A3
Kirkgate..........................C3
Lady Lane........................C3
Lands Lane.......................B3
Leeds Bridge.....................B4
Leighton Street..................A2

Leyland Road....................D2
Little Queen Street.............A3
Lovell Park Hill.................C1
Lovell Park Road...............C1
Lower Basinghall Street.......B3
Lower Brunswick Street......C2
Mabgate..........................D2
Macaulay Street................D2
Mark Lane.......................B3
Marsh Lane......................D4
Maude Street....................C4
Melbourne Street...............C2
Merrion Street...................B2
Merrion Way.....................B2
Millennium Square.............B2
Mill Hill..........................B4
Mill Street........................D4
Millwright Street...............B4
Mushroom Street..............D1
Neville Street....................B4
New Briggate....................C3
New Station Street.............B3
New York Road.................C2
New York Street................C3
Nile Street........................C2
Northern Street.................A4
North Street......................C2
Oatland Drive...................C1
Oxford Place....................A3
Oxford Row.....................A3
Park Cross Street...............A3
Park Lane.........................A3
Park Place........................A3
Park Row.........................B3
Park Square East...............A3
Park Square North.............A3

Park Square West..............A3
Park Street.......................A3
Pilot Street.......................D1
Portland Crescent..............B2
Portland Way....................B2
Princes Square..................A4
Quarry Hill.......................D3
Quebec Street...................B3
Queen Square...................B2
Queen Square Court...........B2
Queen Street.....................A3
Railway Street...................D3
Regent Street....................D2
Richmond Street...............C4
Russell Street....................B3
St Cecilla Street.................D3
St Mary's Street.................D3
St Paul's Street.................A3
St Peter's Square...............D3
St Peter's Street.................D3
Saxton Street....................D4
Sheepscar Grove................D1
Sheepscar Street South........D1
Skinner Lane.....................D2
Somers Street....................A3
South Parade.....................B3
Sovereign Street.................B4
Swinegate.........................B4
Templar Place....................C3
Templar Street...................C3
The Calls..........................C4
The Garth.........................D4
The Headrow.....................B3
The Lane..........................D4
Thoresby Place..................A2
Trafalgar Street.................C2

Trinity Street.....................B3
Union Street......................C3
Upper Basinghall Street........B3
Vicar Lane........................C3
Victoria Quarter.................C3
Wade Lane........................B2
Waterloo Street.................C4
Well Close Rise..................B1
Wellington Street...............A3
Westgate..........................A3
Wharf Street.....................C4
Whitehall Quay..................A4
Whitehall Road..................A4
Whitelock Street.................D1
Willow Terrace Road...........A1
Woodhouse Lane...............A1
York Place........................A3
York Street.......................D3

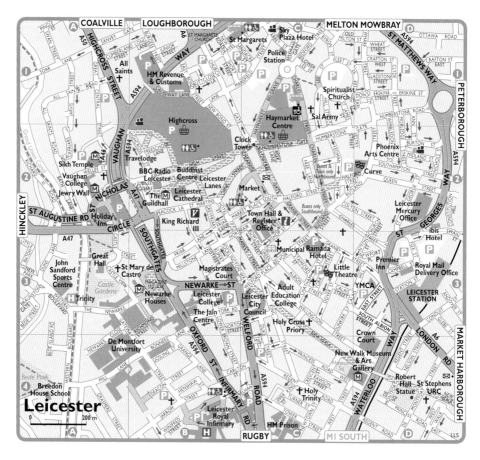

Abbey Street	C1	Conduit Street	D3	Haymarket	C2	Newport Place	D3	South Albion Street	D3
Albion Street	C3	Constitution Hill	D2	Henshaw Street	B4	New Road	B1	Southampton Street	D2
All Saints Road	A1	Crafton Street East	D1	Highcross Street	A1	Newtown Street	C4	Southgates	B3
Andover Street	D3	Crafton Street West	D1	Highcross Street	B2	New Walk	C3	Stamford Street	C3
Ann Street	D1	Crescent Street	C4	High Street	B2	Nichols Street	D2	Station Street	D3
Bath Lane	A2	Cumberland Street	A1	Hill Street	C1	Northampton Street	D3	Swain Street	D3
Bede Island Road	A4	Deacon Street	B4	Horsefair Street	B3	Norton Street	B3	Swan Street	A1
Bede Street	A3	De Montfort Square	D4	Hotel Street	B2	Old Milton Street	C1	The Newarke	A3
Bedford Street	C1	De Montfort Street	D4	Humberstone Gate	C2	Ottawa Road	D1	Tower Street	C4
Belgrave Gate	C1	Dover Street	C3	Humberstone Road	D1	Oxford Street	B3	Turner Street	C4
Belgrave Street	C1	Duke Street	C3	Infirmary Road	B4	Peacock Lane	B2	Upper King Street	C3
Belvoir Street	C3	Dunkirk Street	D2	Jarrom Street	B4	Pelham Street	C4	Vaughan Way	A2
Bishop Street	C3	Duns Lane	A3	Jarvis Street	A1	Pingle Street	A1	Vestry Street	D2
Blackfriars Street	A2	Earl Street	D1	Jubilee Square	B2	Pocklington Walk	B3	Waterloo Way	D4
Bonners Lane	B4	East Bond Street Lane	B1	Junior Street	B1	Princess Road East	D4	Welford Place	C3
Bowling Green Street	C3	East Street	D3	King Street	C3	Princess Road West	C4	Welford Road	C3
Braunstone Gate	A3	Eldon Street	C1	Lee Street	C1	Queen Street	D2	Welles Street	A2
Burgess Street	B1	Erskine Street	D1	Little Holme Street	A3	Rawson Street	C4	Wellington Street	C3
Burton Street	D2	Fleet Street	C1	London Road	D3	Regent Road	C4	Western Boulevard	A3
Buttclose Lane	A1	Fox Lane	C2	Long Lane	B1	Regent Street	D4	West Street	C4
Byron Street	C1	Fox Street	D3	Lower Brown Street	B3	Richard III Road	A2	West Walk	D4
Calais Hill	C3	Free Lane	C2	Lower Lee Street	C1	Richmond Street	B3	Wharf Street South	D1
Calais Street	C3	Freeschool Lane	B2	Magazine Square	B3	Rupert Street	B3	Wheat Street	D1
Campbell Street	D3	Friar Lane	B3	Mansfield Street	B1	Rutland Street	C3	Wimbledon Street	D1
Cank Street	B2	Gallowtree Gate	C2	Market Place South	B2	St Augustine Road	A2	Winifred Street	B4
Carlton Street	B4	Gateway Street	A3	Market Street	C3	St George Street	D2	Yeoman Street	C2
Castle Street	A3	Gladstone Street	D1	Midland Street	D2	St Georges Way	D2	York Road	B3
Castle View	A3	Glebe Street	D3	Mile Street	C4	St James Street	C1	York Street	C3
Causeway Lane	B1	Gosling Street	B4	Mill Lane	A4	St Margarets Church	B1	
Charles Street	C1	Granby Street	C2	Millstone Lane	B3	St Martins	B2	
Chatham Street	C3	Grange Lane	B4	Morledge Street	D1	St Matthews Way	D1	
Cheapside	C2	Grasmere Street	A4	Nelson Street	D4	St Nicholas Circle	A2	
Church Gate	B1	Gravel Street	B1	Newarke Close	A4	Sandacre Street	B1	
Church Street	D3	Great Central Street	A1	Newarke Street	B3	Sanvey Gate	A1	
Clyde Street	D1	Greyfriars	B2	New Bond Street	B1	Short Street	B1	
Colton Street	C2	Halford Street	C2	New Park	A3	Soar Lane	A1	

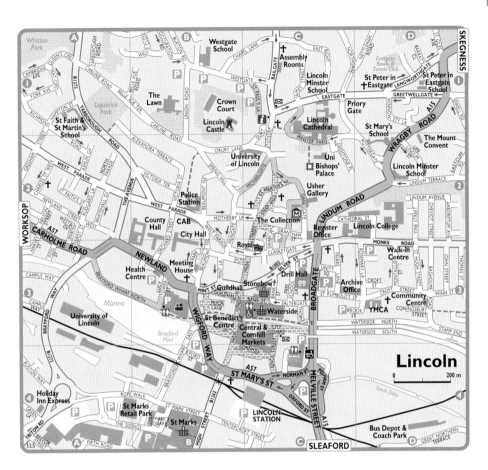

Alexandra Terrace	B2	Cornhill	B4	Lucy Tower Street	B3
Arboretum Avenue	D2	Croft Street	D3	May Crescent	A1
Ashlin Grove	A2	Danesgate	C2	Melville Street	C4
Bagholme Road	D3	Depot Street	A3	Michaelgate	C2
Bailgate	C1	Dury Lane	B2	Minster Yard	C2
Bank Street	C3	East Bight	C1	Mint Lane	B3
Barrat's Close	D1	Eastcliff Road	D2	Mint Street	B3
Beaumont Fee	B3	Eastgate	C1	Monks Road	D3
Bedford Street	B4	Firth Road	A4	Montague Street	D3
Beevor Street	A4	Foss Street	A3	Motherby Lane	B2
Belle Vue Road	B1	Free School Lane	C3	Much Lane	B3
Belle Vue Terrace	A1	Friars Lane	C3	Nelson Street	A2
Brayford Way	A3	Grantham Street	C2	Nettleham Road	D1
Brayford Wharf East	B4	Great Northern		Newland	B3
Brayford Wharf		Terrace	D4	Newland Street	
North	A3	Green Lane	A4	West	A2
Broadgate	C3	Greestone Place	C2	Norman Street	C4
Brook Street	C3	Greetwellgate	D1	Northgate	C1
Burton Road	B1	Gresham Street	A2	North Parade	A2
Cambridge Avenue	A1	Guildhall Street	B3	Occupation Road	B1
Campus Way	A3	Hampton Street	A1	Orchard Street	B3
Carholme Road	A2	Harvey Street	A3	Oxford Street	C4
Carline Road	A1	High Street	B3	Park Street	B3
Cathedral Street	C2	Hungate	B3	Pelham Street	C4
Chapel Lane	B1	James Street	C1	Pottergate	D2
Charles Street West	A2	John Street	D3	Queen's Crescent	A1
Cheviot Street	D2	Langworthgate	D1	Richmond Road	A2
City Square	C3	Lindum Avenue	D2	Rope Walk	A4
Clasketgate	C3	Lindum Road	C2	Rosemary Lane	D3
Coningsbury Street	D3	Lindum Terrace	D2	Rudgard Lane	A2
				Ruston Way	A4
				St Faith's Street	A2
				St Giles Avenue	D1
				St Hugh Street	D3
				St Mark's Square	B4
				St Mark Street	B4
				St Martin's Street	C2
				St Mary's Street	B4
				St Paul's Lane	C1
				St Rumbold's Street	C3
				Saltergate	C3
				Sewell Road	D1
				Silver Street	C3
				Sincil Street	C4
				Spring Hill	B2
				Stamp End	D3
				Steer Hill	C2
				Swan Street	C3
				Tentercroft Street	B4
				The Avenue	A2
				The Sidings	A4
				Thomas Street	D3
				Thorngate	C3
				Triton Road	A4
				Union Road	B1
				Unity Square	C3
				Upper Lindum	
				Street	C2
				Victoria Street	B2
				Victoria Terrace	B2
				Vine Street	D2
				Waterside North	C3
				Waterside South	C3
				Westbourne Grove	A2
				Westgate	B1
				West Parade	A2
				Whitehall Grove	A2
				Wigford Way	B3
				Willis Close	B1
				Winnow Sty Lane	D1
				Winn Street	D3
				Wragby Road	D2
				Yarborough Road	A1
				York Avenue	A1

Addison Street C1
Argyle Street C4
Bartholomew Road C1
Bath Street A1
Benson Street D3
Berry Street D4
Bidder Street D1
Birkett Street D1
Bixteth Street B2
Bold Street D3
Bolton Street D3
Bosnett Street C3
Bridport Street D2
Brook Street A2
Brownlow Hill D3
Brunswick Street A3
Camden Street D2
Canning Place B4
Castle Street B3
Chapel Street A2
Cheapside B2
Christian Street D1
Churchill Way C2
Church Street C3
Cockspur Street B1
College Lane C3
Colquitt Street D4
Comus Street C1
Concert Street C4
Cook Street B3
Copperas Hill D3
Cropper Street D3
Crosshall Street C2
Cunliffe Street B2
Dale Street
   (Queensway) B2

Derby Square B3
Drury Lane B3
Duke Street C4
East Street B1
Eaton Street B1
Eberle Street B2
Edmund Street B2
Elliot Street C3
Fazakerley Street A2
Fenwick Street B3
Fleet Street C3
Fontenoy Street C1
Fraser Street D2
Freemasons Row B1
Gascoyne Street D1
Gerard Street D1
Gilbert Street C4
Gradwell Street C4
Great Crosshall Street C1
Great Howard Street A1
Hackins Hey B2
Hanover Street C4
Harker Street D1
Hartley Quay B4
Hatton Garden B2
Hawke Street D3
Henry Street C4
Highfield Street B1
Hood Street C2
Hotham Street D2
Hunter Street C1
Islington D2
James Street B3
Johnson Street C2
King Edward Street A2
Knight Street D4

Lanyork Road A1
Leece Street D4
Leeds Street A1
Lime Street D2
Liver Street B4
London Road D2
Lord Nelson Street D2
Lord Street B3
Lydia Ann Street C4
Mann Island A3
Mansfield Street D1
Marlborough Street B1
Marybone C1
Midghall Street B1
Moorfields B2
Moor Street B3
Mount Pleasant D3
Naylor Street B1
Newington D3
New Quay A2
North John Street B3
North Street C2
Norton Street D2
Old Hall Street A1
Oldham Place D4
Oldham Street D4
Old Haymarket C2
Old Leeds Street A2
Oriel Street B1
Ormond Street B2
Paisley Street A1
Pall Mall B1
Paradise Street C3
Parker Street C3
Park Lane C4
Parr Street D4

Peover Street C1
Pickop Street B1
Princes Parade A2
Princess Street B2
Pumpfields Road B1
Queensway
   (Birkenhead Tunnel) ... A4
Ranelagh Street C3
Redcross Street B3
Renshaw Street D3
Richmond Lane C3
Rigby Street A1
Roberts Street A1
Rodney Street D4
Roscoe Street D4
Rose Hill D1
Russell Street D2
St Anne Street D1
St Bartholomew Road C1
St John's Lane C2
St Josephs Crescent D1
St Nicholas Place A3
St Paul's Street B2
Salthouse Quay B4
School Lane C3
Scotland Road C1
Seel Street C3
Seel Street C3
Seymour Street D2
Sim Street D1
Sir Thomas Street C2
Skelhorne Street D3
Slater Street C4
Soho Street D1
Springfield D1
Stafford Street D1

Standish Street C1
Stanley Street B2
Strand Street B3
Suffolk Street C4
Tarleton Street C3
Temple Street B2
The Strand A3
Tithe Barn Street B2
Tom Mann Close D1
Trueman Street C2
Union Street A2
Vauxhall Road B1
Vernon Street B2
Victoria Street B3
Wakefield Street D1
Wall Street B3
Waterloo Road A1
Water Street A3
Westmorland Drive B1
Whitechapel C2
William Brown Street C2
William Jessop Way A1
Williamson Square C3
Williamson Street C3
Wood Street C3
York Street C4

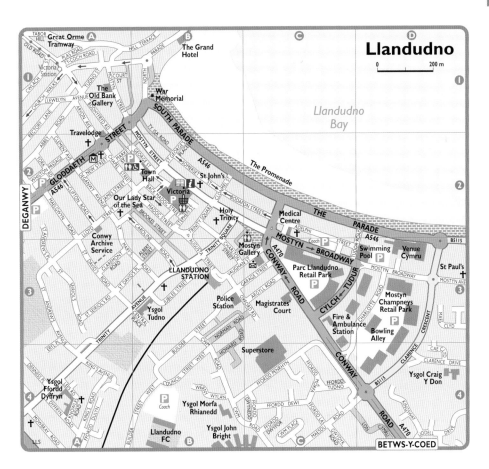

Abbey Road............A2	Cwm Road............B3	Lon Cymru............D4	Trinity Square............B2
Adelphi Street............C2	Cylch Tudur............C3	Madoc Street............B2	Tudno Street............A1
Albert Street............B3	Deganwy Avenue............A2	Maelgwyn Road............A2	Tudor Road............C3
Argyll Road............C3	Denness Place............A4	Maes Clyd............D3	Ty-Coch Road............A1
Arvon Avenue............A1	Dyffryn Road............A4	Maesdu Road............C4	Ty Isa Road............B1
Augusta Street............B3	Eryl Place............A4	Market Street............A2	Vaughan Street............B3
Back Madoc Street............B2	Ffordd Dewi............C4	Mostyn Avenue............D3	Werny Wylan............B4
Bodafon Street............B2	Ffordd Dulyn............A4	Mostyn Broadway............C3	Whiston Passage............A2
Bodhyfryd Road............A1	Ffordd Dwyfor............C4	Mostyn Street............A1	York Road............A2
Brookes Street............B2	Ffordd Gwynedd............C4	Mowbray Road............A4	
Builder Street............B4	Ffordd Las............C4	New Street............A2	
Builder Street West............A4	Ffordd Morfa............C4	Norman Road............B3	
Cae Clyd............D4	Ffordd Penrhyn............C4	North Parade............B1	
Caroline Road............B2	Ffordd Tudno............C4	Old Road............A1	
Central Place............B3	Garage Street............B3	Oxford Road............B3	
Chapel Street............A2	George Street............A2	Plas Road............A1	
Charlotte Road............D3	Gloddaeth Street............A2	Rectory Lane............A1	
Charlton Street............B3	Gwydyr Road............C4	St Andrew's Avenue............A3	
Church Walks............A1	Hill Terrace............A1	St Andrew's Place............A2	
Claremont Road............A3	Howard Road............B4	St David's Place............A3	
Clarence Crescent............D4	James Street............A2	St David's Road............A3	
Clarence Drive............D4	Jubilee Street............B3	St George's Place............B2	
Clement Avenue............A2	King's Avenue............A4	St Mary's Road............A2	
Clifton Road............A2	King's Road............A4	St Seiriol's Road............A3	
Clonmel Street............B2	Kingsway............D4	Somerset Street............B2	
Conway Road............C3	Knowles Road............A4	South Parade............B1	
Council Street West............B4	Lees Road............A4	Stephen Street............B2	
Court Street............A1	Liddell Drive............D4	Tabor Hill............A1	
Cwlach Street............A1	Llewelyn Avenue............A1	The Parade............C2	
Cwm Place............C4	Lloyd Street............A2	Trinity Avenue............A3	

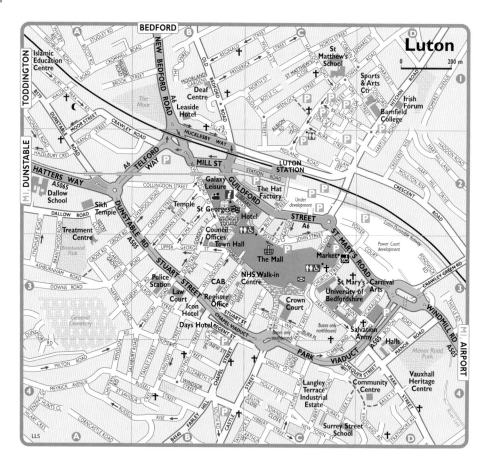

Adelaide Street.............B3	Collingdon Street..........B2	Hartley Road................D2	North Street................C1	Townsley Close C4
Albert Road.................C4	Concorde Street D1	Hastings Street B4	Old Bedford Road........B1	Union Street................C4
Albion Road.................C1	Crawley Green	Hatters Way.................A2	Oxford Road................C4	Upper George
Alma Street B2	Road.........................D3	Havelock Road C1	Park Street..................C3	Street.......................B3
Arthur Street...............C4	Crawley Road A1	Hazelbury Crescent A2	Park Street..................D4	Vicarage Street.............D3
Ashburnham Road.........A3	Crescent Rise...............D2	Hibbert Street..............C4	Park Street West..........C3	Waldeck Road A1
Back Street..................C1	Crescent Road..............D2	Highbury Road..............A1	Park Viaduct................C4	Wellington Street..........B4
Bailey Street.................D4	Cromwell Road.............A1	High Town Road............D1	Pomfret Avenue...........D1	Wenlock Street............C1
Biscot Road.................A1	Cross Street.................C1	Hitchin Road.................D1	Pondwicks Road...........D3	William Street..............C1
Bolton Road.................D3	Cumberland Street........C4	Holly Street.................C4	Power Court.................D2	Windmill Road.............D3
Boyle Close..................C1	Dallow Road A2	Hucklesby Way..............B2	Princess Street.............B3	Windsor Street.............B4
Brantwood Road...........A3	Dudley Street................C1	Inkerman Street............B3	Regent Street...............B3	Winsdon Road.............A4
Brunswick Street..........C1	Duke Street..................C1	John Street...................C2	Reginald Street.............B1	York Street..................C1
Burr Place C3	Dumfries Street............B4	Kelvin Close C4	Rothesay Road.............A3	
Burr Street..................C2	Dunstable Road.............A1	Kingsland Road.............D4	Russell Rise.................A4	
Bury Park Road............A1	Dunstable Road.............A2	King Street...................B3	Russell Street...............B4	
Bute Street..................C2	Edward Street...............D1	Latimer Road C4	St Ann's Street.............C3	
Buxton Road................B3	Essex Close C4	Lea Road......................D3	St Mary's Road.............C3	
Cardiff Road.................A3	Farley Hill.....................B4	Liverpool Road..............B2	St Matthew's Close........C1	
Cardigan Street............B2	Flowers Way.................C3	Manor Road.................C4	Salisbury Road..............A4	
Castle Street................B4	Frederick Street............B1	Melson Street...............C3	Silver Street.................C3	
Chapel Street...............B4	George Street...............B3	Meyrick Avenue A4	Stanley Street...............B4	
Chapel Viaduct.............B3	George Street West......B3	Midland Road...............C2	Station Road.................C2	
Charles Street..............D1	Gillam Street.................C2	Mill Street....................B2	Strathmore Avenue.......D4	
Cheapside C3	Gordon Street...............B3	Milton Road.................A4	Stuart Street.................B3	
Chequer Street.............C4	Grove Road A3	Moor Street.................A1	Surrey Street................C4	
Chiltern Road A4	Guildford Street............B2	Moulton Rise................D2	Tavistock Street............B4	
Church Street...............C2	Haddon Road................D2	Napier Road.................A3	Taylor Street................C1	
Church Street...............C3	Hart Hill Drive..............D2	New Bedford Road........B1	Telford Way.................B2	
Cobden Street..............C1	Hart Hill Lane...............D2	New Town Street..........C4	Thistle Road.................D3	

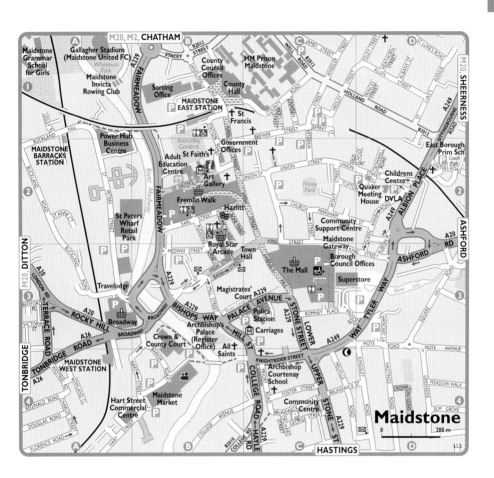

Albany Street	D1	Gabriel's Hill	C3	Princes Street	D1	Wheeler Street	C1
Albion Place	D2	George Street	C4	Priory Road	C4	Woollett Street	C1
Allen Street	D1	Greenside	D4	Pudding Lane	B2	Wyatt Street	C2
Ashford Road	D3	Hart Street	A4	Queen Anne Road	D2		
Bank Street	B3	Hastings Road	D4	Reginald Road	A4		
Barker Road	B4	Hayle Road	C4	Rocky Hill	A3		
Bedford Place	A3	Hedley Street	C1	Romney Place	C3		
Bishops Way	B3	High Street	B3	Rose Yard	B2		
Brewer Street	C2	Holland Road	D1	Rowland Close	A4		
Broadway	A3	James Street	C1	St Anne Court	A2		
Broadway	B3	Jeffrey Street	C1	St Faith's Street	B2		
Brunswick Street	C4	King Street	C3	St Luke's Avenue	D1		
Buckland Hill	A2	Kingsley Road	D4	St Luke's Road	D1		
Buckland Road	A2	Knightrider Street	C4	St Peters Street	A2		
Camden Street	C1	Lesley Place	A1	Sandling Road	B1		
Chancery Lane	D3	London Road	A3	Sittingbourne Road	D1		
Charles Street	A4	Lower Stone Street	C3	Square Hill Road	D3		
Church Street	C2	Market Buildings	B2	Stacey Street	B1		
College Avenue	B4	Marsham Street	C2	Station Road	B1		
College Road	C4	Meadow Walk	D4	Terrace Road	A3		
County Road	C1	Medway Street	B3	Tonbridge Road	A4		
Crompton Gardens	D4	Melville Road	C4	Tufton Street	C2		
Cromwell Road	D2	Mill Street	B3	Union Street	C2		
Douglas Road	A4	Mote Avenue	D3	Upper Stone Street	C4		
Earl Street	B2	Mote Road	D3	Victoria Street	A3		
Elm Grove	D4	Old School Place	D2	Vinters Road	D2		
Fairmeadow	B1	Orchard Street	C4	Wat Tyler Way	C3		
Florence Road	A4	Padsole Lane	C3	Week Street	C1		
Foley Street	D1	Palace Avenue	B3	Well Road	C1		
Foster Street	C4			Westree Road	A4		

Abingdon Street ... C4	Cheapside ... B3	High Street ... C2	Mosley Street ... C3	St Anns Square ... B2
Addington Street ... D1	China Lane ... D3	Hilton Street ... D3	Mount Street ... B4	St Ann Street ... B3
Angel Street ... C1	Chorlton Street ... C4	Hope Street ... D3	Mulberry Street ... B3	St James Square ... B3
Artillery Street ... A4	Church Street ... C2	Houndsworth Street ... D2	Museum Street ... B4	St James Street ... B4
Atkinson Street ... A3	Cobourg Street ... D4	Hunt's Bank ... B1	New Bridge Street ... B1	St Mary's Gate ... B2
Auburn Street ... D4	College Land ... B2	Jackson's Row ... A3	New Cathedral Street ... B2	St Mary's Parsonage ... A2
Aytoun Street ... D3	Collier Street ... A1	John Dalton ... B3	New George Street ... C1	St Mary Street ... B2
Back Bridge Street ... A3	Concert Lane ... B3	John Street ... A1	New Market ... B2	Salmon Street ... C2
Back George Street ... C3	Copperas Street ... C2	John Street ... C2	Newton Street ... D3	Shudehill ... C2
Back Piccadilly ... C2	Corporation Street ... B2	Joiner Street ... C2	New York Street ... C3	Soap Street ... C2
Back South Parade ... A2	Crosskeys Street ... D1	Kennedy Street ... B3	Nicholas Street ... C3	South King Street ... B3
Bendix Street ... D1	Cross Street ... B3	King Street ... A1	Norton Street ... A1	Spear Street ... D2
Blackfriars Road ... A1	Dale Street ... C2	King Street ... B3	Oak Street ... C2	Spring Gardens ... C3
Blackfriars Street ... A2	Dantzic Street ... C2	King Street West ... A3	Old Bank Street ... B2	Station Approach ... D3
Bloom Street ... C4	Deansgate ... A4	Lena Street ... D3	Oldham Road ... D1	Swan Street ... C1
Boond Street ... A1	Dean Street ... D2	Lever Street ... D2	Oldham Street ... D2	Tariff Street ... D3
Booth Street ... B3	Dickinson Street ... B4	Lincoln Square ... B3	Pall Mall ... B3	Thomas Street ... C2
Booth Street ... A4	Dolefield ... A3	Little John Street ... A4	Parker Street ... C3	Thompson Street ... D1
Bow Lane ... B3	Ducie Street ... D3	Little Lever Street ... D3	Peter Street ... B4	Tib Lane ... B3
Brazennose Street ... B3	Edge Street ... C2	Liverpool Road ... A4	Piccadilly ... D3	Tib Street ... C2
Brewer Street ... D3	Exchange Square ... B2	Lloyd Street ... B3	Piccadilly Gardens ... C3	Todd Street ... B1
Bridge Street ... A3	Fairfield Street ... D4	London Road ... D4	Pine Street ... C3	Tonman Street ... A4
Bridgewater Place ... C2	Faraday Street ... D2	Long Millgate ... B1	Police Street ... B3	Trinity Way ... A1
Brown Street ... B3	Faulkner Street ... C4	Longworth Street ... A4	Porchfield Square ... A4	Turner Street ... C2
Bury Street ... A1	Fennel Street ... B1	Loom Street ... D2	Portland Street ... C3	Viaduct Street ... A1
Byrom Street ... A3	Fountain Street ... B3	Lower Byrom Street ... A4	Port Street ... D3	Victoria Bridge Street ... B2
Cable Street ... D1	Gartside Street ... A3	Lower Mosley Street ... B4	Princess Street ... B3	Victoria Street ... B2
Canal Street ... C4	George Street ... B4	Ludgate Street ... D1	Quay Street ... A2	Warwick Street ... D2
Cateaton Street ... B2	Gravel Lane ... A1	Major Street ... C4	Quay Street ... A3	Watson Street ... A4
Cathedral Street ... B2	Great Ancoats Street ... D2	Marble Street ... C3	Queen Street ... A1	Well Street ... C2
Chadderton Street ... D1	Great Ducie Street ... B1	Market Street ... B2	Queen Street ... A3	West Mosley Street ... C3
Chain Street ... C3	Great Northern Square ... A4	Marsden Street ... B3	Reyner Street ... C4	Whitworth Street ... C4
Chapel Street ... A2	Greengate ... A1	Marshall Street ... D1	Richmond Street ... C4	Windmill Street ... B4
Charlotte Street ... C3	Hanover Street ... C1	Mason Street ... D1	Roby Street ... D3	Withy Grove ... C2
Chatham Street ... D3	Hardman Square ... A3	Miller Street ... C1	Rochdale Road ... D1	Wood Street ... A3
	Hardman Street ... A3	Minshull Street ... C3	Sackville Street ... C4	York Street ... C3

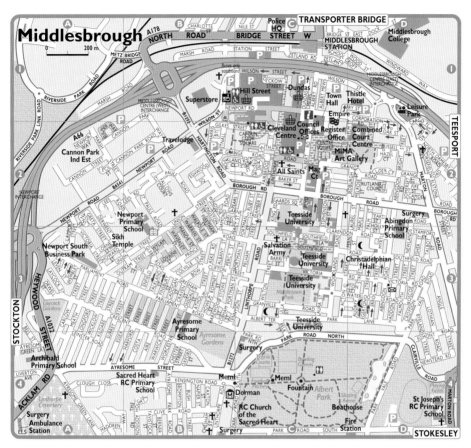

Abingdon Road...................D3	Carlow Street.....................A3	Fry Street...........................D1	Manor Street......................B3	St Aidans Drive..................C2
Acklam Road......................A4	Caxton Street.....................B4	Garnet Street.....................B2	Maple Street......................D3	St Pauls Road.....................B2
Acton Street.......................C3	Centre Square.....................C2	Gilkes Street.......................B2	Marsh Road........................A1	Smith Street.......................C2
Addison Road......................B4	Chester Street.....................B4	Glebe Road.........................B3	Marsh Road........................B1	Somerset Street..................D2
Aire Street.........................B4	Clairville Road....................D4	Grange Road.......................B2	Marsh Street.......................A2	Southfield Lane...................C3
Albany Street......................B3	Clarendon Road..................C3	Grange Road.......................D2	Marton Road.......................C3	Southfield Road..................C3
Albert Mews.......................C1	Clifton Street......................B3	Granville Road....................C3	Meath Street.......................A3	Stamford Street..................C2
Albert Road........................C2	Clive Road..........................B4	Gresham Road.....................B3	Melrose Street....................B3	Station Street.....................C1
Albert Terrace.....................C3	Clough Close......................A4	Greta Street........................A2	Metz Bridge Road................A1	Stephenson Street...............C2
Amber Street......................C2	Colville Street.....................B3	Haddon Street.....................D3	Monkland Close...................B2	Stowe Street.......................B3
Angle Street.......................D3	Corporation Road...............D1	Harewood Street.................B3	Myrtle Street......................D3	Surrey Street......................A4
Aske Road..........................B3	Costa Street........................B4	Harford Street.....................B4	Napier Street......................B4	Talbot Street.......................D3
Athol Street........................B3	Craven Street......................B3	Harris Street........................B2	Newlands Road...................D3	Tavistock Street..................B4
Audrey Street......................B3	Crescent Road....................A3	Hartington Road..................B2	Newport Road.....................A2	Tennyson Street..................B3
Ayresome Park Road...........B4	Croydon Road.....................D3	Head Street.........................C2	Newstead Road...................D4	Ulla Street..........................C3
Ayresome Street.................A4	Derwent Street....................A2	Heywood Street...................A3	North Ormesby Road...........D2	Union Street.......................A3
Baker Street........................C2	Diamond Road....................B3	Horsefield...........................D2	Outram Street.....................A3	University Boulevard...........C2
Barritt Street.......................C3	Dock Street.........................D1	Howard Street.....................A3	Oxford Street......................B4	Upton Street.......................C3
Berner Street......................B4	Dundas Mews.....................C1	Jedburgh Street...................D2	Palm Street.........................D3	Victoria Road......................C3
Bolckow Street....................C1	Egerton Street.....................D3	Kensington Road.................B4	Park Lane...........................C4	Victoria Street.....................A3
Borough Road.....................C2	Egmont Road......................D3	Kildare Street......................A4	Park Road South.................C4	Walpole Street....................B2
Bow Street.........................B3	Elder Court.........................D2	King Edwards Square...........C2	Park Vale Road....................D4	Warren Street......................B2
Bretnall Street....................B2	Elm Street..........................D2	Kingston Street....................B2	Parliament Road..................A3	Warwick Street....................B4
Bridge Street East...............C1	Elstone Road.......................D2	Lamport Street....................A3	Pearl Street........................C2	Waterloo Road....................D3
Bridge Street West..............C1	Emily Street........................C2	Laura Street........................C3	Peel Street..........................B3	Waverley Street...................B3
Bright Street.......................D2	Enfield Street......................B3	Laurel Street.......................D3	Pelham Street......................B3	Wembley Street...................A3
Brompton Street.................B4	Errol Street.........................D3	Laycock Street.....................A3	Percy Street........................B3	Wicklow Street....................A4
Bulmer Way.......................A2	Esher Street........................D3	Lees Road...........................A2	Portman Street....................B3	Wilson Street......................B2
Bush Street.........................B4	Eshwood Square.................B2	Leinster Road......................A4	Princes Road.......................B3	Wilton Street......................C3
Byelands Street...................D3	Essex Street........................A4	Leven Street........................A3	Riverside Park Link Road......A1	Windsor Street.....................B2
Cadogan Street...................B3	Fairbridge Street.................C2	Linthorpe Road...................B4	Riverside Park Road.............A1	Windward Way....................D1
Cannon Park Road..............A2	Falkland Street....................B3	Longford Street...................A4	Romney Street.....................D3	Woodlands Road.................C3
Cannon Park Way................A2	Falmouth Street..................D3	Lonsdale Street...................B3	Roscoe Street......................D3	Worcester Street..................B4
Cannon Street.....................A2	Fern Street.........................D3	Lorne Street........................A3	Ruby Street.........................C2	Wylam Street......................B3
Captain Cook Square...........C2	Finsbury Street....................B3	Lothian Road.......................D3	Russell Street......................D2	Zetland Place......................C1
Cargo Fleet Road................D2	Fleetham Street..................B2	Lovaine Street.....................B3	Rutland Court......................D2	Zetland Road......................C1

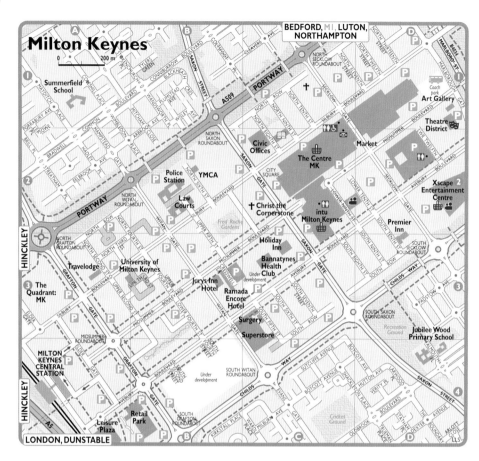

Arbrook Avenue.............B2
Arlott Close.................D4
Avebury Boulevard.......A4
Blackheath Crescent......B1
Boycott Avenue............C4
Bradwell Common
Boulevard.................A2
Brill Place...................A2
Childs Way..................B4
City Square.................C2
Cleavers Avenue...........C1
Coleshill Place..............A1
Coltsfoot Place.............B1
Conniburrow
Boulevard.................B1
Cresswell Lane..............B3
Dexter Avenue.............D4
Eelbrook Avenue..........A2
Elder Gate...................A3
Elder Gate...................A4
Evans Gate..................A2
Falmouth Place............D3
Forrabury Avenue........A1
Grafton Gate...............A3
Hadley Place................A2
Hampstead Gate..........A2
Hutton Avenue............D4
Kirkstall Place..............B4
Larwood Place.............D4
Leasowe Place..............A2

Lower Fourth Street......B3
Lower Ninth Street......C2
Lower Tenth Street......C2
Lower Twelfth
Street.......................D2
Marlborough Gate.......D1
Marlborough Street......D1
Mayditch Place............A1
Midsummer
Boulevard.................B3
Midsummer
Roundabout..............A4
Milburn Avenue...........C4
Mitcham Close.............B1
North Eighth Street......C1
North Eleventh............C1
North Fourth Street......A2
North Grafton
Roundabout..............A3
North Ninth Street........C1
North Row..................A3
North Row..................C1
North Saxon
Roundabout..............B2
North Secklow
Roundabout..............C1
North Second
Street.......................A3
North Sixth Street........B2
North Tenth Street.......C1

North Third Street.......A3
North Thirteenth..........D1
North Twelfth
Street.......................D1
North Witan
Roundabout..............A2
Oldbrook Boulevard....C4
Padstow Avenue..........D3
Plumstead Avenue........B1
Portway.....................A2
Saxon Gate.................B2
Saxon Street................B1
Saxon Street................D4
Secklow Gate..............C1
Shackleton Place..........C4
Silbury Boulevard........A3
Silbury Roundabout......A3
South Eighth Street......C3
South Fifth Street.........C3
South Fourth Street......B4
South Grafton
Roundabout..............B4
South Ninth Street........D2
South Row..................C3
South Row..................D3
South Saxon
Roundabout..............D3
South Secklow
Roundabout..............D3
South Second Street.....B4

South Seventh..............C3
South Sixth Street........C3
South Tenth Street.......D2
South Witan
Roundabout..............C4
Statham Place..............D4
Stokenchurch Place......A1
Streatham Place...........A2
Sutcliffe Avenue...........C4
The Boundary..............D4
Trueman Place.............D4
Tylers Green................B1
Upper Fifth Street.........B2
Upper Fourth Street.....B3
Upper
Second Street...........A3
Upper Third Street.......B3
Verity Place.................D4
Wandsworth Place........B1
Wardle Place...............C4
Wimbledon Place.........A1
Wisley Avenue.............B1
Witan Gate..................B2

Albert Street.................D2	Cross Street....................B3	John Dobson Street.....C2	Oxford Street...............C2	Simpson Terrace...........D2
Argyle Street.................D2	Dean Street....................C3	Jubilee Road...................D3	Pandon...........................D3	South Street...................B4
Back New Bridge	Duke Street....................A4	King Street......................C4	Pandon Bank..................D3	Stepney Lane.................D3
Street..........................D2	Durant Road...................C2	Leazes Crescent............B2	Peel Lane........................A4	Stoddart Street..............D1
Barker Street.................D1	Eldon Square..................B2	Leazes Lane....................B2	Percy Street....................B2	Stowell Street................A3
Barrack Road.................A2	Falconar's Court.............B3	Leazes Park Road...........B2	Pilgrim Street..................C2	Strawberry Place...........A2
Barras Bridge.................B1	Falconer Street...............D2	Leazes Terrace...............A2	Pilgrim Street	Summerhill Terrace.......A4
Bath Lane.......................A3	Fenkle Street..................B3	Lombard Street...............C4	Roundabout.................C3	Terrace Place.................A2
Blackett Street................B2	Forth Banks Close...........B4	Lord Street.....................A4	Pink Lane........................B4	Tower Street..................D3
Blagdon Street...............D3	Forth Street....................B4	Low Friar Street.............B3	Pitt Street.......................A2	Tyne Bridge...................C4
Blandford Square...........A4	Friars Street....................A3	Market Street.................B3	Portland Road................D1	Wakenshaw VC
Blandford Street............A4	Gallowgate.....................A2	Melbourne Street...........D3	Prudhoe Place...............B2	Junction......................A4
Bridge Street..................C4	Gallowgate Junction.......A3	Milburn Junction............A3	Quayside.........................D3	Waterloo Square............A4
Broad Chare...................C3	George Street.................A4	Milton Close...................D1	Quayside.........................D4	Waterloo Street.............A4
Buxton Street.................D3	Gibson Street.................D3	Milton Place...................D1	Queen Street..................C4	Wellington Street...........A2
Byron Street...................D1	Gladstone Terrace..........D1	Mosley Street.................C3	Queen Victoria	Westgate Road...............A3
Camden Street...............D2	Grainger Street...............B3	Naper Street...................D1	Road............................B1	Westmorland Road.......A4
Carliol Square.................C3	Grantham Road...............D1	Nelson Street..................B3	Richardson Road............A1	West Walls.....................A3
Charlotte Square............A3	Great North Road...........C1	Neville Street..................B4	Rock Terrace..................D2	Wretham Place...............D2
Chester Street.................D1	Grey Street......................C3	New Bridge Street...........D2	St Andrew's Street..........A2	
City Road.......................C3	Groat Market..................B3	New Bridge Street	St Ann's Street................D3	
Claremont Road..............B1	Hadrian's Wall	Roundabout.................C2	St James Boulevard........A4	
Clarence Street...............D2	Junction......................A3	Newgate Street...............B3	St Mary's Place...............B1	
Clayton Street................B3	Harrison Place.................D1	Northumberland	St Nicholas Street...........C4	
Clayton Street West.......A4	Helmsley Road.................D1	Road............................C2	St Thomas' Court...........B2	
Cloth Market..................B3	Henry Square..................D2	Northumberland	St Thomas' Street...........B1	
College Street.................C2	High Bridge.....................C3	Street..........................B3	Sandgate........................D3	
Copland Terrace.............D2	Hillgate...........................D4	Nun Street.......................B3	Sandhill...........................C4	
Coppice Way..................D1	Hood Street....................C3	Oakwellgate....................D4	Sandyford Road..............C1	
Corporation Street.........A3	Jesmond Road West.......C1	Orchard Street................B4	Shield Street....................D2	

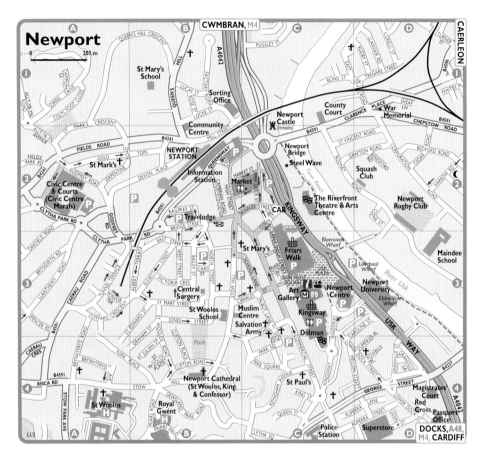

Albert Terrace B3
Allt-Yr-Yn Avenue A2
Allt-Yr-Yn Road A1
Bailey Street B3
Bedford Road D2
Beresford Road D2
Blewitt Street B3
Bond Street C1
Bridge Street B2
Bryngwyn Road A3
Brynhyfryd Avenue A4
Brynhyfryd Road A4
Caerau Crescent A4
Caerau Road A3
Cambrian Road B2
Campion Close A1
Caroline Street D3
Cedar Road D2
Charles Street C3
Chepstow Road D1
Clarence Place C1
Clifton Place B4
Clifton Road B4
Clyffard Crescent A3
Clytha Park Road A2
Clytha Square C4
Colne Street D2
Colts Foot Close A1
Commercial
  Street C4

Corelli Street D1
Corn Street C2
Corporation Road D2
Devon Place B2
Dewsland Park
  Road B4
Dumfries Place D4
East Street B3
East Usk Road C1
Factory Road B1
Fields Park Road A2
Fields Road A2
Friars Field B4
Friars Road B4
Friar Street C3
George Street D4
Godfrey Road A2
Gold Tops A2
Grafton Road C2
Graham Street B4
Granville Lane D4
Granville Street D4
Harrow Road D2
High Street B2
Hill Street C3
Ivor Square C3
John Frost Square C3
John Street D4
Jones Street B3
Keynsham Avenue C4

King Street C4
Kingsway C2
Kingsway C4
Llanthewy Road A3
Locke Street B1
Lower Dock Street C4
Lucas Street B1
Market Street B2
Mellon Street C4
Mill Street B2
North Street B3
Oakfield Road A3
Park Square C4
Powells Place D4
Pugsley Street C1
Queen's Hill B1
Queen's Hill
  Crescent A1
Queen Street C4
Queensway B2
Railway Street B2
Risca Road A4
Rodney Road C2
Rose Street B1
Rudry Street D1
Ruperra Lane C4
Ruperra Street D4
St Edward Street B3
St Julian Street B4
St Mark's Crescent A2

St Mary Street B3
St Vincent Road C2
St Woolos Place B4
St Woolos Road B3
Scard Street B3
School Lane C3
Serpentine Road A2
Sheaf Lane D1
Skinner Street C2
Sorrel Drive A1
Spencer Road A3
Stow Hill B3
Stow Hill B4
Stow Park Avenue A4
Talbot Lane C3
Tregare Street D1
Tunnel Terrace A3
Turner Street D1
Upper Dock Street C2
Upper Dock Street C3
Usk Plaza C3
Usk Way D3
Victoria Crescent B3
West Street B3
Whitby Place D1
Winsor Terrace A3
York Place A4

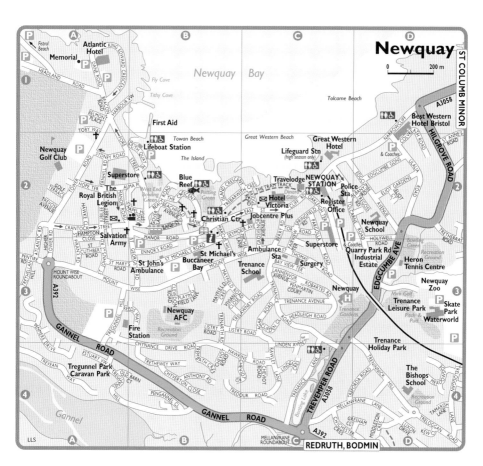

Agar Road..............C3	Eliot Gardens.............D2	Listry Road...............B3	St John's Road.............A3	Treninnick Hill.............D4
Albany Road.............D2	Ennor's Road............B3	Luxon Drive..............D4	St Mary's Road............A3	Trethellan Hill............A3
Alma Place...............A2	Estuary View.............A4	Manor Road..............A2	St Michael's Road.......B3	Tretherras Road..........D2
Anthony Road...........B4	Fairview Terrace........C3	Marcus Hill..............B2	St Piran's Road...........A2	Trethewey Way...........B4
Atlantic Road............A3	Fernhill Road.............A2	Mayfield Crescent......B3	St Thomas' Road.........C3	Trevean Way...............A4
Bank Street..............B2	Fore Street...............A2	Mayfield Road............B3	Seymour Avenue.........B2	Trevemper Road...........C4
Bay View Terrace.......C3	Gannel Road.............A3	Meadowside..............D4	South Quay Hill..........B2	Trevose Avenue...........A2
Beachfield Avenue......B2	Golf Terrace..............A2	Mellanvrane Lane.......C4	Springfield Road..........C2	Ulalia Road.................D2
Beach Road..............B2	Gover Lane..............B2	Mellanvrane	Sydney Road..............A2	Vivian Close...............B3
Beacon Road.............A1	Gresham Close...........C4	Roundabout............C4	Tamarish Lane.............D4	
Belmont Place...........A1	Grosvenor Avenue.......C3	Michel Lane...............C2	The Crescent..............B2	
Berry Road...............C2	Hampton Close...........A2	Middleton Crescent.....D4	The Tram Track...........C2	
Bridge Road..............C2	Harbour View............A1	Mount Wise..............B3	Toby Way..................A1	
Chapel Hill...............A2	Hawke Close.............A2	Mount Wise	Tolcarne Road............C2	
Cheviot Road.............B4	Hawkins Road............B4	Roundabout............A3	Tor Road...................C2	
Cheviot Road.............C4	Headland Road...........A1	Narrowcliff...............D2	Tower Road................A2	
Chichester Crescent....C4	Headleigh Road..........A2	Oakleigh Terrace.........C3	Trebarwith Crescent....B2	
Chynance Drive	Highertower Road........A3	Old Barn Court...........A4	Tredour Road..............B4	
Road.....................B4	Hilgrove Road............D1	Pargolla Road.............C2	Treforda Road.............C4	
Chyverton Close.........B4	Holywell Road............D3	Penganel Close...........B4	Tregoss Road..............D2	
Clevedon Road...........B3	Hope Terrace.............A2	Penmartin Court..........C3	Tregunnel Hill.............A3	
Clifden Close.............C3	Island Crescent..........B2	Penmere Drive............A3	Tregunnel Hill.............A4	
Cliff Road.................C2	Jubilee Street.............A2	Pentire Road..............A3	Trelawney Road...........B3	
Colvreath Road..........D2	Kew Close.................D4	Playing Field Lane........B3	Treloggan Lane............D4	
Crantock Street..........A2	King Edward	Rawley Lane...............C4	Treloggan Road...........D4	
Dane Road................A1	Crescent................A1	Reeds Way................A3	Trembath Crescent.......B4	
East Street...............C2	King Street................B2	Robartes Road............C3	Trenance Avenue.........C3	
Edgcumbe Avenue......D3	Lanhenvor Avenue.......C4	St Anne's Road...........D2	Trenance Lane.............C4	
Edgcumbe Gardens......D2	Linden Avenue............C4	St Cuthbert's Road......A3	Trenance Road.............C3	
Eliot Court...............D2	Linden Crescent..........C4	St George's Road........B3	Trenarth Road.............B3	

Abington Street...........C2	Crispin Street...............B2	Lower Cross Street...... A2	Sheep Street...................B1
Albert Place.................D2	Derngate D3	Lower Harding	Sheep Street...................C2
Albion Place.................D3	Doddridge Street.........A3	Street.............................B1	Spencer Bridge..............A1
Alcombe Road..............D1	Drapery..........................C3	Lower Mounts...............D2	Spencer Bridge
Angel Street C3	Dunster Street...............D1	Marefair A3	Road..............................A1
Arundel Street..............B1	Dychurch Lane..............C3	Margaret Street.............C1	Spencer Parade.............D3
Ash Street.....................C1	Earl Street......................D1	Market Square................C2	Spring Gardens.............D3
Bailiff Street.................C1	Fetter Street..................C3	Mercers Row.................C3	Spring Lane A1
Bath Street....................A2	Fitzroy Place...................A2	Moat Place.....................A2	Swan Street...................C3
Bedford Place...............D3	Foundry Street...............B4	Monkspond Street.......A1	Tanner Street.................A4
Black Lion Hill...............A3	Francis Street.................A1	Newland..........................C1	The Ridings...................D2
Black Lion Hill	Freeschool Lane B3	Notredame Mews..........D2	Towcester Road............A4
Junction A3	George Row...................C3	Overstone Road............D1	Tower Street..................B2
Bradshaw Street...........B2	Gold Street....................B3	Pike Lane.......................B3	Upper Bath Street.........B2
Bridge Street................C3	Grafton Place.................B1	Quorn Way.....................A1	Upper Mounts..............C1
Broad Street..................B1	Grafton Street...............A1	Regent Street.................B1	Upper Priory Street......B1
Campbell Street.............C1	Great Russell Street......D1	Robert Street..................C1	Victoria Gardens...........C4
Castilian Street.............D3	Green Street A3	St Andrew's Road..........A2	Victoria Promenade......C4
Castilian Terrace...........D3	Gregory Street...............A3	St Andrew's Street........B1	Victoria Street...............C1
Castle Street.................B2	Greyfriars........................B2	St George's Street.........B1	Wellington Street..........D2
Chalk Lane....................A3	Guildhall Road C3	St Giles Street................D3	Western Wharf...............B4
Charles Street................D1	Hazelwood Road............D3	St Giles' Terrace............D2	William Street.................C1
Cheyne Walk.................D3	Herbert Street................B2	St John's Street..............C4	
Church Lane..................C1	Horse Market.................B3	St John's Terrace C4	
Cloutsham Street...........D1	Horseshoe Street...........B3	St Katherine's Street.....B3	
College Street................B2	Kingswell Street.............B3	St Mary's Street.............A3	
Commercial Street........B4	Lady's Lane....................C1	St Michael's Road D1	
Connaught Street...........C1	Latymer Court................C1	St Peter's Way...............B4	
Court Road B3	Little Cross Street..........A2	Scarletwell Street...........A2	
Cranstoun Street...........D1	Lower Bath Street A2	Scholars Close...............D4	

Norwich

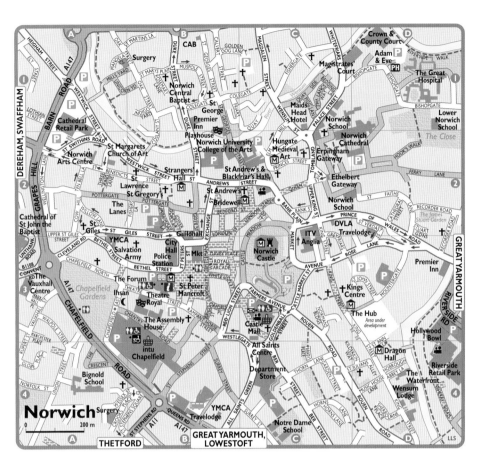

Abbey Lane	D4	Ely Street	A1	Mountergate	D3	St Benedicts Street	A2	Vauxhall Place	A3
All Saints Green	B4	Exchange Street	B2	Music House Lane	D4	St Faiths Lane	D2	Vauxhall Street	A3
Bank Plain	C2	Farmers Avenue	C3	Muspole Street	B1	St Georges Street	B1	Walpole Street	A3
Bank Street	C2	Ferry Lane	D2	Norfolk Street	A4	St Giles Street	A2	Wellington Lane	A2
Barn Road	A1	Fishergate	C1	Normans Buildings	C3	St John Street	D3	Wensum Street	C1
Bedding Lane	C1	Fishers Lane	B2	Oak Street	A1	St Julians Alley	C4	Wessex Street	A4
Bedford Street	B2	Friars Quay	B1	Opie Street	C2	St Martins Lane	B1	Westlegate	B3
Ber Street	C4	Garden Street	C4	Orford Place	B3	St Marys Plain	B1	Westwick Street	A1
Bethel Street	A3	Gentlemans Walk	B3	Palace Street	C1	St Peters Street	B3	Wherry Road	D4
Bishopgate	D1	Globe Place	A4	Pigg Lane	C1	St Stephens Road	B4	White Lion Street	B3
Brigg Street	B3	Goldenball Street	C3	Pottergate	A2	St Stephens Square	A4	Whitefriars	C1
Calvert Street	B1	Golden Dog Lane	B1	Prince of Wales		St Stephens Street	B4	Willow Lane	A2
Castle Meadow	C3	Grapes Hill	A2	Road	C2	St Swithins Road	A2		
Cathedral Street	D2	Greyfriars	C3	Princes Street	C2	St Verdast Street	D2		
Cattle Market Street	C3	Haymarket	B3	Quay Side	C1	Stuart Gardens	D2		
Chantry Road	B3	Heigham Street	A1	Queens Road	B4	Surrey Street	B4		
Chapelfield East	A3	Hobrough	D4	Queen Street	C2	Ten Bell Lane	A2		
Chapelfield North	A3	Hook's Walk	D2	Rampant Horse		Theatre Street	B3		
Chapelfield Road	A3	Horns Lane	C4	Street	B3	The Crescent	A4		
Cleveland Road	A3	Indigo Yard	B1	Recorder Road	D2	Thorn Lane	C4		
Colegate	B1	Kilderkin Way	C4	Red Lion Street	B3	Three King Lane	A2		
Convent Road	A3	King Street	C2	Riverside Road	D3	Tombland	C2		
Coslany Street	B2	London Street	B2	Riverside Walk	D1	Unicorn Yard	A1		
Cow Hill	A2	Lothian Street	A1	Rose Lane	C3	Union Street	A4		
Crooks Place	A4	Lower Goat Lane	B2	Rosemary Lane	B1	Unthank Road	A3		
Davey Place	B3	Magdalen Street	C1	Rouen Road	C3	Upper Goat Lane	B2		
Dove Street	B2	Manchester Place	A3	Royal Arcade	B3	Upper King Street	C2		
Duke Street	B1	Mandela Close	A1	Rupert Street	A4	Upper St Giles			
Earlham Road	A3	Market Avenue	C3	St Andrews Street	B2	Street	A2		
Elm Hill	C2	Mills Yard	A1	St Ann Lane	D4				

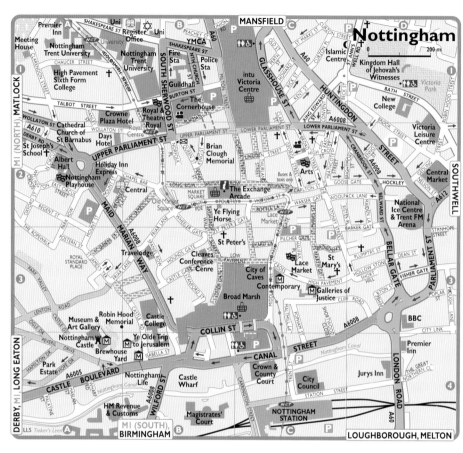

Albert Street	B3	East Street	C2	Low Pavement	B3	Ristes Place	C2	Wilford Street	B4
Barker Gate	D2	Exchange Walk	B2	Maiden Lane	D2	Robin Hood Street	D1	Wollaton Street	A1
Bath Street	D1	Fisher Gate	D3	Maid Marian Way	A2	Royal Standard Place	A3	Woolpack Lane	C2
Beck Street	C1	Fletcher Gate	C3	Maltmill Lane	C3	St Ann's Well Road	D1	
Bellar Gate	D3	Forman Street	B1	Market Square	B2	St James's Street	A3	
Belward Street	D2	Friar Lane	A3	Market Street	B2	St James's Street	B2	
Bottle Lane	C2	Friar Lane	B3	Middle Hill	C3	St James's Terrace	A3	
Brightmore Street	D2	Gedling Street	D2	Milton Street	B1	St Marks Gate	C3	
Broad Street	C2	George Street	C2	Mount Street	A2	St Marks Street	C1	
Broadway	C3	Glasshouse Street	C1	Mount Street	A3	St Mary's Gate	C3	
Bromley Place	A2	Goldsmith Street	A1	Nelson Street	D2	St Peter's Gate	B3	
Brook Street	D1	Goose Gate	C2	Norfolk Place	B2	Shakespeare Street	A1	
Burton Street	B1	Halifax Place	C3	North Church Street	B1	Short Hill	D3	
Byard Lane	C3	Hamilton Drive	A4	North Circus Street	A2	Shortwood Close	C3	
Canal Street	C4	Hanley Street	A1	Ogle Drive	A3	Smithy Row	B2	
Carlton Street	C2	Haslam Street	A4	Old Street	C1	South Parade	B2	
Carrington Street	C4	Heathcote Street	C2	Oxford Street	A2	South Sherwood Street	B1	
Castle Boulevard	A4	High Cross Street	C2	Palatine Street	A4	Spaniel Row	B3	
Castle Gate	B3	High Pavement	C3	Park Row	A3	Stanford Street	B3	
Castle Grove	A3	Hockley	C2	Park Valley	A3	Stanhope Street	D3	
Castle Road	B3	Hollow Stone	D3	Parliament Street	D3	Station Street	C4	
Chapel Bar	B2	Hope Drive	A4	Peachey Street	B1	Stoney Street	C2	
Chaucer Street	A1	Hounds Gate	B3	Pelham Street	C2	Talbot Street	A1	
City Link	D3	Howard Street	C1	Pemberton Street	D3	The Great Northern	
Clarendon Street	A1	Huntingdon Street	C1	Perth Street	C1	Close	D4	
Clare Street	C1	Isabella Street	B4	Peveril Drive	A4	The Ropewalk	A3	
Cliff Road	C3	Kent Street	C1	Pilcher Gate	C3	Thurland Street	C2	
Collin Street	B4	King Edward Street	C1	Plough Lane	D3	Trent Street	C4	
Convent Street	C1	King Street	B2	Plumptre Street	D3	Union Road	B1	
Cranbrook Street	D2	Lennox Street	D1	Popham Street	B3	Upper Parliament Street	A2	
Cumber Street	C2	Lenton Road	A3	Poplar Street	D3	Victoria Street	C2	
Curzon Place	C1	Lincoln Street	C2	Postern Street	A3	Warser Gate	C2	
Curzon Street	C1	Lister Gate	B3	Poultry	B2	Weekday Cross	C3	
Dean Street	D3	London Road	D4	Queen Street	B2	Wellington Circus	A2	
Derby Road	A2	Long Row	B2	Regent Street	A2	Wharf Road	A4	
East Circus Street	A2	Lower Parliament Street	C2	Rick Street	C1	Wheeler Gate	B2	

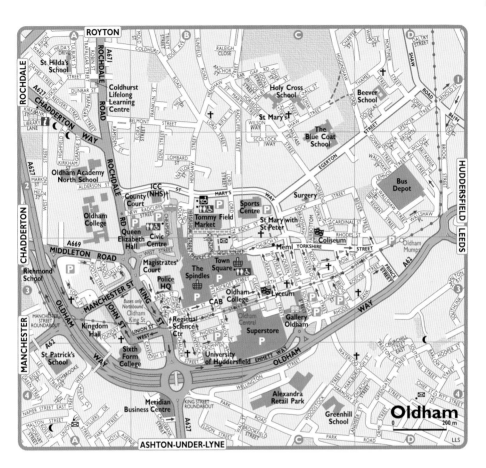

Alderson Street	A2	Crossbank Street	B4	Hornby Street	A4	Park Street	A4	South Hill Street	D4
Anchor Street	B1	Curzon Street	B2	Horsedge Street	C1	Pembrooke Street	A4	Southlink	D3
Arnold Street	D1	Daltry Street	D1	Hoyle Avenue	A4	Peter Street	B3	Spencer Street	D2
Ascroft Street	B3	Davies Street	A1	Hunters Lane	C3	Phoenix Street	B3	Sunfield Road	B1
Bar Gap Road	B1	Douglas Street	D1	Jackson Pit	B3	Pitt Street	D4	Thames Street	D1
Barlow Street	D4	Dunbar Street	A1	John Street	A3	Preston Street	D4	Trafalgar Street	A1
Barn Street	B3	Eden Street	B2	Jones Street	D1	Prince Street	D3	Trinity Street	B1
Beech Street	D2	Edge Avenue	B1	King Street	B3	Queen Street	C3	Tulbury Street	A1
Beever Street	D2	Egerton Street	C2	King Street Roundabout	B4	Radcliffe Street	B1	Union Street	B3
Bell Street	B2	Eldon Street	B4	Kirkbank Street	A1	Raleigh Close	A1	Union Street West	A4
Belmont Street	B1	Emmett Way	C4	Kirkham Street	A2	Ramsden Street	A1	Union Street West	B3
Bisley Street	A4	Fairbottom Street	C3	Landseer Street	C4	Redvers Street	A1	Villiers Drive	A4
Booth Street	A3	Firth Street	C3	Lee Street	A4	Regent Street	D2	Wallshaw Place	D2
Bow Street	C3	Fisher Street	C1	Lemnos Street	D2	Retiro Street	C3	Wallshaw Street	D2
Bradshaw Street	C2	Flora Street	B2	Library Lane	A1	Rhodes Bank	C3	Wall Street	B4
Bridge Street	C3	Foundry Street	A3	Lombard Street	B2	Rhodes Street	D2	Ward Street	A1
Briscoe Street	C1	Fountain Street	B2	Lord Street	B1	Rifle Street	B1	Waterloo Street	C3
Britannia Street	D2	Franklin Street	B1	Malby Street	C1	Ripon Street	A1	Wellington Street	B4
Brookfield Street	C4	Gallick Street	A3	Malpass Street	C1	Robin Street	A1	West End Street	A2
Brook Street	D2	George Street	B3	Malton Street	A4	Rochdale Road	A1	West Street	B3
Brown Street	D2	Gower Street	D2	Manchester Street	A3	Rock Street	B2	Whitehall Street	C1
Brunswick Street	B3	Grange Street	A2	Manchester Street		Roscoe Street	B3	Willow Street	D2
Canon Street	A3	Greaves Street	C3	Roundabout	A3	Ross Street	A4	Wilson Way	C1
Cardinal Street	C2	Greengate Street	D4	Market Place	B3	Ruskin Street	A4	Wimpole Street	D1
Cavendish Street	B3	Green Street	A4	Mark Street	A2	Ruth Street	C1	Woodstock Street	C4
Chadderton Way	A1	Hamilton Street	D3	Marlborough Street	C4	St Hilda's Drive	A1	Yorkshire Street	C3
Charter Street	C1	Hardy Street	D4	Middleton Road	A3	St Marys Street	B1	York Street	A3
Chaucer Street	B3	Harmony Street	C4	Mold Street	B1	St Mary's Way	B2	
Cheapside	B2	Henshaw Street	B2	Mortimer Street	D1	Scotlock Way	C2	
Chief Street	D4	Higginshaw Road	C1	Napier Street East	A4	Shaw Road	D1	
Churchill Street	D4	Highfield Street	A2	Naylor Street	B2	Shaw Street	C1	
Churchill Street East	D4	High Street	B3	New Radcliffe Street	A2	Shield Close	A4	
Church Street	C3	Hilda Street	A2	Nile Street	B1	Shore Street	D2	
Clegg Street	C3	Hobson Street	B3	Oldham Way	A3	Siddall Street	C1	
Coldhurst Road	B1	Hooper Street	D4	Orme Street	D4	Silver Street	B3	
Cromwell Street	B4	Hopkin Street	C2	Park Road	B4	Southgate Street	C3	

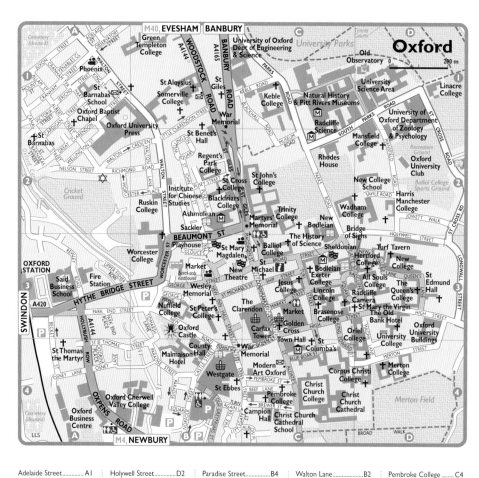

Adelaide Street.............. A1
Albert Street.................. A1
Albion Place.................. C4
Allam Street................... A1
Banbury Road B1
Beaumont Street.......... B3
Becket Street A3
Beef Lane C4
Blackhall Road.............. C1
Blue Boar Street........... C4
Bonn Square................. B4
Brewer Street C4
Broad Street................. C3
Broad Walk D4
Canal Street................. A1
Cardigan Street............ A2
Castle Street................. B4
Catte Street.................. C3
Cornmarket Street....... C3
Cranham Street............ A1
Cranham Terrace......... A1
George Street............... B3
George Street
Mews B3
Gloucester Street B3
Great Clarendon
Street....................... A2
Hart Street A1
High Street C3
Hollybush Row A3

Holywell Street............. D2
Hythe Bridge Street A3
Jericho Street............... A1
Jowett Walk................. D2
Juxon Street.................. A1
Keble Road................... C1
King Edward Street C3
King Street.................... A1
Little Clarendon
Street....................... B2
Littlegate Street........... B4
Longwall Street............ D3
Magdalen Street........... C2
Magpie Lane................. D3
Mansfield Road D2
Market Street................ C3
Merton Street............... D4
Mount Street................ A1
Museum Road C2
Nelson Street................ A2
New College Lane......... D3
New Inn Hall Street...... B3
New Road..................... B3
Norfolk Street............... B4
Observatory Street........ A1
Old Greyfriars
Street....................... B4
Osney Lane................... A4
Oxpens Road................. A4
Paradise Square........... B4

Paradise Street.............. B4
Park End Street A3
Parks Road................... C1
Pembroke Street C4
Pike Terrace B4
Pusey Lane................... B2
Pusey Street.................. B2
Queen's Lane D3
Queen Street................ C4
Radcliffe Square........... C3
Rewley Road A3
Richmond Road............ A2
St Aldate's C4
St Barnabas Street A2
St Cross Road............... D1
St Ebbes Street............. B4
St Giles B2
St John Street............... B2
St Michael's Street........ B3
St Thomas' Street.......... A4
Savile Road................... D2
Ship Street.................... C3
South Parks Road......... C1
Tidmarsh Lane.............. B3
Turl Street.................... C3
Turn Again Lane........... B4
Upper Fisher Row A3
Venables Close.............. A1
Victoria Street A1
Walton Crescent........... A2

Walton Lane.................. B2
Walton Street................ A1
Wellington Square......... B2
Wellington Street A2
Woodbine Place A4
Woodstock Road........... B1
Worcester Place............ A2
Worcester Street........... B3

University Colleges

All Souls College........... D3
Balliol College C3
Brasenose College C3
Christ Church
College C4
Corpus Christi
College D4
Exeter College............... C3
Harris Manchester
College D2
Hertford College D3
Jesus College................. C3
Keble College................ C1
Lincoln College.............. C3
Mansfield College.......... D2
Merton College............. D4
New College................. D3
Nuffield College............. B3
Oriel College D3

Pembroke College C4
Ruskin College.............. B2
St Cross College B2
St John's College........... C2
St Peter's College......... B3
Somerville College........ B1
The Queen's
College D3
Trinity College.............. C2
University College......... D3
Wadham College........... D2
Worcester College......... B3

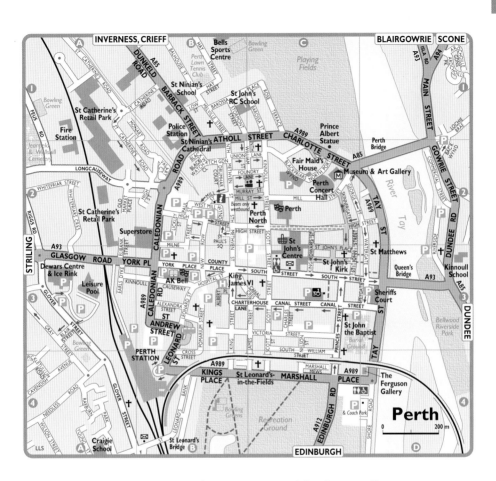

Perth

0   200 m

Albert Place....................B3	Gowrie Street...............D2	North William	Vasart Court.................B2
Alexandra Street...........B3	Gray Street....................A3	Street.........................B2	Victoria Street.............C3
Ardchoille Gardens......D1	Hay Street.....................B1	Old Market Place........A2	Watergate.....................D2
Ardchoille Park............D1	High Street....................B2	Paul Street....................B2	West Mill Wynd...........B2
Atholl Street..................B1	Hospital Street.............B3	Perth Bridge................D2	Whitefriars
Back Wynd.....................D2	Isla Road.......................D1	Picklellum Road.........A4	Crescent....................A2
Balhousie Street............B1	James Street.................C3	Pomarium Street........B3	Whitefriar Street..........A2
Barossa Place................B1	King Edward Street......C3	Princes Street..............C3	Wilson Street................A4
Barrack Street...............B1	Kings Place...................B4	Queen's Bridge............D3	York Place.....................A3
Blackfriars Wynd...........C2	King Street.....................B3	Raeburn Park...............A4	Young Street.................A4
Black Watch Garden.....B2	Kinnoull Causeway.......A3	Riggs Road....................A2	
Caledonian Road...........B3	Kinnoull Street..............C2	Riverside.......................D3	
Canal Street...................C3	Leonard Street...............B3	Rose Terrace................C1	
Cavendish Avenue.........A4	Lochie Brae...................D1	St Andrew Street..........B3	
Charles Street................C3	Longcauseway..............A2	St Catherine's Road.....A1	
Charlotte Street.............C2	Low Street......................B1	St John's Place.............C3	
Charterhouse Lane.........B3	Main Street....................D1	St John Street...............C3	
Commercial Street.........D2	Marshall Mews...............C4	St Leonard's Bank........B4	
County Place..................B3	Marshall Place...............C4	St Paul's Square...........B2	
Cross Street....................B4	Melville Street................B1	Scott Street...................C2	
Dundee Road..................D3	Mill Street......................B2	Shore Road....................D4	
Dunkeld Road.................B1	Milne Street...................B2	Skinnergate..................C2	
Earls Dyke......................A3	Monart Road..................A1	South Methven	
Edinburgh Road..............C4	Murray Street.................B2	Street.........................B2	
Elibank Street.................A3	Needless Road...............A4	South Street..................C3	
Feus Road.......................A1	Nelson Street.................C3	South William Street....C4	
Foundry Lane..................B2	New Row.........................B3	Speygate.......................D3	
George Street.................C2	North Methven	Stormont Street.............B1	
Glasgow Road.................A3	Street.........................B2	Tay Street......................D2	
Glover Street..................A3	North Port......................C2	Union Lane....................B2	

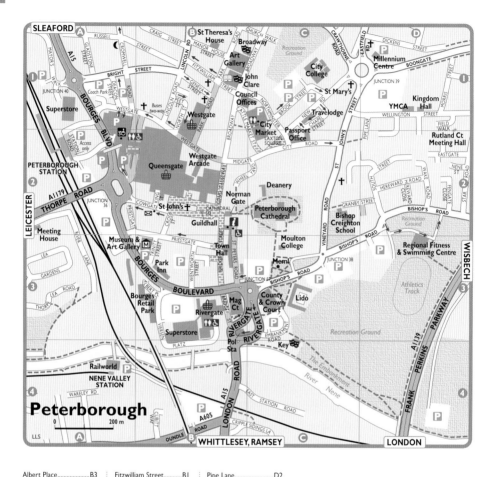

Albert Place....................B3
Bishop's Road................C3
Boongate D1
Bourges Boulevard........A1
Bridge Street..................B3
Bright Street...................A1
Broadway B2
Brook Street...................C1
Cathedral Square B2
Cattle Market Street.....B1
Chapel Street.................C1
Church Street.................B2
Church Walk C1
City Road.......................C2
Cowgate.........................B2
Craig Street....................B1
Crawthorne Road.........C1
Cripple Sidings Lane.....B4
Cromwell Road A1
Cross Street...................B2
Cubitt Way.....................B4
Deacon Street................A1
Dickens Street...............D1
Eastfield Road D1
Eastgate D2
East Station Road..........C4
Embankment Road........C3
Exchange Street.............B2
Fengate Close D2
Field Walk D1

Fitzwilliam Street...........B1
Frank Perkins
   Parkway.....................D4
Geneva Street................B1
Gladstone Street............A1
Granby Street.................C2
Hereward Close.............D2
Hereward Road.............D2
Junction 36....................A2
Junction 37....................C3
Junction 38....................C3
Junction 39....................D1
Junction 40 ....A1
King Street......................B2
Laxton Square................C2
Lea Gardens..................A3
Lincoln Road B1
London Road B4
Long Causeway.............B2
Manor House Street.....B1
Mayor's Walk A1
Midgate..........................B2
Morris Street.................D1
Nene Street....................D2
New Road.......................C1
Northminster.................C1
North Street...................B1
Oundle Road..................B4
Park Road.......................B1
Peet Street.....................B1

Pipe Lane........................D2
Priestgate A2
Rivergate........................B3
River Lane......................A2
Russell Street A1
St John's Street C2
St Peters Road...............B3
South Street....................D2
Star Road D2
Station Road...................A2
Thorpe Lea Road...........A3
Thorpe Road..................A2
Trinity Street B3
Viersen Platz...................B3
Vineyard Road C3
Wake Road.....................D2
Wareley Road A4
Wellington Street...........D1
Wentworth Street..........B3
Westgate A1

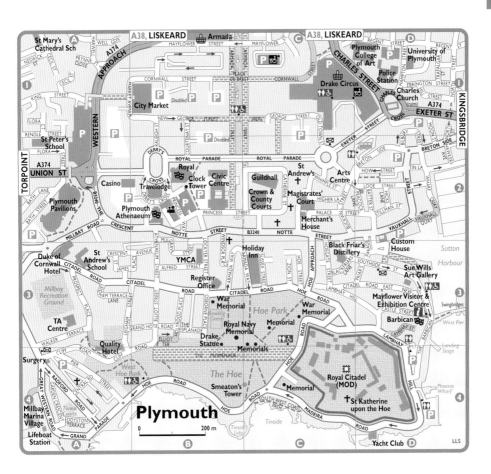

Plymouth

0   200 m

Alfred Street................B3	Flora Street................A2	Mayflower Street..........B1	The Barbican................D4
Armada Way................B1	Friar's Parade................D3	Millbay Road................A2	The Crescent................A2
Armada Way................B3	Garden Crescent........A4	Moon Street................D1	The Esplanade............B3
Athenaeum Street........B2	Grand Hotel Road........B3	Mulgrave Street............B3	The Promenade............B4
Bath Lane................A2	Grand Parade................A4	Neswick Street............A1	Tin Lane................D2
Bath Street................A2	Great Western	New George Street......B1	Trafalgar Street............D1
Batter Street................D2	Road................A4	New Street................D3	Union Street................A2
Bilbury Street................D2	Hampton Street............D1	North Street................D1	Vauxhall Quay................D2
Blackfriars Lane............C3	Harwell Street................A1	Notte Street................B2	Vauxhall Street................D2
Breton Side................D2	Hawkers Avenue............D2	Old Town Street............C1	Walker Terrace................A3
Buckwell Street............C2	Hicks Lane................D2	Osborne Place................B3	Well Garden................A1
Castle Street................D3	Higher Lane................C2	Palace Street................C2	Western Approach........A2
Catherine Street............C2	Hill Street................D1	Peacock Lane................C2	Wharf Quay................D2
Cecil Street................A1	Hoe Approach................C3	Pier Street................A4	Whimple Street................C2
Central Road................A4	Hoegate Street................C3	Place de Brest................B1	Windsor Place................B2
Charles Cross................D1	Hoe Road................B4	Princess Street................B2	Zion Street................C3
Charles Street................C1	Hoe Street................C3	Princess Way................B2	
Citadel Road................A3	Holyrood Place................B3	Prospect Place................A3	
Citadel Road East........C3	How Street................D2	Prynne Close................A1	
Cliff Road................A4	King Street................A1	Radford Road................A4	
Cornwall Street................B1	Lambhay Hill................C3	Raleigh Street................A1	
Courtenay Street............B2	Lambhay Hill................D3	Regent Street................D1	
Crescent Avenue............A3	Lambhay Street................D3	Rendle Street................A1	
Derry's Cross................B2	Leigham Street................A3	Royal Parade................B2	
Ebrington Street............D1	Leigham Terrace	St James Place................A3	
Eddystone Terrace........A4	Lane................A3	Southside Street................D3	
Elliot Street................B3	Lockyer Street................B3	South West	
Elliot Terrace................B3	Looe Street................D2	Coast Path................C4	
Exeter Street................C2	Madeira Road................C4	Stillman Street................D2	
Flora Court................A1	Market Avenue................A1	Sussex Street................C3	

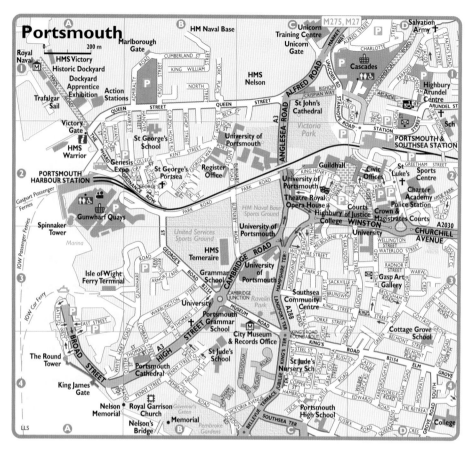

Admiralty Road B1
Alec Rose Lane D2
Alfred Road C1
Alfred Street C1
Anglesea Road C2
Armory Lane B3
Arundel Street D1
Astley Street A3
Bath Square A3
Beck Street B1
Beehive Way B3
Bellevue Terrace C4
Belmont Place D4
Belmont Street D4
Bishop Street B1
Blount Road C4
Britain Street B2
Broad Street A4
Brougham Road D3
Brunswick Street C3
Buckingham Street D1
Burnaby Road B2
Bush Street East C4
Butcher Street B2
Cambridge Junction B3
Cambridge Road B3
Castle Close C4
Castle Road C4
Cecil Place C4
Charlotte Street D1
Chatham Drive B4
Clock Street A2
College Street B2
Commercial Road D1
Copper Street C4
Cottage Grove D3

Cross Street B1
Cumberland Street B1
Curzon Howe Road B1
Earlsdon Street C3
East Street A3
Edinburgh Road C1
Eldon Street D3
Elm Grove D4
Flint Street C4
Gold Street C4
Gordon Road B4
Grand Parade A4
Great Southsea Street C4
Green Road D4
Greetham Street C2
Grosvenor Street D3
Grove Road North D4
Grove Road South D4
Guildhall Walk C2
Gunwharf Road B3
Hambrook Street C4
Hampshire Terrace C3
Hanover Street B1
Havant Street A2
Hawke Street B1
Highbury Street B3
High Street B4
Hyde Park Road D2
Jacob's Street D1
Jubilee Terrace C4
Kent Street B2
King Henry I Street C1
King's Road C4
King's Road Roundabout .. C4
King's Terrace C4
King Street C3

King William Street B1
Landport Terrace C3
Landsdowne Street C3
Lion Street B2
Little Southsea Street C4
Lombard Street B3
Main Road A1
Margate Road D3
Market Way C1
Mary Rose Street D2
Melbourne Place C3
Middle Street D3
Museum Road D3
Norfolk Street C4
North Street B1
Ordnance Row B2
Oyster Street B4
Paradise Street D1
Park Road B2
Park Street C3
Peacock Lane B4
Pelham Road D4
Pembroke Road B4
Penny Street B4
Portland Street B2
Queens Crescent D4
Queens Place D4
Queen Street A1
Radnor Street D3
Sackville Street C4
St Edwards Road C4
St Faith's Road D1
St George's Road B3
St George's Square B2
St George's Way B2
St James's Road D3

St James's Street B2
St Nicholas Street B4
St Paul's Road C3
St Thomas's Street B4
Sedsley Close D3
Slindon Street D2
Somers Road C4
Southsea Terrace C4
South Street C4
Stanhope Road C1
Station Street D2
Steel Street C4
Stone Street C4
Sun Street B2
Surrey Street D1
Sussex Road C4
Temple Street D1
The Hard A2
The Retreat D4
Tyseley Road D2
Unicorn Road C1
Upper Arundel
Street D1
Victoria Avenue B4
Victory Road B2
Waltham Street C3
Warblington Street B3
Warwick Crescent D3
Waterloo Street D3
Wellington Street D3
West Street A3
White Hart Road A4
Wickham Street A2
Wilberforce Road D4
Willis Road C1
Wiltshire Street C3

Winston Churchill
Avenue D2
Woodpath D4
Woodville Drive C4
Worsley Road D4
Yarborough Road D4
Yorke Street C3
York Place B1

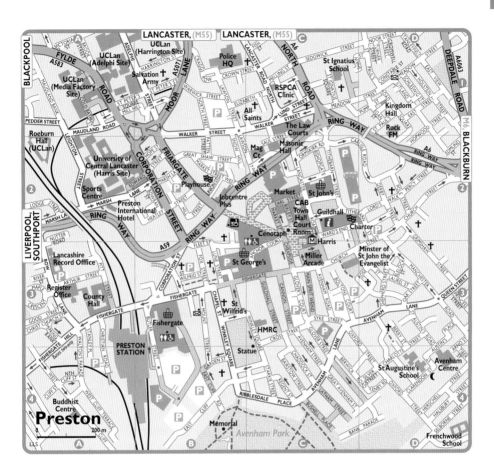

Adelphi Street....................A1	Cromwell Street..................D1	Hopwood Street..................D2	Pitt Street.........................A3	Victoria Street..................A1
Anchor Court......................C3	Cross Street.......................C3	Jutland Street.....................D1	Pole Street........................D2	Walker Street....................B1
Arno Street........................D4	Crown Street......................B1	Lancaster Road...................C2	Princess Street..................D3	Walton's Parade.................A3
Arthur Street......................A3	Deepdale Road...................D1	Lancaster Road North.........C1	Pump Street......................D1	Ward's End.......................C2
Avenham Lane....................C4	Derby Street.......................D2	Latham Street.....................C4	Queen Street......................D3	Warwick Street..................B1
Avenham Road....................C3	Earl Street..........................C2	Laurel Street.......................D3	Regent Street.....................C4	West Cliff..........................A4
Avenham Street...................C3	East Cliff.............................B4	Lawson Street.....................B1	Ribblesdale Place................B4	West Cliff Terrace..............A4
Bairstow Street...................C4	East Cliff Road....................B4	Leighton Street...................A2	Ring Way..........................B2	Winkley Square..................B3
Bank Parade........................C4	East Street..........................D1	Lodge Street.......................A2	River Street.......................A3	
Berry Street.........................D3	East View............................D1	Lord's Walk.........................D2	Rose Street........................D3	
Berwick Road......................C4	Edmund Street....................D1	Lund Street.........................C1	St Austin's Place.................D4	
Birley Street........................C2	Edward Street.....................A2	Lune Street.........................B3	St Austin's Road.................D3	
Bishopgate..........................C2	Egan Street.........................D1	Main Sprit Weind...............C3	St Ignatius Square..............C1	
Bielock Street.....................D3	Elizabeth Street...................B1	Manchester Road................D3	St Paul's Road....................D1	
Boltons Court......................C3	Fishergate..........................A3	Maple Crescent..................A3	St Paul's Square..................D1	
Bow Lane...........................A3	Fish Street..........................C1	Market Street.....................C2	St Peter's Square................A1	
Bowran Street.....................B2	Fleet Street.........................B3	Market Street West.............B2	St Peter's Street.................B1	
Brook Street.......................A1	Fox Street...........................B3	Marsh Lane........................A2	St Wilfrid Street.................B3	
Bushell Place.......................B3	Friargate............................B2	Maudland Bank...................A1	Saul Street.........................D1	
Butler Street.......................B3	Fylde Road.........................A1	Maudland Road...................A1	Schleswig Street.................D1	
Cannon Street.....................C2	Garden Street......................B4	Meadow Street....................C1	Sedgwick Street.................C1	
Carlisle Road.......................C4	Glover's Court.....................C3	Melling Street.....................C1	Selborne Street..................D4	
Chaddock Street..................C4	Glover Street.......................C3	Mill Hill..............................A1	Shaw Street........................D1	
Chapel Street.......................B3	Good Street........................A3	Moor Lane..........................B1	Shepherd Street..................D3	
Charlotte Street...................D4	Great Avenham Street..........C4	Mount Street......................B3	Silver Street........................D3	
Cheapside...........................C3	Great Shaw Street................B2	Noor Street........................D1	Snow Hill...........................B2	
Christ Church Street............A3	Grimshaw Street..................D2	North Cliff Street................A4	Spring Bank........................A3	
Christian Road.....................A3	Guildhall Street...................C3	North Road.........................C1	Stanleyfield Road................D1	
Church Street......................C3	Halsbury Street...................B1	North Street........................B1	Stanley Place......................A3	
Clarendon Street..................D4	Harrington Street.................B1	Nutter Road........................A1	Starkie Street......................C4	
Cliff Street..........................A4	Heatley Street......................B2	Oak Street..........................D3	Syke Street.........................C3	
Cold Bath Street..................A1	Herschell Street..................D4	Ormskirk Road....................C2	Tenby Road.........................D4	
Constable Street..................D1	Hill Street...........................B2	Oxford Street......................C3	Tiber Street........................D4	
Corporation Street...............B2	Holstein Street....................D1	Patten Street.......................B2	Tithebarn Street..................C1	
Corporation Street...............B3	Hope Street........................B2	Pedder Street......................A1	Turner Street......................D1	
Craggs Row........................B1		Percy Street........................D2	Union Street.......................B2	

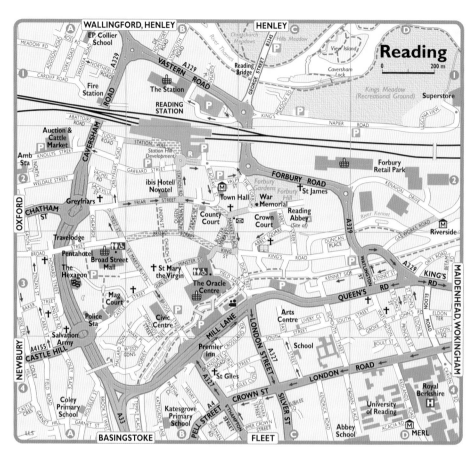

Abattoirs Road	A1	Crown Place	C4	Kennet Side	C3	Redlands Road	D4	Weldale Street	A2
Abbey Square	C3	Crown Street	C4	Kennet Street	D3	Ross Road	A1	West Street	A2
Abbey Street	C2	Deansgate Road	B4	King's Meadow		Sackville Street	A2	Wolseley Street	A4
Acacia Road	D4	De Montfort Road	B1	Road	C1	St Giles Close	B4	Yield Hall Place	B3
Addison Road	A1	Duke Street	C3	King's Road	D3	St John's Hill	D3	York Road	A1
Anstey Road	A3	Duncan Place	C3	King Street	B3	St John's Road	D3	Zinzan Street	A3
Baker Street	A3	East Street	C3	Knollys Street	A2	St John's Street	D3		
Barthia Close	B4	Eaton Place	A3	Livery Close	C3	St Mary's Butts	B3		
Betam Road	D3	Eldon Place	D3	London Road	C4	Sherman Road	B4		
Blagrave Street	B2	Eldon Road	D3	London Street	C3	Sidmouth Street	C3		
Boult Street	D4	Eldon Square	D3	Luscinia View	D1	Silver Street	C4		
Bridge Street	B3	Eldon Terrace	D3	Lynmouth Road	B1	Simmonds Street	B3		
Broad Street	A3	Field Road	A4	Mallard Row	A4	Southampton Street	B4		
Brook Street West	A4	Fobney Street	B4	Market Place	B2	South Street	C3		
Buttermarket	B3	Forbury Road	C2	Meadow Road	A1	Station Hill	B2		
Cardiff Road	A1	Friar Street	B2	Mill Lane	B4	Station Road	B2		
Carey Street	A3	Garnet Hill	A4	Minster Street	B3	Swan Place	B3		
Castle Crescent	A4	Garnet Street	A4	Napier Road	C1	Swansea Road	A1		
Castle Hill	A4	Garrard Street	B2	Newark Street	C4	Temple Place	B4		
Castle Street	A3	Gas Works Road	D3	Norman Place	B1	The Forbury	C2		
Caversham Road	A2	George Street	C1	Northfield Road	A1	The Grove	D3		
Chatham Street	A2	Greyfriars Road	A2	North Street	A1	Tudor Road	A2		
Cheapside	A2	Gun Street	B3	Orts Road	D3	Union Street	B2		
Church Street	B3	Henry Street	B4	Parthia Close	B4	Upper Crown			
Church Street	B4	Howard Street	A3	Pell Street	B4	Street	C4		
Coley Hill	A4	Jesse Terrace	A3	Prince's Street	D3	Vachel Road	A2		
Coley Place	A4	Jubilee Square	C4	Queen's Road	C3	Valpy Street	B2		
Craven Road	D4	Katesgrove Lane	B4	Queen Victoria		Vastern Road	B1		
Crossland Road	B4	Kenavon Drive	D2	Street	B2	Waterside Gardens	B4		
Cross Street	B2	Kendrick Road	C4	Reading Bridge	B1	Watlington Street	D3		

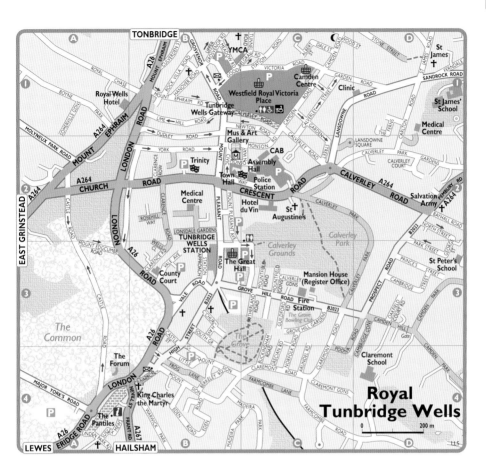

Royal Tunbridge Wells

0　　　　　200 m

Albert Street	C1	Clarence Row	B2
Arundel Road	C4	Crescent Road	B2
Bayhall Road	D2	Culverden Street	B1
Belgrave Road	C1	Dale Street	C1
Berkeley Road	B4	Dudley Road	B1
Boyne Park	A1	Eden Road	B4
Buckingham Road	C4	Eridge Road	A4
Calverley Court	D2	Farmcombe Lane	C4
Calverley Gardens	C3	Farmcombe Road	C4
Calverley Park	C2	Ferndale	D1
Calverley Park		Frant Road	A4
Gardens	D2	Frog Lane	B4
Calverley Road	C2	Garden Road	C1
Calverley Street	C1	Garden Street	C1
Cambridge Gardens	D4	George Street	D3
Cambridge Street	D3	Goods Station Road	B1
Camden Hill	D3	Grecian Road	C4
Camden Park	D3	Grosvenor Road	B1
Camden Road	C1	Grove Hill Gardens	C3
Carlton Road	D2	Grove Hill Road	C3
Castle Road	A2	Guildford Road	C3
Castle Street	B3	Hanover Road	B1
Chapel Place	B4	High Street	B4
Christchurch		Lansdowne Road	C2
Avenue	B3	Lansdowne Square	D2
Church Road	A2	Lime Hill Road	B1
Civic Way	B2	Linden Park Road	A4
Claremont Gardens	C4	Little Mount Sion	B4
Claremont Road	C4	London Road	A2
Clarence Road	B2	Lonsdale Gardens	B2

Madeira Park	B4	Rock Villa Road	B1
Major York's Road	A4	Rosehill Way	B2
Meadow Road	B1	Royal Chase	A1
Molyneux Park		St James' Road	D1
Road	A1	Sandrock Road	D1
Monson Road	C2	Somerville Gardens	A1
Monson Way	B2	South Green	B3
Mount Edgcumbe		Station Approach	B3
Road	A3	Stone Street	D1
Mount Ephraim	A2	Sussex Mews	A4
Mount Ephraim		Sutherland Road	C3
Road	B1	The Ferns	D1
Mountfield Gardens	C3	Tunnel Road	C1
Mountfield Road	C3	Upper Grosvenor	
Mount Pleasant		Road	B1
Avenue	B2	Vale Avenue	B3
Mount Pleasant		Vale Road	B3
Road	B2	Victoria Road	C1
Mount Sion	B4	Warwick Park	B4
Nevill Street	B4	Wells Close	B3
Newton Road	B1	Wood Street	C1
Norfolk Road	C4	York Road	B2
North Street	D2		
Oakfield Court			
Road	D3		
Park Street	D3		
Pembury Road	D2		
Poona Road	D2		
Prince's Street	C3		
Prospect Road	D3		

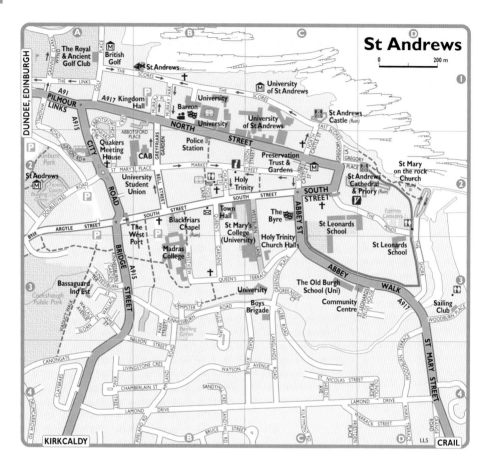

St Andrews

0   200 m

Abbey Street C2	Greyfriars Garden......... B2	St Mary Street D3
Abbey Walk C3	Hope Street.................. A2	St Nicolas Street C4
Abbotsford	Howard Place.............. A2	Sandyhill Crescent B4
Crescent A1	James Street A3	Sandyhill Road.............. B4
Abbotsford Place......... A2	Kilrymont Road............ C4	Shields Avenue C4
Argyle Street A2	King Street A4	Sloan Street A3
Auld Burn B3	Kinkel Terrace D4	South Castle Street C2
Bell Street B2	Kinnessburn Garden A3	South Street B2
Boase Avenue............... C3	Kinnessburn Road......... B3	Station Road................ A2
Bridge Street A3	Kinnessburn Terrace..... A3	The Links A1
Bruce Street................. B4	Lamond Drive............... A4	The Pends D2
Canongate.................... A4	Langlands Road............. C3	The Scores A1
Chamberlain Street A4	Livingstone	The Shore D3
Church Street............... B2	Crescent A4	Union Street................. C2
City Road...................... A2	Logies Lane B2	Viaduct Walk A3
Claybraes...................... A4	Market Street.............. B2	Wallace Avenue A3
Dempster Court............ B3	Murray Park................. B1	Wallace Street............. A3
Doubledykes Road........ A2	Murray Place................ B1	Warrack Street............. C4
Drumcarrow Road........ A4	Nelson Street............... A3	Watson Avenue............ B4
Dunolly Place D4	North Castle Street C2	Westburn Lane............. C2
East Scores C1	North Street................ B1	Westview..................... B3
Glebe Road.................... C3	Park Street................... B3	Windmill Road.............. A1
Golf Place...................... A1	Pilmour Links A1	Woodburn Place D3
Grange Road D4	Pipeland Road B4	Woodburn Terrace D4
Grannie Clarks	Priestden Place C4	
Wynd............................ A1	Queen's Gardens.......... B2	
Greenside Court............ C3	Queen's Terrace........... B3	
Greenside Place............. C3	St Leonards Field	
Gregory Lane................ C2	House......................... D3	
Gregory Place................ C2	St Mary's Place............. A2	

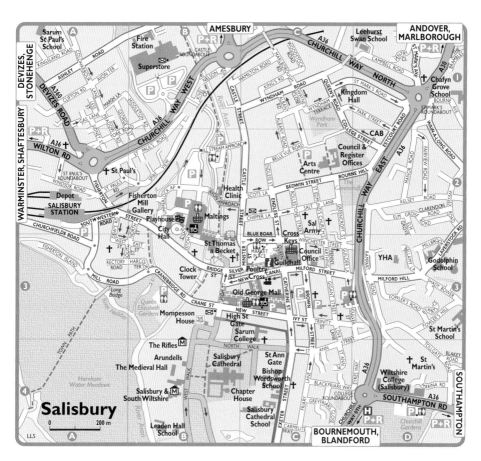

Salisbury

0 ——— 200 m

Albany Road	C1	Coldharbour Lane	A1
Ashley Road	A1	College Roundabout	D4
Avon Approach	B2	College Street	C1
Avon Terrace	A1	Cranebridge Road	B3
Bedwin Street	C2	Crane Street	B3
Bellamy Lane	D3	Culver Street	C3
Belle Vue Road	C2	Dew's Road	A3
Blackfriars Way	C4	East Street	B3
Blakey Road	D4	Elm Grove Road	D2
Blue Boar Row	C3	Endless Street	C2
Bourne Avenue	D1	Estcourt Road	D2
Bourne Hill	C2	Exeter Street	C4
Brambles The	D1	Eyres Way	D4
Bridge Street	B3	Fairview Road	D2
Brown Street	C3	Fisherton Island	A3
Byways Close	D3	Fisherton Street	A2
Campbell Road	D1	Fowler's Hill	D3
Carmelite Way	C4	Fowler's Road	D3
Castle Roundabout	B1	Friary Lane	C4
Castle Street	B1	Gas Lane	A1
Catherine Street	C3	George Street	A1
Chipper Lane	C2	Gigant Street	C3
Churchfields Road	A2	Greencroft Street	C2
Churchill Way		Greyfriars Close	C4
North	C1	Grove Elm	D2
Churchill Way South	C4	Guilder Lane	C2
Churchill Way East	D3	Hamilton Road	B1
Churchill Way West	B2	Harcourt Terrace	B3
Clarendon Road	D2	High Street	B3
Clifton Road	A1		

Hulse Road	B1	Pennyfarthing Street	C3
Ivy Street	C3	Queen's Road	C1
Kelsey Road	D2	Queen Street	C3
Kingsland Road	A1	Rampart Road	D3
King's Road	C1	Rectory Road	A3
Kivel Court	B1	Rollestone Street	C2
Laverstock Road	D3	St Ann Place	C4
Less Street	A1	St Ann Street	C4
Long Bridge	A3	St Edmund's Church	
Love Lane	C3	Street	C2
Malthouse Lane	B3	St Mark's Avenue	D1
Manor Road	D2	St Mark's Road	D1
Marina Road	D4	St Mark's	
Market Place	C3	Roundabout	D1
Marlborough Road	C1	St Pauls Road	A2
Marsh Lane	A1	St Paul's Road	B2
Meadow Road	A1	St Paul's	
Middleton Road	A1	Roundabout	A2
Milford Hill	D3	Salt Lane	C2
Milford Street	C3	Scots Lane	C2
Millbrook	D3	Shady Bower	D3
Mill Road	A3	Sidney Street	A1
Mill Stream Approach	B2	Silver Street	B3
Minster Street	C3	Southampton Road	D4
Nelson Road	B1	South Street	A3
New Canal	B3	South Western	
New Street	B3	Road	A2
North Street	B3	Spire View	B2
North Walk	B4	Summerlock	
Park Street	D1	Approach	B2

Swayne's Close	C1
Tollgate Road	D4
Trinity Street	C3
Ventry Close	D1
Wain-A-Long Road	D1
Wessex Road	C2
West Street	A3
West Walk	B4
Wilton Road	A2
Winchester Street	C3
Windsor Road	A2
Woodstock Road	C1
Wyndham Road	C1
Wyndham Terrace	C1
York Road	A2

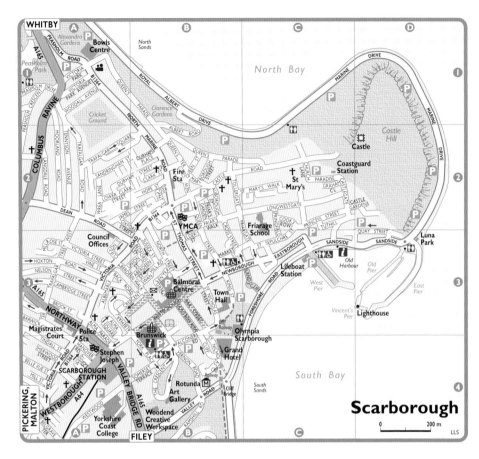

Aberdeen Street.............B3	Durham Street................A2	Oxford Street................A2	Trafalgar Square.............A2
Aberdeen Terrace..........B3	Eastborough...................C3	Paradise........................C2	Trafalgar Street
Aberdeen Walk..............A3	Elder's Street..................B3	Peasholm Crescent.......A2	West.........................A3
Albemarle Back	Falconers Road..............B4	Peasholm Drive..............A1	Tuthill...........................C2
Road..............................A3	Foreshore Road..............C3	Peasholm Road..............A1	Union Street..................B3
Albemarle Crescent.....A3	Friargate.........................B2	Princess Street...............C2	Valley Bridge Road.......A4
Albert Road..................B2	Friar's Garden.................B2	Quay Street...................D3	Valley Road...................B4
Alma Parade..................A3	Friar's Walk....................B2	Queen's Parade..............A1	Vernon Road.................B4
Alma Square..................A3	Graham Close.................C2	Queen's Terrace.............B2	Victoria Park..................A1
Auborough Street..........B2	Hanover Road................A4	Queen Street..................B2	Victoria Park
Bar Street......................B3	Hope Street....................B2	Ramshill Road................B4	Avenue.......................A1
Barwick Terrace.............A3	Hoxton Road.................A3	Regent Street................B2	Victoria Road................A4
Bedford Street...............B3	Huntress Row.................A2	Royal Albert Drive.........B1	Victoria Street...............A3
Belgrave Terrace...........A4	James Street...................A2	St Mary's Walk..............C2	Vine Street....................A3
Belle Vue Street............A4	King Street.....................B3	St Nicholas Cliff.............B4	Westborough.................A4
Bland's Cliff..................C3	Langdale Road................A2	St Nicholas Street..........B3	West Square..................A4
Brook Street..................A3	Longwestgate................C2	St Sepulchre Street........C3	Westwood.....................A4
Cambridge Street...........A3	Lower Clark Street.........A2	St Thomas Street...........B2	Woodall Avenue............A1
Castle Gardens..............C2	Marine Drive..................C1	Sandringham Street........A2	Wrea Lane.....................A2
Castlegate.....................C2	Market Street.................B3	Sandside........................C3	York Place.....................B4
Castle Road..................B2	Marlborough Street........B2	Sherwood Street............A4	
Church Lane..................C2	Melrose Street................A3	Somerset Terrace...........B4	
Clark Street...................B2	Mill Street.......................A4	Springfield......................C2	
Cliff Bridge...................B4	Moorland Road...............A2	Sussex Street.................B3	
Clifton Street................A3	Nelson Street.................A3	Swan Hill Road..............B3	
Columbus Ravine..........A2	Newborough...................B3	Tennyson Avenue...........A2	
Cook's Row...................C2	New Queen Street..........B2	The Crescent.................B4	
Cross Street...................B2	North Marine Road.........A1	Tindall Street.................A4	
Dean Road.....................A2	North Street...................B3	Tollergate......................B2	
Durham Place.................B2	Northway........................A3	Trafalgar Road...............A2	

Allen Street	A1	Copper Street	B1
Angel Street	C2	Corporation Street	B1
Anson Square	D3	Cotton Street	B1
Arundel Gate	C3	Craven Street	A1
Arundel Lane	C4	Cross Burgess Street	B3
Arundel Street	C4	Cupola	B1
Backfields	B3	Cutlers Gate	D1
Bailey Lane	A2	Derek Dooley Way	D1
Bailey Street	A2	Devonshire Street	A3
Balm Green	B3	Division Street	A3
Bank Street	C2	Dixon Lane	C2
Barkers Pool	B3	Doncaster Street	A1
Blonk Street	D1	Duke Street	D2
Bowdon Street	A4	Earl Way	B4
Bridge Street	C1	East Parade	C2
Broad Lane	A2	Ebenezer Street	A1
Broad Street	D2	Edward Street	A2
Brocco Street	A2	Eldon Street	A3
Broom Grove	A4	Ellis Street	A1
Broomhall Street	A4	Exchange Place	D2
Brown Lane	C4	Exchange Street	D2
Brown Street	C4	Eyre Lane	B4
Burgess Street	B3	Eyre Road	C4
Cambridge Street	B3	Eyre Street	B4
Campo Lane	B2	Fig Tree Lane	C2
Carver Lane	B3	Fitzalan Square	C2
Carver Street	B3	Fitzwilliam Street	A4
Castlegate	C1	Flat Street	C3
Castle Street	C2	Furnace Hill	B1
Chapel Walk	C2	Furnival Gate	B4
Charles Street	B4	Furnival Road	D1
Charter Row	A4	Furnival Square	B4
Charter Square	B4	Furnival Street	C4
Church Street	B2	Garden Street	A2
Clay Lane	B4	George Street	C2
Commercial Street	C2	Gibraltar Street	B1
Harmer Lane	C3	North Bank	D1
Harts Head	C2	North Church Street	B2
Hawley Street	B2	Nursery Lane	C1
Haymarket	C2	Nursery Street	C1
Headford Street	A4	Orange Street	A3
High Street	C2	Orchard Lane	B3
Holland Street	A3	Orchard Street	B3
Hollis Croft	A2	Paradise Street	B2
Holly Street	B3	Park Square	D2
Holy Green	B3	Pinstone Street	B3
Howard Lane	C4	Plum Lane	C1
Howard Street	C4	Pond Hill	C3
Hoyle Street	A1	Pond Street	C3
Joiner Street	C1	Portobello Street	A3
Kenyon Street	A2	Queen Street	B2
King Street	C2	Rockingham Lane	A3
Lady's Bridge	C1	Rockingham Street	A2
Lambert Street	B1	Rockingham Way	B4
Leadmill Road	C4	Russell Street	B1
Leopold Square	B3	St James Street	B2
Leopold Street	B3	Scargill Croft	C2
Love Street	B1	Scotland Street	A1
Mappin Street	A3	Shalesmoor	B1
Matilda Lane	B4	Sheaf Street	D4
Matilda Way	B4	Shepherd Street	A1
Meadow Street	A1	Shoreham Street	C4
Meetinghouse Lane	C2	Shrewsbury Road	D4
Millsands	C1	Silver Street	B2
Milton Street	A4	Smithfield Street	A1
Morpeth Street	A1	Snig Hill	C2
Mulberry Street	B4	Snow Lane	B1
Newcastle Street	A1	Solly Street	A2
New Street	C2	South Street Park	D3
Norfolk Road	D4	Stanley Street	C1
Norfolk Row	B3	Sudbury Street	A1
Norfolk Street	C3	Suffolk Road	C4
Surrey Place	C3
Surrey Street	C3
Sussex Street	D1
Sydney Street	C4
Talbot Street	D4
Tenter Street	B2
Townhead Street	B2
Trafalgar Street	A4
Trinity Street	B1
Trippet Lane	B3
Tudor Square	C3
Turner Street	C4
Union Lane	B4
Union Street	B4
Upper Allen Street	A1
Vicar Lane	B2
Victoria Station Road	D1
Waingate	C2
Ward Street	B1
Wellington Street	A4
West Bar	B2
Westfield Terrace	A3
West Street	A3
Wharf Street	D2
White Croft	A2
Wicker	D1
Wicker Lane	C1
Willey Street	D1
Workhouse Lane	B1
York Street	C2

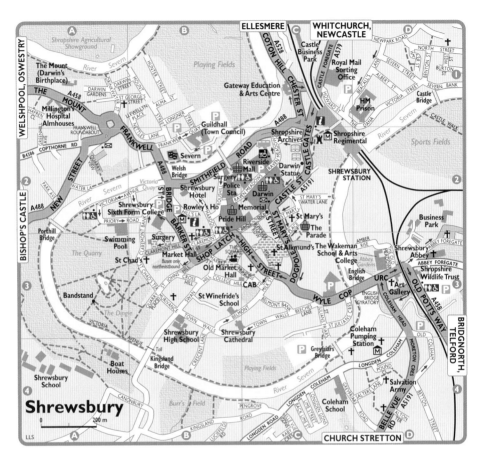

Shrewsbury

0 _____ 200 m

Abbey Foregate D3	Copthorne Road...........A2	Longden Road................C4	St Julians Crescent........C3
Albert Street.................D1	Coton Hill.....................C1	Longner Street................B1	St Julians Friars C3
Alma Street B1	Crescent Lane................B4	Luciefelde Road.............B4	St Mary's Place...............C2
Alton Terrace................D4	Cross Hill......................B3	Mardol..........................B2	St Mary's Street..............C2
Amber Rise...................D3	Darwin Gardens............A1	Market Street.................B3	St Mary's Water
Back Lime Street...........C4	Darwin Street................A1	Milk Street....................C3	Lane........................C2
Barker Street.................B2	Dogpole........................C3	Moreton Crescent..........D4	Salters Lane...................D4
Beacall's Lane D1	Drinkwater Street..........A1	Mount Street.................B1	Severn Bank...................D1
Beeches Lane C3	English Bridge................C3	Murivance......................B3	Severn Street.................D1
Belle Vue Gardens C4	English Bridge	Nettles Lane..................B1	Shop Latch....................B3
Belle Vue Road..............D4	Gyratory..................D3	Newpark Road...............D1	Smithfield Road..............B2
Belmont........................B3	Fish Street.....................C3	New Street.....................A2	Swan Hill.......................B3
Belmont Bank................C3	Frankwell......................A2	North Street..................D1	The Dana D1
Benyon Street...............D1	Frankwell Quay.............B2	Old Coleham..................D3	The Mount.....................A1
Betton Street D4	Frankwell	Old Potts Way D3	The Old Meadow...........D3
Bridge Street.................B2	Roundabout A2	Park Avenue..................A2	The Square.....................B3
Burton Street................D1	Greenhill Avenue..........A2	Pengrove.......................C4	Town Walls....................B3
Butcher Row.................C2	Greyfriars Bridge...........C4	Porthill Bridge................A3	Victoria Avenue.............A2
Canonbury....................A4	Greyfriars Road.............C4	Pound Close...................D4	Victoria Avenue A3
Castle Bridge.................D1	Hafren Close..................A1	Pride Hill.......................C2	Victoria Street................D1
Castle Foregate..............C1	High Street....................C3	Princess Street...............B3	Water Lane....................A2
Castle Gates..................C2	Hill's Lane.....................B2	Priory Road....................A2	Water Street...................D1
Castle Street..................C2	Howard Street...............C1	Quarry Place..................B3	Welsh Bridge..................B2
Castle Walk D1	Hunter Street.................B1	Quarry View...................A2	West Street.....................D1
Chester Street................C1	Kingsland Bridge...........B4	Raby Crescent................C4	Wyle Cop C3
Claremont Bank.............B3	Kingsland Road..............B4	Raven Meadows............B2	
Claremont Hill...............B3	Lime Street....................B4	Roushill.........................B2	
Claremont Street............B3	Llewellyn Place..............B1	St Chad's Terrace...........B3	
Coleham Head................D3	Longden Coleham..........C4	St George's Street...........A1	
College Hill...................B3	Longden Gardens..........C4	St Johns Hill..................B3	

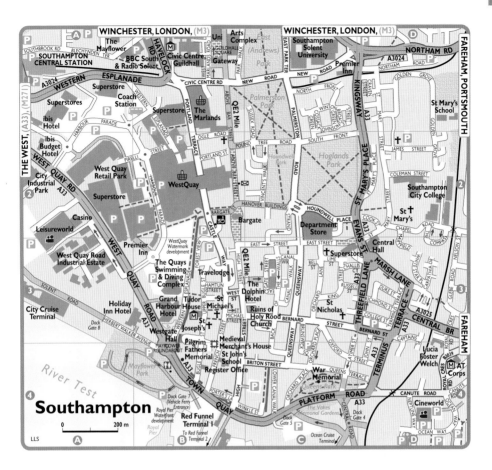

Above Bar Street B1	Forest View B3	Ogle Road.....................B2	Upper Bugle Street.......B3
Back of the Walls C3	French Street B4	Orchard Lane................C3	Vincent's Walk...............C2
Bargate Street................B2	Glebe Road....................D3	Orchard Place...............C4	Western Esplanade A1
Bell Street......................C3	Golden Grove...............D1	Oxford Street...............C4	Western Esplanade B3
Bernard Street...............C3	Hamtun Street..............B3	Palmerston Road...........C1	West Marlands
Blechynden Terrace A1	Hanover Buildings..........B2	Park Walk......................B1	Road........................B1
Briton Street.................C4	Harbour Parade.............A2	Pirelli Street..................A2	West Quay Road...........A2
Broad Green..................C1	Havelock Road...............B1	Platform Road...............C4	West Street...................C3
Brunswick Square..........C3	Herbert Walker	Porter's Lane................B4	White Star Place D3
Bugle Street...................B4	Avenue A3	Portland Street..............B2	Winkle Street................B4
Canal Walk....................C3	High Street....................B4	Portland Terrace............B1	Winton Street...............C1
Canute Road..................C4	Houndwell Place............C2	Pound Tree Road..........B2	
Captains Place...............D3	James Street..................D2	Queens Terrace.............C4	
Carpathia Drive.............D3	Johnson Street...............C1	Queensway.....................C4	
Castle Way.....................B2	John Street....................D4	Richmond Street............D3	
Central Bridge D3	King Street.....................C3	Royal Crescent	
Central Road..................C4	Kingsway........................C1	Road.........................D4	
Challis Court..................C3	Latimer Street................C4	Russell Street C3	
Chapel Road...................D2	Lime Street....................C3	St Mary's Place..............D2	
Civic Centre Road..........B1	Lower Canal Walk..........C4	St Mary Street...............D1	
Coleman Street..............D2	Marsh Lane....................D3	St Michael Street...........B3	
College Street................D3	Maryfield.......................D2	Solent Road...................A3	
Cook Street....................D2	Mayflower	Southbrook Road...........A1	
Cossack Green................C1	Roundabout................B4	South Front...................C2	
Craven Street.................D1	Nelson Street.................D3	Strand............................C2	
Duke Street....................D3	Neptune Way.................D4	Sussex Road...................C1	
Eastgate Street...............C3	New Road......................C1	Terminus Terrace...........D4	
East Park Terrace...........C1	Northam Road...............D1	The Compass.................D2	
East Street.....................C2	North Front...................C1	Threefield Lane..............D3	
Evans Street...................C2	Ocean Way....................D4	Town Quay....................B4	

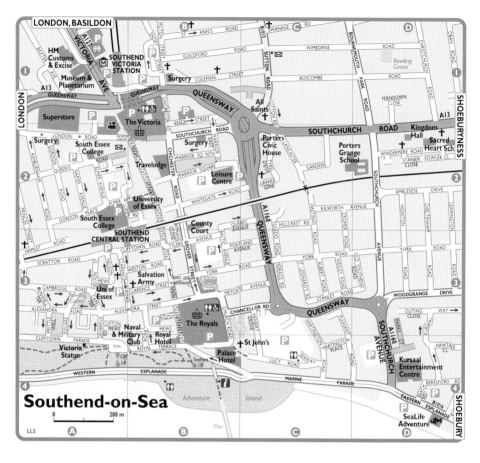

Albert Road C3
Alexandra Road A3
Alexandra Street A3
Ambleside Drive D2
Ashburnham Road A2
Baltic Avenue B3
Baxter Avenue A1
Beach Road D4
Beresford Road D4
Boscombe Road C1
Bournemouth Park
Road D1
Cambridge Road A3
Capel Terrace A3
Chancellor Road B3
Cheltenham Road D2
Chichester Road B1
Christchurch Road D1
Church Road B3
Clarence Road A3
Clarence Street B3
Clifftown Parade A4
Clifftown Road B3
Clifton Mews A3
Coleman Street B1
Cromer Road C2
Devereux Road A4
Eastern Esplanade D4
Elmer Approach A2
Elmer Avenue A2

Essex Street B1
Ferndown Close D1
Fowler Close D2
Gordon Place A2
Gordon Road A2
Grange Gardens C2
Grover Street B3
Guildford Road B1
Hamlet Road A3
Hartington Place C4
Hartington Road C3
Hastings Road A2
Hawtree Close D4
Heygate Avenue B3
High Street B2
Hillcrest Road C2
Honiton Road D2
Horace Road C3
Kilworth Avenue C2
Kursaal Way D4
Lancaster Gardens C2
Leamington Road D2
London Road A2
Lucy Road C4
Luker Road A2
Marine Parade C4
Marks Court D3
Milton Street B1
Napier Avenue A2

Nelson Mews A3
Nelson Street A3
Oban Road D1
Old Southend Road D3
Outing Close D3
Pitmans Close B2
Pleasant Road C3
Portland Avenue B3
Princes Street A2
Prittlewell Square A3
Quebec Avenue B2
Queen's Road A2
Queensway A1
Royal Mews B4
Royal Terrace B4
Runwell Terrace A3
St Ann's Road B1
St Leonard's Road C3
Scratton Road A3
Seaway C4
Short Street B1
Southchurch Avenue ... D2
Southchurch Road B2
Stanier Close D2
Stanley Road C3
Sutton Road C1
Swanage Road C1
Toledo Road C2
Tylers Avenue B3
Tyrel Drive C2

Victoria Avenue A1
Warrior Square East B2
Warrior Square
North B2
Warrior Square B2
Wesley Road C3
Western Esplanade A4
Weston Road B3
Whitegate Road B2
Wimborne Road C1
Windermere Road D2
Woodgrange Drive D3
York Road B3

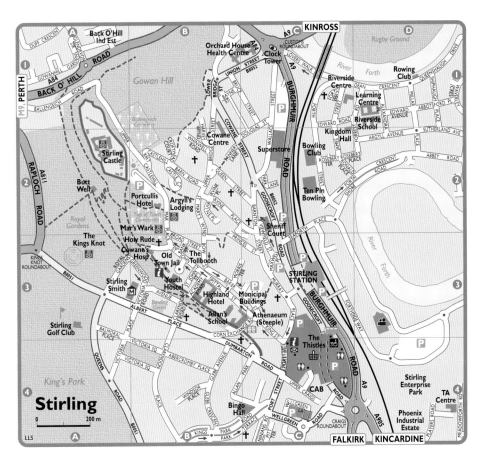

Abbey Road...................D2	Dean Crescent.............D1	Millar Place...................D1	Victoria Place..............A4
Abbotsford Place..........D1	Douglas Street.............C2	Morris Terrace..............B3	Victoria Road................B3
Abercromby Place..........B4	Duff Crescent...............A1	Murray Place.................C3	Victoria Square............A4
Academy Road..............B3	Dumbarton Road...........B4	Ninians Road.................C4	Viewfield Street............C2
Albert Place..................A3	Edward Avenue.............D1	Park Lane.....................C2	Wallace Street...............C2
Alexandra Place.............D1	Edward Road................C1	Park Terrace.................B4	Waverley Crescent.......D1
Allan Park.....................B4	Forrest Road.................D2	Pitt Terrace..................C4	Wellgreen Lane.............C4
Argyll Avenue................D2	Forth Crescent.............C2	Players Road.................D4	Wellgreen Road.............C4
Back O' Hill Road..........A1	Forth Street..................C1	Port Street....................C4	Whinwell Road..............B2
Baker Street..................B3	Forth View...................C1	Princes Street...............B3	Windsor Place...............B4
Ballengeich Road...........A1	Glebe Avenue...............B4	Queenshaugh Drive.......D1	
Balmoral Place..............A3	Glebe Crescent.............B4	Queens Road.................A4	
Bank Street...................B3	Glendevon Drive...........A1	Queen Street.................B2	
Barn Road.....................B2	Goosecroft Road...........C2	Raploch Road................A2	
Barnton Street..............C2	Gowanhill Gardens........A1	Ronald Place.................C2	
Bayne Street.................B1	Greenwood Avenue.......A3	Rosebery Place..............C2	
Bow Street....................B3	Harvey Wynd................B1	Rosebery Terrace..........C2	
Broad Street.................B3	Irvine Place..................B2	Royal Gardens..............A3	
Bruce Street..................B1	James Street.................C2	St John Street................B3	
Burghmuir Road............C1	Kings Knot	St Mary's Wynd............B2	
Castle Court..................B2	Roundabout..............A3	Seaforth Place...............C3	
Clarendon Place............B4	Kings Park Road............B4	Shiphaugh Place............D1	
Clarendon Road............B3	King Street...................C3	Shore Road...................C2	
Corn Exchange	Lovers Walk.................C1	Spittal Street.................B3	
Road.........................B3	Lower Bridge Street.......B1	Sutherland Avenue........D2	
Cowane Street...............B2	Lower Castlehill...........B2	Tannery Lane................B2	
Craigs Roundabout.........C4	Mar Place.....................B2	Union Street.................B1	
Crofthead Court.............B2	Maxwell Place...............C3	Upper Bridge Street......B2	
Customs	Meadowforth Road.......D4	Upper Castlehill............A2	
Roundabout...............C1		Upper Craigs.................C4	

1825 Way	B4	Derby Street	A2	Lodge Street	B3	Raddcliffe Crescent	D3	Vane Street	B2
Allison Street	B1	Dixon Street	A2	Major Street	B1	Ramsgate	B3	Vicarage Avenue	A1
Alma Street	B1	Dovecot Street	A3	Mandale Road	D4	Riverside	C3	Vicarage Street	A1
Bakery Street	A3	Dugdale Street	D1	Manfield Street	A3	Robert Street	D4	Victoria Bridge	C4
Balaclava Street	B1	Dunmail Road	A1	Maritime Road	C1	Russell Street	B2	Wade Avenue	C1
Baltic Close	C1	Durham Road	A1	Massey Road	D3	Ryan Avenue	C1	Webster Close	A3
Bath Lane	C1	Durham Street	A2	Mellor Street	A1	Sabatier Close	D3	Wellington Square	B2
Bath Place	B2	Eastport Road	D1	Melbourne Street	A2	St Ann's Terrace	D1	Wellington Street	A2
Bedford Street	A1	Edwards Street	A4	Middle Street	B2	St Johns Close	B1	Westbourne Street	A4
Bickersteth Close	B4	Eleanor Place	A4	Millbank Close	B2	St Bernard Road	A3	Westcott Street	B4
Bishop Street	B2	Ewbank Drive	A3	Mill Street West	A2	St Mark's Court	C3	Westpoint Road	C3
Bishopton Lane	A1	Farrer Street	B1	Moat Street	C4	St Pauls Road	A1	West Row	B3
Bishopton Road	A1	Finkle Street	B3	Nelson Terrace	B2	St Paul's Street	A1	Wharf Street	B4
Boathouse Lane	C4	Frederick Street	B1	Newton Avenue	A1	Samuel Street	A1	William Street	B3
Bone Street	B1	Fudan Way	D3	Northport Road	D1	Shaftesbury Street	A4	Woodland Street	A4
Bowesfield Lane	A4	Goosport Road	D1	North Shore Gyratory	C2	Silver Street	B2	Worthing Street	A3
Bridge Road	B3	Grove Street	A4	Northshore Link	C2	Skinner Street	B3	Yale Crescent	C4
Bridge Road	C4	Haffron Avenue	B1	North Shore Road	D2	Spring Street	A4	Yarm Lane	A4
Bright Street	B2	Hartington Road	A3	Norton Road	B1	Stamp Street	A2	Yarm Road	A4
Britannia Road	A1	Harvard Avenue	D3	Orde Wingate Way	A1	Stanford Close	D4	Yarm Street	B3
Brunswick Street	B3	High Street	B2	Outram Street	A4	Station Street	D4	York Street	B3
Buchanan Street	A3	Hill Street East	D1	Oxbridge Lane	A4	Stephenson Street	D4	
Bute Street	B2	Hutchinson Street	A2	Palmerston Street	A2	Sydney Street	B2	
Carlton Close	B2	John Street	B2	Parkfield Road	B4	Tarring Street	A3	
Cecil Street	C3	King Street	B2	Park Road	A4	The Black Path	C1	
Chalk Close	B4	Knightport Road	D1	Park Terrace	B4	The Square	C2	
Chapel Street	C4	Knowles Street	B2	Parliament Street	B4	Thistle Green	C2	
Church Road	D1	Laing Street	B1	Pearson Close	C4	Thomas Street	B1	
Claremont Close	D4	Lawrence Street	A4	Petch Street	A2	Thompson Street	B1	
Clarence Row	C1	Lawson Street	A3	Phoenix Sidings	A2	Tower Street	B4	
Columbia Drive	C3	Leeds Street	B2	Portrack Lane	D1	Trinity Mews	D3	
Corporation Street	A2	Leyburne Terrace	A3	Prince Regent Terrace	B3	Trinity Street	B4	
Council of Europe		Lightfoot Grove	B4	Princess Avenue	C1	Union Square	B2	
Boulevard	C2	Limeoak Way	D1	Princess of Wales Bridge	C2	Union Street East	C1	
Cragg Street	A1	Lobdon Street	B2	Princeton Drive	D4	University Boulevard	C3	
Cromwell Avenue	B1			Quayside Road	C3	University Roundabout	D3	

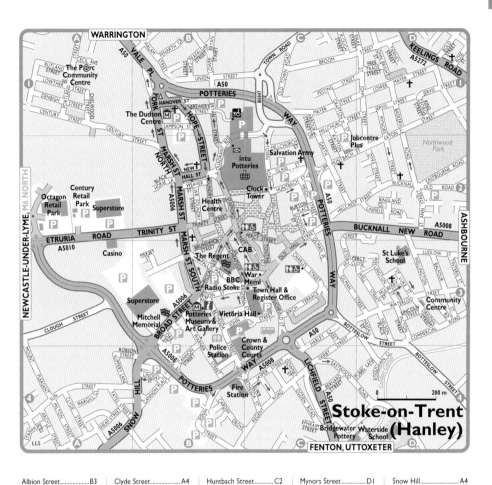

Stoke-on-Trent
(Hanley)

Albion Street................B3	Clyde Street A4	Huntbach Street............C2	Mynors Street................D1	Snow Hill........................A4
Arbour Street C1	Commercial Road...........D3	Jasper Street..................C4	Nelson Place D3	Stafford Street................B2
Argyle Street..................A4	Denbigh Street................A1	Jervis Street...................D1	New Hall Street.............B2	Stanhope Street.............A4
Bagnall Street.................B3	Derby Street C4	John Bright Street.........D1	Ogden Road C4	Stubbs Lane...................D4
Balfour Street.................D3	Dilke Street C1	John Street......................B3	Old Hall Street C3	Sun Street.......................A4
Baskerville Road............D1	Downey Street................C4	Keelings Road.................D1	Old Town Road..............C1	Tierney Street D1
Bernard Street................C4	Dresden Street................D3	King George Street........D1	Orb Street.......................B3	Tontine Street...............C3
Bethesda Street..............B3	Dyke Street D2	Lichfield Street...............C3	Pall Mall..........................B3	Town Road.....................C2
Birch Terrace C3	Eastbourne Road............D2	Lincoln Street.................D3	Penarth Grove................B1	Trafalgar Street..............B1
Black Horse Lane...........B2	Eastwood Road...............C4	Lindsay Street.................B4	Percy Close C3	Trinity Street..................B2
Bold Street.....................D1	Eaton Street D2	Linfield Road D2	Percy Street....................C2	Union Street...................B1
Botteslow Street.............C3	Ephraim Street................C4	Lower Bethesda	Piccadilly.........................B3	Upper Hillchurch
Brewery Street...............B1	Etruria Road A2	Street...........................C4	Picton Street..................D3	Street............................C2
Broad Street...................B3	Festing Street..................C1	Lower Bryan Street.......B1	Plough Street..................C1	Upper Huntbach
Broom Street..................C1	Foundry Street................B2	Lower Foundry	Portland Street A1	Street............................C2
Brunswick Street............B3	Free Trade Street D1	Street...........................B2	Potteries Way.................B1	Vale Place.......................A1
Bryan Street...................B1	Garth Street....................C2	Lower Mayer Street D1	Quadrant Road...............B2	Warner Street................B3
Bucknall New Road........C2	Gilman Place....................C2	Lowther Street...............A1	Ratton Street..................C2	Waterloo Street.............D3
Bucknall Old Road.........D2	Gilman Street...................C3	Ludlow Street..................D3	Regent Road...................C4	Weaver Street................B2
Burton Place...................C2	Glass Street.....................C2	Malam Street...................B1	Ringland Close................D2	Well Street......................D3
Cannon Place B4	Goodson Street...............C2	Margill Close...................A4	Robson Street.................A4	Wellington Road.............D3
Cannon Street................B4	Grafton Street.................C1	Marsh Street...................B2	Rose Street.....................D1	Wellington Street...........D3
Cape Street.....................B1	Hanover Street................B1	Marsh Street North........B2	Rosedawn Close.............D4	Yates Street....................A4
Cardiff Grove..................B4	Harley Street...................C4	Marsh Street South........B3	Rutland Street.................A1	York Street.....................B1
Cecil Avenue...................A1	Hassall Street..................D3	Mayer Street...................C1	St Ann Street..................D2	
Century Street................A1	Hillchurch........................C2	Meigh Street....................C2	St John Street..................D1	
Charles Street.................C3	Hillcrest Street................C2	Mersey Street..................B3	St Luke Street.................D3	
Cheapside B3	Hinde Street....................B4	Milton Street...................A4	Sampson Street...............B1	
Chelwood Street............A1	Hope Street.....................B1	Mount Pleasant A4	Sheaf Street A4	
Clough Street..................A3	Hordley Street.................C3	Mulberry Street..............C4	Slippery Lane...................A4	

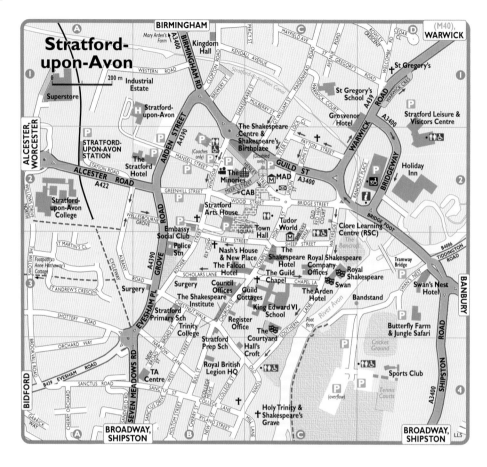

Albany Road	A3	Greenhill Street	B2	Sanctus Drive	B4	Willows Drive
Alcester Road	A2	Grove Road	B3	Sanctus Road	A4	North	A2
Arden Street	B2	Guild Street	C2	Sanctus Street	B4	Windsor Street	B2
Avenue Road	C1	Henley Street	B2	Sandfield Road	A4	Wood Street	B2
Bancroft Place	C2	High Street	C3	Scholars Lane	B3	
Birmingham Road	B1	Holtom Street	B4	Seven Meadows	
Brewery Street	B1	John Street	C2	Road	A4	
Bridge Foot	D2	Kendall Avenue	B1	Shakespeare Street	B1	
Bridge Street	C2	Lock Close	C2	Sheep Street	C3	
Bridgeway	D2	Maidenhead Road	C1	Shipston Road	D4	
Broad Street	B4	Mansell Street	B2	Shottery Road	A3	
Brookvale Road	A4	Mayfield Avenue	C1	Shrieves Walk	C3	
Bull Street	B4	Meer Street	B2	Southern Lane	C3	
Cedar Close	D1	Mill Lane	C4	Station Road	A2	
Chapel Lane	C3	Mulberry Street	C1	Swan's Nest	D3	
Chapel Street	C3	Narrow Lane	B4	The Willows	A3	
Cherry Orchard	A4	New Broad Street	B4	Tiddington Road	D3	
Cherry Street	B4	New Street	B4	Town Square	B2	
Chestnut Walk	B3	Old Red Hen Court	C2	Tramway Bridge	D3	
Church Street	B3	Old Town	C4	Tyler Street	C2	
Clopton Road	B1	Orchard Way	A4	Union Street	C2	
College Lane	B4	Payton Street	C2	Warwick Court	C1	
College Mews	B4	Percy Street	C1	Warwick Crescent	D1	
College Street	B4	Rother Street	B3	Warwick Road	C2	
Ely Gardens	B3	Rowley Crescent	D1	Waterside	C3	
Ely Street	B3	Ryland Street	B4	Welcombe Road	D1	
Evesham Place	B3	St Andrew's		Wellesbourne	
Evesham Road	A4	Crescent	A3	Grove	B2	
Garrick Way	A4	St Gregory's Road	C1	Western Road	B1	
Great William Street	C1	St Martin's Close	A3	West Street	B4	

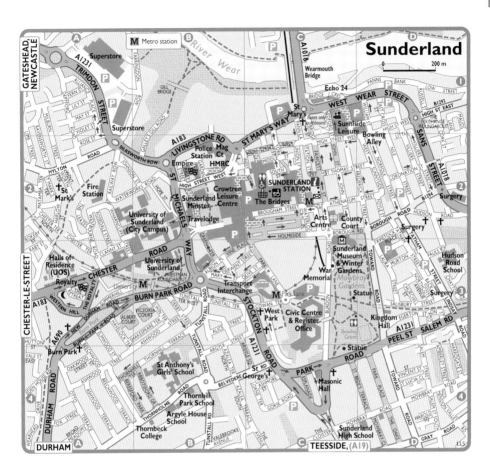

Abbotsford Grove B4	Deptford Road........................A1	John Street..............................C2	Ravensworth Street..................A1	Toward Road...........................D3
Albert Court A3	Derby Street B3	Laura Street.............................D3	Rokeby Street A2	Trimdon Street........................A1
Albion Place............................B3	Derwent Terrace.....................B3	Lily Street................................A1	Rosedale Street A2	Tunstall Road...........................B3
Alice Street..............................B3	Durham Road..........................A4	Lime Street..............................A1	Rose Street..............................D2	Tunstall Terrace........................B3
Alliance Place A1	East Cross Street.....................D1	Lindsay Road............................D3	Russell Street D1	Tunstall Terrace West................B3
Amberley Street......................D4	Eden House Road....................A4	Little Villiers Street.................D2	St Bede's Terrace C4	Union Street.............................C2
Argyle Square..........................B3	Egerton Street D3	Livingstone Road.....................B2	St Lucia Close..........................D4	Valebrooke Avenue..................B4
Argyle Street...........................B4	Elmwood Street......................A3	Lorne Terrace..........................C4	St Mark's Terrace A2	Vale Street East........................A4
Ashmore Street C4	Elwin Terrace..........................B3	Low Street...............................D1	St Mary's Way..........................B2	Victoria Court..........................B3
Ashwood Street A4	Esplanade................................C4	Mary Street.............................B3	St Michaels Way.......................C2	Villiers Street............................D2
Ashwood Terrace.....................A4	Farringdon Row.......................B1	Matamba Terrace.....................A2	St Thomas' Street.....................C2	Vine Place................................B3
Athenaeum Street....................C2	Fawcett Street.........................C2	Mauds Lane.............................D1	St Vincent Street......................D4	Violet Street.............................A1
Azalea Terrace North................B4	Fern Street...............................A1	May Street...............................A1	Salem Road..............................D3	Waterloo Place........................C2
Azalea Terrace South................B4	Fox Street................................A4	Middle Street...........................C2	Salem Street.............................D4	Waterworks Road....................A2
Bedford Street.........................C1	Foyle Street.............................D2	Milburn Street.........................A1	Salem Street South...................D4	Wearhead Drive.......................A4
Beechwood Street...................A3	Frederick Street.......................C2	Mowbray Close........................D4	Salisbury Street.........................D2	Wearmouth Bridge...................C1
Beechwood Terrace..................A4	Galley's Gill Road.....................B2	Mowbray Road........................C4	Sans Street...............................D2	Wentworth Terrace..................A2
Belvedere Road........................B4	Garden Place...........................B2	Murton Street..........................D3	Shakespeare Terrace.................B3	Westbourne Road....................A2
Beresford Park.........................B4	Gill Bridge...............................B1	New Durham Road...................A3	Silksworth Row........................A2	Western Hill.............................A3
Borough Road..........................C2	Gorse Road..............................C4	Nile Street................................D2	South Street.............................C2	West Street..............................B2
Bridge Crescent.......................C1	Gray Road................................D4	Norfolk Street..........................D2	Station Street...........................C2	West Sunnyside........................D2
Bridge Street C1	Green Terrace..........................B2	Northcote Avenue....................A4	Stockton Road..........................B3	West Wear Street.....................C1
Broad Meadows.......................A4	Harlow Street A2	Oakwood Street.......................A4	Summerhill...............................A3	Wharncliffe Street A2
Brougham Street......................C2	Harold Square..........................D4	Olive Street.............................B3	Tatham Street..........................D2	William Street...........................D1
Burdon Road............................C3	Harrogate Street......................A3	Otto Terrace...........................A4	Tatham Street Back..................D2	York Street..............................C2
Burn Park Road........................A3	Havelock Terrace.....................A3	Paley Street..............................B2	Tavistock Place.........................D3	
Chaytor Grove........................A3	Hendon Valley Road.................D4	Pann Lane................................C1	The Avenue..............................C4	
Chester Road...........................D3	High Street East........................D1	Panns Bank..............................D1	The Cloisters............................C4	
Chester Terrace........................A2	High Street East.......................D1	Park Lane.................................C3	The Exchange	
Chester Terrace North..............A2	High Street West......................C2	Park Place................................D4	Roundabout.........................D1	
Churchill Street........................D3	Holmeside...............................C2	Park Road................................C4	The Leazes...............................A2	
Clanny Street...........................A3	Hope Street.............................B2	Pauls Road...............................D3	The Oaks.................................A3	
Cork Street..............................D1	Hudson Road...........................D2	Peel Street...............................D3	The Retreat..............................A3	
Coronation Street....................D2	Hutton Street...........................A3	Priestman Roundabout.............B3	The Royalty..............................A3	
Cowan Terrace........................C3	Hylton Road.............................A2	Raby Street..............................A3	Thornhill Terrace......................A4	
Coxon Street...........................D3	Johnson Street.........................A2	Railway Row.............................A2	Thornholme Road.....................B4	

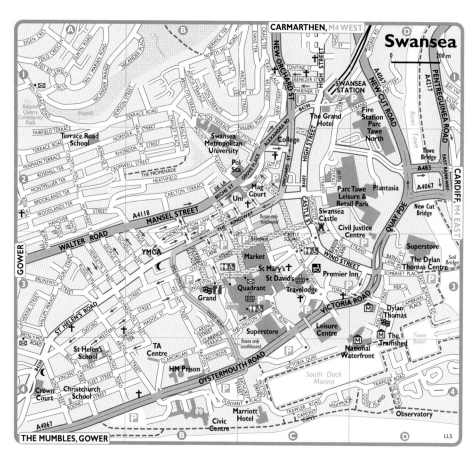

Adelaide Street............D3	Craig Terrace................C1	High Street...................C2	Park Street.....................B3	Stanley Terrace..............B1
Albert Row.................C3	Crole Street..................A2	Hill Street.....................B1	Paxton Drive.................C4	Strand.............................C1
Alexandra Road...........C2	Cromwell Street............A2	Humphrey Street..........A2	Paxton Street.................B4	Strand Row....................C2
Argyle Street...............A4	De La Beche Street........B2	Islwyn Road..................A1	Penmaen Terrace..........A2	Tan Y Marian Road........A1
Bath Lane...................D3	Dillwyn Street...............B3	John Street....................C1	Pentreguinea Road........D1	Tawe Bridge..................D2
Bathurst Street............C4	Duke Street..................A3	Jones Terrace...............C1	Pen-Y-Graig Road.........A1	Teilo Crescent...............A1
Bay View....................D1	Dunvant Place..............B4	Kilvey Terrace...............D1	Phillips Parade...............A3	Terrace Road.................B1
Beach Street...............A4	East Bank Way..............D2	Llewelyn Circle.............A1	Picton Arcade...............B3	Terrace Road.................A2
Belle Vue Way.............C2	East Burrows Road........D3	Madoc Street................B3	Picton Lane...................B3	The Kingsway................B2
Berwick Terrace..........B1	Ebenezer Street............C1	Mansel Street...............B2	Picton Terrace...............B1	The Promenade.............B2
Bond Street.................A4	Eigen Crescent.............A1	Mariner Street..............C1	Pier Street....................D3	The Slipway..................D4
Brooklands Terrace......A2	Elfed Road....................A1	Milton Terrace..............B1	Portia Terrace...............B1	Tontine Street................C1
Brunswick Street.........A3	Evans Terrace...............C1	Montpellier Terrace......A2	Pottery Street...............D1	Trawler Road.................C4
Bryn-Syfi Terrace.........B1	Fairfield Terrace...........A2	Morfa Road...................B1	Primrose Street.............A2	Trinity Place..................C2
Bryn-Y-Mor Road.........A3	Ferry Street..................D3	Mount Pleasant............B2	Princess Way.................C3	Victoria Quay................C4
Burman Street..............A2	Firm Street...................B1	New Cut Bridge...........D2	Quay Parade.................D2	Victoria Road................C3
Burrows Road..............A4	Fleet Street..................A4	New Cut Road..............D1	Recorder Street.............B4	Vincent Street...............A4
Caer Street..................C3	Fullers Row..................C1	New Orchard	Rhondda Street............A2	Walter Road..................A3
Cambrian Place...........D3	George Street................A3	Street........................C1	Richardson Street..........A3	Watkin Street................C1
Camona Drive..............C4	Glamorgan Street..........B4	New Street....................C1	Rodney Street...............A4	Wellington Street...........C3
Carlton Terrace............B2	Goose Island................D4	Nicander Parade............A1	Rose Hill.......................A2	Western Street...............A4
Castle Square...............C3	Green Lane Dragon......C3	Nicander Place..............B1	Rosehill Terrace.............A2	West Way......................B3
Castle Street................C2	Grove Place..................C2	Nicholl Street...............A3	Russel Street.................A3	White Street..................A2
Catherine Street..........A3	Hanover Street.............A2	Norfolk Street...............A3	Sail Bridge...................D3	William Street................B3
Clarence Street............B3	Harcourt Street.............B2	Northampton Lane.......B2	St Helen's Road.............A3	Wind Street..................C3
Clarence Terrace..........B4	Heathfield....................B2	North Hill Road.............B1	Short Street..................B1	Woodlands Terrace........A2
Clifton Hill..................C2	Henrietta Street............A3	Orchard Street..............C2	Singleton Street.............B3	Worcester Place.............C2
Constitution Hill..........B2	Hewson Street..............A1	Oxford Street................A3	Somerset Place.............D3	York Street....................C3
Cradock Street.............B2	Highmoor.....................C4	Oystermouth Road........B4	Spring Terrace...............B3	
Craig Place..................C1	High Street...................C1	Page Street...................B3	Stanley Place.................B1	

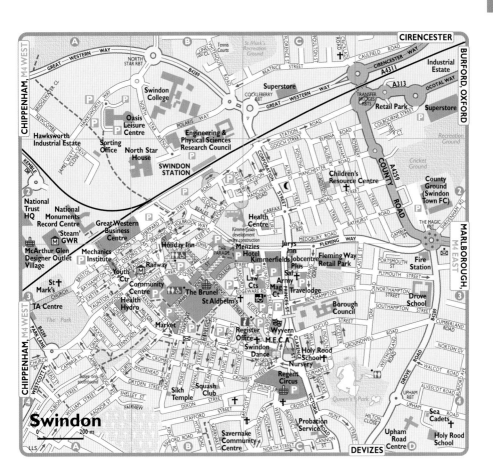

Albion Street...............A4	Cricklade Road...............C1	Haydon Street...............C2	Ponting Street...............C2	Victoria Road...............C4
Alfred Street...............C2	Crombey Street...............B4	Hilton Close...............D4	Portsmouth Street...............D3	Villett Street...............B3
Alvescot Road...............D4	Cross Street...............C4	Holbrook Way...............B2	Poulton Street...............C1	Volta Road...............C2
Amber Court...............D1	Cumberland Road...............D3	Hunt Street...............C4	Princes Street...............C3	Walcot Road...............D4
Ashford Road...............B4	Curtis Street...............A4	Hythe Road...............B4	Prospect Hill...............C4	Wells Street...............C3
Aylesbury Street...............B2	Deacon Street...............B4	Islington Street...............C3	Queen Street...............B3	Westcott Place...............A4
Bathampton Street...............A3	Dixon Street...............B4	James Watt Close...............A2	Radnor Street...............A4	Western Street...............C4
Bathurst Road...............C2	Dover Street...............C4	John Street...............B3	Reading Street...............A3	Westmorland Road...............D4
Beales Close...............B2	Dowling Street...............B4	Kemble Drive...............A2	Read Street...............A4	Whale Bridge...............C3
Beatrice Street...............C1	Drove Road...............D4	Kent Road...............B4	Regent Circus...............C4	Whitehead Street...............B4
Beckhampton Street...............C3	Dryden Street...............A4	King Street...............B3	Regent Close...............C3	Whitehouse Road...............B1
Belgrave Street...............C4	Durham Street...............C4	Leicester Street...............C3	Regent Place...............C3	Whitney Street...............B4
Bridge Street...............B2	Eastcott Hill...............C4	Lincoln Street...............C3	Regent Street...............B3	William Street...............A4
Bridgewater Close...............A1	East Street...............B2	London Street...............A3	Rosebery Street...............C2	York Road...............D3
Bristol Street...............A3	Edgeware Road...............B3	Lorne Street...............A4	Salisbury Street...............C2	
Broad Street...............B2	Edmund Street...............C4	Manchester Road...............C2	Sanford Street...............B3	
Brunel Close...............B1	Elmina Road...............C1	Market Street...............B3	Savernake Street...............B4	
Burford Avenue...............D4	Emlyn Square...............A3	Maxwell Street...............B4	Shelley Street...............A4	
Cambria Bridge Road...............A4	Euclid Street...............C3	Medgbury Road...............C2	Sheppard Street...............B2	
Cambria Place...............A4	Exeter Street...............A3	Milford Street...............B2	Shrivenham Road...............D2	
Canal Walk...............B3	Fairview...............A4	Milton Road...............B3	Southampton Street...............D3	
Cannon Street...............C4	Faringdon Road...............A3	Morley Street...............B3	Spring Gardens...............C3	
Carfax Street...............C2	Farnsby Street...............B3	Morse Street...............B4	Stafford Street...............B4	
Carr Street...............B3	Fleet Street...............B2	Newcastle Street...............D3	Stanier Street...............B4	
Caulfield Road...............D1	Fleming Way...............C3	Newcombe Drive...............A1	Station Road...............B2	
Chester Street...............A3	Florence Street...............C1	Newhall Street...............B4	Swindon Road...............C4	
Church Place...............A3	Gambia Street...............D2	Northampton Street...............D3	Taunton Street...............A3	
Church Street...............A4	Gladstone Street...............C2	North Star Avenue...............B1	Tennyson Street...............A3	
Cirencester Way...............D1	Gloucester Street...............B2	North Star Roundabout...............B1	The Magic Roundabout...............D2	
Clarence Street...............C3	Gooch Street...............C2	North Street...............C4	Theobald Street...............A3	
Cockleberry Roundabout...............C1	Graham Street...............C2	Norton Grove...............D1	The Parade...............B3	
Colbourne Street...............D1	Great Western Way...............A1	Ocotal Way...............D1	Turl Street...............C2	
College Street...............B3	Groundwell Road...............C3	Oxford Street...............A3	Transfer Bridges	
Commercial Road...............B3	Harding Street...............B2	Park Lane...............A3	Roundabouts...............D1	
Corporation Street...............C2	Havelock Street...............B3	Plymouth Street...............D3	Upham Road...............D4	
County Road...............D2	Hawksworth Way...............A1	Polaris Way...............B1	Upham Roundabout...............D4	

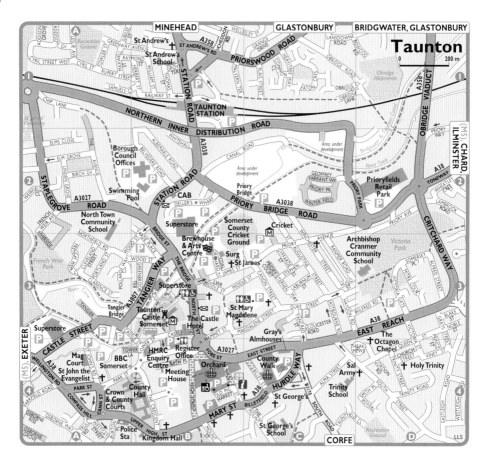

Addison Grove	A1	Eastbourne Road	C3	Lansdowne Road	C1	Priorswood Road	B1	The Bridge	B3
Albemarle Road	B2	Eastleigh Road	D4	Leslie Avenue	A1	Priory Avenue	C3	The Crescent	B4
Alfred Street	D3	East Reach	D3	Linden Grove	A2	Priory Bridge	B2	The Mount	C4
Alma Street	C4	East Street	C4	Lower Middle Street	B3	Priory Bridge Road	B2	Thomas Street	B1
Bath Place	B4	Eaton Crescent	C1	Magdalene Street	B3	Priory Court	C3	Toneway	D2
Belvedere Road	B2	Elm Grove	A2	Malvern Terrace	B1	Priory Park	C2	Tower Lane	A4
Billetfield	C4	Elms Close	A2	Mary Street	B4	Priory Way	D2	Tower Street	B4
Billet Street	C4	Fore Street	B4	Maxwell Street	A1	Queen Street	D4	Trevor Smith Place	D4
Birch Grove	A2	Fowler Street	A1	Middle Street	B3	Railway Street	B1	Trinity Road	D4
Blake Street	D3	French Weir Avenue	A2	Mitre Court	D3	Ranmer Road	C3	Trinity Street	D4
Bowood Road	C1	French Weir Close	A3	Mount Street	B4	Raymond Street	A1	Trull Road	A4
Bridge Street	B2	Geoffrey Farrant		Noble Street	D3	Riverside	A3	Upper High Street	B4
Burton Place	C4	Walk	C2	Northern Inner		St Andrew's Road	B1	Victoria Gate	D3
Canal Road	B2	Gloucester Road	C3	Distribution Road	B1	St Augustine Street	C3	Victoria Street	D3
Cann Street	A4	Gordon Road	D4	Northfield Road	A3	St James Street	B3	Viney Street	D4
Canon Street	C3	Grange Drive	D1	North Street	B3	St John's Road	A4	Weirfield Close	A2
Castle Green	B3	Grays Street	D3	Obridge Close	C1	Samuels Court	A1	Wellesley Street	B1
Castle Street	A4	Greenbrook Terrace	B3	Obridge Lane	C1	Somerset Place	D3	Wellington Road	A4
Cheddon Road	B1	Greenway Avenue	A1	Obridge Road	C1	South Road	C4	Westgate Street	A4
Chip Lane	A1	Grove Terrace	B1	Obridge Viaduct	D2	South Street	C4	Westleigh Road	D4
Church Street	D4	Gyffarde Street	C3	Old Pig Market	B4	Staplegrove Road	A2	Wheatley Crescent	D2
Clarence Street	A3	Hammet Street	B4	Osborne Grove	A4	Station Road	B2	Whitehall	B2
Cleveland Street	A3	Haydon Road	C3	Osborne Rise	A4	Stephen Street	C3	Wilfred Road	C3
Coal Orchard	B3	Heavitree Way	C1	Osborne Way	A4	Stephen Way	C3	William Street	B1
Compass Hill	A4	Herbert Street	B1	Parkfield Road	A4	Tancred Street	C3	Winchester Street	C2
Compton Close	C1	High Street	B4	Park Street	A4	Tangier	A3	Winter Field	C2
Critchard Way	D2	Hugo Street	C3	Paul Street	B4	Tangier Bridge	A3	Wood Street	B3
Cyril Street	A1	Hurdle Way	C4	Plais Street	C1	Tauntfield Close	C4	Yarde Place	B2
Cyril Street West	A1	Jubilee Street	A1	Pollards Way	A3	Theaks Mews	D4		
Deller's Wharf	B2	Laburnum Street	C3	Portland Street	A3	The Avenue	A2		
Duke Street	C3	Lambrook Road	D2	Princes Street	D3				

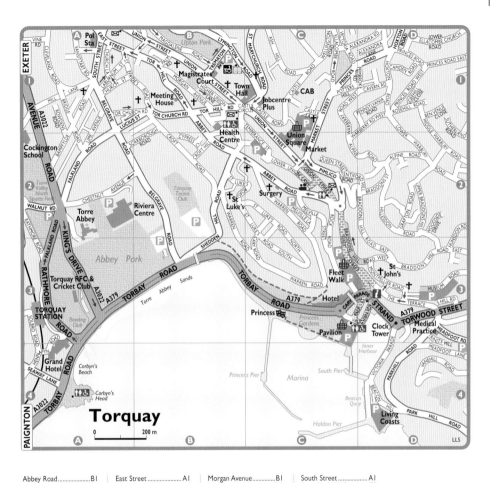

Torquay

0   200 m

Abbey Road................B1	East Street A1	Morgan Avenue..............B1	South Street A1
Alexandra Lane.............D1	Ellacombe Road............C1	Museum Road D3	Stentiford Hill Road......C2
Alexandra Road............C1	Falkland Road................A2	Palk Street C3	Strand..............................D3
Alpine Road..................C2	Fleet Street C3	Palm Road......................B1	Sutherland Road............D1
Ash Hill Road................C1	Grafton Road................D2	Parkhill Road................D4	Temperance Street C2
Avenue Road................A1	Hennapyn Road A4	Pembroke Road............C1	The Terrace..................D3
Bampfylde Road............A2	Higher Union Lane B1	Pennsylvania Road........D1	Torbay Road A4
Beacon Hill..................D4	Hillesdon Road..............D2	Pimlico..........................C2	Tor Church Road..........A1
Belgrave Road A1	Hoxton Road................D1	Potters Hill C1	Tor Hill Road................B1
Ben Venue Close............D1	Hunsdon Road................D3	Princes Road C1	Torwood Street............B1
Braddons Hill Road	King's Drive A3	Princes Road East D1	Trematon Ave................B1
East..............................D3	Laburnum Street A1	Princes Road West........D1	Trinity Hill....................D3
Braddons Hill Road	Lime Avenue A2	Queen Street C2	Union Street..................B1
West C2	Lower Ellacombe	Rathmore Road A2	Upper Braddons Hill....D2
Braddons Street D2	Church Road D1	Rock Road C2	Vanehill Road................D4
Bridge Road..................A1	Lower Union Lane........C2	Rosehill Close................D1	Vansittart Road............A1
Camden Road................D1	Lower Warbury	Rosehill Road................D1	Vaughan Parade C3
Cary Parade..................C3	Road..........................D2	Rowdens Road..............A1	Victoria Parade............D4
Cary Road......................C3	Lucius Street A1	St Efride's Road A1	Victoria Road C1
Castle Circus................B1	Lymington Road............B1	St Luke's Road..............B2	Vine Road A1
Castle Lane....................C1	Magdalene Road............B1	St Luke's Road	Walnut Road A2
Castle Road....................C1	Market Street................C2	North C2	Warberry Road
Cavern Road D1	Meadfoot Lane..............D4	St Luke's Road	West C1
Chestnut Avenue..........A2	Meadfoot Road..............D3	South C2	Warren Road................B2
Church Lane..................A1	Melville Lane..................C2	St Marychurch Road......C1	Wellington Road............C1
Church Street................A1	Melville Street................C2	Scarborough Road........B2	Woodside Drive............D2
Cleveland Road..............A1	Middle Warbury	Seaway Lane A4	
Croft Hill......................B2	Road..........................D1	Shedden Hill Road........B3	
Croft Road....................B2	Mill Lane........................A1	Solbro Road..................A3	
Cypress Close................B2	Montpellier Road..........D3	South Hill Road............D3	

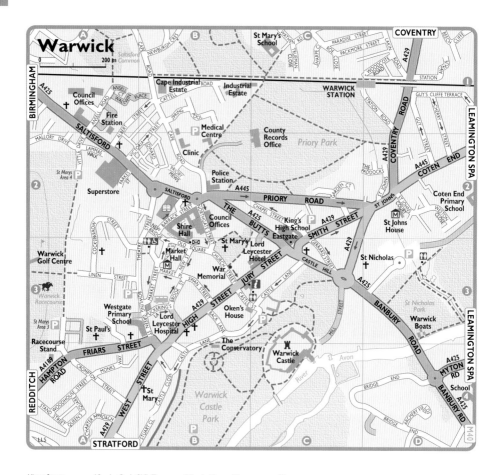

Albert Street A2
Ansell Court A1
Ansell Road A1
Archery Fields............. D4
Back Lane B3
Banbury Road D3
Barrack Street............. B2
Beech Cliffe D1
Bowling Green
  Street....................... B3
Bridge End D4
Brook Street B3
Cape Road.................. B1
Castle Close................ B4
Castle Hill C3
Castle Lane................. B4
Castle Street B3
Cattell Road B1
Chapel Street.............. C2
Charter Approach........ A4
Cherry Street.............. D1
Church Street.............. B3
Cocksparrow Street.... A3
Coten End.................. D2
Coventry Road............ D2
Crompton Street A4
Edward Street............. B2
Friars Street A4
Garden Court.............. C2
Gerrard Street............. C3

Guy's Cliffe Terrace........ D1
Guy Street D1
Hampton Road A4
High Street.................... B3
Jury Street..................... B3
Lakin Road.................... D1
Lammas Walk A2
Linen Street................... A3
Mallory Drive................ A2
Market Place................. B3
Market Street................. B3
Mill Street C3
Monks Way.................... A4
Myton Road................... D4
New Bridge................... B2
Newburgh Crescent...... B1
New Street..................... B3
Northgate Street........... B2
Old Square.................... B3
Packmore Street........... C1
Paradise Street............. C1
Parkes Street................. A2
Priory Mews.................. B2
Priory Road.................. C2
Puckering's Lane........... B3
Queen's Square............. A4
Roe Close...................... C1
St Johns......................... D2
St Johns Court................ D2
Saltisford........................ A1

Sharpe Close................. C1
Smith Street.................. C2
Spring Pool.................... B1
Stand Street................... A4
Station Avenue.............. D1
Station Road................. D1
Stuart Close B4
Swan Street.................... B3
Theatre Street B3
The Butts....................... B2
The Paddocks................ D2
Trueman Close.............. C1
Victoria Street............... A2
Vittle Drive.................... A2
Wallwin Place................ A1
Wathen Road................ C1
Weston Close................. D2
West Street.................... A4
Woodcote Road........... D1
Woodhouse Street A4

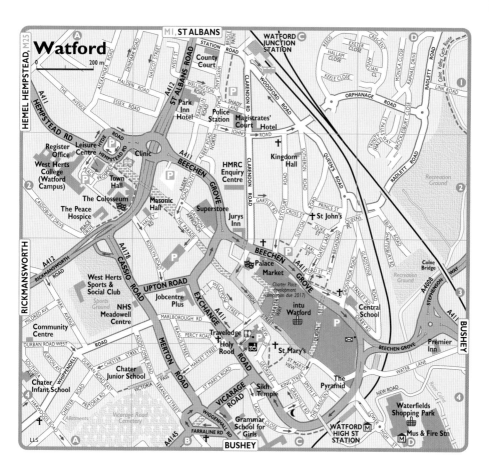

Addiscombe Road..........B3
Albert Road North........B2
Albert Road South.........B2
Alexandra Road............A1
Anglian Close.................D1
Beechen Grove...............C3
Brocklesbury Close......D2
Burton Avenue..............A4
Cassiobury Drive...........A2
Cassio Road...................A3
Charter Way..................C3
Chester Road.................A4
Chester Street...............A4
Clarendon Road.............C1
Cross Street...................C2
Denmark Road...............A1
Derby Road....................C3
Duke Street....................C2
Durban Road East..........A4
Durban Road West........A4
Earl Street......................C3
Ebury Road....................D2
Essex Road.....................A1
Estcourt Road................C2
Exchange Road...............B3
Farraline Road................B4
Feranley Street...............B4
Francis Street.................B3
Franklin Road.................B1
Gartlet Road..................C2

Gaumont Approach.......B2
George Street................C4
Gladstone Road.............D3
Granville Road...............C4
Grosvenor Road.............C3
Halsey Road...................B2
Harwoods Road..............A4
Hempstead Road............A1
High Street.....................C3
Hyde Road......................A2
Keele Close.....................C1
King Street.....................C4
Lady's Close...................C4
Link Road.......................D1
Loates Lane....................C3
Lord Street.....................C3
Lower High Street..........D4
Malborough Road...........B3
Malden Road...................A1
Market Street.................B4
Merton Road..................B3
Mildred Avenue..............A3
Monica Close..................D1
Nascot Street.................B1
New Road........................D4
New Street......................C3
Orphanage Road.............C1
Park Avenue...................A3
Peace Prospect...............A2
Percy Road......................B3

Pretoria Road.................A4
Prince Street..................C2
Queen's Road.................C2
Queen Street..................C3
Radlett Road...................D2
Raphael Drive.................D1
Reeds Crescent..............C1
Rickmansworth
Road...........................A3
Rosslyn Road..................B3
St Albans Road...............B1
St John's Road................B1
St Mary's Road...............B4
St Pauls Way..................D1
Shady Lane.....................B1
Shaftesbury Road...........D2
Smith Street...................C4
Sotheron Road...............C2
Southsea Avenue...........A4
Stanley Road...................C3
Station Road...................B1
Stephenson Way.............D3
Sutton Road...................C2
The Avenue....................A1
The Broadway.................C3
The Crescent..................C4
The Parade.....................B2
Upton Road.....................B3
Vicarage Road................B4
Water Lane.....................D4

Wellington Road.............B1
Wellstone Street.............B3
Westland Road................B1
West Street.....................B1
Whippendell Road..........A4
Wiggenhall Road.............B4
Woodford Road...............C1

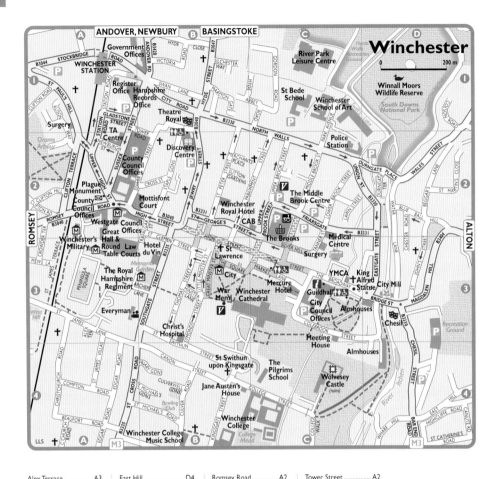

Alex Terrace A3	East Hill D4	Romsey Road A2	Tower Street A2
Alison Way A1	Edgar Road A4	St Catherine's Road D4	Trafalgar Street B3
Andover Road B1	Friarsgate C2	St Clement Street B2	Union Street C2
Archery Lane A3	Friary Gardens B4	St Cross Road A4	Upper Brook Street C2
Bar End Road D4	Gladstone Street A1	St George's Street B2	Upper High Street A2
Beaufort Road A4	Gordon Road C1	St James' Lane A3	Victoria Road B1
Beggar's Lane D2	Great Minster	St James Terrace A3	Wales Street D2
Blue Ball Hill D2	Street B3	St James' Villas A4	Water Lane D3
Bridge Street D3	Highcliffe Road D4	St John's Street D3	Wharf Hill D4
Canon Street B4	High Street B2	St Martin's Close D2	
Canute Road D4	Hyde Abbey Road B1	St Michael's Gardens B4	
Chesil Street D3	Hyde Close B1	St Michael's Road B4	
Chester Road D2	Hyde Street B1	St Paul's Hill A1	
Christchurch Road A4	Jewry Street B2	St Peter Street B2	
City Road B1	Kingsgate Street B4	St Swithun Street B3	
Clifton Hill A2	Lawn Street C2	St Thomas Street B3	
Clifton Road A1	Little Minster Street B3	Silchester Way B1	
Clifton Terrace A2	Lower Brook Street C2	Silver Hill C3	
Colebrook Street C3	Magdalen Hill D3	Southgate Street B3	
College Street B4	Market Lane C3	Staple Gardens B2	
College Walk C4	Marston Gate B1	Station Road A1	
Colson Road D1	Mews Lane A3	Stockbridge Road A1	
Compton Road A4	Merchants Place B2	Sussex Street A2	
Cross Street B2	Middle Brook Street C2	Sutton Gardens B2	
Crowder Terrace A3	Minster Lane B3	Swan Lane B1	
Culver Road B4	Newburgh Street A2	Symonds Street B3	
Culverwell Gardens B4	North Walls B1	Tanner Street C3	
Durngate Place D2	Parchment Street B2	The Broadway C3	
Durngate Terrace D2	Park Avenue C2	The Square B3	
Eastgate Street D3	Peninsula Square A3	Tower Road A1	

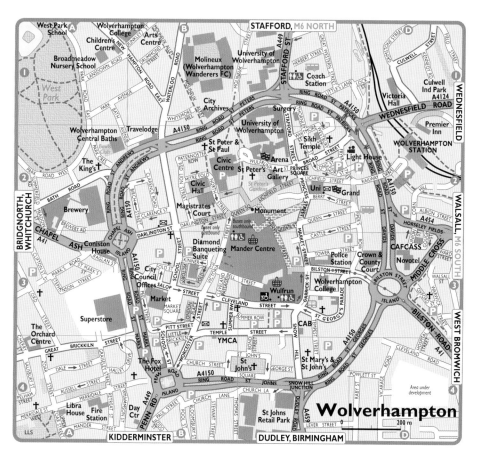

Albion Street..............D2	Drummond Street..........B1	Lord Street..................A3	Powlett Street..............D4	Snow Hill Junction......C4
Bath Avenue................A1	Dudley Road................C4	Mander Street..............A4	Princes Square..............C2	Stafford Street..............C1
Bath Road....................A2	Dudley Street................C2	Market Square..............B3	Princess Street..............C2	Stephenson Street........A3
Bell Street....................B3	Dunkley Street..............A1	Market Street................C2	Queen Square..............B2	Stewart Street..............B4
Berry Street..................C2	Field Street....................D1	Meadow Street............A2	Queen Street................C2	Summerfield Road........A2
Bilston Road................D3	Fold Street....................B3	Melbourne Street..........C4	Raby Street..................D4	Summer Row................B3
Bilston Street..............C3	Fryer Street..................C2	Merridal Street..............A4	Raglan Street................A3	Tempest Street..............C3
Bilston Street Island....D3	Garrick Street................C3	Merridal Street	Railway Drive................D2	Temple Street................B3
Birch Street..................B2	George Street................C4	West..........................A4	Red Lion Street............B2	Thomas Street..............B4
Bloomsbury Street........B4	Gough Street................D3	Middle Cross................D3	Retreat Street................A4	Thornley Street..............C1
Bond Street..................C4	Graiseley Street............A4	Mitre Fold....................B2	Ring Road	Tower Street................C3
Brewery Road..............A2	Great Brickkiln	Molineux Alley..............B1	St Andrews................A2	Union Street................D3
Broad Street..................C2	Street........................A4	Molineux Street............B1	Ring Road St Davids....D2	Upper Zoar Street........A4
Camp Street..................C1	Great Western	New Hampton Road	Ring Road	Vicarage Road..............D4
Castle Street..................C3	Street........................C1	East............................A1	St Georges................C4	Victoria Fold................B3
Chapel Ash..................A3	Grimstone Street..........D1	North Street..................B2	Ring Road St Johns......B4	Victoria Street..............B3
Chapel Ash Island........A3	Hallet Drive..................D4	Oxford Street................D3	Ring Road St Marks......A3	Walsall Street................D3
Cherry Street................A4	Herbert Street................C1	Park Avenue................A1	Ring Road St Patricks....C1	Ward Street..................D3
Church Lane................B4	Horseley Fields............D2	Park Crescent..............A2	Ring Road St Peters......B2	Warwick Street..............D3
Church Street................B4	Hospital Street..............D4	Park Road East............A1	Russell Street................A4	Waterloo Road..............B1
Clarence Road..............B2	Jeddo Street..................B4	Park Road West............A2	St George's Parade........C3	Wednesfield Road........D1
Clarence Street..............B2	Kennedy Road..............D1	Paternoster Row............B2	St John's Square............B4	Westbury Street............C2
Cleveland Passage........B3	Lansdown Road............A1	Paul Street....................B4	St Mark's Road............A3	Whitemore Hill..............B1
Cleveland Road............D4	Lever Street..................C4	Peel Street..................B3	St Mark's Street............A3	Whitmore Street............C2
Cleveland Street............B3	Lichfield Street..............C2	Pelham Street................A4	Salisbury Street............A4	Williamson Street..........A4
Clifton Street................A3	Little Brickkiln Street....B4	Penn Road....................B4	Salop Street................B3	Worcester Street............B4
Corn Hill......................D2	Little's Lane..................C1	Penn Road Island........B4	School Street................B3	Wulfruna Street..............C2
Culwell Street................D1	Lock Street..................D1	Piper's Row..................D2	Short Street..................B3	Zoar Street..................A4
Dale Street..................A4	London Place................B3	Pitt Street....................B3	Skinner Street................B3	
Darlington Street..........B3	Long Street..................C2	Pool Street..................B4	Snow Hill....................C3	

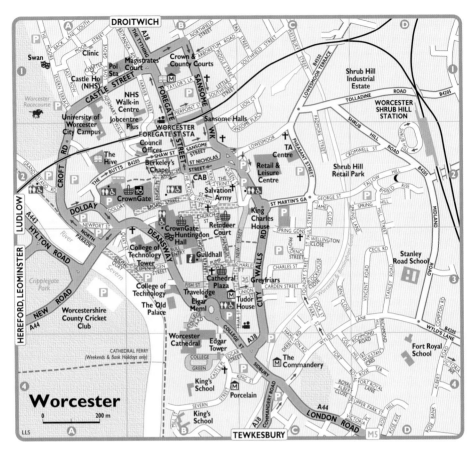

Worcester

Albert Road	D4	
Angel Place	B2	
Angel Street	B2	
Arboretum Road	B1	
Back Lane South	A1	
Blockhouse Close	C3	
Britannia Road	B1	
Broad Street	B2	
Bull Entry	B3	
Byfield Rise	D2	
Carden Street	C3	
Castle Place	B4	
Castle Street	A1	
Cathedral Ferry	A4	
Cecil Road	D3	
Charles Street	B3	
Charter Place	A1	
Church Street	B2	
City Walls Road	C3	
Cole Hill	C4	
College Green	B4	
College Street	B3	
College Yard	B3	
Commandery Road	C4	
Compton Road	D3	
Copenhagen Street	B3	
Croft Road	A2	
Cromwell Street	C2	
Deansway	B3	
Dent Close	C3	

Derby Road	C4	
Dolday	A2	
East Street	B1	
Easy Row	A1	
Edgar Street	B4	
Farrier Street	B1	
Fish Street	B3	
Foregate Street	B1	
Fort Royal Hill	C4	
Fort Royal Lane	D4	
Foundry Street	C3	
Friar Street	C3	
George Street	C2	
Grandstand Road	A2	
Hamilton Road	C3	
High Street	B3	
Hill Street	D2	
Hylton Road	A3	
Infirmary Walk	A1	
James Close	C2	
King Street	B4	
Lion Court	C1	
Little Southfield		
Street	B1	
Lock Street	C3	
London Road	C4	
Love's Grove	A1	
Lowesmoor	C2	
Lowesmoor Terrace	C1	
Middle Street	B1	

Midland Road	D2	
Mill Street	B4	
Moor Street	A1	
Newport Street	A2	
New Road	A3	
New Street	C3	
Northfield Street	B1	
North Parade	A3	
Padmore Street	C1	
Park Street	C3	
Pheasant Street	C2	
Pierpoint Street	B1	
Providence Street	C3	
Pump Street	B3	
Quay Street	A3	
Queen Street	B2	
Richmond Hill	D3	
Richmond Road	D4	
Rose Avenue	D4	
Rose Bank	D4	
Rose Hill	D4	
Rose Terrace	D4	
Royal Albert Close	C4	
St Martin's Gate	C2	
St Nicholas Street	B2	
St Paul's Street	C3	
St Swithin Street	B2	
St Wulstan's		
Crescent	D4	
Sansome Place	B2	

Sansome Street	B2	
Sansome Walk	B1	
Severn Street	B4	
Severn Terrace	A1	
Shaw Street	B2	
Shrub Hill	D2	
Shrub Hill Road	C1	
Sidbury	C4	
Southfield Street	C1	
South Quay	A3	
Spring Gardens	C3	
Spring Hill	D2	
Spring Lane	D2	
Stanley Road	D3	
Tallow Hill	D2	
Taylor's Lane	B1	
The Butts	A2	
The Cross	B2	
The Moors	A1	
The Shambles	B2	
The Trinity	B2	
The Tything	B1	
Tolladine Road	C1	
Trinity Street	B2	
Union Street	C3	
Upper Park Street	D4	
Victoria Avenue	D4	
Victoria Place	C4	
Vincent Road	D3	
Wellington Close	C3	

Westbury Street	C1	
Wyld's Lane	C4	

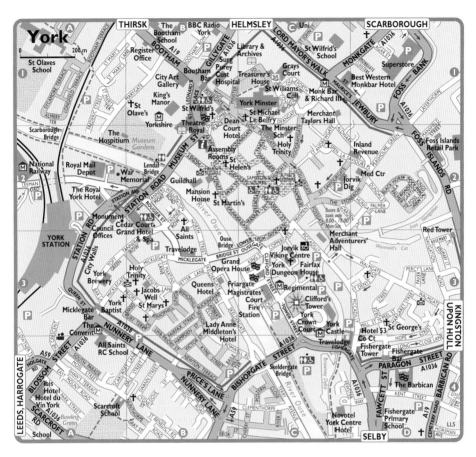

Agar Street	D1	Ebor Street	B4	Lord Mayor's Walk	C1	Postern Close	C4	Sycamore Terrace	A1
Aldwark	C2	Fairfax Street	B3	Lower Ousegate	C3	Price's Lane	B4	Tanner Row	B3
Almery Terrace	A1	Fawcett Street	D4	Lower Priory Street	B3	Priory Street	C3	Tanners Moat	B2
Baile Hill Terrace	B4	Feasegate	C2	Low Petergate	C2	Queen Street	A3	The Crescent	A4
Bar Lane	A3	Fetter Lane	B3	Lowther Terrace	A3	River Street	C4	The Stonebow	C2
Barbican Road	D4	Fewster Way	C4	Mansfield	D2	Rosemary Court	D3	Toft Green	A3
Bishopgate Street	B4	Finkle Street	C2	Margaret Street	D3	Rougier Street	B2	Tower Street	C3
Bishophill Junior	B3	Fishergate	C4	Market Street	C2	St Andrewgate	C2	Trinity Lane	B3
Bishophill Senior	B3	Foss Bank	D1	Marygate	B1	St Benedict Road	B4	Victor Street	B4
Black Horse Lane	D2	Fossgate	C2	Micklegate	B3	St Denys' Road	D3	Walmgate	D3
Blake Street	B2	Foss Islands Road	D2	Mill Street	D3	St Helen's Square	B2	Wellington Road	B2
Blossom Street	A4	Foss View	D2	Minster Yard	B1	St John Street	C1	Willis Street	D4
Bootham	B1	Frederic Street	A1	Monkgate	C1	St Leonard's Place	B1	
Bootham Row	B1	Garden Place	C2	Moss Street	A4	St Martins Lane	B3	
Bootham Terrace	A1	George Street	D3	Museum Street	B2	St Mary's	A1	
Bridge Street	B3	Gillygate	B1	Navigation Road	D2	St Mary's Lane	A1	
Buckingham Street	B3	Goodramgate	C2	New Street	B2	St Marys Terrace	A1	
Cemetery Road	D4	Hampden Street	B4	Newton Terrace	A4	St Maurice's Road	C1	
Cherry Street	C4	High Ousegate	C3	North Street	B2	St Sampson's Square	C2	
Church Street	C2	High Petergate	B1	Nunnery Lane	A3	St Saviourgate	C2	
Clementhorpe	C4	Holgate Road	A4	Nunthorpe Road	B4	St Saviours Place	C2	
Clifford Street	C3	Hope Street	B4	Ogleforth	C1	Scarborough Bridge	A2	
College Street	C1	Horsman Avenue	D4	Ouse Bridge	C3	Scarcroft Lane	A4	
Colliergate	C2	Hungate	D2	Palmer Lane	D2	Scarcroft Road	A4	
Coney Street	B2	Jewbury	D1	Palmer Street	D2	Shambles	C2	
Coppergate	C3	Kent Street	D4	Paragon Street	D4	Shaw's Terrace	A4	
Cromwell Road	B4	Kings Pool Walk	D2	Park Street	A4	Skeldergate	B3	
Cygnet Street	B4	King Street	C3	Parliament Street	C2	Skeldergate Bridge	C4	
Dale Street	B4	Kyme Street	B4	Pavement	C2	South Parade	A4	
Davygate	B2	Lambert Close	B3	Paver Lane	D2	Spen Lane	C2	
Deangate	C1	Layerthorpe	D1	Peasholme Green	D2	Spurriergate	B2	
Dewsbury Terrace	B4	Leeman Road	A2	Peckitt Street	C3	Station Avenue	A2	
Dove Street	B4	Lendal	B2	Peel Street	D3	Station Road	A3	
Duncombe Place	B2	Lendal Bridge	B2	Percy's Lane	D3	Stonegate	C2	
Dundas Street	D2	Long Close Lane	D4	Piccadilly	C3	Swann Street	B4	
East Mount Road	A4	Longfield Terrace	A1	Ponds Garth	D2	Swinegate	C2	

Major airports

London Heathrow Airport

16 miles west of London

Information: visit
heathrowairport.com
Parking: short-stay, long-stay
and business parking is
available.
Public Transport: coach, bus,
rail and London Underground.
There are several 4-star and
3-star hotels within easy reach
of the airport.
Car hire facilities are available.

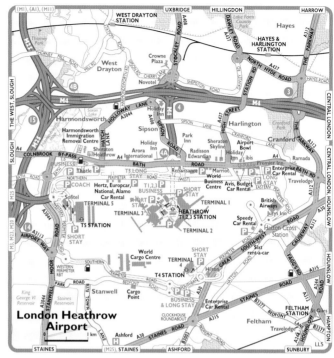

London Gatwick Airport

35 miles south of London

Information: visit
gatwickairport.com
Parking: short and long-stay
parking is available at both the
North and South terminals.
Public Transport: coach, bus
and rail.
There are several 4-star and
3-star hotels within easy reach
of the airport.
Car hire facilities are available.

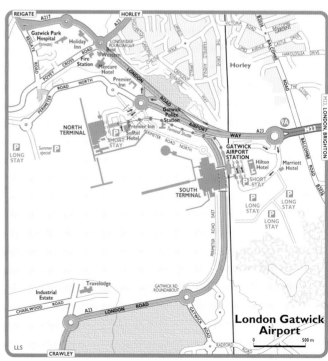

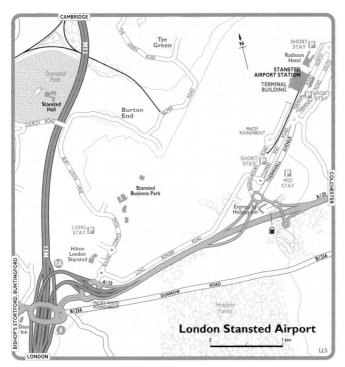

London Stansted Airport

London Stansted Airport

London Stansted Airport

36 miles north east of London

Information: visit *stanstedairport.com*
Parking: short, mid and long-stay open-air parking is available.
Public Transport: coach, bus and direct rail link to London on the Stansted Express.
There are several hotels within easy reach of the airport.
Car hire facilities are available.

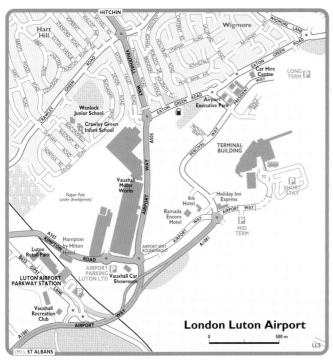

London Luton Airport

London Luton Airport

33 miles north of London

Information: visit *london-luton.co.uk*
Parking: short-term, mid-term and long-stay parking is available.
Public Transport: coach, bus and rail.
There are several hotels within easy reach of the airport.
Car hire facilities are available.

London City Airport

7 miles east of London

Information: visit
londoncityairport.com
Parking: short and long-stay
open-air parking is available.
Public Transport: easy access
to the rail network, Docklands
Light Railway and the London
Underground.
There are 5-star, 4-star and
3-star hotels within easy reach
of the airport.
Car hire facilities are available.

London City Airport

Birmingham International Airport

8 miles east of Birmingham

Information: visit
birminghamairport.co.uk
Parking: short, mid-term and
long-stay parking is available.
Public Transport: Air-Rail Link
service operates every 2 minutes
to and from Birmingham
International Railway Station
& Interchange.
There is one 3-star hotel
adjacent to the airport and
several 4 and 3-star hotels
within easy reach of the airport.
Car hire facilities are available.

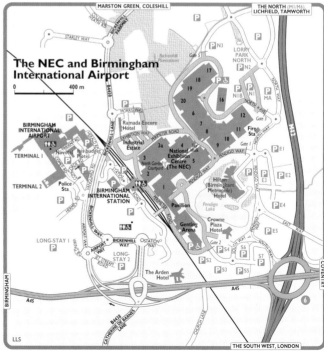

The NEC and Birmingham International Airport

East Midlands Airport

East Midlands Airport

15 miles south west of Nottingham, next to the M1 at junctions 23A and 24

Information: visit *eastmidlandsairport.com*
Parking: short and long-stay parking is available.
Public Transport: bus and coach services to major towns and cities in the East Midlands. There are several 3-star hotels within easy reach of the airport. Car hire facilities are available.

Manchester Airport

Manchester Airport

10 miles south of Manchester

Information: visit *manchesterairport.co.uk*
Parking: short and long-stay parking is available.
Public Transport: coach, bus and rail.
There are several 4-star and 3-star hotels within easy reach of the airport.
Car hire facilities are available.

Leeds Bradford International Airport

7 miles north east of Bradford and 9 miles north west of Leeds

Information: visit *leedsbradfordairport.co.uk*
Parking: short, mid-term and long-stay parking is available.
Public Transport: bus service operates every 30 minutes from Bradford, Leeds and Otley.
There are several 4-star and 3-star hotels within easy reach of the airport.
Car hire facilities are available.

Aberdeen Airport

7 miles north west of Aberdeen

Information: visit *aberdeenairport.com*
Parking: short and long-stay parking is available.
Public Transport: regular bus service to central Aberdeen.
There are several 4-star and 3-star hotels within easy reach of the airport.
Car hire facilities are available.

Edinburgh Airport
7 miles west of Edinburgh

Information: visit
edinburghairport.com
Parking: short and long-stay parking is available.
Public Transport: regular bus services to central Edinburgh, Glasgow and Fife and a tram service to Edinburgh.
There are several 4-star and 3-star hotels within easy reach of the airport.
Car hire and valet parking facilities are available.

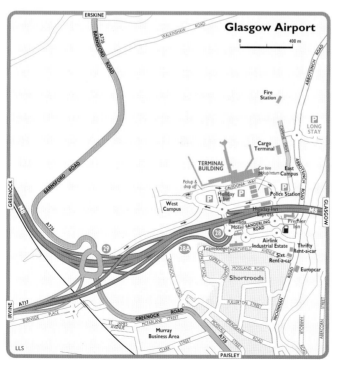

Glasgow Airport
8 miles west of Glasgow

Information: visit
glasgowairport.com
Parking: short and long-stay parking is available.
Public Transport: regular coach services operate direct to central Glasgow and Edinburgh.
There are several 3-star hotels within easy reach of the airport.
Car hire facilities are available.

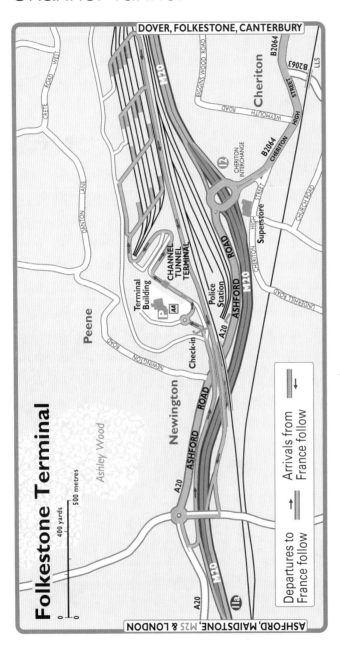

Folkestone Terminal

DOVER, FOLKESTONE, CANTERBURY

ASHFORD, MAIDSTONE, M25 & LONDON

Ashley Wood

Peene

Newington

CRETE ROAD WEST

DANTON LANE

NEWINGTON ROAD

ASHFORD ROAD

A20

M20

M20

A20

Terminal Building

CHANNEL TUNNEL TERMINAL

Check-in

Police Station

ASHFORD ROAD

A20

M20

Cheriton

CHERITON INTERCHANGE

B2064

CHERITON

HIGH STREET

WEYMOUTH ROAD

BIGGINS WOOD ROAD

B2064

B2063

CHURCH ROAD

CHERITON HIGH STREET

UNDERHILL ROAD

Superstore

12

11a

500 metres

400 yards

Departures to France follow

Arrivals from France follow